Derrida From Now On

John D. Caputo, *series editor*

PERSPECTIVES IN
CONTINENTAL
PHILOSOPHY

MICHAEL NAAS

Derrida From Now On

FORDHAM UNIVERSITY PRESS
New York ■ 2008

Library of Congress Cataloging-in-Publication Data

Naas, Michael.
    Derrida from now on / Michael Nass.
       p.   cm.
    Includes bibliographical references (p.   ) and index.
    ISBN 978-0-8232-2958-1 (cloth : alk. paper)—
    ISBN 978-0-8232-2959-8 (pbk. : alk. paper)
    1. Derrida, Jacques.   I. Title.
  B2430.D484N32   2008
  194—dc22

                                                      2008034763

Printed in the United States of America
10 9 8   5 4 3 2 1

In gratitude for the lives of three men, each unique,
each for me at the origin of a world

•

Jacques Derrida
1930–2004

•

Pierre Brault
1922–2005

•

Bruce Naas
1934–2006

Contents

Acknowledgments

Several chapters of this book were initially presented as lectures at various institutions or conferences, and many were subsequently published in earlier versions in different journals or collections. They all benefited enormously from the conversations that followed these lectures and the suggestions received from various editors and copyeditors. All but the Conclusion were significantly rewritten for this volume.

Parts of the Introduction were presented at a special session at the Modern Language Association (MLA) in December 2005 at the invitation of Claudia Brodsky. Chapter 1 was first presented in January 2005 at the Alliance Française in Chicago at the invitation of Norah Delaney and published in *SubStance* #106, 34, no. 1 (2005): 6–17. Parts of Chapter 2 were presented at a conference organized by Tanja Stähler in June 2005 at the University of Sussex. Chapter 3, first presented at the Society for Phenomenology and Existential Philosophy (SPEP) in October 2006, and then in April 2007 at Marquette University at the invitation of Pol Vandervelde, and then again in October 2007 at Northern Arizona University at the invitation of Julie Piering, was published in *The New Centennial Review* 7, no. 2 (Fall 2007): 21–42. Chapter 4 was first presented at Slippery Rock College at the invitation of Bernie Freydberg and Richard Findler and was published in *Theory & Event* 8, no. 1 (2005): 1–19. Chapter 5, first presented in February 2005 at the Tate Museum in London at the invitation of Simon Glendinning and then at the Midwest meeting of the American Philosophical Association (APA) in Chicago in

April 2005, at a session organized by Penelope Deutscher, was published in *Derrida's Legacies*, ed. Simon Glendinning and Robert Eaglestone (London: Routledge, 2008), 118–37. Chapter 6 was first published in French under the title "Un philosophe à son tour" in the *Cahier de l'Herne* devoted to Derrida (Paris: l'Herne, 2004), 131–36), and then in English as "A Philosopher at the Wheel," in *Mosaic* 39, no. 3 (September 2006): 59–68. Chapter 7 was first presented at the International Symposium on Deconstruction and National Contexts, organized by Alcides Cardoso dos Santos in Araraquara, Brazil, in June 2005, and then at the Collegium Phaenomenologicum in Città di Castello, Italy, in July 2005 at the invitation of Dennis Schmidt; it was subsequently published in *Research in Phenomenology* 36 (2006): 15–44. Chapter 8 was initially written for the conference Postmodernism at Wofford College in March 2004 at the invitation of Vivian Fisher, and it benefited greatly from my conversations there with Karen Goodchild, Stephen Michelman, and Jim Neighbors. Chapter 9 was originally written for the July 2002 conference on Derrida at Cerisy-la-Salle, organized by Marie-Louise Mallet, and was published in French as "Les restes de l'histoire: Comment faire son deuil des inconnus," in *La démocratie à venir: Autour du travail de Jacques Derrida* Paris: Galilée, 2004), 549–65, and then rewritten in English as "History's Remains: Of Memory, Mourning, and the Event," for *Research in Phenomenology* 33 (2003): 75–96. Chapter 10 was first presented at a conference organized by Dawne McCance at the University of Manitoba in October 2006 and was published in *Mosaic* 40, no. 2 (June 2007): 1–26. "Lifelines," Chapter 11, initially written in French at the invitation of René Major for *Mélanges* (Paris: Stock, 2007), 63–81, was subsequently presented in English at the October 2004 meeting of SPEP and published in *Epochē* 10, no. 2 (Spring 2006): 221–36. Finally, the Conclusion was first presented at a memorial session for Derrida at SPEP in October 2004 and was published in its present form as "The World Over" in *Radical Philosophy Review* 8, no. 2 (2005): 123–30.

I would also like to express my profound gratitude for the many exchanges I have had over the years with my colleagues and students at DePaul University. Most of the ideas in this work were either first conceived or first developed in conversations or seminars with them. My thanks in particular to Peg Birmingham, Rick Lee, Bill Martin, Will McNeill, David Pellauer, Peter Steeves, and, especially, Elizabeth Rottenberg. I owe a special word of thanks to Pascale-Anne Brault and David Krell, who demonstrated their generosity and friendship by reading the entirety of this work and offering many excellent suggestions. This work also profited from many conversations with friends outside DePaul. To name just a few, Geoff Bennington, Martin Hägglund, Samir Haddad, Peggy Kamuf, Matthias Fritsch, Len Lawlor, Dawne McCance, Ginette Michaud, Jeff Nealon, Alan Schrift, Sam Weber, and David Wood.

My thanks also to DePaul's College of Liberal Arts and Sciences and its dean, Chuck Suchar, for the summer grant program that facilitated the completion of this work.

Finally, I owe a great debt of gratitude to Helen Tartar at Fordham University Press, who not only improved the writing and form of this book but who, with her impeccable knowledge of the work and life of Jacques Derrida, informed and clarified the content throughout.

This book is dedicated to my father, Bruce Naas, whose love and attention always sustained my work, and whose memory animates every page of what follows. From now on, I think toward him.

Abbreviations of Works by Jacques Derrida

A   *Adieu to Emmanuel Levinas*. Trans. Pascale-Anne Brault and Michael Naas. Stanford, Calif.: Stanford University Press, 1997.

AF   *Archive Fever*. Trans. Eric Prenowitz. Chicago: University of Chicago Press, 1996.

"AI"   "Autoimmunity: Real and Symbolic Suicides—a Conversation with Jacques Derrida." Trans. Pascale-Anne Brault and Michael Naas. In *Philosophy in a Time of Terror*, ed. Giovanna Borradori, 85–136. Chicago: University of Chicago Press, 2003.

"AID"   "As *if* I were Dead: An Interview with Jacques Derrida." In *Applying: To Derrida*, ed. John Brannigan, Ruth Robbins, and Julian Wolfreys, 212–26. New York: St Martin's Press, 1996.

AL   *Acts of Literature*. Ed. Derek Attridge. London: Routledge, 1992.

"AO"   "Abraham, the Other." Trans. Gil Anidjar. In *Judeities: Questions for Jacques Derrida*, ed. Bettina Bergo, Joseph Cohen, and Raphael Zagury-Orly, 1–35. New York: Fordham University Press, 2007.

AOA   *Athènes à l'ombre de l'Acropole*. Text by Jacques Derrida with photographs by Jean-François Bonhomme. Athens: Editions OLKOS, 1996.

AP   *Aporias*. Trans. Thomas Dutoit. Stanford, Calif.: Stanford University Press, 1993.

"AT"   "Of an Apocalyptic Tone Recently Adopted in Philosophy." Trans. John P. Leavey, Jr. *Oxford Literary Review* 6, no. 2 (1984): 3–37.

C   *Cinders*. Trans. Ned Lukacher. Lincoln: University of Nebraska Press, 1991.

CF   *On Cosmopolitanism and Forgiveness*. Trans. Mark Dooley and Michael Hughes. London: Routledge, 2001.

CFU   *Chaque fois unique, la fin du monde*. Ed. Pascale-Anne Brault and Michael Naas. Paris: Editions Galilée, 2003.

CP   *Counterpath: Traveling with Jacques Derrida*. With Catherine Malabou. Trans. David Wills. Stanford, Calif.: Stanford University Press, 2004.

D   "Demeure: Fiction and Testimony," in *The Instant of My Death / Demeure: Fiction and Testimony*, Maurice Blanchot / Jacques Derrida, trans. Elizabeth Rottenberg, 15–103. Stanford, Calif.: Stanford University Press, 2000.

"DA" "Deconstruction in America: An Interview with Jacques Derrida." With James Creech, Peggy Kamuf, and Jane Todd. *Critical Exchange* no. 17 (Winter 1985): 1–33.

"EH" "A Europe of Hope." Trans. Pleshette DeArmitt, Justine Malle, and Kas Saghafi. *Epochē* 10, no. 2 (Spring 2006): 407–12.

EIRP *Ethics, Institutions, and the Right to Philosophy*. Trans. Peter Pericles Trifonas. Lanham, Md.: Rowman & Littlefield Publishers, 2002.

ET   *Echographies of Television*. With Bernard Stiegler. Trans. Jennifer Bajorek. Cambridge: Polity Press, 2002.

EU   *Eyes of the University: Right to Philosophy 2*. Trans. Jan Plug and others. Stanford, Calif.: Stanford University Press, 2004.

"FF" "La forme et la façon." Preface to Alain David, *Racisme et antisémitisme*. Paris: Ellipses Édition, 2001.

"FK" "Faith and Knowledge: The Two Sources of 'Religion' at the Limits of Reason Alone." Trans. Samuel Weber. In *Religion*, ed. Jacques Derrida and Gianni Vattimo, 1–78. Stanford, Calif.: Stanford University Press, 1998.

"FL" "Force of Law: The 'Mystical Foundation of Authority.'" Trans. Mary Quaintance. In *Deconstruction and the Possibility of Justice*, ed. Drucilla Cornell, Michel Rosenfeld, and David Gray Carlson, 3–67. New York: Routledge, 1992.

FWT *For What Tomorrow. . . .* With Elisabeth Roudinesco. Trans. Jeff Fort. Stanford, Calif.: Stanford University Press, 2004.

G   *Of Grammatology*. Trans. Gayatri Chakravorty Spivak. Baltimore: Johns Hopkins University Press, 1976.

GD   *The Gift of Death*. Trans. David Wills. Chicago: University of Chicago Press, 1995.

GD2   *The Gift of Death*, 2d ed., and *Literature in Secret*. Trans. David Wills. Chicago: University of Chicago Press, 2008.

GG   *Geneses, Genealogies, Genres, and Genius: The Secrets of the Archive*. Trans. Beverley Bie Brahic. New York: Columbia University Press, 2006.

GL   *Glas*. Trans. John P. Leavey, Jr., and Richard Rand. Lincoln: University of Nebraska Press, 1986.

GT   *Given Time*. Trans. Peggy Kamuf. Chicago: University of Chicago Press, 1992.

H   *Of Hospitality*. With Anne Dufourmantelle. Trans. Rachel Bowlby. Stanford, Calif.: Stanford University Press, 2000.

HCFL   *H. C. for Life, That Is to Say. . . .* Trans. Laurent Milesi and Stefan Herbrechter. Stanford, Calif.: Stanford University Press, 2006.

"HI"   "Une hospitalité à l'infini." In *Manifeste pour l'hospitalité—aux Minguettes, Autour de Jacques Derrida*, ed. Mohammed Seffahi, 97–106. Grigny: Éditions Paroles de l'Aube, 1999.

IS   *Inconditonnalité ou souveraineté*. Athens: Editions Patakis, 2002.

JD   *Jacques Derrida*. With Geoffrey Bennington. Chicago: University of Chicago Press, 1993.

"K"   "*Khōra*." Trans. Ian McLeod. In Jacques Derrida, *On the Name*, ed. Thomas Dutoit, 89–127. Stanford, Calif: Stanford University Press, 1995.

LI   *Limited Inc*. Evanston, Ill.: Northwestern University Press, 1988.

LLF   *Learning to Live Finally*. Trans. Pascale-Anne Brault and Michael Naas. Hoboken, N.J.: Melville House Publishing, 2007.

"M"   "Mondialisation: La guerre ou la paix?" *Divinatio*, no. 15 (Spring–Summer 2002): 157–76.

MAR   *Moscou aller-retour*. La Tour d'Aigues: Éditions de l'aube, 1995.

MB   *Memoirs of the Blind*. Trans. Pascale-Anne Brault and Michael Naas. Chicago: University of Chicago Press, 1993.

"MC"   "Mes chances." *Confrontation* 19 (Spring 1988): 19–45.

MJ   *Marx en jeu*. Paris: Descartes & Cie, 1997.

MO   *Monolingualism of the Other; or, The Prosthesis of Origin*. Trans. Patrick Mensah. Stanford, Calif.: Stanford University Press, 1998.

MP   *Margins of Philosophy*. Trans. Alan Bass. Chicago: University of Chicago Press, 1982.

MPD   *Memoires for Paul de Man*. Trans. Cecile Lindsay, Jonathan Culler, Eduardo Cadava, and Peggy Kamuf. New York: Columbia University Press, 1989.

MS   *Marx & Sons*. Paris: Presses Universitaires de France / Galilée, 2002.

N   *Negotiations*. Trans. Elizabeth Rottenberg. Stanford, Calif.: Stanford University Press, 2002.

"NA"   "No Apocalypse, Not Now." Trans. Catherine Porter and Philip Lewis. *Diacritics* 14, no. 2 (Summer 1984): 20–31.

"NW"   "The Nightwatch." Trans. Pascale-Anne Brault and Michael Naas. In *Joyce and Derrida: Between Philosophy and Literature*, ed. Andrew J. Mitchell and Sam Slote. Stanford, Calif.: Stanford University Press, forthcoming.

"O"   "Otobiographies." Trans. Avital Ronell. In Jacques Derrida, *The Ear of the Other*, 1–38. New York: Schocken Books, 1985.

OH   *The Other Heading: Reflections on Today's Europe*. Trans. Pascale-Anne Brault and Michael Naas. Bloomington: Indiana University Press, 1992.

OS   *Of Spirit*. Trans. Geoffrey Bennington and Rachel Bowlby. Chicago: University of Chicago Press, 1991.

"P"   "Passions." In *Derrida: A Critical Reader*, ed. David Wood, 5–35. Malden, Mass.: Blackwell Publishers, 1992.

P   *Points . . . : Interviews, 1974–1994*. Ed. Elisabeth Weber. Trans. Peggy Kamuf and others. Stanford, Calif.: Stanford University Press, 1995.

PC   *The Post Card: From Socrates to Freud and Beyond*. Trans. Alan Bass. Chicago: University of Chicago Press, 1987.

PF   *Politics of Friendship*. Trans. George Collins. New York: Verso, 1997.

PG   *The Problem of Genesis in Husserl's Philosophy*. Trans. Marian Hobson. Chicago: University of Chicago Press, 2003.

PM   *Paper Machine*. Trans. Rachel Bowlby. Stanford, Calif.: Stanford University Press, 2005.

"PMS"   "Peine de mort et souveraineté." *Divinatio*, no. 15 (Spring–Summer 2002): 13–38.

POS   *Positions*. Trans. Alan Bass. Chicago: University of Chicago Press, 1981.

"PP"   "Plato's Pharmacy." Trans. Barbara Johnson. In Jacques Derrida, *Dissemination*, 61–171. Chicago: University of Chicago Press, 1981.

PSY   *Psyche: Inventions of the Other*. 2 vols. Ed. Peggy Kamuf and Elizabeth Rottenberg. Stanford, Calif.: Stanford University Press, 2007.

R   *Rogues: Two Essays on Reason.* Trans. Pascale-Anne Brault and Michael Naas. Stanford, Calif.: Stanford University Press, 2005.

RES   *Resistances of Psychoanalysis.* Trans. Peggy Kamuf, Pascale-Anne Brault, and Michael Naas. Stanford, Calif.: Stanford University Press, 1996.

"SA"   "The Spatial Arts: An Interview with Jacques Derrida." In *Deconstruction and the Visual Arts: Art, Media, Architecture,* ed. Peter Brunette and David Wills. Cambridge: Cambridge University Press, 1994.

SM   *Specters of Marx: The State of the Debt, the Work of Mourning, and the New International.* Trans. Peggy Kamuf. New York: Routledge, 1994.

"SN"   "Sauf le nom." Trans. John P. Leavey, Jr. In Jacques Derrida, *On the Name,* ed. Thomas Dutoit, 33–85. Stanford, Calif.: Stanford University Press, 1995.

SP   *Speech and Phenomena and Other Essays on Husserl's Theory of Signs.* Trans. David B. Allison. Evanston, Ill.: Northwestern University Press, 1973.

SQ   *Sovereignties in Question: The Poetics of Paul Celan.* Ed. Thomas Dutoit and Outi Pasanen. New York: Fordham University Press, 2005.

"SST"   "Some Statements and Truisms about Neologisms, Newisms, Postisms, Parasitisms, and Other Small Seismisms." Trans. Anne Tomiche. In *The States of "Theory": History, Art, and Critical Discourse,* ed. David Carroll, 63–94. New York: Columbia University Press, 1990.

SUR   *Sur Parole.* Paris: Éditions de l'Aube, 1999.

TM   *Tourner les mots: Au bord d'un film.* With Safaa Fathy. Paris: Éditions Galilée, 2000.

TS   *A Taste for the Secret.* With Maurizio Ferraris. Trans. Giacomo Donis. Ed. Giacomo Donis and David Webb. Cambridge: Polity Press, 2001.

"UG"   "Ulysses Gramophone." In Jacques Derrida, *Acts of Literature,* ed. Derek Attridge, 253–309. New York: Routledge, 1992.

WA   *Without Alibi.* Ed., trans., and introd. Peggy Kamuf. Stanford, Calif.: Stanford University Press, 2002.

WAP   *Who Is Afraid of Philosophy?: Right to Philosophy 1.* Trans. Jan Plug. Stanford, Calif.: Stanford University Press, 2002.

WD   *Writing and Difference.* Trans. Alan Bass. Chicago: University of Chicago Press, 1978.

WM   *The Work of Mourning.* Ed. Pascale-Anne Brault and Michael Naas. Chicago: University of Chicago Press, 2001.

Derrida From Now On

Introduction

Bénédictions—*"traces in the history of the French language"*

In the days immediately following the death of Jacques Derrida in October 2004, I imagined that my mourning would go otherwise. ("My mourning," I say, as if I knew what mourning was and could identify it as "my own.") I imagined myself continuing to speak and write about the importance of Derrida's work for me personally and for contemporary thought more generally. I imagined myself bearing witness to the kindness and hospitality Derrida always showed me and my work. I even imagined myself in the wake of Derrida's death recounting some more personal stories about him—something I had never allowed myself to do before. And I also saw myself, of course, continuing to read him, especially, I thought, those final interviews, texts, and seminars, works that I imagined might tell me something about how he himself thought about a death he knew was approaching and how I myself should understand that death or my own work of mourning. In short, I imagined myself as a more or less "faithful heir," bearing witness to Derrida's life and work, introducing that work to students who have never had the chance to read it before, and defending it before those in the academy and the media who so often blindly criticize it.

Today, more than a couple of years after the death of Jacques Derrida, it has become unmistakably clear that I had imagined wrongly, that my mourning has gone otherwise, demonstrating, no doubt, that mourning is never so predictable and that, in this case at least, it was never simply my own. Indeed the one thing I did not imagine myself doing in those

1

early days was returning to Derrida's work—to all his work, early as well as late—with the same passion I had had for it before his death. I simply did not see myself having the heart to study him in that way again, at least not for a long time to come. But events dictated otherwise. In the days and weeks immediately following October 9, 2004, I was invited on numerous occasions to speak or to write on Derrida for various memorial sessions, conferences, and special journal issues. Out of what I considered to be a certain fidelity to Derrida's work and memory, I accepted most every one of these generous invitations—and that's when things began to change. What began each time as an attempt to say a few choice words about a person and an oeuvre I thought I knew well turned into a rereading, a rethinking, and, very quickly, a renewed passion for an incomparably rich and, I came to realize, still very much intact and unread corpus. What began each time as an exercise in memory and mourning ended up becoming an attempt to think along with Derrida about various themes and relationships in his corpus—themes such as sovereignty, hospitality, phantasms, autoimmunity, and the list goes on, and relationships such as that between Europe and the United States, religion and secularism, and so on—themes and relationships that are prominent in Derrida's very last texts, to be sure, but that can all be traced back to very early ones as well. This work is the result of these rereadings of Derrida, rereadings that no doubt *could* have been carried out before Derrida's death but that have been motivated and, the reader will hear, inflected by his death and by the events that have followed it.

What I feel today is thus still, to be sure, an aching melancholy and a deep gratitude for the life and work of Derrida, but also a renewed desire to read and to encourage others to read him. At a time when Derrida's work—indeed when Theory more generally—risks being forgotten, declared passé or irrelevant, it is important, I believe, to read ever more closely in order to demonstrate the extraordinary inventiveness and coherence, as well as the essential reserve and potential, of a work that has, for the most part, yet to be read and is still waiting for us out there in the future. While there will continue to be other appropriate ways to remember Derrida, other ways to pay tribute to his enormous influence in philosophy, literary theory, or the academy more generally, reading him is, I believe, the best way of doing justice to the traces he left in language, the best way of resurrecting or reanimating not him (there can be no illusions here) but his corpus, and the only way of receiving—and I hope this word can be heard without presumption or piety—his *benediction*.

Reading him: that, I believe, is the only absolute condition for receiving a benediction. We must thus begin or begin again, I believe, with the traces Derrida left us in language—and first of all in the French language. In Derrida's final interview, printed in *Le Monde* in August 2004 and subsequently published as *Learning to Live Finally*, Derrida declares in an almost testamentary tone that what interested him most was "to leave traces in the history of the French language" (*LLF* 37).[1] At the outset of a book *in English* on Derrida, it is important to recall Derrida's desire to leave traces in the only language for which he ever professed his love, a language that, like tradition itself, will have preceded and succeeded him, a language, then, that helped him define such notions as trace, spectrality, tradition, inheritance, living on, and so on but that would then itself be defined in turn by these notions. What ultimately interested Derrida was thus not, or not simply, to influence the history of philosophy or literary theory, to leave, as we say, "his mark" on history, or even to "learn to live finally"—something Derrida confesses in this final interview never having learned to do—but to leave traces in the history of the French language, a language that will be marked from now on by Jacques Derrida's unique passage through it.

But how exactly are we to understand this desire and these traces? Several possibilities, none of them mutually exclusive, suggest themselves. We might consider, first, all those traces Derrida will have left upon the French language of his time, words he inflected, inhabited, and signed otherwise, words he countersigned or retraced in his own hand, words, precisely, like *trace, pharmakon, supplement, aporia, crypt, adieu, salut,* and, even more definitively, more uniquely, *différance, dissemination, deconstruction,* and so on. Word traces, then, but also phrases that functioned as signatures, little signs of "poetic invention," idioms that can today be read as dated signatures, little signature-events that came to him from elsewhere, often at the very beginning or end of a text, right in the place of the signature: *il y a là cendre, il y va d'un certain pas, nous nous devons à la mort, comment voulez-vous que je meure?, apprendre à vivre enfin,* and so on.[2] Derrida will have left us countless words and phrases like these, though also, more discreetly, a certain way of punctuating the French sentence, of giving it an élan, of letting it breathe and, at times, and always at the right time, interrupting it and taking its breath away. If what interested Derrida was to leave traces in the history of the French language, that is, in the only language whose purity he ever sought, indeed, whose purity was the only purity he ever sought (*MO* 46), who could deny that he was not successful in leaving such traces, in making such a mark, upon the French language?[3] If, as Derrida claims in this final interview, "love in general passes by way of the love of language" (*LLF* 36), then who could deny that Derrida demonstrated his love by leaving a long series of traces within it?

Yet I believe that what Derrida meant was something quite different when he said in his final interview that what interested him most was to leave traces in the history of the French language. I believe that Derrida did not just want to be *remembered* by means of such traces but that such traces would *themselves* bear memory—his memory and the memory of others—in an even more essential way. For the trace is always, Derrida demonstrated, Derrida believed, not just the inscription of memory and legacy but the mark of abandon or loss, a way of marking not just one's presence but one's absence and death. In other words, the trace—every trace—is testamentary. In a text written in 2002 in memory of Hans-Georg Gadamer, Derrida reflects upon the trace in its relationship to testimony, testament, friendship, and mourning through a reading of a poem by Paul Celan that both he and Gadamer had previously interpreted.[4] In this beautiful and moving memorial essay, Derrida speaks of the way in which the death of the friend that Gadamer was interrupted—and, in fact, will have interrupted from the very beginning—their relationship, their friendship, or, indeed, borrowing a word from Gadamer, their *dialogue*. Derrida writes:

> The dialogue, virtual though it may be, will forever be wounded by an ultimate interruption. Comparable to no other, a separation between life and death will defy thought right from a first enigmatic seal, which we will endlessly seek to decipher. No doubt the dialogue continues, following its course in the survivor. . . . But survival carries within itself the *trace* of an ineffaceable incision. (*SQ* 139; my emphasis)

"The trace of an ineffaceable incision": while one might be tempted to think of this as just one kind of trace among others, I think it could be demonstrated that Derrida always and everywhere, from his first writings to his last, considered every trace to be the trace of an ineffaceable incision, the trace of an interruption. For Derrida every trace entails in its very structure the absence of every possible or foreseeable addressee as well as the disappearance—the death—of the addressor. As Derrida put it back in 1971 in "Signature Event Context," writing—the trace—"must continue to 'act' and to be readable even if what is called the author of the writing no longer answers for what he has written, for what he seems to have signed, whether he is provisionally absent, or if he is dead" (*MP* 316). More than thirty years later, in *Learning to Live Finally*, Derrida puts this now canonical thesis of deconstruction into an even more poignant and personal form. Responding to a question about his work as a kind of "writing of survival," Derrida says:

> The trace I leave signifies to me at once my death, either to come or already come upon me, and the hope that this trace survives me. This is not a striving for immortality; it's something structural. I leave a piece of paper behind, I go away, I die: it is impossible to escape this structure, it is the unchanging form of my life. Each time I let something go, each time some trace leaves me, "proceeds" from me, unable to be reappropriated, I live my death in writing. (*LLF* 32–33)

It is thus not the case that we spend our lives producing traces and then, one day, on the day of our death, we bequeath those traces to the future. Rather, says Derrida, "we are structurally survivors, marked by this structure of the trace and of the testament" (*LLF* 51). The trace is bequeathed, to be sure, but it is also from the beginning structured by this bequeathal, this testament or this testimony.

The desire to leave traces in the history of the French language would thus have to do less with leaving one's mark, leaving little bits of one's idiom or one's body in the language for posterity, than with bearing witness within language to this structure of the trace, to events, places, names, and dates that are themselves so many testaments within language. The desire Derrida expresses in his final interview would thus have to do with leaving within language, and above all within the French language, the "only language he was taught to cultivate" (*LLF* 36), a language he spoke, inhabited, and cultivated but that was precisely not *his own*, so many crypts to mark the singularity of an event. In this sense, a discourse on mourning such as the one we find on Gadamer is not simply one genre of discourse among others but the only genre we ever speak, all language being testamentary and in mourning. Derrida expresses this with Cartesian clarity in an interview from 1990 when he says "I mourn therefore I am" (*P* 321), suggesting that mourning is more originary than the cogito, more originary than thinking, more originary than the soul's silent dialogue or conversation with itself, more originary than being for death or being toward death.

Because even the trace I myself produce is left in a language that is not my own, it suggests not only my death, my death to come or already having come upon me, my mourning or a mourning for myself, but an originary mourning for the other; it suggests or bears the loss of the world that comes upon me with the death of the other, the end of all ethical codes and thus, for Derrida, the beginning of my responsibility. This is precisely how Derrida, reading and translating Celan in the text on Gadamer I cited above, interprets the famous final line of a poem by Celan, "Die Welt ist fort, ich muss dich tragen," a line Derrida reads in terms of an originary mourning for the other and, as a result, an originary responsibility for the other and affirmation of the other. He there writes:

> I must carry [*porter*] the other, and carry *you* . . . even there where the world is no longer between us or beneath our feet. . . . I am left with the immediacy of the abyss that engages me on behalf of the other wherever the "I must"—"I must carry you"—forever prevails over the "I am," over the *sum* and over the *cogito*. Before I *am*, I carry. Before *being me, I carry the other*. I carry *you*. (*SQ* 161–62)

What we can hear in this passage—as if Derrida were pursuing a kind of autobiography or self-interpretation through Celan—is nothing other than a meditation on what it means to leave traces in the history of a language, for Celan, a colleague of Derrida's for several years at the École Normale Supérieure and his partner in a silent and perpetually interrupted dialogue, the history of the German language, and for Derrida, as a reader of Celan and a bearer of his memory, a French language that brings together—and this is just one of its gifts—the vocabulary of mourning with that of birth and responsibility. The "great French language," as Derrida calls it in *Learning to Live Finally* (36), is thus always more prescient or more telling than the one who uses it, but also always more telling than itself, in communication both with other languages, calling out always for translation, and with the "elsewhere" from which it speaks.[5]

In the course of reading or rereading all these texts after the disappearance of Jacques Derrida, many things sound so very different to me today, but one word stands out for me in particular, a word that, better even than *trace* perhaps, expresses this conjunction of memory, mourning, interruption, testament, and testimony that each trace is, and, perhaps in exemplary fashion, the poetic trace. That word, whose religious signification must be not effaced but suspended, and whose etymology must be thought otherwise, is—I dare use it again—*benediction*.[6] Though Derrida came to use the word in his own idiom, though he came to mark and countersign the word in his own name, it is in many ways the word of another—just as most of his words were—in this case, the word of an author writing in another language. In "Shibboleth," a text of 1984 devoted to the poetry of Paul Celan, Derrida writes: "the poem speaks beyond knowledge. It writes, and what it writes is, above all, precisely this:

that it is addressed and destined beyond knowledge, inscribing dates and signatures that one may encounter, in order to bless them, without knowing everything of what they date or sign. Blessing [or benediction] beyond knowledge" (SQ 34). In reading the poem, Derrida suggests, the dates and signatures that are consigned there are blessed by an act of reading, but one that would be beyond all knowledge and, thus, beyond all performative power. When Derrida says that he was always interested in leaving traces in the history of the French language, what I believe he could have said, what I believe he says otherwise, is that he was interested in leaving in language a benediction, not so much a "good word" or some "good news" but a saying that is good because it comes from beyond our power and our knowledge, a saying that does not first and foremost express, like a constative, or even perform or make happen, like a performative, but that bears witness and, in bearing witness, "is" an *event*. Benediction as affirmation, benediction as yes-saying—that is what it would mean to leave traces in the history of a language. Though these traces might be gathered together and marked by a common signature, by what we call a "work," they would themselves always work in the absence of their signatory and thus always beyond the signatory's power to sign their work. Though this does not make the signatory any less responsible for what has been written—indeed quite the contrary—the "event" always goes beyond the signatory's "act."

Such a benediction within the poem—within the work—would thus precede or exceed both the addressor and the addressee, the giver and the receiver. Hence there can be no science of the benediction, no theory of reading to take it into account, no context to assure its success, no criteria for judging when it has taken place. A benediction—*if there is one*, as Derrida might have said—is never uttered to or from a living present. Later in "Shibboleth," Derrida writes: "To address no one is not exactly not to address any one. To speak to no one, *risking*, each time, singularly, that there might be no one to bless, no one who can bless—is this not the only chance for blessing [or benediction]? for an act of faith? What would a blessing be that was sure of itself? A judgment, a certitude, a dogma" (SQ 42). To utter a word that goes beyond the sovereignty of the self, beyond one's powers or one's promises, to leave or to abandon a trace that does not necessarily announce some good word but that *says* a life open to its own undoing, and thus to living on, to another life, or to the life of another—that is, I believe, what Jacques Derrida in so many later texts meant by the word *benediction*.

Such an abandoned trace, which is never granted or received once and for all, is thus anything but a source of comfort or security, certainly not a sign of election or salvation. If all traces are vulnerable to being effaced or destroyed, the archive incinerated or blown to smithereens, the trace as benediction remains vulnerable to effacement or forgetting, even when the archive remains perfectly intact. At the end of an interview a couple of years back on Paul Celan, Derrida ventured:

> Each poem is a resurrection, but one that engages us to a vulnerable body, one that may be forgotten again. I believe that all Celan's poems remain in a certain way indecipherable, retain some indecipherability, and the indecipherable can either call endlessly for a sort of interpretation, resurrection, or new interpretative breath, or, on the contrary, it can perish or waste away once more. Nothing insures a poem against its own death, either because the archive can always be burnt in crematoria or in flames, or because, without being burnt, it can simply be forgotten, or not interpreted, or left to lethargy. Oblivion is always possible. (*SQ* 107)

To read or not to read is thus first and foremost an ethical alternative, and even when we *choose* the former we can never be certain that we are not doing the latter. When it comes to reading Derrida, then, the future remains necessarily uncertain, as he himself well knew. In *Learning to Live Finally* he expresses this uncertainty with clarity and sobriety:

> At my age, I am ready to entertain the most contradictory hypotheses in this regard: I have simultaneously—I ask you to believe me on this—the *double feeling* that, on the one hand, to put it playfully and with a certain immodesty, one has not yet begun to read me, that even though there are, to be sure, many very good readers (a few dozen in the world perhaps, people who are also writer-thinkers, poets), in the end it is later on that all this has a chance of appearing; but also, on the other hand, and thus simultaneously, I have the feeling that two weeks or a month after my death *there will be nothing left*. (*LLF* 33–34)

Because the trace is always testamentary, destined for a future beyond both the addressee and the addressor, its fate is always uncertain, a living on that is always *to be determined*. "Who is going to inherit, and how? Will there even be any heirs?" asks Derrida in *Learning to Live Finally* (33), questions we might rephrase, "Who is going to read, and how? Will there even be anyone to read?" Jacques Derrida knew what it meant to bequeath traces to an uncertain future, but he also knew better than anyone what it means to occupy the uncertain position of an heir. He knew the paradoxes that await the one who thinks him or herself capable of inheriting a thought or taking on a tradition.

If the benediction is always consigned to a text, beyond the capacity of the giver to give it or the receiver to receive it, if the benediction always marks an event, then the only way to bear witness to that event is to attempt a countersignature. Though the risk is always an appropriation that consigns the other's work in yet another way to oblivion (the book you are reading is *mine*, not Derrida's), it is the only way, it would seem, of remaining faithful to the singular law of the other. The only way to bear witness to the text of another is thus to attempt to provoke an event of "one's own." In an interview from 1996, Derrida says that it was this gesture of the countersignature that—like leaving traces in the history of the French language—interested him more than all else.

> I try to think the language in which I write, as well as the singular works of others as they are produced in a particular language, in a faithful way, that is, by trying to encounter that which has happened there before me—just as language is before me, the work of the other is before me—and to countersign these events. The counter-signature is itself a performative, another performative: it is a performative of gratitude toward language or toward the work of the other. Such gratitude always involves becoming implicated oneself, it always involves writing something else in one's turn. This has always interested me much more than all the philosophical theories, even deconstructionist theories, that I have been concerned with.[7]

If forgetting and oblivion are always possible when it comes to a work, the risk is perhaps even greater in a work like Derrida's. If what interested Derrida was leaving behind not a theoretical knowledge or philosophical system but, to take him at his word, countersignatures, traces within language, then our own countersignature must be up to the task of bearing witness to these, even if the success of our own countersignature can never be assured.

While Derrida's death in October 2004 must thus be lamented and his absence mourned, it must also be understood as a unique opportunity for his work. It is perhaps now possible as it never was before to read that work on its own terms, to think and speculate about it, without the specter—indeed, as I argue at the end of this book, the *phantasm*—of Derrida's presence at some colloquium or other, in some new book or other, coming to confirm or refute our hypotheses about it. In other words, it is perhaps now possible as it never really was before to read his work without the phantasm of an author or a father coming to master our reading. The question remains, of course, whether we are ready for such a reading, whether we really can read him from now on without trying to bring him back, whether we really can from now on read without him, or rather, since I hope never to read without him, without the phantasm of him.

It should be clear by now: this work is nothing like an attempt at a final assessment of Derrida's work. It is a work of mourning, true, and a work of celebration, but first and foremost, I would like to think, a work of responsible scholarship and of *reading*. Written at different times and at various distances from that early morning phone call on October 9, 2004, these essays contain varying degrees of reflection and testimony, analysis and emotion. All but one have been reworked to accommodate the demands of a book and in the interest of drawing connections between the various themes and chapters. In no case, however, has this intermingling of analysis and testimony, of reflection and affection, been effaced or attenuated. I will make no apologies for this, even if it will not be to everyone's taste, or will seem to some out of place in a work of scholarship. But since no one will have done more than Derrida to open up the norms and possibilities of scholarship, I am consoled by the thought that, in this regard at least, I have Derrida on my side. That his spirit or spirits will have accompanied me not just in this guiding intention but throughout this work—that must remain an unverifiable hope, what Derrida might have characterized from the one side as a *prayer*, and from the other, a *benediction*.

Derrida From Now On opens and closes with the two texts written closest in time to Derrida's death, indeed, written in the days and weeks just after, two texts initially read in public—veritable "works of mourning," where feelings (and not just mine) were still all too raw. I have decided to include these texts here because of what I think they *say about Derrida*, that is, because of certain things that could really only be said in public on these unique occasions, and because of what these things say about a man who was able to elicit in me and in so many others not just admiration but such an enduring affection. I include them even though they run the risk of transgressing today's unspoken law of scholarly writing—the avoidance at all cost of any pathos. In Chapter 1, then, "*Alors, qui êtes-vous?*: Jacques Derrida and the Question of Hospitality," I recount my first meeting with Jacques Derrida in the context of an analysis of Derrida's work on the theme of hospitality and a thesis about Derrida's work *as* hospitality. In the Conclusion, "The World Over," I end as I began, on a more personal, testamentary note, and reproduce—with only minor alterations—the words I pronounced at a memorial session for Derrida just a couple of weeks after his death. I read these two texts today—and hope others can do the same—as traces not just of a personal mourning but of the originary mourning Derrida had given us to think from the very beginning of his work. I thus read them—and hope others can do the same—as signs and affirmations of life.

The eleven chapters placed between these two eulogies or memorials are more traditional essays, aimed at certain themes in Derrida's work, from his views on analogy and sovereignty to his evolving relationship to Europe and the United States to, finally, his use of the notions of auto-immunity and the phantasm to rethink and remark that strange "thing" that had come to be known for more than forty years as "deconstruction." These essays often begin with a provocation from a relatively late text of Derrida, but they almost always turn back rather quickly to earlier texts. That is the case in Chapter 2, "Analogy and Anagram: Deconstruction as the Deconstruction of the *as*," which begins with comments made by Derrida in "The University Without Condition" (2001) and *Rogues* (2003) about the nature of analogy in his work but which then returns to "Plato's Pharmacy" (1968) and, especially, "*Khōra*" (1987), where, I argue, Derrida engages in a critique of Plato and of Platonism as a philosophy of analogy, indeed, as a *reign of analogy* that is coextensive with the history of Platonic metaphysics. I demonstrate the way in which Derrida moves in this text from the question of writing to a critique of *analogy* as the linchpin of Plato's philosophy to, finally, the articulation of a "philosophy" of the *anagram*—that is, a "philosophy" of *writing*. This analysis of Derrida's work on Plato will allow us, I argue in conclusion, to understand why Derrida in several later texts is so insistent on distinguishing in Plato the Good (which he reads as sustaining the "reign of analogy") from *Khōra* (which, though always approachable only in terms of analogy, resists and undermines all analogy in the name of *writing* or the *anagram*).

In the following several chapters I turn toward a series of more explicitly political themes in Derrida's work. I begin in Chapter 3 by demonstrating how Derrida systematically relates the question of sovereignty to its theologico-political origins and how much of his work over the last couple of decades consisted in ferreting out the theological origins of so many of our political concepts and practices. Arguing that Derrida tries to develop his own version of what is known in France as *laïcité* (roughly translated as "secularism"), or what I will call a "radical secularity without secularism," the chapter demonstrates that almost all of Derrida's analyses over the past couple of decades, from his reading of Schmitt on political sovereignty to his critique of the death penalty and his rereading of democracy, are motivated by a critique of the unthematized or unthought conflation of theological and political concepts in our political institutions and practices. In these works Derrida attempts to bring about a clarification of the theological origins of political concepts, beginning with the concept of sovereignty, which is always related, for Derrida, to the decisive exceptionality of a sovereign subject and thus, in the end, to a subject who begins always to resemble—in what is always a sovereign analogy—a sovereign God. I thus argue that Derrida's brand of laïcité consists in a radical critique of the "theologico-political" in the name or under the aegis of an unconditionality (the other, the event, justice) that exceeds and ultimately disrupts all sovereignty, whether of the self, the nation-state, or God. Derrida's laïcité would thus go well beyond the mere separation of church and state and the protection of the state from religious dogma and authority; it would entail both a critical examination of the state in its theological heritage and a notion of justice that would be the very force behind this laïcité and the nonteleological end toward which it moves.

Because Derrida seems over the last couple of decades to have identified this notion of laïcité more with Europe than with anywhere else in the world, including the United States, I turn briefly in Chapter 4 to Derrida's rethinking of Europe in works such as The Other Heading (1992), Rogues (2003), and, even more recently, "A Europe of Hope" (2004). Since the two earlier works are so much better known and because this topic has been the object of much excellent work in recent years, I spend the majority of this chapter on the last of these works, which will no doubt turn out to have been Derrida's final words on Europe and which distills in a very concentrated form Derrida's ideas on this subject. Initially presented by Derrida in Paris at a fiftieth-anniversary celebration for the French publication Le monde diplomatique, this text articulates a critique of contemporary American political culture and develops what Derrida considered to be the unique "promise" of Europe. At the same time, then, as he criticizes not just the unholy alliance of theology and politics in America more generally but, especially, the prevailing American political climate circa 2004—an even greater identification of politics and religion (the famous "axis of evil"), the continuance of a vastly flawed policy in the Middle East, American manipulation of the United Nations and its Security Council, the invasion of Iraq, and so on—Derrida begins putting more and more of his "hope" in Europe as a counter to all of this, or rather, to be clear, in "Europe," a proper name that Derrida writes almost always in quotation marks and that he challenges us to think beyond its geographical designation and current political incarnation. While Derrida reminds us in this brief text that deconstruction is, in many ways, co-extensive with a critique of Eurocentrism, he seems to see in the promise that goes by the name "Europe" the best hope we have for developing and transforming international law and institutions and for resisting both the theocratism of certain Arab-Islamic states and the politico-theocratic hegemony of the United States.

Having briefly sketched out Derrida's affirmation of what might be called a "Europe to come," I look in Chapter 5 in some detail at "Derrida's America," that is, at the complex history of Derrida and deconstruction in America. Those familiar with Derrida's life and work already know that, while Derrida lived the first eighteen years of his life in colonial Algeria, while he went to university in France and subsequently taught for over forty years in Paris, it was in many ways only in America, or through his success in America—by which I mean here the United States—that Derrida became the internationally renowned intellectual figure that he was when he died in 2004. In other words, America was the place of a relationship without equivalent in the life of Derrida and in the adventure of his work. Since, as Derrida himself once acknowledged, "no theoretical work, no literary work, no philosophical work, can receive a worldwide legitimation without crossing the [United] States, without being first legitimized in the States" (*EIRP* 29), it was in some sense in America that Jacques Derrida, professor at the École Normale Supérieure and École des Hautes Études in Paris, came to be known, indeed renowned, throughout the world as Jacques Derrida, "the founder of deconstruction." In trying to retell the story of Derrida's work and of deconstruction more generally in America, as well as the place occupied by America in Derrida's thought, I attempt to separate fact from fiction, sober reality from journalistic hyperbole, and I end by asking why Derrida, who often identified the adventure of deconstruction with America, tended in the final years of his life to identify it more and more with the promise of a certain "Europe." What changed in Derrida's relationship in America—or what changed in America—to warrant this shift?

In Chapter 6, "Derrida at the Wheel," I step away briefly from these more political themes in order to explore a somewhat playful aside in *Rogues* where Derrida expresses his admiration for the craft of the potter and where he compares the potter's work to that of the philosopher. This chapter attempts to develop Derrida's aside in the same playful spirit, following the theme or trope of the potter and his products in Western literature (from Homer to Wallace Stevens), religion (from Genesis to Romans), and philosophy (from Plato through Heidegger). It also attempts not just to speak of the potter's craft in Derrida's work but to mold a jar, pot, or, perhaps, funeral urn of its own—another way of demonstrating, here at the dead center of the book, the performative nature of Derrida's work.

In Chapter 7 I return to Derrida's rethinking and reevaluation of both America and Europe under the pressure of changing political realities in order to bring Derridean deconstruction into even more direct contact with the American context. In "'One Nation . . . Indivisible': Of Autoimmunity, Democracy, and the Nation-State," I look less at Derrida's thoughts about America than at Derrida's thought in relationship to America as I try to ask how deconstruction can help us think what is happening today in America. I thus examine here Derrida's notion of autoimmunity in order to rethink questions of American identity and mourning post–9/11. For it today appears that *autoimmunity*—a trope Derrida came to use with greater and greater frequency during the last two decades of his life—was the last iteration of what for more than forty years Derrida called *deconstruction*. This chapter looks at the consequences of this terminological shift for understanding not only Derrida's final works (such as *Rogues*) but his entire corpus. By taking up a term from the biological sciences that describes the process by which an organism turns in quasi-suicidal fashion against its own self-protection, Derrida was able to rethink the very notion of *life* otherwise and to demonstrate the way in which every sovereign identity, from the self to the nation-state to, most provocatively, God, is open to a process that both threatens to destroy it and yet gives it its only chance of living on.

In Chapter 8, I use Derrida's work on notions of identity and autoimmunity to read Don DeLillo's *Cosmopolis*, a novel that, I argue, puts Derrida's ideas to the test in a most remarkable and poignant way. *Cosmopolis* illustrates what Derrida argued for in many texts, from early to late, namely, the essential self-destruction or autoimmunity of every *autos* as a self-affirming identity. Set in New York City in the year 2000 and published in 2003, *Cosmopolis* can be read, I argue, as a post–9/11 fable about the inevitable destruction or self-destruction of every *autos* that attempts to protect itself from all compromise, contamination, or corruption. And the *autos* at the center of DeLillo's novel is not just any *autos* but the one that still today defines a certain American dream or phantasm of autonomy, autarky, and automobility—namely, the automobile, in this case, the super-stretch limo of twenty-eight-year-old billionaire Eric Packer.

Chapter 9, "History's Remains: Of Memory, Mourning, and the Event(s) of 9/11," takes Derrida's insights into mourning in general and collective mourning in particular—especially in the wake of 9/11—in order to ask about the relationship between mourning and politics. Taking a lead from a text of Derrida on Jean-François Lyotard, I develop my reading through two examples, one from ancient Greece and one from twentieth-century America: first, the "beautiful death" of Greek culture and the role mourning plays in the constitution and maintenance of the state in Plato's *Laws*, and second, the controversy surrounding the consecration of the Tomb of the Unknown Soldier of Vietnam in Arlington National Cemetery. The latter example will allow me to question the relationship between mourning and identification, the possibilities of mourning the unknown or the unidentifiable for both an individual and a state, and it will provide a unique opportunity for asking about the ways in which the United States has mourned or failed to mourn, remembered or failed to remember, after the attacks in 2001 on the Pentagon and the World Trade Center. This and the previous chapter thus attempt to use Derrida's thinking about America, but also his thinking of politics and of mourning, to reflect upon what has happened in America post–9/11. They are offered not as examples of something like "applied Derrida" but as attempts to think through or along with Derrida the perils America faces not just in its politics but, it seems to me, in the way it organizes (or not) its mourning.

Chapter 10 is in many ways the culmination of several of the previous chapters. It is an attempt to think the logic by which the essential autoimmunity of all identity is occluded, forgotten, or "repressed" by the mechanisms that produce sovereignty in all its guises, that is, by what Derrida calls the *phantasm* of sovereignty. I argue that, for Derrida, sovereignty is always and everywhere a fiction or a phantasm and that to understand the effects and affects of sovereignty we must take this phantasm seriously. The power of sovereignty lies not in its truth value or substantive reality but precisely in the elision of its fictional origin and its real effects, the elision of its performative fiction (an "as if," a *comme si*) and its constative results (an "as such" or a "like that," a *comme ça*). From *comme si* to *comme ça*: that is the movement, I argue, of every fiction and the constitution of every sovereign power. In this chapter I look at three such fictions or phantasms in Derrida's work—the sovereignties of the self, the nation-state, and God—in order to understand Derrida's insistence that we must ultimately relinquish our notion of sovereignty in the name of the very thing that has traditionally been identified with it, that is, the *unconditional*. We thus return in this chapter to some of the themes raised back in Chapter 2 involving the relationship in Plato between the sovereign Good as the ultimate place of the onto-theological phantasm and *Khora* as the unconditional that resists all phantasm. By examining the relationship between sovereignty and unconditionality in many of Derrida's works, from *Speech and Phenomena* to *Glas*, "Faith and Knowledge," and *Sovereignties in Question*, I ask whether a deconstructive *thinking* of sovereignty can help determine and change for the better the deconstructive processes already at work in ourselves and our political institutions. And, finally, I ask in this chapter whether a work such as this one can ever completely resist the temptation of turning its object, namely, Derrida or the memory of Derrida, into a phantasm of its own, into the figure of a father whose sovereign gaze would silently preside over everything being done *in his name*.

In the final chapter, "Lifelines," I return from the more explicitly sociopolitical questions of the previous chapters to the more personal, to the questions of autobiography, poetry, and benediction raised earlier in this Introduction. I attempt here to bear witness to the extraordinary life and work of Derrida by reading what is no doubt his shortest published work—a one-line poem of 1986—in conjunction with several texts of Derrida from the same period, including "Shibboleth" and "How to Avoid Speaking: Denials." I thus attempt to read this one-line poem as precisely one of those "traces in the history of the French language" I mentioned above, a single line that raises so many questions for us about life and work, living speech and the dead letter, life and living on, the French language and its translation, the destiny inscribed in a lifeline and the life or living on of a work.

If *Derrida From Now On* seems to follow a trajectory from France and an emphasis on the French language to a thinking of Europe and, then, America, it is perhaps because I believe, as I believe Derrida believed, that if Derrida's thought is to survive it will do so only by being read in its letter and its spirit so as to be transformed and transplanted *elsewhere*.[8] From now on—though this has *always* been the case—Derrida must always be elsewhere, repeated elsewhere, translated and transformed. From now on, Derrida must always be where he has always been, and where he has always beckoned us to be, drawn toward this elsewhere that goes by the name of the other, or justice, or the trace, or, perhaps, benediction.

I spoke earlier of Derrida's rethinking and reinscription of the notion of *benediction* from "Shibboleth" on, and especially in his readings of Celan. At the very end of *Learning to Live Finally*—an interview, let me recall, from August 2004—Derrida spoke yet again of the notion of benediction, this time in reference to his own life.[9] He ends that interview:

> When I recall my life, I tend to think that I have had the good fortune to love even the unhappy moments of my life, and to bless

them. Almost all of them, with just one exception. When I recall the happy moments, I bless them too, of course, at the same time as they propel me toward the thought of death, toward death, because all that has passed, come to an end. (*LLF* 52)

Yet again—this time for perhaps the last time—Derrida will have spoken *about* the benediction, that is, spoken about it in the constative mode, as he did in "Shibboleth" and in numerous other places afterward. But beyond all these references to benediction, Jacques Derrida's final words, his final performative utterance, in some sense his final act, will have also been a benediction, beyond knowledge and beyond power, spoken through another and not even in the first person, breaking every rule of the successful performative utterance. In words presumably written not long before his death, Derrida thanked those who had come to his burial, and he gave them a benediction, or rather, having left traces to be read by his eldest son over his tomb, he offered those in attendance and no doubt beyond a benediction through his son. Derrida wrote and his son Pierre read: "Il me demande de vous remercier d'être venus, de vous bénir"; "He asks me to thank you for coming, to bless you [to give you a benediction]." Speaking through his son, not knowing to whom he would be speaking, Derrida speaks here as he *will have* always spoken—beyond the living present, beyond the present indicative where one might say "I am." Speaking, therefore, from a future anterior proper to the trace, or rather, speaking from beyond the present—"wherever I may be [*d'où que je sois*]," as he says in the subjunctive just a couple of lines later to conclude—Derrida offers a benediction through his son, demonstrating one last time how the trace comes always before our own generation and is already beyond the next.[10]

Today, this benediction—beyond the power and knowledge of Jacques Derrida—is given to us by the traces Derrida will have left in the history of the French language and, once again beyond him, in so many other languages—including this one. But to receive that benediction one must read him, one must begin or begin again to read him, and if the machine is working well, something just may click and, unpredictably, and perhaps without one even realizing it, it just may happen. "Derrida From Now On," then, or rather, as the title of this work first came to me on a beautiful spring day in Paris in 2006, a phrase that came well in advance of the book itself, indeed that came almost as a way of announcing the book to come, *Derrida Désormais*.[11]

Alors, qui êtes-vous?

Jacques Derrida and the Question of Hospitality

I could not begin these reflections on the life and work of Jacques Derrida without recalling at least one further phrase in French, the only language for which Derrida ever expressed his fidelity and his love and the only language I ever spoke with him. I could not begin without letting at least one more of those traces resonate within me, one of those traces of a French language in which I will never feel absolutely at home but which I nevertheless have also come to love—and in large part thanks to Jacques Derrida. Indeed, I could not cross this threshold without letting this simple phrase—*Alors, qui êtes-vous?*—reverberate within me, since it was the very first Jacques Derrida ever addressed to me, on the verge of what would become—and I feel fortunate to be able to use the terms—a relationship of hospitality and of friendship.

Alors, qui êtes-vous? I must emphasize here at the outset that these are Jacques Derrida's words, not my own, so that no one is misled by the title of this chapter into thinking that I would have the temerity of asking this question of Jacques Derrida, or the audacity to think I could actually provide a response. *Qui êtes-vous?* "Who are you?" That is a question I never posed and will never pose to Jacques Derrida.[1] I underscore this because it is so tempting today, in the wake of Derrida's death, to want to claim some special privilege, some unique intimacy, with the man or his work, in order to say something definitive about him or it. It is tempting to think that one can offer some final judgment, now that that life and that work have, it seems, come to an end. As Maurice Blanchot writes at the end of *Friendship*, a text Derrida knew very well, this unique time just after the death of a thinker we've read, known, and admired is typically "the moment of complete works," the terrible moment when "one wants to publish 'everything,' one wants to say 'everything,' . . . as if the 'everything is said' would finally allow us to stop a dead voice, to stop the pitiful silence that arises from it."[2] It is the moment when we are tempted to give a final evaluation, a final reckoning, the moment when we feel more licensed than usual to go beyond the facts, to say something more than just "Jacques Derrida was born in 1930, in El-Biar, Algeria; he went to France in 1949, graduated from the École Normale Supérieure and later took a teaching position at that same institution, eventually becoming known in France and, indeed, throughout the world through his more than seventy books, translated into dozens of languages, for a type of philosophical and literary analysis known as 'deconstruction.'" It is the moment when the living feel justified, even entitled, to go beyond these facts to assess the merits of the man and his work and assign them some definitive place in the *history* of French letters or of Western philosophy. Faced with such a temptation, we would do well to recall what Blanchot wrote after the death of his friend Georges Bataille, near the very end, once again, of *Friendship*:

> How could one agree to speak of this friend? Neither in praise nor in the interest of some truth. The traits of his character, the forms of his existence, the episodes of his life, even in keeping with the search for which he felt himself responsible to the point of irresponsibility, belong to no one. There are no witnesses. Those who were closest say only what was close to them, not the distance that affirmed itself in this proximity, and distance ceases as soon as presence ceases.

Alors, qui êtes-vous? These words and the gestures and tone that accompanied them live on today—Blanchot is right—only in me, in my memory, so that everything I say reveals much more about me than about Jacques Derrida. And yet I would like to believe that having been so profoundly marked by the thought and person of Jacques Derrida, touched in a way that goes well beyond what we so blithely call "influence," something of who Jacques Derrida *was* or *is* cannot help but be conveyed by these words, something like a secret we shared—a secret that would not be anything like an answer to the question *Alors, qui êtes-vous?* but that just might tell us something about the question itself.

Alors, qui êtes-vous? Though I had been reading Jacques Derrida for several years and had heard him speak in public on numerous occasions, indeed, had even attended his seminar in Paris for an entire year, I had never spoken to him directly before the fall of 1988, when I approached his desk one day after class in the Salle Dussane at the École Normale Supérieure in order to volunteer—in order to be "volunteered," really, for it was an act of divine madness—to give an exposé in his seminar later that year. After a brief description of that exposé in halting and embarrassed French, Derrida looked at me kindly, with a light and I think somewhat amused smile, and asked, *Alors, qui êtes-vous?* Little did I know at the time that these very simple, common words, this everyday question, would end up transforming so radically my evolving answer to that question, so that it would be impossible for me to answer that question today without recalling that conversation of 1988 and everything it ultimately led to or portended.

I have thus tried over the years to hear those words as they were spoken on that day, without the successive overlays of so many subsequent memories, conversations, readings, and interactions. I have tried to recall the nuances and inflection of this everyday, threshold phrase. Spoken not at all out of impatience or irritation, as a way of asking me, *Alors, qui êtes-vous? Vous vous prenez pour qui?* "Just who are you or who do you think you are?" but, rather, out of what I would like to call a certain hospitality, it was offered—or at least this is how I heard it—as an invitation, as a way of saying *Dites-moi un peu plus. Dites-moi qui vous êtes;* "Tell me a bit more. Tell me who you are," for example, "Tell me your name." It was, in short, a welcoming, hospitable phrase, an invitation to tell him not exactly *who I was* but just a little more about myself, beginning with my name, what I was doing in France, in Paris, in his class, proposing to give an exposé in his seminar later that year on the topic of friendship in Homer.

Yes, when Jacques Derrida asked me that day in the fall of 1988 *Alors, qui êtes-vous?* he was in effect asking me, there on the threshold of an introduction and an invitation, and I heard it in precisely this way, "What is your name?" *Comment t'appelles-tu?* That is, he was asking me with this very common, everyday phrase what he would come to call in a book of 1997 entitled *Of Hospitality* the question of hospitality itself, a question that, depending on the inflection, can either exclude or invite, repel or draw in. Derrida there writes:

> The foreigner . . . who has the right to hospitality in the cosmopolitan tradition which will find its most powerful form in Kant [in, for example, *Perpetual Peace*] . . . is someone with whom, to receive him, you begin by asking his name; you enjoin him to state and to

guarantee his identity, as you would a witness before a court. This is someone to whom you put a question and address a demand, the first demand, the minimal demand being: "What is your name?" . . . What am I going to call you? It is also what we sometimes tenderly ask children and those we love. (*H* 27–28)

The threshold question is thus the question of the name, a seemingly banal, everyday question that can be asked and/or heard as either an invitation or a threat, a welcoming or an interrogation. In an interview published in *Le Monde* shortly after the publication of *Of Hospitality*, Derrida was asked to elaborate upon this question, to explain whether hospitality consists in "questioning the one who arrives, and first of all by asking him his name," or whether it begins "with the welcome that is without question." He was asked, in other words, a question about the necessary conditions of hospitality, and he responded:

The decision is made at the heart of what looks like an absurdity, impossibility itself (an antinomy, a tension between two equally imperative laws that are nonetheless not opposed). Pure hospitality consists in welcoming the *arrivant*, the one who arrives, before laying down any conditions, before knowing or asking anything of him, whether this be a name or a piece of identification. But this pure hospitality also presupposes that one addresses him, and singularly so, that one thus calls him and acknowledges a proper name for him. "What is your name?" [*Comment t'appelles-tu, toi?*] Hospitality consists in doing everything to address the other; it consists in granting him, indeed, in asking him, his name, all the while trying to prevent this question from becoming a "condition," a police interrogation, an inquest or an investigation, or a border check. The difference is subtle and yet fundamental, a question asked on the threshold of one's home [*chez soi*] and on the threshold between two inflections.[3]

For Derrida, then, hospitality—a theme he treated in several works during the last decade of his life—consists in what might be called a negotiation between two seemingly contradictory imperatives, the imperative to welcome the other unconditionally, before any knowledge, recognition, or conditions, indeed, before any names or identities, and the imperative to welcome someone in particular and not some indefinite anyone, someone, then, with a particular name, identity, and origin. The question of hospitality, *Comment t'appelles-tu?* "What is your name?" thus appears stretched between "two equally imperative laws," its offering and its reception suspended on the lip "between two inflections," between the conditional and the unconditional, possibility and the impossible. But since any notion of hospitality that refers to the "unconditional" can so easily be written off as naïve, utopian, impractical, or, simply, impossible, I would like to linger a bit here on this threshold of hospitality in order to ask about the relationship between unconditional and conditional hospitality in Derrida. I do so because I cannot help but think that Derrida is right when he claims that unconditional hospitality is impossible, or *the* impossible, but that it nonetheless takes place, indeed, all the time, and sometimes through the most everyday and unremarkable gestures, such as the one I experienced in the Salle Dussane of the École Normale Supérieure that fall day in 1988. If unconditional hospitality is impossible, or *the* impossible, it is the only hospitality that can give any meaning to the concept of hospitality itself and, thus, the only possible hospitality, the only one worthy of this name.

What then "is" hospitality for Derrida? The first thing to note is that, for Derrida, the concept of hospitality must be rigorously distinguished from any relation of reciprocity or exchange between two parties, whether we are talking about an exchange of goods and services, or a more symbolic exchange of words and assurances, or simply an exchange of names. There would be no hospitality, no rigorous concept of hospitality, no hospitality worthy of the name, without an unconditional welcoming of the other before any exchange, a welcoming of an other whose identity and character are thus not assured, an other, therefore, who may in fact pose a threat to us, who may cause us to question our right to what we call "our home," or who may in fact try to evict us from that home and from everything we consider "our own." At the limit, then—and to define a concept rigorously one must always think the limit—there would be no hospitality without this *exposure* to an *arrivant* who arrives or comes even before he or she can even be identified or greeted as "our guest," since any identification of this other would already take back, betray, or nullify the hospitality being extended. In *Aporias* Derrida elaborates upon this unconditional welcoming of the *arrivant*, of the one who arrives, a welcoming that would take place before all interrogations and identifications and would thus seem to be the essence of hospitality, the only true, genuine, or pure hospitality, the only one worthy of the name:

> I am talking about the absolute *arrivant*, who is not even a guest.
> He surprises the host—who is not yet a host or an inviting power—
> enough to call into question, to the point of annihilating or rendering indeterminate, all the distinctive signs of a prior identity,

beginning with the very border that delineated a legitimate home and assured lineage, names and language, nations, families and genealogies. The absolute *arrivant* does not yet have a name or an identity. (*AP* 34)

Hospitality thus seems to require this unconditional welcoming of the other *before* any powers or possibilities, any identities or identifications, before the French word *hôte*, for example, has been read or interpreted to mean *either* host *or* guest, before any difference between host and guest, the one who invites and the one invited, before, it seems, any *power* or *capacity* to ask a question like *Comment t'appelles-tu?* It appears to make no sense to speak of *hospitality*—as opposed, say, to relations of exchange, interaction, and commerce—without this unconditional invitation where nothing is expected in return, without this absolute or hyperbolic opening of the host to the guest, an opening so radical that the host must give up even his or her identity as host.

And yet, as we can see, this radical or absolute exposure to the other in unconditional hospitality actually threatens the very categories that make it possible. For if it makes no sense to speak of hospitality, as opposed to commerce or exchange, without this notion of an unconditional welcome, it *also* appears to make *no sense* to speak of hospitality without, precisely, a *hand* being extended or a good being offered *from* host *to* guest, that is, without a *difference* between host and guest and an orientation, if not a direction, being established between the one offering or welcoming and the one being offered or welcomed. Indeed, there would seem to be no hospitality worthy of the name in a general invitation or welcome that is not extended by some particular host with a name and an identity to some particular guest, to someone, therefore, who might well be asked there on the threshold, who perhaps must be asked in order for the invitation to be effective, effectively offered and received, *Alors, qui êtes-vous?* or *Comment t'appelles-tu?*

It thus appears that what Derrida calls pure or absolute hospitality has its chance only in the impure or conditional hospitality that then conditions and threatens it. That is why Derrida speaks in the passage cited above of a "tension" or an "antinomy" between "two equally imperative laws." Unconditional or pure hospitality is at once betrayed or perverted by impure or conditional hospitality and yet also given its only chance *as pure hospitality* by it. Similarly, conditional hospitality can only ever be *called* hospitality and *experienced as* hospitality by means of the pure or absolute hospitality toward which it is drawn and by which it is inspired. As Derrida puts it in *Paper Machine*, without a certain "impossible," without, in this case, *unconditional hospitality*, the "desire, the concept, and experience, the very thought of hospitality, would be meaningless" (*PM* 131).

Hence unconditional hospitality is not some goal or telos toward which we must strive; it is not some utopic ideal on which we must keep our eyes fixed. It is what accounts for the very concept and experience of hospitality itself, and it is what drives all "progress" toward a more universal hospitality, such as we find it, for example, in Kant's *Perpetual Peace*. Even though absolute or unconditional hospitality becomes conditioned the moment it is codified, the moment it is put into practice or law, the moment it becomes effective (and so, in Kant, the moment it is extended to citizens of other nation-states but not to noncitizens, or the moment nation-state citizens are granted a temporary right to asylum but not a permanent one), this unconditional hospitality remains that which draws and inspires all effective hospitality, and it remains the only hospitality *in the name of which* any hospitality can be offered.

It is important to underscore this relationship between unconditional and conditional hospitality, since so many of Derrida's other analyses of what we take to be ethical concepts—from the gift to friendship—rely upon a similar articulation. Whereas unconditional hospitality, like the gift, is irreciprocal, absolute, and hyperbolic—that is, beyond or transgressive of all norms, customs, and laws—conditional hospitality always entails a relationship of exchange and reciprocity, a regime of norms, customs, laws, and proportion. Whereas unconditional hospitality is offered to the anonymous *arrivant*, to the absolute other, before any identities or names have been given, before the other has been identified as either human, god, or animal, as either living or dead, conditional hospitality is always offered by a figure with some power or sovereignty, some means of identification, selection, and determination, to someone with a name, family, and social status—and, thus, *not* to others. Whereas unconditional hospitality is thus an impossible hospitality, that is, a hospitality beyond or before all possibilities and all powers, the only one, therefore, truly worthy of the name, and thus the only possible hospitality, every conditional hospitality, every hospitality determined by laws, codes, and powers, is, as possible, impossible, that is, a hospitality unworthy of the name and thus no hospitality at all. Whereas unconditional hospitality, like a kind of grace or absolute form of respect, corresponds to an absolute desire for hospitality, to what Derrida would elsewhere call justice or, in this context, a just hospitality, conditional hospitality entails laws, rights, duties, and debts, pacts made between individuals or groups on the basis of names, lineages, and histories, in a word, laws of hospitality that are inscribed in a particular language and culture and so are always subject to history and change.

Unconditional hospitality would thus seem to correspond to a call for justice that the law or the laws of conditional hospitality can never heed and yet can never do without. Justice is thus always heterogeneous to and yet inseparable from the law it both makes possible and perpetually interrupts. Recall that in the passage cited above Derrida called unconditional hospitality and conditional hospitality "two equally imperious *laws*" (my emphasis), laws that, he will go on to say in *Of Hospitality*, are "heterogeneous but inseparable," "irreducible" and "antinomic," forming a "nondialectizable antinomy." The question concerning the link or relation, the articulation, between these two laws, these two regimes of hospitality, must thus be constantly raised, and the language to describe this relation perpetually reinvented.

In *Of Hospitality* Derrida calls the law of unconditional hospitality a kind of law above all laws, an *anomos nomos*, a law, a singular law, above all conditioned plural laws. It is this law that accounts for the desire for hospitality and justice; like the law above all laws that inspires all civil disobedience (though this is just an analogy, since civil disobedience typically relies upon one conditioned law being placed above another, a respect for human rights, for example, above some law of the nation-state), the law of unconditional hospitality "inspires," "draws," and "guides" the many conditional laws of hospitality. It is thus *in the name* of the law of unconditional hospitality that conditional laws are made effective and inscribed *in history*, even if these conditional laws inevitability betray the law of the unconditional and even if they not only expose the perfectibility of this law to pervertibility but sometimes hinder its progress and even lead to its regression. Indeed, for Derrida, progress toward greater and greater universality in hospitality is hardly inevitable and can always be reversed. Hostility, inhospitality, and xenophobia are always possible, and history offers no guarantees that the intrinsic perfectibility of the laws of hospitality will not be developed or will go unheeded. Vigilance is thus always required, because things can always get worse.

If it is always in the name of the law of unconditional hospitality that conditional laws are inscribed in history, then the laws of hospitality must be thought of as a response to the undeniable though always vulnerable and pervertible *experience of the other*. It is, therefore, in the becoming-law of justice, in the becoming-law of the law of the other, in the becoming-effective of absolute hospitality, that language (the name of hospitality), history (the movement "toward," say, a perpetual peace), and experience (the experience of the other as other, as stranger, as absent, or as dead) are first opened up. *Comment t'appelles tu?* would thus be *the* question of hospitality not simply because it is asked on the threshold of the house or the nation-state, because it is on the verge of a relationship, whether of hospitality or hostility, but because it is an *articulation* between the unconditional law of hospitality, for which there are no protocols, and conditional laws that begin to determine and condition that unconditional law. *Comment t'appelles tu?* This question is already a response, perhaps responsible and perhaps not, to the experience of the other. It is already a response in a particular time and place, in a particular language and not another, indeed, in a language that might well not be the language of the one being questioned. Because there is no law to prescribe the words of a hospitable question, no language beyond languages in which to ensure its just reception, the question of hospitality—the question *as* hospitality— comes down to a matter of *inflection*.

There is thus, on the one hand, an inevitable perversion of unconditional hospitality by conditional hospitality, an ineluctable violence, even if, as we have seen, conditional hospitality is the only chance for the unconditional, the only chance for its inscription in history and in language. But there is also the risk that within this inevitable perversion the hospitable question "Hey you, what's your name?" will get turned into a police interrogation, that is, that the hospitable question that aims to welcome the other and open the self up to difference and surprise will turn into an interrogation bent on protecting and enforcing one's borders and affirming one's identity. Because the law of hospitality can never be inscribed as such in laws, because this law has no "as such," nothing can ever assure us that this negotiation will not go terribly awry, either for the host or for the guest. Because we are negotiating here between two antinomic imperatives, and because the conditions and circumstances of this negotiation are each time unique, there can be no law or formula, no categorical imperative, to ensure that hospitality does not cross over into hostility. Derrida thus writes in yet another text on hospitality, entitled "Une hospitalité à l'infini," that is, "An Infinite Hospitality" or "A Hospitality to the Infinite," "hospitality must be so inventive, adjusted to the other, and to the welcoming of the other, that each experience of hospitality must invent a new language" ("HI" 101). Such an emphasis on novelty and invention helps explain, I think, why Derrida speaks in the next sentence of the *Le Monde* interview I cited above of hospitality not as a science or law but as "an art and a poetics," even if, as he says, "an entire politics depends on it and an entire ethics is determined in it."

If hospitality is thus, for Derrida, more of "an art and a poetics" than a science or a law, then Derrida's *thinking* about hospitality, his *articulation* of hospitality, is itself perhaps more of an "art and a poetics" than a theory or a theorem. It is a thinking that invents at the limits or on the threshold of the concept and an articulation that attempts to give voice to "two equally imperious laws" and to two inflections. There is then, I think we can see, more than just an analogy between the form of Derrida's thinking about hospitality and hospitality itself. I will try to spell this out in more detail in a moment, but before doing so let me return to my own narrative about Derrida. I do so in order again to insist that the laws of hospitality I have been speaking of condition not only the policy of nation-states but our most everyday practices and relations—from greeting another to asking his or her name.

I would thus like to believe—though, of course, this must remain a matter of belief and can never be proven or justified—that I received a hospitality worthy of its name in the seminar of Jacques Derrida on that day in 1988 and then later that year when I delivered that exposé, that I received it in his home on numerous occasions thereafter, in the cafés or restaurants where we would sometimes meet, and in the telephone calls he never failed to make either from France or whenever he was visiting the United States. Jacques Derrida was indeed, among so many other things, a man of hospitality or, to use his words, an artist or a poet of hospitality, someone who knew how to offer and to accept hospitality, who was receptive to hospitality in all its gestures and guises, who experienced the hospitality of language and tradition, though also, it has to be said, its opposite. Hence Jacques Derrida was sensitive, as well he should have been, to being expelled at the age of twelve from his school in colonial Algeria for being Jewish, his French citizenship, accorded to French Jews by the Crémieux decree of 1870, suddenly revoked. He was sensitive, as well he should have been, to the fact that he was never really accepted by a certain academic establishment in France, and to the fact that most of his students are still not accepted by it to this day. And he was sensitive, as well he should have been, to being labeled in the United States an "abstruse theorist," by which was meant a fancy French stylist who concealed his lack of rigor with word-play and mystification, and to being labeled in France an intellectual "superstar" of the United States, by which was meant a marketing sensation within an American academy that cannot tell the difference between genuine learning and its flashy simulacrum.[4]

And yet he was also extremely sensitive to and appreciative of, I believe, the hospitality that was often shown him and his work in France, at the École Normale Supérieure or the École des Hautes Études, where he taught for close to four decades, at the Collège International de Philosophie, which he helped found in 1983, or at Cerisy-la-Salle, where four major colloquia were devoted to his work—in France, then, but also throughout the world, and perhaps particularly in the United States, from New Haven, Baltimore, and New York to Los Angeles, Santa Monica, and Irvine, not to mention here in Chicago, to which I will return. Despite all of the exclusions and attacks, he was sensitive, I think, to the fact that he, an Algerian Jew, should become a renowned teacher in an elite French institution, in the capital of the French nation-state, welcomed within it just enough to be able to welcome others—as hundreds, indeed thousands, of students from around the world can testify, many of whom will have received the benediction of a welcoming phrase like *Alors, qui êtes-vous?*

If I have spent so much time on this one personal memory and on an interpretation of it in terms of hospitality, it is because, of all the ways in which deconstruction might be presented—none of them definitive, each provisional and determined by context—the one that strikes me as most appropriate today is this one: *deconstruction is inviting* or *deconstruction is hospitality.*[5] Though Derrida did not invent this word *deconstruction*, he is certainly the one most responsible for making it a staple of academic discourse and even of popular culture. Often mischaracterized as a philosophy of negation or destruction, deconstruction can perhaps best be described as a philosophy of affirmation, an affirmation of what is best in the tradition and of what is most living in life—a philosophy, therefore, of thoughtful and responsible reflection and reception, a thinking par excellence *of* hospitality. Deconstruction would thus be not simply a mode of philosophical reflection that thinks, among other things, hospitality, the theme of hospitality and the traditional texts concerning it, but a thinking that *is* hospitality—hospitality to the tradition, to be sure, but also to what exceeds and cannot be identified within that tradition.

From the early 1960s onward, Derrida taught and inspired philosophers, literary critics, political theorists, artists, and so on to turn back to the tradition, to reread and reflect upon it, in order to criticize what needed to be criticized in the name of a promise or secret harbored within the tradition itself. Hence Derrida became known for seminal works in philosophy (on Plato, Aristotle, Augustine, Descartes, Rousseau, Kant, Hegel, Kierkegaard, Nietzsche, Freud, Husserl, Heidegger, Benjamin, and Levinas, to name just some of the most prominent) and literary criticism (for example, on Joyce, Ponge, Celan, and Blanchot) that attempted to find resources within canonical figures and texts to rethink such important social, political, and ethical themes as friendship, hospitality, forgiveness, community, sovereignty, and so on.

In each case, Derrida sought to draw our attention to—indeed, he invited us to welcome—something that exceeds the explicit argument of these texts, something that might at once function as a place of critique or resistance and call for a new understanding of our traditional concepts, oppositions, and structures. Whether this something went by the name of "justice" or the "Other," the *arrivant* or the "event," Derrida welcomed something within the tradition that can never be appropriated, made present, or identified. Each time, Derrida welcomed something from "elsewhere," or, rather, he welcomed the "elsewhere." In a text entitled *Monolingualism of the Other*, Derrida says that deconstruction would not have been possible without this "strange reference to an 'elsewhere [*ailleurs*]' of which the place and the language were unknown and prohibited even to myself, as if I were trying to *translate* into the only language and the only French Western culture that I have at my disposal, the culture into which I was thrown at birth, a possibility that is inaccessible to myself" (*MO* 70). Hence Derrida always attempted to welcome the "elsewhere" in an *unconditional* way, but he did so always from within a context or text that was specific, marked by a particular epoch and language—in a word, within a context that was always *conditioned*. It is in this sense that we might see hospitality not simply as a delimitable theme within the corpus of Derrida but as the very "activity" of Derrida's work. Even when, for whatever reason, deconstruction was not welcome, it remained in the hands of Derrida always welcoming, turning us back to the tradition in order to reread and remark it in a patient and responsible fashion, in order to launch it anew and so be faithful to the *event* it harbors. For the event—like the guest or *arrivant*—is something that visits us but cannot ultimately be identified, anticipated, or foreseen against the backdrop of any horizon. It is something that befalls us, that falls upon us vertically, from an abyssal height, disrupting all our expectations—an uninvited guest that is the only guest worthy of the name and, indeed, the only guest capable of providing us with a future rather than a moribund repetition of the past. Unconditional hospitality is thus always hospitality to the event—and the event, I would argue, is what was always at the heart of Derrida's thought. To cite *Aporias* again, the word *arrivant* describes, says Derrida, "the neutrality of *that which* arrives, but also the singularity of *who* arrives, he or she who comes, coming to be where s/he was not expected, where one was awaiting him or her without waiting for him or her, . . . without knowing what or whom to expect . . .—and such is hospitality itself, hospitality toward the event" (*AP* 33).

Alors, qui êtes-vous? In a sense, that is the question Derrida asked of everyone he read, not in order to evaluate, assess, or define once and for all, not so as to learn or speak the truth of Plato or Hegel or Heidegger, but in order to bear witness to the singularity of a proper name and the promise it bears. Between two equally imperious laws: to read a text in the terms the text itself lays out, as if in response to the ontological question "Who or what are you?" to read according to all the respected and time-honored protocols of interpretation and good scholarship, emphasizing the historical context, the original language of the text, the hidden assumptions and presuppositions, and so on, but then to try to discover another logic organizing the text, beyond the intention or self-conscious presentation of the author, something that would *not* be a truer, more definitive answer to the question *Alors, qui êtes-vous?* "Who are you, Plato?" or "Who are you, Heidegger?" but an open question that would invite us to rethink the tradition and countersign it in our turn. All in the name, as Derrida would put it, of a promise or a secret sealed in the name, in the name of what within the tradition resists every answer to the question *Alors, qui êtes-vous?*—something like the event, or, perhaps especially today, *life.*

In all his work, though in a renewed and more insistent fashion over the last decade, Jacques Derrida was a thinker of *life.* As was his wont, as was his art or his poetics, he spoke about it by questioning it, by receiving but then criticizing the terms in which it has been thought, the neat opposition, for example, between life and death, the living breath and the dead letter, what is called the living animal and its others. Which is why Derrida spoke so often, and especially in later texts, of living on, of ghosts, phantoms, and specters, of memory and mourning, of a notion of lifedeath that would precede the oppositions between nature and convention, the original and the artificial, the animal and the machine, living speech and the dead letter. Derrida was an heir to the tradition, to the "life" it had given him, but he was an heir or guest who thought it necessary *not* to leave intact that into which he was invited, the kind of heir or guest who believed it necessary to return the hospitality he had been offered by countersigning the tradition in his own name. In an interview with Elisabeth Roudinesco in *For What Tomorrow*, Derrida speaks of himself as just such a guest or heir:

> Whether it's a question of life or work or thought . . . I have always recognized myself in the figure of the heir—and more and more so, in a way that is more and more deliberate, and often happy. By insistently confronting this concept or this figure of the heir, I came to think that, far from the secure comfort that we rather too quickly associate with this word, the heir must always respond to a sort of

double injunction, a contradictory assignation: It is necessary first of all to know and to know how to *reaffirm* what comes "before us," which we therefore receive even before choosing, and to behave in this respect as a free subject. Yes, it is necessary [*il faut*] (and this "it is necessary" is inscribed directly on and within the received heritage), it is necessary to do everything possible to appropriate a past even though we know that it remains fundamentally inappropriable, whether it is a question of philosophical memory or the precedence of a language, a culture, and a filiation in general. What does it mean to reaffirm? It means not simply accepting this heritage but relaunching it otherwise and keeping it alive. Not choosing it (since what characterizes a heritage is first of all that one does not choose it; it is what violently elects us), but choosing to keep it alive. (*FWT* 3)

We begin to see here, I think, a convergence of all the themes I've introduced thus far—the double injunction of deconstruction, hospitality, and reception, affirmation of the past and a past that cannot be appropriated, and, finally, life. Derrida continues his response in *For What Tomorrow*, which I cite again at length both because of what it says about life and because citation, incorporating the words of another into one's own, incorporating as a kind of mourning *and* melancholy, is another way of letting the other live on in us, that is, another kind of hospitality . . .

Life—being-alive—is perhaps defined at bottom by this tension internal to a heritage, by this reinterpretation of what is given in the gift, and even what is given in filiation. This reaffirmation, which both continues and interrupts, resembles (at least) an election, a selection, a decision. One's own *as* that of the other: signature against signature. But I will not use any of these words without placing quotation marks and precautions around them. Beginning with the word "life." It would be necessary to think life on the basis of heritage, and not the other way around. It would be necessary therefore to begin from this formal and apparent contradiction between the passivity of reception and the decision to say "yes," then to select, to filter, to interpret, and therefore to transform; not to leave intact or unharmed, not to leave *safe* the very thing one claims to respect before all else. . . . to save it, perhaps, yet again, for a time, but without the illusion of a final salvation. (*FWT* 3–4)

If deconstruction is indeed hospitality, then it is not a hospitality that leaves what is welcomed intact or unharmed, that leaves it safe and sound, and that, while allowing it perhaps to live on, offers the illusion of some final salvation. Indeed, for Derrida fidelity to the tradition consists precisely in *not* leaving it safe and sound, intact or unharmed. It is important to underscore this, so that no one is tempted to hear my equation of deconstruction with hospitality, my equation of deconstruction as the unconditional welcoming of the other, as something innocuous, heartwarming, pacific, or pacifying. Nothing could be more inimical to the letter or the spirit of Derrida's work. My intention is thus not to make Jacques Derrida into some spokesperson for good liberal, democratic values—even if, when push came to shove, when it came to voting yes or no, signing a petition or not signing, it was often on the side of liberal democracy that Derrida most often spoke and lent his support. For even when it is characterized, as it is here, as hospitality, deconstruction is hardly reassuring. If hospitality consists in an exposure to the event of what comes, in an unconditional opening to the Other, before any recognition or cognition, then we can never know—indeed, must not know—whether the one we are welcoming into our home or into our nation is a friend or an enemy, someone who will help us or harm us, aid us or destroy us. Hospitality, Derrida suggests, can be extended only at the price of this risk—a risk to ourselves, our families, and our nations, as well as to the very principle of identity that first defines these.

Let me give one more example, one of the most recent, from Derrida's 2003 book *Voyous* (*Rogues*). In this work Derrida questions the concept of democracy, the philosophical tradition of defining this concept, the practices of democracy, and the rhetorical uses and abuses of everything that goes under this name or this banner. Derrida develops this "critique" of democracy by means of yet another figure or inflection for deconstruction, which, as I said earlier, can be described in no single, definitive fashion. The term Derrida chooses to describe or inflect deconstruction in *Rogues* is thus not hospitality, a term from politics or ethics, but autoimmunity, or the autoimmune, a term known to most of us from the biological sciences, which use it to describe the way in which certain diseases, such as AIDS, cause the organism not simply to turn against itself in an act of auto-aggression or suicide but, more radically, to turn against the forces or principles that protect and define the organism so that it becomes compromised in its identity and made vulnerable to external aggression. This is, it has to be admitted, a curious and far less reassuring way of understanding deconstruction, even if it is not as different from a thinking of deconstruction as hospitality as one might initially think. For if deconstruction as hospitality always entails the risk of welcoming someone or something who has not yet been identified, an *arrivant* who might radically destabilize or compromise one's own identity, then hospitality, the perfectibility of hospitality, is always, we could say, open to an auto-immune pervertibility. To reverse the proposition, if autoimmunity describes the way in which an organism, an individual, a family, or a nation, some identity, compromises its own forces of self-affirmation so as to become open and vulnerable to its outside, then autoimmunity is always a kind of hospitality—the welcoming of an event that might well change the very identity of the self, of the *autos*, the welcoming of an event that may thus bring good or ill, that may invite a remedy or a poison, a friend or a foe. To be open to the event, to offer hospitality, it is essential *not to know* in advance what is what or who is who.

Deconstruction as hospitality or deconstruction as autoimmunity thus helps explain not only how we live, how we remain open to the future and to a renewal of life in the future, how we remain open to innovation and invention through the reception of others, but how we die, how we inevitably turn against ourselves, against the very principles that constitute and sustain our selves and our identities. In what was to be his final interview, first published in *Le Monde* in August 2004, Derrida expressed quite well this aspect of deconstruction, of a body, so to speak, in deconstruction, alluding both to the antinomic exigencies of deconstruction and to the pancreatic cancer that was killing him, *Je suis en guerre contre moi-même*, "I am at war with myself" (*LLF* 47).[6] Though internecine war and hospitality would seem to be mutually exclusive notions, they are in fact the conditions of one another: only someone at war with himself can offer refuge to that which is not the self, and only by welcoming that which is not the self can one hope to live on for a time, to live on, that is, through this internal tension that gives us all time.

Jacques Derrida—the words and works of Jacques Derrida, the traces I spoke of in the Introduction—will live on, at least for a time, like little machines that will have survived him, provoking "living" thought in others in the absence of their author. He will live on, but for what tomorrow we do not know—indeed, we cannot know and must not claim to know. For he will live on only by being transformed, as we the survivors emphasize certain things and develop his work in certain directions and not others—for example, here, trying to read deconstruction in terms of hospitality (something I imagine he would have endorsed *only to a point*, an interpretation he would have welcomed *only conditionally*). Hence he will live on but always differently, always now only "in us." There will thus be living on but there will be no salvation or resurrection, only a certain hospitality, and we owe it to his memory to recall this.

I began by saying that I could not begin without letting the words Jacques Derrida first addressed me, those words *Alors, qui êtes-vous?* "resonate" within me, words that resonate for me today a bit like Vinteuil's little musical "phrase" in Proust, words that bear today not so much a meaning as a past, or, rather, a trace of what was already immemorial in that past. There are, to be sure, many here in Chicago like me, many who walk around today with memories, images, and sounds from Jacques Derrida's extraordinary life and, more specifically, from his unique passage through this city. Many of us remember him at the various universities of this city, from Hyde Park to Evanston, at the University of Chicago, for example, speaking about the gift or the death penalty, or at Northwestern University, speaking about language and his childhood in Algeria, or at Loyola University, speaking about Heidegger, or at DePaul, speaking in 1991 at a conference on philosophy and architecture, engaging in a dialogue with Daniel Libeskind, the architect who would go on to win the design contest for rebuilding the site of the World Trade Center, or again at DePaul in 1996, speaking about politics and mourning and about the texts of mourning he had written over the past two decades in memory of dead friends and colleagues, from Emmanuel Levinas and Roland Barthes to Gilles Deleuze and Paul de Man.

We have memories of Derrida in Chicago and, of course, Derrida had memories of us and of this city. One of the most poignant of these memories is recalled by Derrida in a text written in memory of his friend Paul de Man, a text that, in the wake of de Man's death, reflects on the French idiom *la mort dans l'âme*. While we tend to say in English after the death of a friend or family member that we are "heartbroken" or that we have "a heavy heart," it seems truer to the unique nature of the event to say that we have *la mort dans l'âme*, that is, "death in our soul." In January 1984, writing not long after the death of his friend, Derrida recounts the following memory of having death in the soul, a memory that cannot but resonate within *us* today in the wake of Jacques Derrida's own death:

> I had known for a long time, even though he spoke of it very rarely, that music occupied an important place in Paul's life and thought. On that particular night—it was 1979 and once again the occasion was a colloquium—we were driving through the streets of Chicago after a jazz concert. My older son, who had accompanied me, was talking with Paul about music, more precisely about musical instruments. This they were doing as the experts they both were, as technicians who know how to call things by their name. It was then I realized that Paul had never told me he was an experienced musician

and that music had also been a practice with him. The word that let me know this was the word *âme* [soul] when, hearing Pierre, my son, and Paul speak with familiarity of the violin's or the bass's soul, I learned that the "soul" is the name one gives in French to the small and fragile piece of wood—always very exposed, very vulnerable—that is placed within the body of these instruments to support the bridge and assure the resonant communication of the two sounding boards. I didn't know why at that moment I was so strangely moved and unsettled in some dim recess by the conversation I was listening to: no doubt it was due to the word "soul," which always speaks to us at the same time of life and of death and makes us dream of immortality, like the argument of the lyre in the *Phaedo*.

And I will always regret, among so many other things, that I never again spoke of any of this with Paul. How was I to know that one day I would speak of that moment, that music and that soul, without him, before you who must forgive me for doing it just now so poorly, so painfully, when already everything is painful, so painful? (*WM* 75)

These are the closing words of Derrida's very beautiful little memorial text on Paul de Man, one of the nearly twenty such texts I had the honor and privilege to collect with Pascale-Anne Brault and Kas Saghafi and publish under the title *The Work of Mourning*, and then later in French under the title *Chaque fois unique, la fin du monde*. I was tempted to end my own reflections here with these words, with Derrida's thoughts about the soul as he drove through the streets of Chicago, with the pain he himself felt at the death of a friend, or else with other works of Derrida where he teaches us that with the death of a friend what we lose is not this or that friend within the world but the world itself, a unique way of opening up the world, as he put it, "each time unique, the end of the world." But to end with these words today would perhaps not be to offer the kind of hospitality that I myself have been offered; in simply repeating Derrida's words, it would not take the *risk* of an invitation, the risk of a hospitality poised between two inflections.

Today, in the wake of the death of Jacques Derrida, what I feel instead or in addition to sadness and melancholy is gratitude, gratitude for this life, this work, but also for everything it made possible and everything that made it possible. So let me conclude, as I began, with another memory, another experience of hospitality, and another French phrase, another liminal, threshold phrase—one that preceded even my first conversation with Jacques Derrida. Again, it is a common, everyday phrase, one that can be heard by almost any traveler or visiting student to France trying to get a visa, student card, *carte de séjour*, or any number of other official documents. You arrive at some government building, a commissariat, for example, with your papers, you hope, in order, and you ask one of the security people where to go to apply for your card and you are inevitably told, *à l'accueil*, "go to the reception desk," *renseignez-vous à l'accueil*, "go inquire at the reception desk." If *Alors, qui êtes-vous?* was the first phrase Jacques Derrida ever addressed me, *à l'accueil* was the first phrase of official French spoken to me in France, in the commissariat of the Fourteenth Arrondissment, to be exact. *A l'accueil*: like *Alors, qui êtes-vous?* I can still today hear these words reverberating, resonating, within me, within what I would be tempted to call my "soul." I can hear them as they were spoken to me on the threshold of my first extended stay in France—a stay that would allow me to attend Derrida's seminar and eventually meet Jacques Derrida. Though they were not, as I recall, spoken in the friendliest or most welcoming of tones, I will always be grateful for what they made possible, something I would be tempted to call *un autre accueil*, another reception, another reception of thinking, the thought of another reception and another thinking *as* reception.

Though he cannot hear me today, or, as he reminds us, though he can hear me today only in me, I cannot resist ending these reflections by making explicit words that silently preceded everything I ever said to him, words that I hope, I believe, he was able to make out beneath everything I ever said to him, beginning that day in 1988 with my name.

Merci, Jacques, merci infiniment pour votre accueil.

2

Analogy and Anagram

Deconstruction as Deconstruction of the as

Though I tried to argue in the previous chapter that the double gesture of deconstruction might helpfully be compared to the antinomy between a conditional and an unconditional hospitality, that deconstruction as such might be thought of *as* a kind of hospitality, there is, it has to be said, something woefully inadequate about this comparison, indeed, something fundamentally mistaken about the notion that deconstruction might be understood through any such comparison or analogy. For it is as if deconstruction itself, deconstruction *as such*, before being a critique of phonocentrism or logocentrism, of phallogocentrism or carnophallologocentrism, were first of all, and much more simply, a critique of the *as such*; as if Derridean deconstruction *as* philosophy, *as* critique, before being a critique of the so-called metaphysics of presence, were first of all a critique of being *as* presence, or more simply still, a critique of the *as* that makes all presence possible; as if Derridean deconstruction, before being a critique of individualism, humanism, nationalism, or Eurocentrism, were first of all a critique of the *as if*, a critique of the performative fiction that gives rise to the phantasms of autochthony and property, of the self-same of any self, species, state, or sovereign god; as if, in short, Derridean deconstruction, before being a critique of the analogies of sovereignty, were first of all, and from the very beginning, a critique of the "as," the "as such," and the "as if" that make all comparison and analogy possible.

One need go no further than what Derrida himself has said about deconstruction to make such a case. Near the end of "The University Without Condition," for example, Derrida argues that the little word "as" in "as if" or "as such" might well be or have been the name of the real *target* of deconstruction, since it is, he says, "authoritative" in all phenomena and all philosophy *as* science or *as* knowledge.[1] Hence Derrida in that and other texts will discreetly but unmistakably separate the "as" from the "if" in order to argue that the proper modality of the event, of the unconditionality of the event, is neither "as," the event *as* past, present, or future, the event *as* this or that, nor "as if," the event as possibility, performative fiction, or virtuality, but, more simply, "if," the event, as Derrida liked to say, "*if* there is any." Yes, it is "as if" deconstruction *as* philosophy were from the very beginning a critique of this authoritative or sovereign "as," a critique, then, not only of analogies of sovereignty but of the sovereignty of analogy, of what I will call here the "sovereign reign of analogy."

But since Derrida was not often given to speaking so generally about deconstruction, because he preferred more local, contextualized analyses, and because I think he appreciated it even less when others spoke so generally, I would like to demonstrate in this chapter that such an interpretation of Derrida is justified already by Derrida's 1968 reading of Plato in "Plato's Pharmacy" and by his subsequent readings of Plato, from his 1987 essay "*Khōra*," right up through one of his very last works, in 2003, *Rogues*.[2] Since, as I will argue, the premises for so many of Derrida's readings of canonical texts in the history of philosophy can be related in some way to this critique of analogy, it is essential to return to these texts on Plato in order to understand both the terms and the form of these readings and this critique. Moreover, because a reading of the *khōra* or, as we will see, of *Khōra* in Plato's *Timaeus* became so central to Derrida's late political works, because the *unconditionality* of *Khōra* is so often opposed in these later works to the *sovereignty* of the Good, it is important to understand the *philosophical* background of this political critique. As we will see much later, in Chapter 10, it is this very "reign of analogy" initiated by Platonic metaphysics that will feed the sovereignty of every phantasm and allow the Good to become the ultimate phantasm of sovereignty, and it is *Khōra*—*Khōra* not exactly *beyond* all being but "before" all being— that will allow us to call into question both the phantasms of sovereignty and the sovereignty of the phantasm. This reading of analogy in Plato, I will argue, will ultimately give Derrida the terms he needs, in *Rogues* and elsewhere, to call into question various forms of sovereignty, including that of the nation-state, as well as the phantasms upon which that sovereignty is based. Before turning to Derrida's earlier texts on Plato, then, let me simply cite two references from *Rogues*, which will have turned out to contain some of Derrida's very last reflections on Plato.

In *Rogues*, Derrida reads several classic philosophical texts on democracy with an eye to the way in which each ends up defining sovereignty in terms of self-identity, autonomy, freedom, power, and, in the end, unconditionality: sovereignty is unconditional, and the unconditional is another way of thinking and naming what is most free, most powerful, most autonomous, and most self-identical. Against this entire tradition, then, Derrida argues that we must try to think the unconditional—the unconditional as event, as justice, as other, or, precisely, as the democracy to come—without these attributes, as an unconditional that is powerless, that has relinquished its sovereignty, even its self-identify. Unconditionality and sovereignty must be distinguished, Derrida argues, not unlike the way the "if" must be separated from the "as."

Now, in this philosophical history, Derrida identifies the first moment or first figure of the unconditional in Plato's *Republic* under the name of the sovereign Good. Derrida thus writes near the end of *Rogues*, concerning the idea of this sovereign Good as it is presented by Socrates at the end of book 6 of the *Republic*:

> [My use of] the word *sovereign* is further justified by the fact that Plato actually qualifies as *kurion* (508a) this Sun and this Good, which produce, analogically, sensible visibility and intelligible visibility. But it is also, and especially, justified by the fact that, at the moment of defining the idea of the Good in a literally hyperbolic fashion as *epekeina tēs ousias* (beyond being or beingness), Plato couches this idea in the language of power or, rather, super-power. It is a question of a power more powerful than power, conveyed in a sovereign superlative that undercuts in an exceptional fashion the analogy and hierarchy it nonetheless imposes. That is the essence without essence of sovereignty. (*R* 138)

I will return to this passage later in order to emphasize this identification of the unconditional with not only sovereignty and power but productivity and, indeed, fertility and life. For the moment, let me simply underscore that Derrida is drawing attention here to the *analogical* structure of Plato's text, to the analogy between sensible visibility and intelligible visibility, the realm of the sun and that of the Good. Whether analogy is understood as proportion according to the divisions of the divided line or as mere relation, Derrida is drawing our attention not just to the analogies used by Plato but to the way in which analogy structures Plato's metaphysics: what the sun is in the realm of sensible visibility, the Good is in the realm of intelligible visibility—an analogical structure that permits such similes as "the Good is like the sun" or metaphors such as "the Good is the intelligible sun."

Derrida also underscores here the way in which the Good is both part of this analogical structure and, in some sense, sovereign over and independent of it as *epekeina tēs ousias*, that is, as beyond or otherwise than being. The Good at once imposes *and* undercuts analogy and hierarchy, imposing them, we might say, by providing the "light" by which a comparison between itself and the sun, intelligible visibility and sensible visibility, might be understood or "read," and undercutting them by withdrawing beyond all light, as the invisible source of all visibility. We have here, then, a reading of the sovereign or the unconditional as what is at once the highest, as what grounds or establishes all analogies, *and* as that which must always be absent—like a King or like a Father whose absence or withdrawal from light and comparison is at once the very condition of his absolute sovereignty and incomparable authority *and* that which allows the Father to be replaced.

Yes, "like a Father," I just said, an analogy to which we will return after a long detour through "Plato's Pharmacy."

The second reference to Plato in *Rogues* to which I wish to draw attention can be found around the middle of the book, where Derrida, referring implicitly both to Plato's *Timaeus* and to his own work on that dialogue, says, in a very striking though initially cryptic formulation: "The democracy to come would be *like* the *khōra* of the political" (*R* 82; my emphasis on *like*). Whereas the first passage I cited draws attention to the analogical structure of Plato's text, the second uses the Platonic *khōra* in a simile or analogy that would run something like this: what the *khōra* is in Plato's cosmological-philosophical discourse, the democracy to come is in my, Derrida's, political discourse. Such an analogy thus invites the following speculation: if *khōra* is what gives place or space for phenomena to appear, if it is the third *genos* between *genesis* and *to on*, between the world of becoming and the intelligible models that are copied in the sensible world, then Derrida would seem to be suggesting that the democracy to come would be *like that*, not a sensible, actualized, or actualizable thing, some past, present, or future regime, and yet not an idea or ideal or intelligible model either—which no doubt helps explains why Derrida spends so much time in *Rogues* and elsewhere distinguishing the democracy to come from a Kantian regulative idea. The democracy to come would be, *like khōra*, it seems, the place or space or perhaps the space-time in which all democratic regimes, more or less good, might arrive or appear. As the space-time in which they might appear, it would thus be irreducible to any of these regimes. And like *khōra* in the *Timaeus*, we might continue to speculate, it would be understandable or graspable only through a kind of bastard discourse—perhaps a kind of deconstruction—and, as that which has no proper meaning of its own, no "as such," named only through a series of *irreducible analogies*—beginning, perhaps, with *Khōra*. Such analogies would be irreducible; indeed, such analogies would hardly be ana*logies* any more but ana*grams*, precisely insofar as their material, signifying bodies, insofar as their *names*, cannot be written off in the name of some meta-linguistic meaning or signified. Such *irreducible analogies* or such *anagrams* would thus signal not the ultimate height and power of the sovereign reign of analogy but the beginning of its end or at least its suspension. As Derrida might have put it, it signals the end of a reign of sovereign speech and the beginning of a practice of writing. The democracy to come would thus be, for Derrida, *like* the *khōra* of the political, *like* that which, in the *Timaeus*, is said to be *like* a nurse or *like* a mother.

Yes, "like a mother," I just said, whereas earlier I said "like a Father." If sovereignty and unconditionality are to be distinguished, as I said Derrida in *Rogues* suggests they must, does this then mean that we, as readers of Plato and Derrida, must ultimately choose, like the children of feuding parents, between the sovereign Father and the unconditional mother, between the Good and *Khōra*? I will leave that question in suspense. For the moment, let me simply note this family resemblance between the family scene that Derrida lays out in such detail in "Plato's Pharmacy" and the more discreet mise-en-scène of a Father and a mother in *Rogues* some thirty-five years later. In the end, I will argue, everything will come down to how we read this resemblance, and the reign of analogy that either imposes or undercuts it.

Like Glaucon in book 2 of the *Republic*, then, let me simply polish up and then leave these two statues alone for a while, that of a sovereign Father and an unconditional mother, and turn to the courtship or foreplay of this odd couple in "Plato's Pharmacy." For it is in "Plato's Pharmacy" that we will be able to locate the premises of Derrida's critique of analogy, whose traces we have just seen in *Rogues* and which is at the very center of Derrida's 1987 work "*Khōra*." The only question that will remain after this reading, or the only one I will ask in the end, will be whether Derrida in 1968 was not still tempted to identify the source or site of all analogy with the sovereign Good—the Good beyond being—

while in later works, from *"Khōra"* to *Rogues*, he will be suspicious of this identification, suspicious precisely because of the light and sovereignty of the Good, because of the productivity, power, fecundity, and paternity associated with it *through analogy.*

Sovereign Analogies: "The Father of Logos" and the Good Beyond Being

Derrida's reading in "Plato's Pharmacy" of the Platonic critique of writing in the *Phaedrus* and elsewhere is so well known that it merits only the briefest recapitulation here. What is important about that reading for the argument I wish to make is the way Derrida inscribes the Platonic critique of writing into a much more comprehensive system of hierarchies and oppositions that runs throughout the Platonic corpus and, indeed, throughout Greek thought more generally. The Platonic claim that writing leads to forgetting, corruption, and, ultimately, death, that it is sterile, unthinking, merely repetitive, unaristocratic, and so on, is of a piece, Derrida shows, with Plato's emphasis in the *Phaedrus* and elsewhere on the intelligence and fertility of live speech and the living breath and his suspicion of the imitative arts, rhetoric, and democracy. Though writing may thus appear to be a rather marginal theme in the Platonic text, especially next to such important themes as the forms, anamnesis, the philosopher king, and so on, Derrida shows how the system that informs this theme is the same one that frames Plato's entire ontology, epistemology, aesthetics, ethics, and politics. Writing has less being than speech (and so is ontologically inferior); it is but a shadowy object of knowledge (and so is epistemologically inferior); it is a form of imitation or representation rather than genuine expression (and so is far removed from the truth it would claim to represent); it is morally corrupting (and so must be made to serve dialectic or else be exiled from the city); and it exhibits democratic tendencies (and so must be mastered for the good of the *polis* by an aristocratic or philosophical sovereign). Less real, less true, less beautiful, less legitimate, and less useful than speech, writing left to itself is as ignorant, indiscriminate, and unruly as the *dēmos* itself. To understand the Platonic critique of writing, indeed simply to understand what writing "is" for Plato, one cannot help but rethink Plato's entire philosophy, that is, the complex system of hierarchies, relations, and oppositions that goes by the name of "Plato."

The extraordinary interpretative power of "Plato's Pharmacy" thus resides in the way in which Derrida, following each of these relations or oppositions, shows the critique of writing to be part of a general structure or system that extends well beyond the explicit critique of writing in the *Phaedrus*. Because the Platonism that Derrida is trying to explicate is not a theory of forms, located, say, in a series of claims made in the dialogues, but, first and foremost, a vast system or structure of relations and oppositions, and, perhaps especially, of *analogies*, Derrida underscores these structural elements throughout his essay. Hence Derrida speaks of certain "structural laws" that "govern and articulate these oppositions" ("PP" 85), of a "structural analogy" or "structural resemblance," of a "more deeply buried necessity" that relates these terms and oppositions to one another in Plato's philosophy and more generally in the Greek language ("PP" 86). Hence writing is *like* the imitative arts insofar as it is removed from the truth of the speaker; it is *like* the *dēmos* in its indiscriminate, unruly, and unthinking repetition of language; it is *like* the flowering of seeds in the gardens of Adonis—alluring and attractive to the eye but ultimately unproductive, unfruitful, merely playful, and fast fading.

For Derrida in "Plato's Pharmacy," Platonism is an enormous system of hierarchically ordered oppositions sustained by the structure of *analogy*, that is, by a network of seemingly *reducible analogies*, what we might call *mere analogies*, which would seem to point back to an essential meaning that precedes, exceeds, and governs them. But to read or interpret analogy in this way in the Platonic text is already to assume, Derrida claims, the very terms the Platonic text attempts to establish, beginning with the priority of spoken over written language, thought over expression, and so on. To resist reading and interpreting in this way, to resist naively adopting a Platonic theory of interpretation in reading the Platonic text, one must no longer take for granted the categories that make these "mere analogies" possible. One must begin instead to pay greater attention to the linguistic and rhetorical means by which the Platonic text, and, thus, Platonic metaphysics, uses analogy *of necessity* in order to establish a system in which analogy appears contingent, that is, a system in which "mere analogies" are possible. Hence Derrida goes on in "Plato's Pharmacy" to demonstrate that, just as Plato could not completely reduce writing to an inferior, bastard form of speech, so analogy cannot be reduced to the meaning that would appear to sustain it. Derrida demonstrates the way in which the analogical structure with which Plato sustains his philosophical project is itself situated and sustained by an *anagrammatical web* that exceeds that structure. This anagrammatical structure includes everything that Plato wished to reduce and consign to the inessential: rhetoric, the signifier, language, in a word, *writing*. Hence Derrida does not, as some have thought, simply reverse all the values and hierarchies of the Platonic text to claim, for example, that writing is superior to speech and so on, since that would simply leave the analogical structure in place. Rather, he tries to displace or resituate this structure without liquidating it, resituating it within an anagrammatical texture that *at once* makes possible and undermines or undercuts the analogies of Platonism and the hierarchies they sustain. This displacement begins with Derrida's rereading of the *pharmakon*, whose appearance in the Platonic text cannot be reduced to its *meaning* (for example, *either* remedy *or* poison) but which must instead be *read* in its fundamental ambivalence, put into communication with other sometimes contradictory inscriptions of the word in the Platonic text and beyond. The result of this reading is to show that the *pharmakon*, as *both* remedy and poison, as a milieu whose meaning cannot be reduced, fixed, or definitively determined, is the medium or pivot point between values that can never be completely neutralized or stabilized by the decisions of philosophy, by a manipulation that would always try to turn this trace that goes by the name of "pharmakon" toward some presence or repeatable identity. The pharmakon *as such*, then, would have no *as such*, no identity of its own, and so would defy all philosophical appropriation, all attempts to give it a single or identifiable meaning ("PP" 97).

Resituated within a much larger "chain of significations" ("PP" 95), one that goes beyond the single line, passage, or dialogue in which it is found, that goes beyond the intentional structure of the text, the first question to be asked of the *pharmakon* in any particular instance—for example, in those crucial passages of the *Phaedrus* in which writing is called a *pharmakon*—is not necessarily "What does it mean?" but "How is it *written*?" Though the determination of the speaker's apparent intention or the author's intended meaning is obviously important in any reading, the textual web in which these intentions or meaning are caught goes well beyond the speaker or the author.

Derrida thus moves, in "Plato's Pharmacy," from analogy to anagrammatology or, better, from the analogical to the anagrammatical—from a language where what is essential is the signified to a text where the sign is at once signifier and signified, where the signifier, the *grammē*, is irreducible to the signified. When Socrates in the *Phaedrus* thus declares speech—that is, good, productive, living speech—to be "writing in the soul," Derrida refuses to take this as a mere metaphor or analogy. He refuses to make the signifier reducible to the signified, the rhetorical or linguistic form of the text reducible to its philosophical content—despite Plato's apparent intentions that we read these in this way. When Plato in the *Phaedrus* opposes writing to what he calls "writing in the soul," what he *meant*, what he meant us to *hear* or *understand*, was no doubt that "writing in the soul" is another way of speaking of "live speech." But what he *wrote* was precisely "*writing* in the soul," thus using the very term he just criticized to characterize what he wishes to privilege. Rather than *hear* this, then, as a mere metaphor or analogy, rather than *understand* it as merely contingent, Derrida tries to *read* the appearance of "writing" in this metaphor in terms of another necessity. Derrida writes: While "[Plato's] intentions are always apparently didactic and analogical," "they conform to a constant necessity, which is never thematized as such: what always makes itself apparent is the law of difference, the irreducibility of structure and relation, of proportionality, of analogy" ("PP" 159).[3] The metaphor of writing thus cannot be written off. As Derrida writes earlier in "Plato's Pharmacy," "What we are provisionally and for the sake of convenience continuing to call a metaphor thus in any event belongs to a whole system" ("PP" 79).

The question of what "pharmakon" *means* in a certain context or place in Plato's corpus thus cannot simply be determined by asking about Plato's or Socrates' intentions or voluntary or conscious meaning. Though these categories are still operative, they are now inscribed within a much larger textual network or web, where signifiers have relations that exceed intentional or conscious meaning. Though Platonism no doubt always tries to regain the upper hand by transforming an uncontrollable ambivalence into a controlled polysemy, though it tries always to reimpose its reign of analogy, Derrida shows that at the level of the pharmacy such mastery is always an illusion or royal phantasm—which does not, of course, make the power wielded by that phantasm any less real or less effective.

Thus even if Plato might have thought all these graphic references to be "mere" images or "analogies," that is, controllable by the intentional structure of the text, by a regulated, philosophical parasitism of terms, Derrida's analysis demonstrates that such images or analogies borrow *of necessity* from the anagrammatical structure of the text. Platonism borrows from what it condemns *of necessity*; it needs *pharmaka* to exorcise *pharmaka*, needs the anagram to construct its analogies. The meaning of analogies thus can never simply be precipitated out without remainder; each brings along with it an irreducible anagrammatical structure, a signifying structure or texture that can never be reduced to a signified meaning, a history and a language that can never be overcome by some transhistorical meaning. Analogy as a structure of resemblance—that is, of resemblances that can never be reduced to a common *meaning*—now appears to have been made possible by an irreducible anagram that at once opens up and undercuts every *as such*, *as if*, and *as*. Anagrammaticality would thus be the condition of possibility and impossibility of all analogy.

Nevertheless—or as a result—analogy remains, and it remains incomparably powerful. Even if analogy is always irreducible, always subject to the anagrammatical web that makes it possible, the phantasm of the reducible analogy remains, the phantasm of a language that can ultimately be reduced to thought, and especially, in Plato, the phantasm of a master analogy that provides the legitimacy, the presence, and the light for all the others. That master analogy is in Plato the one between the father and the son, on the one hand, and a speaker and his words, on the other, an analogy that will be extended in the *Republic* to that between the sun and the phenomenal world, on the one hand, and the Good and the sun, on the other. Indeed, among all the analogies Derrida reads in "Plato's Pharmacy" to demonstrate what I have called the sovereign reign of analogy in Plato, none are more highly charged than those surrounding this family scene. Recalling the myth of writing in the *Phaedrus*, where the speaker is said to be a *father* of his *logos* ("PP" 78), Derrida speaks of the "permanence of a Platonic schema that assigns the origin and power of speech, of *logos*, to the paternal position" ("PP" 76)—and, by extension, the paternal position to one of sovereignty and, ultimately, divinity.

But again, as Derrida demonstrates, all these distinctions and oppositions can—indeed *must*—be read against the backdrop of the anagrammatical web as the products of writing and difference. Hence the paternal metaphor can and must be read precisely *as a metaphor*. The speaker *as* "father of his logos" cannot be reduced to some premetaphorical meaning; the father's role in such a metaphor cannot simply be precipitated out in order to retrieve some more original notion of "origin," "source," or "procreator." For it is precisely the *logos* that gives meaning to all these terms, the *logos* that determines the meaning of its own source. As Derrida puts it, such "'metaphors' must be tirelessly questioned" ("PP" 78), for perhaps, as Joyce—already cited in an exergue of "Plato's Pharmacy"—once said and Derrida often cited, even "paternity is a legal fiction," which means, I take it, that it is the effect of discourse, of *logos*, the very thing that is presented in Plato as being the son or offspring of a living, speaking father. Hence the expression "'father of logos' is not a simple metaphor," writes Derrida, because if "the father is always father to a speaking/living being. . . . it is precisely *logos* that enables us to perceive and investigate something like paternity" ("PP" 80–81). In other words, it would be from the son, from *logos*, that the father would be able to be *called* a father, that the father would come to be identified *as* a father.

Hence the supplement—here the son, *logos*—always risks supplanting: the son always risks replacing the father, usurping his sovereign position, just as writing always risks contaminating and replacing speech. That is the risk that Platonism always runs and, I think, Derrida ultimately argues in "Plato's Pharmacy," the necessity to which it must always yield. For *that too* is part and parcel of Platonism—the father must give way to the son; the Good, the Beautiful, and the True must be supplemented and supplanted by *logoi*. Socrates in the *Phaedo* thus says that, because he is unable to look at reality directly for fear of being blinded by it, he must take refuge in *logoi*, *logoi* that, he says in an analogy, would be *like* images that reflect and protect us from the real. Just as one can look at the midday sun only through images or reflections of it, so one can approach the ideas, and particularly the idea of the Good, only through *logoi*. *Logos*, says Derrida, is what shelters us from the Good in a way that is *analogous* to the way images shelter us from the sun ("PP" 83–84). The only way to approach what is beyond difference and diacriticity is thus through the difference and diacriticity (in a word, through writing, through the anagram) to which the father-king-Good gives rise and which he will try desperately to stabilize and control after the fact. As in the *Sophist*, then, truth must always come to terms with nontruth, and ontology must reckon with grammar ("PP" 166). The impossibility of a full intuition of the truth (or of the sun), the withdrawal of the father-sun-Good, this parricide—as Derrida calls it—of the father, is thus the condition of all difference and all writing ("PP" 168–69).[4] The system—if we still want to call it that—thus now includes both this withdrawal and the hierarchies it makes possible, this sovereign absence of a father beyond being and the reign of analogy it imposes, *along with* the patricide-regicide-deicide that replaces the father-king-god by his son, that contaminates all these hierarchies with their opposites, and that thus ushers in not another reign of analogy but a series of *irreducible analogies* of and in writing.

Such a reading of Derrida's 1968 "Plato's Pharmacy" appears to bring us right back to where Derrida ended up in 2003 in *Rogues*, back to the *Republic* and to the analogy between the sun and the Good. In the *Republic*, you will recall, Socrates says that he will not, that he cannot, talk of the father, that is, of the Good, but only of his offspring [*tokos*], that is, only of "the visible sun, the son that resembles the father, the *analogon* of the intelligible sun" ("PP" 82). The visible sun is the *analogon* of the intelligible sun, that is, of the Good, and it is only through this *analogon* that the Good can be approached. For in and of itself, if we can say this, the Good is not visible, not even intelligibly visible. This "Good (father, sun, capital)," whose presence would be so blinding that it would efface all difference and render one mute, is thus "the hidden illuminating, blinding source of *logos*," and the only way of gaining a glimpse of it is by taking refuge in *logoi* and analogies ("PP" 82). Derrida writes in "Plato's Pharmacy":

> The absolute invisibility of the origin of the visible, of the Good-sun-father-capital, the unattainment of presence or beingness in any form, the whole surplus Plato calls *epekeina tēs ousias* (beyond being-ness or presence), gives rise to a structure of replacements such that all presences will be supplements substituted for the absent origin, and all differences, within the system of presence, will be the irre-ducible effect of what remains *epekeina tēs ousias*. ("PP" 167)

But it is here that the question I alluded to at the outset of this chapter returns, the one question with which, whether explicitly or implicitly, I believe Derrida continued to struggle between "Plato's Pharmacy" and *Rogues*. If the withdrawal of the father-king-Good is indeed the condition of all discourse, of the reign of replacements and analogies, what is the nature of this withdrawal? In what way is the Father absent? What does *epekeina tēs ousias* mean, exactly? Or is it a question here, as it is with *Khōra*, not of meaning but of a singular *name*, a sort of signifier without signified? Is the Good the super-powerful sovereign whose power is con-firmed precisely *by* his sovereign withdrawal beyond all being, his removal to a height that rises above even the highest level of being on the divided line, or is the Good more *like* writing, a writing that first opens up all the differences of the divided line? Is the Good the ground or origin of all resemblance and all analogy, or the anagrammatical "origin" of all differ-ence—including the notion of "origin" itself?

In "Plato's Pharmacy" there are signs that suggest that Derrida was trying to think the father-king-capital-sun in both of these ways, that is, as both the sovereign Good and that third *genos* that goes by the name of writing, or perhaps by the name of *Khōra*. On the one hand, Derrida seems tempted to put writing and, perhaps inspired by a certain Levinas, the Other in the place of the Good. Derrida writes, near the end of "Plato's Pharmacy," "The disappearance of the Face" (a term that appears to substitute for "the Good-father-capital-sun" in the previous paragraph) "or the structure of repetition can thus no longer be dominated by the value of truth" ("PP" 168). And in the paragraph just above: "writing (is) *epekeina tēs ousias*," that is, to risk a translation, "writing (is) otherwise than being." *Like* the Good, writing makes possible or is perhaps even productive of all relations, and yet it itself withdraws from these relations, or withdraws by being inscribed within them, withdraws through differ-ence and deferral, withdraws, therefore, through and within history and language but not before or beyond them.

The Good would thus be *like* writing—beyond or otherwise than being. And yet one has to wonder—and I think Derrida wondered—about the *authority*, *power*, and, ultimately, the *fecundity* of such an analogy. Recall the passage from *Rogues* with which I began: the Good not only provides the light for analogies but provides the analogy between the realm over which the sun is sovereign and the one over which it itself is sovereign. The Good that is *epekeina tēs ousias* is characterized by Plato as *sovereign*, as *kurios*, as a sovereign power that remains completely in reserve, that is, as a kind of productive excess, a Good that is able to spend or sow its seed without losing any of its potency or substance, a capital Good that generates offspring—interest—from itself without losing anything of itself, a Good that would pretend, at least, to give itself to analogy without being contaminated by analogy.

That is why, I think, already in "Plato's Pharmacy," though much more clearly and insistently in "*Khōra*," as we will see in a moment, Derrida seems to identify writing and difference, in short, the anagrammatical, *not* with this paternal Good in withdrawal, absent as "beyond being," but with *Khōra*, which is neither sensible nor intelligible, neither being nor nonbeing, but that which or the one who first opens up these distinctions. In "Plato's Pharmacy," the *khōra* is already identified with the milieu of the pharmakon, with that which has no proper identity and so can be described only through irreducible analogies or metaphors, or else suspended in quotation marks that can never be lifted. Derrida writes: "The 'essence' of the *pharmakon* lies in the way in which, having no stable essence, no 'proper' characteristics, it is not, in any sense (metaphysical, physical, chemical, alchemical) of the word, a *substance*" ("PP" 125–26). Neither a simple nor a composite, it is always "undecidable," analogous to a "prior medium in which differentiation in general is produced"; with no stable identity of its own, irreducible to an either/or and thus to any "as" or "as such," it both defies *and* invites analogy, both within Plato and within the history of philosophy ("PP" 138, 126). In modern philosophy, the pharmakon is thus a mixed medium that is "*analogous* to the one that will, subsequent to and according to the decision of philosophy, be reserved for transcendental imagination" ("PP" 126),[5] and in Plato it is analogous—and this already in "Plato's Pharmacy"—to *khōra*, which in the *Timaeus* escapes the opposition between sensible and intelligible and can be thought only in a kind of dream mode or bastard discourse as "the 'impression-bearer'" or "formless 'base'" of all impressions ("PP" 160). *Khōra*, *like* writing—which we just saw in the position of the Good as *epekeina tēs ousias*—is thus the "place" of all impressions or inscriptions, the place of "the *production of the son*," that is, of phenomena, and "at the same time the constitution of *structurality*" ("PP" 161). On the one hand, then, writing is situated in the place of the Good beyond being and, on the other, in the place of *Khōra*. On the one hand, it is like the Good that sows or disseminates its seed, and, on the other, it is like *Khōra*, which is, as Derrida puts it, "big with everything that is disseminated here" ("PP" 161). Derrida then adds, anticipating, it seems, the essay "*Khōra*," which would appear some two decades later: "We will go into that elsewhere [*Nous y pénétrons ailleurs*]."

Thus the seeds, so to speak, are certainly there in "Plato's Pharmacy" for thinking the separation of the Good and *Khōra*, sovereignty and the unconditional. But in this essay of 1968 Derrida seems to hesitate to mark this separation, identifying writing and the pharmakon at once with *Khōra* and with the Good. Such a critique of the sovereign Good in the name of the unconditional—whether this be called *Khōra*, justice, or the event—will become explicit only later, in "*Khōra*," "How to Avoid Speaking: Denials," *Rogues*, and other works.

Irreducible Anagrams: *Khōra*—"this strange mother"

If the question of analogy returns at regular intervals throughout "Plato's Pharmacy," it is a central theme of the "*Khōra*" essay. In the opening footnote, Derrida makes a methodological point that governs the entirety of the essay, even though, as I've tried to demonstrate, it was already working in the background of "Plato's Pharmacy." Derrida writes, in words that might have stood as an epigraph to this entire chapter:

> It is not a question here of criticizing the use of the words *metaphor, comparison,* or *image*. It is often inevitable, and for reasons which we shall try to explain here. It will sometimes happen that we too will have recourse to them. But there is a point, it seems, where the relevance of this rhetorical code meets a limit and must be questioned as such, must become a theme and cease to be merely operative. It is precisely the point where the concepts of this rhetoric appear to be constructed on the basis of "Platonic" oppositions (intelligible/sensible, being as *eidos*/image, etc.), oppositions from which *khōra* precisely escapes. The apparent multiplicity of metaphors (or also of mythemes in general) signifies in these places not only that the proper meaning can only become intelligible via these detours, but that the opposition between the proper and the figurative, without losing all value, encounters here a limit. ("*K*" 147n1)

Throughout the "*Khōra*" essay, Derrida both follows Plato's analogies in the *Timaeus*—especially those related to the *khōra*—and poses critical questions with regard to the "rhetorical code" that would have us read them as mere analogies or metaphors. He follows, for example, the "formal" analogy between the guardians of the *Republic*, who themselves own nothing, and the *khōra* ("*K*" 105), the structural analogy between Socrates as the recipient of discourse and the *khōra*, and, of course, the "'comparison' of *khōra* with the mother" ("*K*" 105). He thus follows these analogies at the level of "content" and others at the level of "form," noting, for example, how the general *mise-en-abyme* of places and roles in the preamble to the *Timaeus* follows a "scheme analogous to the one which will later order the discourse on *khōra*" ("*K*" 110). These analogies or analogical relations suggest to Derrida that the discourse on *khōra*, which takes up a very small portion of the *Timaeus*, actually organizes or dictates the content and form of the dialogue from the very beginning. Derrida can thus say of the preamble to the *Timaeus*, "Although the word was already uttered (19a), the question of *khōra* as a general place or total receptacle (*pandekhes*) is, of course, not yet posed. But if it is not posed *as such*, it gestures and points already" ("*K*" 109; my emphasis).

What interests Derrida in all of this is thus not so much the dramatic art of Plato, which, whether consciously or unconsciously, will have created all these resemblances, but the constraints of language and of rhetoric that will have imposed themselves upon him—either with or without his conscious, voluntary control or knowing consent. After all, what is control, and what would it mean to say that Plato consciously embedded all these analogies, one inside the other, in order to draw attention to the structure of *khōra*? Derrida writes:

> These formal analogies or these *mises-en-abyme*, refined, subtle (too subtle, some will think), are not considered here, *in the first place* [en premier lieu], as artifices, boldness, or secrets of formal composition: the art of Plato the writer! This art interests us and ought to do so more still, but what is important in this very place [*ici même*], and first of all, independently of the supposed intentions of a composer, are the constraints which produce these analogies. Shall we say that they constitute a *programme*? A *logic* whose authority was imposed on Plato? Yes, up to a point only. . . . Thus one cannot calmly, with no further ado, call by the name *programme* or *logic* the form which dictates to Plato the law of such a composition: programme and logic are apprehended in it, *as such*, though it be in a dream, and put *en abyme*. ("*K*" 106)

Like "Plato's Pharmacy," then, which begins by looking not at the forms or anamnesis or the ideal city but at writing, "*Khōra*" concentrates on a relatively marginal notion within the Platonic corpus. Though the *khōra* plays an important role in the *Timaeus*, it appears nowhere else in Plato in this form, and it takes up relatively few pages in the *Timaeus* itself. Derrida's design in concentrating on these apparently marginal notions is nonetheless to uncover the inner workings of Platonism itself, Platonism as a whole, evident both in Plato and in readers of Plato who understand Plato's metaphors and analogies as "mere" metaphors and analogies, that is, who understand the metaphors and analogies used to construct Platonism by means of Platonic categories.

As in "Plato's Pharmacy," then, Platonism is the movement by which analogies and resemblances are reduced to "mere" analogies and resemblances, the philosophical movement—the very movement of philosophy—whereby the signifier is but a mere supplement to the signified, where writing is always controlled by speech, *and*, as we also saw in "Plato's Pharmacy," where these oppositions and hierarchies are established and undone, undercut, by means of a supplemental, "hidden" reserve. Derrida thus writes, some twenty years after "Plato's Pharmacy": "'Platonism' is not only an example of this movement, the first 'in' the whole history of philosophy. It commands it, it commands this *whole* history. A philosophy as such would henceforth always be 'Platonic.' Hence the necessity to continue to try to think what takes place in Plato, with Plato, what is shown there, what is hidden, so as to win there or to lose there" ("*K*" 121).

Just as the appearance of the *pharmakon* in the *Phaedrus* brings along with it all the relations Derrida follows in "Plato's Pharmacy," the appearance of *khōra* in the *Timaeus* introduces all the relations and resemblances Derrida follows in "*Khōra*." For all these relations, all these analogies and resemblances, are "in" Plato's text, including, in the *Timaeus*, an explicit evocation of the relationship—the analogy—between modes of being and modes of discourse, an analogy Derrida will at once follow and question. This analogy is absolutely crucial in the *Timaeus*, because it already raises the question of the relationship between the objects of discourse and discourse itself, a question that Derrida will be particularly keen to pick up when he turns to *khōra*. For if the intelligible can give rise to a discourse about it that is *certain*, and the sensible or phenomenal can give rise to a discourse that is only *probable*, what kind of discourse will be appropriate or suitable for approaching that which is neither intelligible nor sensible? The *Timaeus* itself raises this question in a more or less explicit way. When Timaeus, for example, compares the receptacle to a mother, he comments first on the appropriateness of this comparison, preceding the comparison itself with the claim that it would be fitting, appropriate, or suitable to compare the intelligible model to a father, the receptacle (*khōra*) to a mother, and what is between to a child ("*K*" 124). In what follows, Derrida will at once affirm and question the appropriateness of these comparisons and will narrow in on the question of comparison as such. He will thus at once question various metaphors, analogies, and resemblances in the Platonic text and "ponder the reasons for resemblance as such" ("*K*" 109–11). As in "Plato's Pharmacy," then, he will look at the way the *khōra* is *inscribed* in the Platonic text in order to expose the question of metaphor, analogy, and resemblance *as such*, the question of the *as*, the *as such*, even the *as if*.[6]

On the one hand, then, *khōra* as receptacle does seem to be *like* a mother or a nurse, forming a pair or couple with the intelligible father and giving rise or giving birth to phenomena within her. And yet, on the other hand, Derrida insists on the fact that, as this third *genos*, as this interval or spacing between *genē*, *khōra* is "so virginal that it does not even have the figure of a virgin any longer" ("*K*" 126). And this goes for all the other figures to which she—or it—gives rise: "it is from this cosmos that the proper—but necessarily inadequate—figures will be taken for describing *khōra*: receptacle, imprint-bearer, mother, or nurse" ("*K*" 126). Derrida then continues, and notice here how he decouples *khōra*—or actually the discourse on the *khōra*, a discourse that, in *Timaeus*, must be analogous to the *khōra* itself—from philosophy, that is, from the father *and* the son.

> These figures are not even true figures. Philosophy cannot speak directly, whether in the mode of vigilance or of truth (true or probable), about what these figures approach. The dream is between the two, neither one nor the other. Philosophy cannot speak philosophically of that which looks like its "mother," its "nurse," its "receptacle," or its "imprint-bearer." As such, it speaks only of the father and the son, as if the father engendered it all on his own. ("*K*" 126)

As such . . . as if: philosophy *as such* would speak only of the father and the son, that is, only of the intelligible and of the phenomena to which the intelligible gives rise or gives birth—*as if* the father engendered the son all by himself, all on his own, *as if* the mother played no role in generation. It is *as if* we have returned to the family scene of "Plato's Pharmacy" where the father, where the Good, is productive of everything by himself. And yet if philosophy *as such* cannot speak philosophically of the "mother," of the *khōra*—or, as Derrida sometimes writes it, without a definite article and capitalized as a proper name, of *Khōra*—since *Khōra* is neither simply intelligible nor sensible, Plato's text nonetheless speaks of her, or *writes* of her—or it. Neither intelligible nor sensible, neither the father nor the son, neither a power in reserve nor simply empty space, *Khōra* is that which withdraws and, through this withdrawal, makes space for this self-relation between the father and himself, for this self-sowing of the father as his son.[7] *Khōra* withdraws, and yet, as neither an intelligible idea nor the sensible copy of such an idea, her *name*—this unique name—remains absolutely irreducible. Neither a concept nor a common name, *Khōra* is, rather, the proper name of that which has nothing proper to it. Neither itself an analogy nor something that can be captured by an analogy, *Khōra* would be that which supports and undercuts the reign of analogy. As such, as that which has no "as such" and threatens every "as such," *Khōra* would be yet another name for what elsewhere goes by the name of "writing," yet another name not for the *same thing* but for the anagrammacality that makes all resemblances and identities possible.

Khōra thus gives rise to the figures that will then be used to approach her, but she "herself" cannot be any of the things to which she is compared—mother, nurse, woman. If she "gives place to all the stories, onto-logic or mythic, that can be recounted on the subject of what she receives and even of what she resembles," "*khōra* herself, so to speak, does not become the object of any *tale*, whether true or fabled. A secret without secret remains forever impenetrable on the subject of it/her [*à son sujet*]" ("*K*" 117). Though Derrida promised in "Plato's Pharmacy," with a cer-tain irony, no doubt, to "penetrate" the question of *khōra* elsewhere, he says in "*Khōra*" that the *khōra* or *Khōra* remains forever "impenetrable," "a secret without secret," a "desert within the desert." Derrida thus capi-talizes her name throughout this essay in order to underscore the fact that she is a "unique individual," not a member of a *genos*, not a member of the feminine sex, indeed not even a member of the human species. *Khōra* "gives place without engendering" ("*K*" 124). It is precisely in this, I think, that *Khōra* can never be taken for the Good. Because she or it does not engender like the Father does, *Khōra* can never be understood as the Good or put in the place of the Good. With no power, authority, auton-omy, or identity even, *Khōra* gives space to the Father and the son but can never be confused with either. And because she or it opens a place for *and* undercuts the categories by which she is approached—mother, nurse, receptacle—she—it—can never be considered an origin and can never be appropriated by any anthropomorphism or taken up by any anthropo-theology: "*Khōra* marks a place apart, the spacing which keeps a dissym-metrical relation to all that which, 'in herself,' beside or in addition to herself, seems to make a couple with her. In the couple outside of the couple, this strange mother who gives place within engendering can no longer be considered as an origin. She/it eludes all anthropo-theological schemes, all history, all revelation, and all truth" ("*K*" 124).

Khōra is thus not the female version or inversion of the Good; she— it—is not the matriarchal underside of Plato's patriarchal philosophy, where philosophy as such speaks only of the Father and the son. *Khōra* ushers in no matriarchy for the simple reason that she—it—has no –archy, no power or no sovereignty. As I once heard Derrida say in response to a question during a conference, "*Khōra* s'en fout complètement," that is, "*Khōra* is completely indifferent," it—she—"doesn't give a damn" about what takes place "within" her. That's how far she—it—is away from either an engendering or fertile mother or an all-powerful or loving father. If one wants to speak of *Khōra* one must go back before the origin, just as, in the *Timaeus*, if one wants to speak of ancient Athens one must go back before Athens' own memory of itself—"a homology or analogy," writes Derrida, "that is at least formal" ("*K*" 126). If one wants to speak of *Khōra* it will be with a discourse that is neither certain nor probable, that will have neither truth nor likelihood, a discourse that will thus be "like" its object or that will "resemble" its object—its object that can never be an object—only in the most unlikely, improbable, and unpredictable of ways.

Separating the Sovereign Father and the Unconditional "mother"

In the essay "*Khōra*," Derrida seems to make certain that *Khōra* and the Good will never get back together again, will never couple or be taken again as a couple. If *Khōra* forms any kind of a "couple" at all, it would be not with the Good or with the intelligible model, that is, with the Father, but with the Father *and* the son taken together. On the one hand, there would be philosophy speaking of itself, the Father and the son, and, on the other hand—a hand that is dissymmetric with the first—there would be that which, though inscribed in the Platonic text, can never be spoken of by philosophy as such, namely, *Khōra*. While the Father thus engenders the son in his image, while he takes care always to bring the son back into his orbit, while he tries always to give meaning to his son, *Khōra*, as that which first opens up this relationship between *logos* and itself, as the space between the Father and the son, the place of abandon, barrenness, nonidentity, and powerlessness, *Khōra* couldn't care less.

While the question of analogy is thus posed in both "Plato's Pharmacy" and "*Khōra*," though even more explicitly in the latter, what appears markedly different between these two texts is this decoupling of the Good and *Khōra*, the Father and the "mother," this decoupling, in the end, of two kinds of unconditional, the one sovereign and the other not. The reasons for this decoupling are no doubt multiple, but one surely has to do with what Derrida always saw to be the *power of analogy*, the power of analogies of sovereignty and the sovereignty of analogy that makes all power possible. In "*Khōra*," *Rogues*, and "Faith and Knowledge," therefore, Derrida will show himself to be even more suspicious than in "Plato's Pharmacy" of the metaphors of life, fecundity, and productivity attached to the Good. He will become even more suspicious of the sovereignty and value attached to *life*—suspecting, I think, that behind this value there is the drive to go beyond life, to sacrifice life in the name of what is believed to be a higher life or in the name of the giver and origin of life. Because the Platonic Good is irreducibly attached to this power, this sovereignty, this life-giving and productive force, it was open in a way that *Khōra* never was, Derrida believes, to theological appropriation, to an apotheosis of the Good, the Beautiful, and the True, and to a life beyond life, that is, to a kind of death.

This difference between a discourse that lends itself to theological appropriation and one that does not causes Derrida in "How to Avoid Speaking: Denials," a text first presented in Jerusalem in 1986, one year before the initial publication of "*Khōra*," to contrast even more explicitly and directly Plato's discourses on the Good and on the *khōra*.[8] Intent on explaining himself for the first time in this essay on the oft-noted relationship between the language of deconstruction and that of negative theology, Derrida contrasts in rather bold terms a Platonic discourse that lends itself to the language of negative theology, namely, the discourse of the Good in Plato's *Republic*, and one that resists such appropriation, a Platonic discourse that even—though Derrida does not put it in exactly this way—anticipates many of the traits of deconstruction, namely, the discourse on the *khōra* in Plato's *Timaeus*. More clearly here than anywhere else, more clearly even than in "*Khōra*," in "How to Avoid Speaking: Denials" Derrida distinguishes sharply "between *two* movements or *two* tropics of negativity," two "structures" in Plato that are not only different but, he says, "radically heterogeneous" (*PSY II* 168).

Derrida begins his analysis of these two "structures"—and there is no coincidence in this—with the more metaphysical, indeed, hypermetaphysical or "hyperessential" of the two. Referring to the famous characterization of the Good as that which is "beyond being" in the *Republic*, Derrida interprets the Good not as that which interrupts or withdraws beyond all metaphysical categories but as that which reinscribes these categories on a higher level. Derrida thus speaks of a "*hyperbolization*" of the beyond that "the Good gives one to think, to know, and to be" (*PSY II* 168). Though the Good is "beyond being," everything that "is or is known *owes* its being and its being-known to this Good" (*PSY II* 169). The hyperbolization that makes this super- or hyperessentialism possible is thus that which establishes the ground of all being, knowing, and analogy, including the analogies that allow the Good itself to be glimpsed and named. The Good conditions all analogy and *lends itself* to analogical appropriation and understanding. As Derrida argues, because of the "analogous relation between being and (what is) beyond being," the "analogical continuity allows for translation; it allows one to compare the Good to the intelligible sun, and the latter to the visible sun" (*PSY II* 169): "the excellence [of the Good] is not so foreign to being or to light that the excess itself cannot be described in the terms of what it exceeds. . . . This analogy between the visible sun and the intelligible sun allows one to have confidence in the resemblance between the Good (*epekeina tēs ousias*) and that to which it gives birth, being and knowledge" (*PSY II* 169).

Whereas Derrida will later underscore the way in which the "third kind" that is *khōra* undercuts all analogical reappropriation, the *Republic*'s reference to light as a "third kind" (507e) between sight and the visible object plays "a role of analogical mediation." As such, the "third kind" of the *Republic* (the sun's light in the visible realm, the Good in the intelligible realm) is a very different "third kind" than that found in the *Timaeus*: while one assures mediation between the two sides by means of analogy, the other does not.

It is this hyperbolization or hyperbolic movement, along with the possibilities of analogy to which it gives rise, that ultimately made the Good susceptible, argues Derrida, to Christian appropriation, to reinscription by Dionysius and others within the register of negative philosophy. As Derrida argues, the *epekeina tēs ousias* "inaugurates an immense tradition" (*PSY II* 167); as that which "obeys the logic of the *super*, of the *hyper*," the Good is that which "heralds all the superessentialisms of Christian apophases" (*PSY II* 169).

Having laid out this reading of a superessential Good in the *Republic*, Derrida turns next, in "How to Avoid Speaking: Denials," to the second "movement," "tropic of negativity," or "structure" in Plato, "another way," as he puts it, "of treating the beyond (*epekeina*) of the limit, the third kind and place" (*PSY II* 170). Derrida contrasts the discourse on the *khōra* in the *Timaeus* with that on the Good in the *Republic* on almost every count. In the *Timaeus* Plato emphasizes the difficulty of adapting a "true or firm *logos*" to this third kind (*PSY II* 170), calling into question the status of any discourse about *khōra* and calling for a third kind of discourse, a bastard sort of discourse, to address this third kind that is neither sensible nor intelligible—nor hyperessential. Though the language of *khōra* surely can be and in fact has been appropriated by philosophy, assimilated to a philosophical discourse on space as *extension* (Descartes) or pure sensible form (Kant), there is in this discourse, Derrida argues, "something that no dialectic . . . or analogy would allow one to rearticulate with any philosopheme whatsoever" (*PSY II* 172). It is, again, the very structure of analogy that separates the discourse of the Good from that of the *khōra*. Whereas the Good exceeds but also still makes possible and nourishes the analogies to which it gives rise, or rather, to which it "gives birth," *like a Father*, *khōra* provides the place for the sensible forms that inform all figures to take place while remaining herself—or itself—completely withdrawn from these figures. Though *khōra* will be compared to a nurse, a mother, a receptacle, and so on, she remains, *like a mother*, unproductive of everything that takes place "within" her, though also, because she—it—participates in neither intelligible nor sensible being, completely untouched by these various figures, *including that of the mother*. As Derrida argues, "the so-called metaphors are not only inadequate, in that they borrow from the sensible forms inscribed in the *khōra* figures that are without pertinence for designating the *khōra* itself, they are also no longer metaphors" (*PSY II* 172). Whereas the Good supports a structure of analogical resemblance, a sovereign reign of analogy, as I have called it, allowing us to think, for example, the relationship between sensible visibility and intelligible visibility, *khōra* brings that reign to an end or else indefinitely defers its sovereign ascension. Because *khōra* remains untouched by or indifferent to the various "figures" used to name her, because speaking of *khōra* requires recourse to "tropic detours that are no longer rhetorical figures" (*PSY II* 173), she or it, unlike the Good, remains inappropriable by "every theomorphic or anthropomorphic schema" (*PSY II* 173). *Khōra* is neither mother nor nurse—not even metaphorically. She—it—is neither a supersensible being nor a superessential origin. Thus "*khōra* does not in truth form a couple with the 'father' to whom Plato 'likens' the model," for "the *khōra* does *not engender* the sensible forms that are inscribed in it" (*PSY II* 175).

And yet the *khōra*—or *Khōra*—"appears" in language, in a philosophical language to which she or it *also* remains heterogeneous. It is in this sense, I think, that *Khōra* might be understood not as an analogy but as an *anagram* in the sense that Derrida developed this term in "Plato's Pharmacy," an anagram or, indeed, a "trace" in the sense I spoke of in the Introduction to this work. As Derrida argues in "How to Avoid Speaking: Denials," to obey the injunction to think or name *khōra*, "one must think that which—standing beyond all given philosophemes—would have nevertheless left a trace in language, for example, the word *khōra* in the Greek language, insofar as it is caught up in the network of its usual meanings" (*PSY II* 174). Unlike some superessentiality that *could* have done without language, that gestures beyond all language, *khōra* is marked uniquely in the Greek language, in the Platonic text, all the while calling for iteration, transplantation, and translation. It is precisely *because* this mark in the Greek language is not a sign of some transcendental meaning or essence but the unique name of that which gives place to *and* withdraws from the difference between expression and meaning, the signifier and the signified, from the difference upon which all analogy or metaphor is based, that *khōra* as trace calls for repetition and displacement. "This trace and this promise are always inscribed in the body of a language, in its lexicon and its syntax, but one must be able to discover the trace, still unique, in other languages, in other bodies, in other negativities as well" (*PSY II* 174). Though it may be tempting to read the "Good" as another such reinscription, Derrida seems to suggest—for all the reasons mentioned above—that such a reading would be mistaken and would overlook the theological appropriation to which the Good, unlike the *khōra*, has lent itself.[9]

The difference between the Good and the *khōra* is thus really that between the reign of analogy and the coming of the anagram, the difference between a metaphysical sign that lends itself to anthropomorphic and theomorphic appropriation in negative theology—a Good beyond being that lends itself to the "hyperessentiality of God"—and a trace that does not. What in the end distinguishes the Good from *khōra* is the "ontological wager of hyperessentiality" (*PSY II* 147), which brings with it all the values of presence and immediacy that make vision and intuition possible, the values of presence, resemblance, and light that make all analogy possible, and the values of productivity and life that always mark the discourse of sovereignty. Unlike the Good, *khōra*, while giving place to everything that takes place within her, herself gives nothing. Whereas the being of the Good is not simply negated by the designation of a "beyond" (*epekeina*) but hyperbolized, its "being" one of excess and abundance, its hyperessentiality suggesting at once "no more being" and "being more than being: being more" (*PSY II* 158), superior to and sovereign over all the things that are, one cannot even say "there *is* the *khōra*," much less *es gibt*, which "still announces or recalls too much the dispensation of God, of man" (*PSY II* 173). Unlike the Good, *khōra*—at once "indifferent" and "impassive"—"does not create or produce anything" (*PSY II* 173). Unlike the Good, which in the writing of Dionysius the Areopagite becomes "not a life" but, rather, "superabundant Life" (*PSY II* 175), *khōra* gives life to nothing. With the *khōra* "there is reference to neither an event nor a gift" (*PSY II* 174).

What distinguishes the Good from *khōra*, what makes these two figures of negativity "radically heterogeneous," is indeed a difference in "structure," the difference between a structure that associates being, power, goodness, sovereignty, light, height, and, ultimately, life and one that does not. Indeed, it is this emphasis on sovereignty and life, on superabundant life, on what can easily become sacrifice in the name of that life, that has to be questioned if not countered, I believe Derrida believed, by a relentless, vigilant, and affirmative interrogation of the way in which life as such is only ever itself or only ever possible in relation to death. Already in "Plato's Pharmacy" this rethinking of life was in evidence. Derrida speaks, for example, of the Platonic *eidos* as a repetition of the same that "gives itself out to be a repetition of *life*," while tautology was understood— already, again, in Plato—as "*life* going out of itself to come home to itself" ("PP" 168; my emphasis in both cases). What Derrida then goes on to show in that essay of 1968—an essay that must be read and reread today—is that the good, philosophical repetition of eidetic memory always requires the bad repetition of *hypomnesis* (a *hyper* that always requires the *hypo*), a repetition that introduces writing and thus death into the life of the *eidos*—death as the very possibility of survival or living on and iteration in time as the condition of any eternal life. In that essay, Derrida shows that the return of tautology to itself always involves a "life going out of itself beyond return," an *autos*—even the *autos* of tautology—that always involves a heteron, an other that scans the same and gives it, as Derrida often put it, its very respiration ("PP" 169).[10]

In *Rogues* Derrida will thus want to sever the unconditional from sovereignty, and thus the event, the other, justice, writing, and so on from the Good and from a life that would claim or pretend to be purely present to itself. More and more suspicious of the language of sovereignty, even of a sovereignty of excess and expenditure, as one might find it in Bataille, Derrida will want to sever the unconditional from every *analogy of sovereignty* and from the *sovereignty of analogy*, from everything that would identify the unconditional as self-identical, sovereign, powerful, productive, life giving, and salutary. That is the reason, I believe, why Derrida in *Rogues* will *not* say that the democracy to come is like the Good but that it is like "the *khōra* of the political," as if the Good, unlike *Khōra*—and perhaps despite Plato's intentions—were still too determined by the reign of analogy it itself imposes, still too fecund and productive, still too sovereign, still too apt to be *thought* as an idea rather than *read* as an analogy, and thus inappropriate for the kind of *irreducible analogy* Derrida was seeking for the democracy to come. "The democracy to come would be *like* the *khōra* of the political"—that, I think we can now hear, is the *irreducible* analogy, the anagram, which at once inscribes political thinking into history, language, and culture and opens that history to a radically undetermined future. For what the "democracy to come" and *Khōra* would share, what they would have in common, what makes the "analogy" between them possible, is not their participation in some shared quality or idea, the reduction of both to some shared meaning, but a shared contingency and a common necessity: like proper names marking an absolutely unique historical configuration, Plato's *Khōra* and Derrida's democracy to come, his *démocratie à venir*, are themselves events, "traces in the history of language" that of necessity call for their own reiteration and transformation and themselves already *name* this necessary replacement or supplementarity: *Khōra* on the side of space, making space or giving place to what will of necessity replace it, to what will of necessity come to be inscribed within it, and the *démocratie à venir* on the side of time, opening up the political—making it hospitable—to future discourses, institutions, and practices that themselves keep the future open. Only such irreducible analogies, only such anagrams, only such names of an unconditionality *without sovereignty*, can at once do justice to history by naming the unconditional and history to justice. Only such anagrams have the "weak force" to contest or undercut the sovereign reign of analogy that sustains and guarantees the power of every sovereign reign. If Plato's *Republic* thus provided Western philosophy with its first figure of unconditional sovereignty, and so inaugurated, through a discourse on the sovereign Good, a reign of analogy whose power still determines so much of our thinking today, Plato's *Timaeus* provided Western thought with its first anagram in the name of "*khōra*," that is, with an "unconditional" that is no longer sovereign and that thus brought Western philosophy already at its outset to a close—two and a half millennia before and after itself. Which means that between Plato and Plato the phantasm of sovereignty, the phantasm of a Father who can give birth all on his own to a son, will have found the time and space to impose its reign.

3

Derrida's *Laïcité*

The controversy in France in 2003–4 surrounding a proposed law ban-
ning the wearing of headscarves and other "conspicuous signs of religious
affiliation" in primary and secondary public schools triggered a very lively
debate about the place of religion in French educational institutions and
in French society more generally. The rallying cry for many supporters
of the ban was the French notion of *laïcité*.[1] Though often translated as
"secularism," *laïcité* entails more than just the separation of church and
state and the protection of French institutions from religious dogma and
authority. It involves the promotion of a certain civic and republican ideal
of French politics, culture, and, perhaps especially, education.

In this chapter, I would like to suggest that Jacques Derrida, a product
of the French educational system and for much of his life a citizen of the
French nation-state, was strongly committed to this notion of *laïcité*, or
rather—because I can already hear the objections—to a reworked, en-
larged, call it "deconstructive" notion of *laïcité* that has itself been submitted to critique, its own theologico-political origins exposed through a
radical desacralization that leads, in the end, not to a reason divorced from
religion but to the origins of religion itself.[2] I frame my analysis of Derrida
here in terms of the question of *laïcité* in order both to provide a larger
context for Derrida's critique of the theologico-political and to focus attention on an aspect of Derrida's work that has received less attention
than it ought. While many commentators have rightly argued that over
the past couple of decades Derrida's work became more explicitly political

and more focused on politico-ethical issues, what has been less noticed is the accompanying critique of the theological origins of these political or politico-ethical issues. Indeed, if one had to point to a single motivating force behind almost *all* of Derrida's work over the last two decades—and in many cases well before—it might just be his commitment to a critique of what he considered the pervasive and still unthought or unthematized conflation of religious concepts and the supposed secularism of the modern nation-state. What motivated Derrida's work was thus not the desire to promote an ideology of secularism or *laïcité* in France, the United States, or elsewhere but the imperative to submit to critique and to *clarify* the hidden and often overlooked relationship between the political and its theological origins—origins that, after a couple hundred years of Enlightenment thought, still inform and define political institutions and their founding concepts. To invoke the title of Jean-Luc Nancy's most recent project, what motivated Derrida for at least the last two decades—though one could argue that this is as old as deconstruction itself—is a certain "deconstruction of Christianity,"[3] or, as Derrida preferred to call it, a deconstruction of the "Abrahamic filiation," a deconstruction that took aim at both the theoretical underpinnings of the theologico-political and the policies and institutional practices supported by it, not only in France but also, and perhaps especially, in the United States. This deconstruction of the Abrahamic filiation was carried out, I will argue, not in the name of *laïcité* as it is commonly understood in France or secularism as it is understood in the United States but in the name of what I will hazard to call an originary or, better, a radical secularity that inscribes faith (though not religion) at the very origin of the sociopolitical and thus, Derrida argues, at the very origin of all sovereignty.

Indeed, in Derrida's insistent critique of the theologico-political, the concept that came under the most scrutiny was surely that of sovereignty. It thus did not take the publication of a volume by Derrida entitled *Sovereignties in Question* to know that sovereignty had been for some time a privileged theme in his work. Whether Derrida was looking at discourses on the self, the nation-state, or God, whether he was addressing questions of individual identity formation, politics, or theology, the question of "sovereignty" was at the center of his analysis. Whether understood in relation to its theological origins in a sovereign God or to its philosophical origins in egological ipseity or self-mastery, sovereignty appears to have been at the root of many of the philosophical concepts Derrida wished to reread and many of the contemporary ethical and political issues he wished to rethink. Hence Derrida's analyses of phenomena as seemingly diverse as democracy, globalization, the death penalty, cosmopolitanism, religious tolerance, hospitality, and even monogamy—which I will save for the end as a tease—were all motivated by what he perceived to be the unavowed influence of a theologico-political notion of sovereignty upon our philosophical concepts and discourses as well as our ethical and political practices.

Now, before going any further, let me try to answer a potential objection to the thesis I am trying to support here. While I don't think anyone will dispute the claim that Derrida's work during the past two decades has become more explicitly political and that it often involves a critique of the theological origins of political concepts, it might also seem that Derrida's work became more religious during this very same period. In texts such as "Circumfession," "Faith and Knowledge," "How to Avoid Speaking: Denials," "The Gift of Death," and so on, religious or theological images, themes, and questions come to the forefront of Derrida's work. Whether or not one takes this interest to have been motivated or nourished by Derrida's continuing dialogue with Levinas, it is hard to ignore the fact that questions of faith and religion emerge in so many of Derrida's texts on hospitality, witnessing, the gift, messianicity without messianism, and so on. Indeed, a certain religious language seems so omnipresent and developed in his work that it would be easy to conclude that Derrida too took that famous "theological turn" in French phenomenology.[4] How are we to square this turn or this apparent turn with what I wish to characterize as Derrida's radical secularity or reworked and originary *laïcité*? Let me suggest in anticipation that the apparent contradiction will disappear once we make the case for an originary or radical secularity that includes a critique or questioning of religious dogma *by means of* a more primordial or originary faith that first opens up the dimension of *both* religion *and* the state, *both* faith *and* knowledge. In other words, Derrida's secularity will have to be considered not in complete opposition to religion but in relation to a faith that first opens up religious experience, a faith in the coming of the event or the other that Derrida believes to be at the origin of every relation worthy of its name. Hence Derrida will not simply clarify and critique the religious origins of political concepts so as then to leave these religious origins alone, so as to consign them, for example, to the realm of the private or the personal as opposed to the public or the political. Rather, he will, in a series of texts from "How to Avoid Speaking: Denials" to "Faith and Knowledge," criticize the dogmatic aspects of these religious origins in order to clarify an originary faith that is at the origin of both the political and religion. If *laïcité* or secularism is thus not a very good name for a type of thinking that first opens the dimension of faith, that is perhaps because it is at once still too tainted by its theologico-political origins *and* still too divorced from the originary faith that makes it possible *in our world today*.[5]

Derrida's originary *laïcité* or radical secularity helps explain, I believe, his choice of both authors and themes over the last couple of decades. Derrida's frequent return to Carl Schmitt, for example, from *Politics of Friendship* onward, can be explained in large part by Schmitt's thesis concerning the theological origins of political sovereignty. Though Derrida distances himself in many places from Schmitt's prescriptions regarding this political sovereignty, it seems to me that he generally accepts Schmitt's diagnoses on the issue. As Schmitt succinctly puts it in *Political Theology*: "All significant concepts of the modern theory of the state are secularized theological concepts . . . whereby, for example, the omnipotent God became the omnipotent lawgiver. . . . The exception in jurisprudence is analogous to the *miracle* in theology"[6] (my emphasis). What interests Derrida about Schmitt is his claim that sovereignty is always related to the sovereign exception to suspend rights and laws and that this relationship between sovereignty and exceptionality is inextricable—even in modern democracies—from the theological notion of a sovereign God. "Analogous," says Schmitt, "to a *miracle*"—a word that will return, as we will see, in Derrida's own text. Whether one agrees or disagrees with Schmitt's—and thus Derrida's—diagnosis of sovereignty, it is hard to contest that it is this conjunction of sovereignty and theology in Schmitt that interests Derrida. In an interview in *For What Tomorrow . . .* Derrida makes this unmistakably clear:

> Without this category of exception, we cannot understand the concept of sovereignty. Today, the great question is indeed, everywhere, that of sovereignty. Omnipresent in our discourses and in our axioms, under its own name or another, literally or figuratively, this concept has a theological origin: the true sovereign is God. The concept of this authority or of this power was transferred to the monarch, said to have a "divine right." Sovereignty was then delegated to the people, in the form of democracy, or to the nation, with the same theological attributes as those attributed to the king and to God. (*FWT* 91–92)[7]

It is thus necessary, says Derrida in the same interview, "to deconstruct the concept of sovereignty, never to forget its theological filiation and to be ready to call this filiation into question wherever we discern its effects. This supposes an uncompromising critique of the logic of the state and of the nation-state" (*FWT* 92).[8]

Though one may disagree with this understanding of modernity and argue that Western political thought is not nearly as beholden to or informed by these theological notions as Derrida claims, this critique of the theologico-political surely plays a significant, motivating, even determining role in Derrida's work. In so many of Derrida's texts of the past couple of decades, deconstruction became almost coextensive with the deconstruction of an unthought and still-operative theological heritage in Western political thought—that is, with a critique of "the theological and hardly secularized principle of the sovereignty of nation-states" ("M" 166), a sovereignty "of ontotheological origin, though more or less secularized in one place and purely theological and non-secularized in another" ("AI" 111). As Derrida puts it in *Paper Machine*, "sovereignty remains a theological inheritance" and it is "in this concept of sovereignty (either indivisible or 'partially' divided) that phallogocentric theology has always built its nest" (*PM* 105). Sovereignty thus means, according to Derrida, "omnipotence, self-determination of the will, unlimited and unconditional power," and so on—notions with a clearly theological filiation (*PM* 118). Hence it appears today that Derrida was fully engaged in the "prudent, patient, differentiated, strategically complex deconstruction of political onto-theology" that he himself called for ("PMS" 14).

Central to this critique of theological sovereignty, this "theo-logic of sovereignty" (*PM* 107), is the claim that sovereignty is, in essence, always indivisible, unshareable, and unlimited—a sovereignty, then, whose first figure would be the indivisible, unshareable, and unlimited sovereignty of God. The theological notion of indivisible sovereignty is thus at the very heart of the deconstructive project, whether this be the sovereignty of the self, the nation-state, or God. This deconstruction is not simply a theoretical project to be undertaken or not but a process that is already underway in every attempt to think or put into practice a division, sharing, or limitation of sovereign power. Hence Derrida moves perpetually between the prescriptive and the constative, telling us that the "onto-theological foundations [of democratic sovereignty] *must* be deconstructed" and that this deconstruction "has been underway for a long time, and it will continue for a long time" ("AI" 115, 131).

Derrida was in fact relentless in his questioning of the sources and effects of this theological filiation in our ethical and political discourses and practices. The deconstruction of the theologico-political notion of sovereignty thus became central to Derrida's rethinking not only of democracy in works such as *Rogues* but of more specific political practices and institutions. In a series of lectures and seminars on the death penalty, for example, Derrida wished to expose the theological vestiges of a form of state sovereignty that asserts its power, cruelty, and exceptionality most visibly in putting citizens to death or, in the case of war, sending them off to face death. A vocal opponent of the death penalty, particularly in the United States, Derrida demonstrated not only the way the canonical philosophical discourses of Hobbes and Kant, for example, try to justify the death penalty through Scripture but, more importantly, the way "the essence of sovereign power as political power but, *first of all, as theologico-political power*, presents itself, represents itself, as the right to pronounce and execute a death penalty.[9] Or else to grant pardon: in an arbitrary, sovereign fashion" ("PMS" 34; my emphasis). Derrida's emphasis not on the immorality or inhumanity of the death penalty but on the ultimately theological basis for the state's arrogation to itself of this exceptional right helps explain why Derrida's four paradigmatic cases for the death penalty—Socrates, Jesus, al-Hallâj, and Joan of Arc—are all cases in which the condemned was accused of impiety or worshipping false gods. Each had a message that was at once political and theological; in opposing the state, each brought to light what Derrida calls the "phantasmatico-theological" essence of sovereignty; each was thus condemned in the name of a certain transcendence for worshiping or claiming a relationship to another transcendence or a counter-transcendence ("PMS" 18). In each case, then, writes Derrida, the blasphemer must be "brought back down to earth, led back to the laws of the city or the Church or the clergy or worldly organization—and that is the politics of the State. . . . This condemnation is carried out at once *in the name* of transcendence and *against* transcendence" ("PMS" 37). The cases of Socrates, Jesus, al-Hallâj, and Joan of Arc are thus exemplary of the state's opposition to any claim to a counter-relationship to the sacred within the state (or the city-state, or the empire, or the Church). Such claims cannot be tolerated, not because the state, even the secular state, is opposed to any and all claims of transcendence, but because, being itself a theologico-political formation, it cannot tolerate any counter-claims to its own theological origins. Rather than simply opposing the theological, the state wishes to have a monopoly over it. It thus uses the death penalty not so much to protect the lives of its citizens as to take or sacrifice natural life in the name of an excess or hyperbolization of life, that is, in the name of a certain transcendence. Again, whether one agrees or disagrees with Derrida's analyses, I think it is pretty clear that a deconstruction of the theologico-political origins of sovereignty motivates them.

Derrida thus discerns traces of the theologico-political in everything from discourses on globalization, where the Abrahamic and especially

Christian filiation "of the concept of the world" and the "ethico-politico-juridical concepts" related to it tend "to regulate the process of globalization or *mondialisation*" ("M" 164), to literature, which Derrida calls "a religious remainder, a link to and relay for what is sacrosanct in a society without God" (*GD2* 157). Just as Derrida saw a transfer of the sacred from the divine right of the monarch to the people in democracy, so he sees a relay between sacred texts and the institution of literature. In an interview in *Paper Machine*, he observes that "the quasi-sacralization of literature appeared at a point in time when an apparent desacralization of biblical texts had begun" (*PM* 163). Summarizing an argument he develops at some length in *The Gift of Death*, Derrida claims that "literature, in the strict modern and European sense of the term, preserves the memory of the sacred texts. . . . No critic, no translator, no teacher, has, in principle, the right to touch the literary text once it is published, legitimated, and authorized by copyright: this is a sacred inheritance, even if it occurs in an atheistic and so-called secular milieu" (*PM* 142). This sacred inheritance stems from the fact that the text of the other comes from the other—untouchable in its alterity. As Derrida writes elsewhere in the course of an analysis of the writing, the literature, of Hélène Cixous:

> Literature . . . [an] heir both more than faithful and unpardonably blasphemous of all the Bibles, remains the absolute place of the secret of this heteronomy, of the secret as experience of the law that comes from the other, of the law whose giver is none other than the coming of the other, in this test of unconditional hospitality which opens us to it before any condition, any norm, any concept, any genre, any generic and genealogical belonging. (*GG* 48)

Derrida's analyses of democracy in *Rogues*, of hospitality or forgiveness, even work and globalization, even, as we see, literature, must thus all be read as part of the same patient, differentiated deconstruction of politico-theological notions such as life, sacrifice, transcendence, sovereignty, the sacred, and even salvation.[10] At the end of *Rogues*, for example, Derrida is concerned with an unavowed relation between democracy and the Judeo-Christian notion of salvation, a salvation that, he argues, needs to be distinguished from the unconditionality of the other or the event—that is, from an unconditional that is neither sovereign nor sacred. Having followed a continual relationship throughout the tradition between god or the gods and democracy—from Aristotle's description of the truly virtuous man as a god among men to Rousseau's people of gods to Heidegger's famous reference in the *Der Spiegel* interview to a god who can save us—Derrida wishes to oppose the democracy to come, with all its messianic overtones, to any notion of a sovereign or sacred saving power within the political, that is, to any notion of Judeo-Christian salvation within the state.

The effect of this is to open up an essential difference between sovereignty and the unconditional, between any kind of saving *power* and the weak *force* of the democracy to come, just as, elsewhere, Derrida will want to open up a difference between the theological notion of resurrection and living on (*R* 110–14). In his short preface to *Chaque fois unique, la fin du monde*, for example, Derrida contests a certain Christian notion of resurrection, refusing to reject it outright but trying instead to transform it through a notion of living on without sovereignty, that is, without egological ipseity, a "resurrection," if you will, that structures life itself and would precede every actual death. Whereas the democracy to come would thus be like the historically determined, secular analogue of a transcendent saving force, living on would be, so to speak, like the secular counterpart of resurrection, a living on that would be a structural possibility—though one that would never be assured and would never be final—for every living being capable of leaving a trace. Derrida thus speaks of the *adieu* addressed to the other as "a farewell that resigns itself to welcoming [*saluer*], as I believe every farewell worthy of its name must, the always open possibility, indeed the necessity, of a possible non-return, of the end of the world as the end of all resurrection" (*CFU* 11).

Under the aegis of the "theologico-political," then, Derrida attempts to bring about not exactly a more radical secularization of political thought but rather a clarification of the theological origins of political concepts, beginning with the concept of sovereignty, which is always related, for Derrida, to the decisive exceptionality of a sovereign subject and thus, in the end, to a sovereign God. It is because of the theological filiation of sovereignty, and even in democracy in the figure of "the people," that Derrida ultimately worries at the end of the first part of *Rogues* whether the democracy to come might be understood as, or translated into, a "god to come" (*R* 110–14).[11] If such a translation were possible, it would require a rethinking of such a god in terms of everything a *sovereign* god must *not be*—that is, in terms of a god who is vulnerable, divisible, powerless, and so on—in short, a god who has undergone deconstruction, or perhaps even a radically *secular god*.

Though it would be silly to attribute this radical critique of the theologico-political to mere biography, biography no doubt played a crucial role, from Derrida's unique experience growing up in colonial Algeria to his education in French institutions, where a certain republican, secular ideal was no doubt espoused. In "Abraham, the Other," Derrida speaks of a certain "uprooting" in his upbringing or education, a *déracinement* that was the result of being an Algerian Jew, at once French and not-French, undecidably French, an uprooting that he would later cultivate, he says, through the thought of a "New International" beyond cosmopolitanism, or the thought of the desert in the desert, of *khōra* or of a messianicity without messianism, and so on ("AO" 29). Estranged from both the Christian and Muslim communities in Algeria, though also, to a certain extent, from the Jewish community, Derrida was suspicious of communities in general and, perhaps especially, of religious communities. When Derrida thus came to question the philosophical discourses on community or communism, it was often the religious, eschatological undertones of these discourses that drew his attention and critique. The same holds true for certain evangelistic critiques of those discourses, for example, as we see in *Specters of Marx*, Francis Fukuyama's neo-evangelistic liberalism and his eschatological vision of the end of history.

Derrida thus had an extraordinarily developed sense of smell, so to speak, for the theological assumptions or presuppositions, undertones or underpinnings, of philosophical, political, and ethical discourses. The French would say that he had *du pif* for the legacies of a sovereign God in the most seemingly secular discourses and institutions. In many places, even concepts that seem to have developed out of an Enlightenment tradition *explicitly opposed* to religious dogma are considered suspect for their theological origins. Hence cosmopolitanism, which would appear to move beyond the nation-state and beyond the particularities of ethnicity and religion, is marked, in Derrida's eyes, by its Judeo-Christian history, from Saint Paul to Kant, and by the notion of a World-State that would be in its concept "theologico-political or secular (that is, secular in its filiation, though secretly theologico-political)." This does not mean that we must not support such a cosmopolitan spirit, but it does mean that we must not do so without also submitting it to critique. Derrida concludes: "If we must in fact cultivate the spirit of this tradition (as I believe most international institutions have done since World War I), we must also try to adjust the limits of this tradition to our own time by questioning the ways in which they have been defined and determined by the ontotheological, philosophical, and religious discourses in which this cosmopolitical ideal was formulated" ("AI" 130).

What Derrida calls the democracy to come or messianicity without messianism would be, it seems, an attempt to cultivate cosmopolitanism's international spirit, its drive toward universality, while at the same time, and precisely in the name of that universality, submitting any kind of international or cosmopolitan *ideal* to critique. Hence Derrida's democracy to come would attempt to move beyond cosmopolitanism itself, beyond the notions of world citizenship or world citizens defined as "lawful 'subjects'" in a state or legitimate members of a nation-state ("AI" 130). In going beyond cosmopolitanism in this way, the democracy to come would go "beyond the 'political' as it has been commonly defined," beyond a political determined by a theological conception of sovereignty and a conception of the world as what needs to be saved or redeemed ("AI" 130). For at the same time as we try to think beyond the nation-state we must also ask, "What is the philosophical, theological, and political history of this concept of *world*?" ("AI" 107).[12]

This critique of citizenship and of sovereignty was not to be carried out, it must be emphasized, to the exclusion of initiatives to expand citizenship and extend rights and protections to more and more people throughout the world. Derrida's response to those in need of rights and citizenship would surely not be to proclaim the sovereignty of the nation-state to be a phantasm to be dispelled and citizenship a theological concept to be abandoned. On the contrary, one must extend the rights and protections of citizenship to as many as possible *at the same time* as one submits these notions to critique. And the same could be said about most other Enlightenment concepts: they must be supported and expanded at the same time as their theological origins are questioned and clarified.

Hence even a principle such as religious tolerance—a secular concept if ever there was one, since it would seem to be motivated by a belief that the state must protect the individual rights of citizens to practice the religion of their choice and, thus, that the state must not be in the business of endorsing or supporting any particular religion—is, for Derrida, and not just in practice but in *theory*, theological in its origins and inspiration. In the interview he gave just after 9/11, Derrida hesitates to subscribe without reservation to the notion of religious tolerance because of its Judeo-Christian provenance. Because it is always granted from a position of power, from the side of the "reason of the strongest," tolerance is a "form of charity, a form of Christian charity, even if Jews and Muslims might seem to appropriate this language as well." Tolerance is thus, argues Derrida, "a supplementary mark of sovereignty, the good face of sovereignty, which says from its height to the other: I am letting you be, you are not insufferable, I am leaving you a place in my home, but do not forget that this is my home" ("AI" 127). For Derrida, then, tolerance is not a condition of hospitality but "the opposite of hospitality" or, at best, "a conditional, circumspect, careful hospitality," which, as we saw in Chapter 1, is in Derrida's idiom hardly a hospitality worthy of the name

("AI" 127–28). We would thus need to be extremely circumspect in using this notion of *tolerance*, since it is not as value neutral and secular as it might seem. Referring to Voltaire's famous article on tolerance in his *Philosophical Dictionary* Derrida writes:

> We would have to be extremely vigilant, it seems to me, in interpreting this heritage. I would be tempted to say "yes and no" to each sentence, "yes but no," "yes, although, however," and so forth. . . . The word "tolerance" is first of all marked by a religious war between Christians, or between Christians and non-Christians. Tolerance is a *Christian* virtue, or for that matter a *Catholic* virtue. The Christian must tolerate the non-Christian, but, even more so, the Catholic must let the Protestant be. . . . Peace would thus be tolerant cohabitation. ("AI" 126–27)

Again, this is not to say that tolerance is not to be preferred to intolerance or that it should not be promoted in the state, but it is to say that we need to remain vigilant with regard to the Christian origins of the discourse that supports it. For "it is a discourse with religious roots; it is most often used on the side of those with power, always as a kind of condescending concession" ("AI" 127). While Derrida argues that we must thus "be faithful to the memory of the Enlightenment" and "not forget certain exemplary models [from Voltaire to Zola to Sartre] in the struggle against intolerance," we must at the same time question "the very concept of tolerance" ("AI" 125).

Because Western political concepts have been most heavily marked and influenced by Judeo-Christian theology, it is no surprise that this theology and its influence on political concepts is most often at the center of Derrida's critique. But Derrida's vigilance with regard to questionable theologisms in politics did not end with Judeo-Christianity. Indeed, if there is one thing Derrida finds dubious and dangerous about a certain Islam, it is precisely its conflation of politics and religion. Again in the 9/11 interview, Derrida says that what he finds unacceptable about the Bin Laden "strategy" is "not only the cruelty, the disregard for human life, the disrespect for law, for women, the use of what is worst in techno-capitalist modernity for the purposes of religious fanaticism," but an impoverished notion of the future put in the service of a "dogmatic interpretation . . . of the Islamic revelation of the One" ("AI" 113). Invoking secularization and yet issuing a characteristic caution with regard to it, Derrida argues: "Nothing of what has been so laboriously secularized in the forms of the 'political,' of 'democracy,' of 'international law,' and even in the nontheological form of sovereignty (assuming, again, that the value of sovereignty can be completely secularized or detheologized, a hypothesis about which I have my doubts), none of this seems to have any place whatsoever in the discourse 'Bin Laden'" ("AI" 113). Though the secularization of sovereignty might not yet be complete, though it might still be marked by the theological even if it were complete, radicalized, perfected, Derrida seems to bank on another secularization or another *laïcité*, one that, as we will see in a moment, would not simply purify the state of all faith but seek out the original faith or originary engagement at the origin of *both* the state *and* religion. Today's institutions of international law and human rights must thus be championed for the way they promote secularization in the more limited sense of the term *in the name* of what we might venture to call a *laïcité* to come, perhaps even a messianic *laïcité* or, better still, a radical secularity without secularism.

To show just how far this secularizing thought goes in Derrida, consider his final interview, published in *Le Monde* in August 2004 and subsequently published as *Learning to Live Finally*. In that interview, Derrida appears to endorse—without any real provocation to do so—polygamy or, rather, multiple civil unions with either the opposite or the same sex, simply because the notion of monogamous, heterosexual civil unions seems to be a theological holdover from heterosexual religious marriage. Asked about why, in June 2004, he supported the celebration of a gay marriage in the French town of Bègles—a marriage that was later declared illegal and nullified by the French courts—Derrida explains his support by appealing not simply to principles of equality or equal rights but to the unacknowledged theological origins of the concept of marriage in the state. He argues:

> "Marriage" as a religious, sacred, heterosexual value—with a vow to procreate, to be eternally faithful, and so on—is a concession made by the secular state to the Christian church, and particularly with regard to monogamy, which is neither Jewish (it was imposed upon Jews by Europeans only in the nineteenth century and was not an obligation just a few generations ago in Jewish Maghreb), nor, as is well known, Muslim. (*LLF* 43–44)

Derrida thus supported this gay or same-sex "marriage" because of what he considered to be the unjustified theological origins behind the state's sanctioning of heterosexual marriage alone. But because the concept of marriage is itself of theological origin, Derrida goes on to suggest, as many others have done, simply doing away altogether with the religious concept of "marriage" in France's civil codes and replacing it with the secular notion of "civil union." Marriages would then be performed in churches, temples, and synagogues, and civil unions by state officials in public institutions. The state would thus no longer "marry" anyone—whether homosexual or heterosexual—though it would legitimate both opposite-sex and same-sex civil unions.

But, for Derrida, this would still not go far enough. In order to remove even more of the theological heritage of marriage from civil union, in order to draw an even sharper line between *religious* marriage and *civil* union, Derrida takes the further step of endorsing not just same-sex civil unions but, more provocatively, *multiple* civil unions, whether between partners of the opposite sex or the same sex or both. Derrida argues:

> By getting rid of the word and concept of "marriage," and thus this ambiguity or this hypocrisy with regard to the religious and the sacred—things that have no place in a secular constitution—one could put in their place a contractual "civil union," a sort of generalized *pacs*,[13] one that has been improved, refined, and would remain flexible and adaptable to partners whose sex and number would not be prescribed. As for those who want to be joined in "marriage" in the strict sense of the term—something, by the way, for which my respect remains totally intact—they would be able to do so before the religious authority of their choosing. (*LLF* 44)

One can see how a thoroughgoing critique of the theological origins of political concepts and institutions—in this case marriage—leads Derrida to this position. Once civil union and religious marriage have been distinguished, all the theological attributes typically attached to the latter—including heterosexuality and monogamy—must, in all good logic, be removed from the former.[14]

Hence Derrida's flair for sniffing out the theological origins of seemingly secular concepts, from cosmopolitanism to tolerance to civil union, knew practically no bounds. Indeed, in those places where Derrida considers this secularization for itself, it is *itself* rejected as being too theological. "The opposition between sacred and secular is naïve," he says. Indeed, "contrary to what we think we know, we have never entered into a secular era. The very idea of the secular is religious through and through—Christian really" (*PM* 141). At the end of "Faith and Knowledge," Derrida speaks again of the *naiveté* involved in simply becoming an advocate of secularism or *laïcité*. The reason for this yet again is that *laïcité* is itself defined in relationship to the theological, indeed, to Christianity. Derrida writes:

> If belief [*croyance*] is the ether of the address and relation to the utterly other, it is to be found in the experience itself of non-relationship or of absolute *interruption* (indices: "Blanchot," "Levinas" . . .).

Here as well, the hypersanctification of this non-relation or of this transcendence would come about by way of desacralization rather than secularization or laicization, concepts that are too Christian; perhaps even by way of a certain "atheism," in any case by way of a radical experience of the resources of "negative theology"—and going beyond even this tradition. . . . It designates disenchantment as the *very resource of the religious*. . . . Nothing seems therefore more uncertain, more difficult to sustain, nothing seems here or there more imprudent than a self-assured discourse on the age of disenchantment, the era of secularization, the time of laicization, etc. ("FK" 64–65)

But it is here, in this relationship between a hypersanctification and a vigilant desacralization, that things become more complicated and, to my eyes, more *promising*. It is here that a desacralization of the political, of religion, and even of the secular leads, perhaps, to a "hypersanctification" of the nonrelation of a certain transcendence or absolute interruption. As I suggested in the beginning, Derrida's vigilant "secularizing" of theological concepts goes hand in hand with a claim that at the very origins of not only religion but science is a kind of originary faith. "Believe what I say as one believes in a miracle," writes Derrida in the passage of "Faith and Knowledge" I just cited ("FK" 83–84). What Derrida means by this is that every testimony, even a perjurious one, is in effect preceded by this plea or this promise: "believe in me as you would believe in a miracle." Whether or not what I say is true, whether or not I know it to be true, every testimony, every bearing witness, every appeal to my experience—even in science—asks the other to believe in what I say as one believes in a miracle. This is not the miracle that comes from the sovereign who declares a state of exception, as in Schmitt; it is not a miraculous exceptionality but the miracle of every performative, even the least exceptional, the most ordinary or banal, indeed, the most secular. In the end, it is the miracle of every *event*, for, as Derrida writes in *Paper Machine*, the event that arrives beyond the possible "is as extraordinary as a miracle" (*PM* 161).

Once we recognize that every act of language presupposes a responsibility in the form of a *sworn faith*, an "I promise the truth," an "I engage myself to address the other," then we have, in Derrida's words, "engendered God quasi-mechanically" ("FK" 27). Even a secular oath cannot but produce, invoke, convoke, or engender this unengenderable God, that is, God as *already there*, even before being. The unengenderable is thus perpetually re-engendered as God is *called* to witness, called as the *present-absent* witness, says Derrida, of every oath. Hence a certain faith is inscribed into the very heart of what one would take to be secular knowledge—the knowledge, say, of the university or of the state, as opposed to the faith of the church.

There thus appears to be no contradiction in Derrida between this claim of a fundamental faith that would precede all testimony and all science and a thoroughgoing critique or deconstruction of the theological origins of so many seemingly secular institutions. Indeed, the former would even be necessary for the latter. Hence it should come as no surprise that Derrida can, in the very same section of "Faith and Knowledge," at once affirm the sworn faith of every response and reject the notion of secularism because of its theological origins. Derrida in fact claims that we will fail to understand religion today if we continue to believe in the opposition between reason and religion, or techno-scientific modernity and religion—that is, if we continue to remain in a *certain age* of Enlightenment, within a certain antireligious, dogmatically secularizing filiation that runs, say, from Voltaire and Marx to Nietzsche, Freud, and beyond. We must instead ask how techno-science *supports* religion rather than opposes it and show that religion *and* reason have the same source, a common source—the testimonial engagement (*gage*) of every performative, which commits or engages one to respond *before* the other and *for* the performativity of techno-science.

"*Belief*," says Derrida, "is the *ether* of the address and the relation to the utterly other": it is thus the very experience of nonrelation and of absolute interruption, a belief that is at the origin of both faith and knowledge, and so is always related to a certain reason. This is perhaps the place to speculate that such a notion of a reason that does not exclude faith, that is the result of a radical desacralization, might have led to a fruitful conversation between Derrida and the best-known critic of his supposedly secular or secularizing thought, a critic who is not only well known but globally known, though not specifically as a critic of Derrida. I am speaking—if you can believe it—of Pope Benedict XVI, formerly Joseph Cardinal Ratzinger, who, on June 6, 2004, the sixtieth anniversary of D-day, wrote an article for the German newspaper *Frankfurter Allgemeine Zeitung* entitled "In Search of Freedom: Against Reason Fallen Ill and Religion Abused," in which he argued that, in a world where reason has become detached from God, from faith, "all that remains is reason's dissolution, its deconstruction, as, for example, Jacques Derrida has set it out for us."[15] The criticism here is clear: Derrida belongs to the long line of secular thinkers from Voltaire to Nietzsche who detached reason from faith and who thus led to a crisis of both reason and faith in the twentieth century. Now, it is hardly my intention to show that the pope is, or at least was as Joseph Cardinal Ratzinger, a poor reader or interpreter of Derrida. Indeed, I probably would not have mentioned the pope at all had he not drawn attention to himself not so long ago (in September 2006) with what were taken to be some inflammatory words with regard to Islam. I mention him because, despite their enormous differences, I think there might have been the possibility of a serious if not fruitful dialogue between him and Derrida—a bit like, though there are certainly limits to the analogy, the dialogue Derrida imagines at the end of *Of Spirit* between Heidegger and some Christian theologians (*OS* 109–13). Despite their many and very deep differences, what Derrida and Ratzinger shared is an abiding interest in the relationship between religion and science, reason and faith, and, thus, in a renewed or enriched notion of reason that would not be divorced from faith. "Faith and Knowledge," Derrida's title, could actually be the title of Ratzinger's entire intellectual project, as I know it, an attempt to think an enriched reason that goes beyond mere technical reason. While Derrida and Ratzinger would surely disagree over how to characterize or achieve this enriched reason, with Ratzinger speaking of a *logos* in conformity with God's reasonable nature, and Derrida, in *Rogues*, for example, speaking of a form of the "reasonable" that goes beyond the merely rational, I think there would have been reason for a conversation on this subject between them. Were such a conversation to take place, were Ratzinger now to pursue this conversation alone, he might conclude that reason's deconstruction is not the same as reason's dissolution, and that a deconstructive reason might in fact be more promising than a return to Greek *logos* for the kind of interfaith dialogue the pope himself was seeking to promote in his perhaps ill-advised quotation of a fourteenth-century Byzantine emperor in his dialogue with an educated Persian on the subject of faith in Christianity and Islam. And, perhaps ironically, the Pontiff might find in Derrida a *more hopeful* voice than his own. For while Ratzinger's discourse is, as I have heard it, one of crisis and dissolution, coupled with a call for reform and conversion or salvation, Derrida's secular thought, his unique brand of *laïcité*, argues for a kind of originary faith at the origin of both religion and science not simply as they *should be* but, in some sense, as they *already are*. Instead of diagnosing a crisis of European reason and proposing a reform, rehabilitation, or redemption of it, Derrida wishes to demonstrate the faith—which would be neither Jewish nor Christian nor Muslim—that makes science and religion possible in the first place and that is at the origin of our belief in these *today*.

What Derrida's critical enterprise appears to promote is thus a certain *laïcité* without theological dogma but also without the dogmatism of secularism, a *laïc* notion of democracy, hospitality, or living on that would not be defined through or even in opposition to the theologico-political heritage but that would act as a critical or deconstructive lever within these. This *laïcité* thus led Derrida not to some dogmatic separation of church and state but to a radical critique of the "theologico-political" in the name or under the aegis of an unconditionality (the other, the event, justice) that exceeds and ultimately disrupts all sovereignty. It thus entails both a critical examination of the state in its theological origins or heritage and a notion of *justice* that would be the very force behind this *laïcité* and the nonteleological end toward which it moves.

An originary or radical secularity, then, or a secularity without secularism: I am not exactly happy with any of these formulations, but I advance them nonetheless because they mark a tension between the origin of the world and a particular opening or formulation of the world, much as, in many of Derrida's texts of the last two decades, the name "Europe" marks *both* a historical space and the universalizing movement that goes beyond this space. I advance and retain these terms also because of the origins of the word *secular* in the Latin *saecularis,* meaning worldly, belonging to an age or generation. And I retain them because in *our* world, in *this* world, this political climate, the word *secular* needs to be, I believe, won back from those discourses on the right that equate it with godlessness and immorality. Rather than think of the secular as that which is without God and without morals, we need to think of it as that which is without dogmatism, whether religious or secular, though not at all without faith and responsibility—indeed, as that which opens the very dimension of faith and interrupts every attempt to reduce faith to dogmatic belief. Derrida's thought is of this world in this sense, and while the secular had its origins in a particular world, an originary or radical secularity points to the roots of that world in the coming of the other and an originary profession of faith—a radical secularity, then, *without* secularism. And as for this "without," it would have to be understood in the sense that Derrida understands it in the phrase "messianicity without messianism." In *Marx & Sons* he explains:

> It no longer has *any* essential relationship with what we might mean by messianism, which means at least two things: on the one hand, the memory of a historically determined revelation, whether Jewish or Judeo-Christian, and, on the other, a relatively determined figure of the Messiah. Messianicity *without* messianism excludes, in the

purity of its very structure, these two conditions. Not that one must reject these, not that one must necessarily denigrate or destroy the historical figures of messianism, but these are possible only against the universal and quasi-transcendental backdrop of this structure of the "*without* messianism." (*MS* 73)

If messianicity without messianism points toward a universality or quasi-transcendentality unhinged from any determined messianism, a radical secularity without secularism would point toward an origin of the world *without* either religious or secular dogmatism, an origin of the world that would be—in its response to the other—something like a *secular leap of faith*: a leap, as in Kierkegaard, beyond all epistemological and ethical codes and assurances, but also, like the miracle we spoke of earlier, a leap that first engages all knowledge and ethics, a leap not in a world but a leap *to* a world, or rather, a leap that opens the world—miraculously.

꒳

Near the end of Derrida's interview on 9/11, Giovanna Borradori asks Derrida whether he isn't in fact following Kierkegaard in his skepticism toward the Kantian *as if*, and Derrida responds:

> No doubt, as always. But a Kierkegaard who would not necessarily be Christian, and you can imagine how difficult that is to think. . . . I always make *as if* I subscribed to the *as if*'s of Kant (which I am never quite able to do), or *as if* Kierkegaard helped me to think beyond his own Christianity, *as if* in the end he did not want to know that he was not Christian or refused to admit that he did not know what being Christian means. (In the end, I cannot quite bring myself to believe this, indeed I cannot quite bring myself to believe in general, that is, what is normally called "to believe.") ("AI" 135)

"*As if* Kierkegaard helped me to think beyond his own Christianity": that is, I would like to believe, not quite a principle of deconstruction, not quite one of its articles of faith, but one of its performative fictions—reading Plato, as we saw in the previous chapter, *as if* Plato were to help us think beyond his own Platonism, or Kierkegaard to think beyond Judeo-Christianity. To read Kierkegaard, then, in terms of a leap of faith that would no longer be Christian and would exceed, as Derrida puts it, "what is normally called 'to believe.'" Not a faith or a belief in secularism, then, but something like a secular belief, a belief in this nonrelation or this absolute interruption in my encounter with the other, the radical secularity at the origin of faith and knowledge, religion and science. Call it what you will—there is perhaps no *right* name—but the name at least recalls us to a world, and calls us today to a vocation, to a secular vocation, even a political mission, the very one on which, I continue to believe, the opening of *our* world still hinges.

A Last Call for "Europe"

It is still far too early even to begin to take the measure of Jacques Derrida's extraordinary life and work—and particularly with regard to the political. It is still too early, not just because Derrida's work continues to be disseminated and read throughout the world, and so continues to have an enormous influence on so many disciplines within academia and so many areas outside it, and not just because the institutions Derrida helped found or the causes he championed are still in the process of transforming our world, but, more essentially still, because the "measure" of Derrida's work is yet to come, or, better, because the measure of his work is the "to come." It is still too early to assess the significance, to take the measure, of Jacques Derrida's work with regard to the political or anything else because the event of his work, its living-on, so to speak, is still open to iteration, to reinscription, to a future that might well change just about everything we now think about it.

Were one to give in, however, to the temptation to offer an initial assessment of Derrida's political thought during just the last decade or so, one would no doubt want to begin with a systematic reading of his thoughts about Europe, starting with his 1991 *The Other Heading: Reflections on Today's Europe* and going up through his 2003 *Rogues*, two works that would help us measure just how much Derrida's thinking about world politics in general and Europe's role in the world in particular will have changed over the course of the last decade of his life. Indeed, these two works today appear in retrospect as the bookends of a twelve-year period that would see the publication of many explicitly political works, from *Specters of Marx* in 1993 to *Politics of Friendship* in 1994 to "On Cosmopolitanism" in 1997, a period that runs roughly from the founding of the European Union through the European and American military interventions in the Middle East during the first Gulf War and in the former Yugoslavia to the events of 9/11 and the various European responses to the U.S. doctrine of unilateral preemption, which, during the summer of 2002, when *Rogues* was written, already foretold the American invasion of Iraq. Whereas *The Other Heading* attempted to articulate the dangers and promises of a united Europe, a Europe that must, according to Derrida's maritime metaphor, hold fast to its inheritance in the Enlightenment in order to set sail for a radically "other heading," *Rogues*, written in the wake of 9/11, looking back at a first Gulf War and in anticipation of a second, tried to define even more clearly this new role for Europe in an age when nation-state sovereignty is compromised and sometimes threatened by, on the one hand, nonstate or extra-state entities such as terrorist networks and antiglobalization movements and, on the other, transnational corporations and international organizations such as the World Trade Organization or the United Nations.

Because my ultimate destination in this book is less Derrida's Europe than Derrida's America and the place or fate of deconstruction in America, I will not undertake the kind of thorough and rigorous analysis of texts ranging from *The Other Heading* to *Rogues* that would be required to understand the trajectory of Derrida's work with regard to Europe in particular and the political more generally. I will only say that such an analysis, while concentrating on these later texts, would have to return to the premises of this thinking of Europe in Derrida' s earlier works, indeed, in some of very first works, especially with regard to European exceptionality or *exemplarity*.[1] But in order to understand Derrida's developing thought over the past couple of decades with regard to America or the United States, it is important to give at least some idea of Derrida's thinking of Europe. For if not quite a dialectical pair, Europe and the United States often appear together in Derrida's thinking, with a certain hope in the one being coupled with a skepticism or growing dissatisfaction with regard to the other. Some hint of this was already provided in the previous chapter insofar as the radical secularity Derrida was trying to think came to be identified, in his final works, much more with Europe than with the United States. The reasons for this will become clearer in the next chapter, where I look in some detail at Derrida's complex relationship to the United States. But before turning to the United States, I wish to provide a brief treatment of what was most likely the final iteration of Derrida's thinking on Europe, a short article suggestively entitled "A Europe of Hope."

Delivered in May 2004, just five months before Derrida's death, and published in November of the same year, just one month after his death, what Derrida gives us in this short essay is not so much a developed thesis about Europe but a final call for it, a final prayer or hope for its future.[2] In order, then, to understand in the next chapter why Derrida during the final years of his life began to look at the United States—or at least a certain United States, at certain dominant trends within the United States—with greater and greater suspicion, I propose simply *to read* this short text here, or, rather, *to begin* to read, citing it sometimes at some length and then providing a first, very provisional and inadequate commentary along the way, allowing Derrida thus to speak his "hope" for Europe through these pages and allowing us to accompany him in his thought.

"A Europe of Hope" is a short essay first delivered at a gathering to celebrate the fifty-year anniversary of the highly respected publication *Le Monde diplomatique* and subsequently published on a single page in that newspaper. Having published essays in this monthly newspaper on a couple of other occasions, Derrida was invited to speak about the importance of this publication, which regularly addresses issues of social and political concern—as the name *Le Monde diplomatique* would suggest. But here is already a first surprise, especially from an American perspective, where the university and the media are so separated, particularly with regard to the political, where newspapers and other media outlets provide a forum for political pundits and think-tank representatives and the occasional expert to speak about politics but rarely, very rarely, for a university professor and almost never for a philosopher. It is perhaps worth recalling in this regard, and in order to highlight this difference, that when Derrida died on October 9, 2004, not only other intellectuals but politicians spoke of his passing, from Jack Lang, former Minister of Culture, to President Jacques Chirac. Though it is perhaps not unthinkable that certain of our own political authorities would admit, either publicly or privately, to having read and been influenced by, say, Tocqueville on democracy in America, or, better, Francis Fukuyama on the march of democracy throughout the world, it is difficult to imagine our president or one of his cabinet members making a public statement about the death of a prominent intellectual or university professor.

"A Europe of Hope," then, "Une Europe de l'*espoir*." Early on in his work, Derrida treated with some apprehension the two most common

French words for hope, *espoir* and *espérance*, aligning them with a kind of redemptive thought he found suspect and politically dangerous. But in works such as *Specters of Marx* Derrida seems to begin the rehabilitation of these words, using them much more frequently and associating them not with some redemptive vision of the future but with what he dared to call in various places a "messianicity without messianism," that is, a hope that would be rooted in some tradition, history, and language but that would gesture or call us toward something that must remain heterogeneous to that particular tradition, history, or language, a messianicity, a call and opening toward the future that would be detached from the trappings of any particular messianism, any particular dogmatism, whether Judaic, Christian, or Islamic. By "A Europe of Hope" Derrida would thus seem to be gesturing toward a Europe with a particular tradition, a particular language—or particular languages, beginning with Greek and Latin—and a particular history, but a Europe that calls out for or calls us toward a Europe that exceeds any particular European or Eurocentric vision, a Europe that might be rooted in certain European ideals, notably those of the Enlightenment (democracy, freedom of thought and expression, freedom of the press, liberal education, and so on) but that would call all those who hear the promise and hope of these values beyond their current understanding and development—whether in what is called Europe today or anywhere else in the world.

"A Europe of Hope" would thus refer at once to this historical thing called Europe, this continent identifiable on a map, as well as this political configuration or union of ten, fifteen, twenty-five, or, today, twenty-seven nations, *and* to a Europe that remains to come—not only in France or Germany, Italy or Spain, but in the United States or Australia, in Algeria or in China.[3] In other words, the "Europe" to which Derrida is referring is not simply for Europeans but for anyone in the world, whether in or out of Europe, who hears this call. But because of the unique, irreplaceable history of Europe, because the values of the Enlightenment were first elaborated on European soil, "Europe" (here in quotation marks) still remains a good name for this promise, a good name to attach to this hope, even if, as Derrida recognizes, it might someday be necessary to change the name. This is a good example of a practice Derrida sometimes referred to as "paleonomy,"[4] the practice of reinscribing an old name in the name of a *promise* or even a *secret* harbored within that name. In an interview given shortly after 9/11, Derrida makes it perfectly clear that such a "Europe" goes well beyond the commonly defined geographical and political boundaries of what is today called Europe. And notice that Derrida begins his comments—and this is hardly a gratuitous rhetorical gesture—with a reference to "hope." Having spoken of the need to question in the wake of 9/11 certain outdated concepts such as "war" or "terrorism," Derrida declares:

> I hope that there will be, "in Europe," "philosophers" able to measure up to the task (I use quotation marks here because these "philosophers" of European tradition will not necessarily be professional philosophers but jurists, politicians, citizens, even European noncitizens; and I use them because they might be "European," "in Europe," without living in the territory of a nation-state in Europe, finding themselves in fact very far away, distance and territory no longer having the significance they once did). But I persist in using this name "Europe," even if in quotation marks, because, in the long and patient deconstruction required for the transformation to-come, the experience Europe inaugurated at the time of the Enlightenment (*Lumières, Aufklärung, Illuminismo*) in the relationship between the political and the theological, or, rather, the religious, though still uneven, unfulfilled, relative, and complex, will have left in European political space absolutely original marks with regard to religious doctrine. . . . Such marks can be found neither in the Arab world nor in the Muslim world, nor in the Far East, nor even, and here's the most sensitive point, in American democracy, in what *in fact* governs not the principles but the predominant reality of American political culture. ("AI" 116–17)

If "A Europe of Hope" is thus not simply about what we call Europe, and if it is addressed to "Europeans" who may not even live in Europe, then there is nothing that excludes "us" from being among those addressed.

Derrida begins his piece in a phrase without a main verb, working with the journalistic convention of beginning an article with the city and country from which it was written—yet another way of recognizing the rootedness of discourse in a particular context: *Paris, en France, parlant sa langue, et la France en Europe*; "Paris, in France, speaking its language, and France in Europe." He then asks of this name "Europe": "Can the places that bear and take responsibility for this name, places where a relatively free public discourse and political responsibility are held and taken up, become without presumption, without paradox or contradiction, the thoughtful, active, irradiating sources of an *altermondialisation* worthy of this name? To this question, my hypothesis, my hope, will answer 'yes.'"

I have left the word *altermondialisation* untranslated for the moment in order to underscore the stakes of translation. Why does Derrida himself draw attention to this word by speaking of an *altermondialisation* "*worthy of this name*"? The first thing to note is that the French language has two words for what is called in the English-speaking world "globalization," the first a word that might be taken for the English word itself, spelled with an *s* rather than a *z*, *globalisation*, and the other the distinctively French *mondialisation*. Since what is at stake in "globalization" is the hegemony of not only certain economies and their corresponding economic and political models but certain languages, English first among them, we can understand something of the strategic necessity of using the word *mondialisation* rather than *globalisation*. But even more importantly, as Derrida reminds us in several texts, including the interview on 9/11 I just cited, within the philosophical tradition he is working with, *mondialisation* has connotations very different from *globalization* insofar as a globe is precisely not a *monde*, not a world. Kant, for example, speaks of the world, not the globe, as a regulative idea of understanding, while Heidegger speaks of the world as what opens up our experience and makes possible any horizon of understanding, including the one that would allow us to understand the world as a globe. Finally, to recall the context again, the newspaper Derrida is celebrating is entitled, after all, *Le Monde diplomatique*, not *Le Globe* or *Le Globe diplomatique*.

With the name *altermondialisation* Derrida is asking whether Paris, France, or Europe is capable of *another*—pardon the awkward translation—worldwidization, *an other* (*alter* meaning in Latin not just another, an "alternative," but "other") worldwide movement that might run counter to or that would at least be different from, and perhaps compete differently with, what we call globalization. Derrida is trying to rethink, in Europe, in France, in Paris, what "world" might mean apart from our predominant conception of it as a world economy or global market. Just as he looks to a "Europe" of hope that will remain heterogeneous to the continent called Europe, even if it has developed out of its soil, so he looks to a *mondialisation* that will remain heterogeneous to—that will actually provide a place of resistance to—what is called globalization.

Derrida goes on to bear witness to the significance of this French newspaper for himself, for France, and for the world. Referring to himself as a "faithful friend and appreciative reader of *Le Monde diplomatique*," he praises the newspaper as "the most remarkable journalistic venture and aspiration of this half century—that is, of my entire adult life and life as a citizen—and not only in France, in Paris, and in Europe." He continues:

> During these past fifty years . . . *Le Monde diplomatique* will have epitomized for me the honor and courage of what was, through the rigor and integrity of its reporting, often unavailable elsewhere,

more than a journalistic model inherited from the best of the past but, at the same time, in the same movement, a call and an injunction for the future.

Derrida thus bears witness to the values of a free press that not only carries certain past models into the future but that calls us toward the future—in the name, we could say, of a "Europe" to come, a "Europe" that might function today as a point of resistance and critique everywhere this freedom of the press is smugly touted or simply taken for granted, everywhere, for example, the concentration of media outlets and sources gives the lie to this freedom and imposes new and insidious forms of corporate censorship. A Europe of Hope, what Derrida once called a Europe of an Other Heading, would thus function as a point of resistance to all those whether inside or outside Europe who mouth platitudes about freedom and democracy as mere alibis for ignoring the truth, that is, for ignoring the very real pain and suffering, the countless crimes and injustices, of our world.

This call or this injunction is, as Derrida says, for "the future of the world, that of France and of Europe, certainly, but also well beyond," and *Le Monde diplomatique* has been important in helping us heed or recall this injunction. Derrida continues:

> This recall, this reporting, this analysis without concession and without "unilateralism" of the facts has no doubt been the rule, but also, by the same token, the call to do what has not been done and thus remains to be done—the call to affirm, reaffirm, evaluate, and decide. It is thus not only the past of this great newspaper that I would like to recognize, but also what it asks and demands of us and the world regarding the future. That is why these few words will be not only words of recognition and homage but wishes for tomorrow.

Yet again, Derrida emphasizes the past in order to point us toward the future; the point is not, as we like to say, that those who do not learn about the past are doomed to repeat it, but that there is something about the past that actually calls us toward the future, a "Europe of Hope" within what is today called Europe, a "Europe" of an Other Heading even within the current course of the European Union—however off course it may be.

To provide a greater context for this injunction, Derrida recalls the history of *Le Monde diplomatique*, quoting from its founding statement of 1954 and then referring to a recent, fiftieth anniversary editorial entitled

"Resistances" by its current editor, Ignacio Ramonet. In his May 2004 editorial, Ramonet runs through a litany of principles or positions to which the newspaper is committed, a series of fors and againsts, eighteen yeses, by Derrida's count, and thirty-six nos, an unmistakable "call to resist" that Derrida cannot but affirm. For Derrida too will have taught us the value and necessity of resistance, the value not simply of saying "no" but of slowing down, of not rushing under the pretext of having to be or appear decisive, of having to display unwavering core beliefs and values. He will have taught us, for example, to criticize every manifestation of Eurocentrism without, however, rejecting or leaving Europe altogether. Though Derridean deconstruction continues to be mischaracterized as a philosophy of destruction or negation, it is in fact a relentless philosophy of affirmation, an affirmation that precedes all critique and every "no," and that in fact—and precisely as affirmation—calls for critique. Derrida thus began "A Europe of Hope," recall, by saying that to the question of whether there is hope for an "*altermondialisation* worthy of this name" he would ultimately answer "yes."

Derrida then refers us to his own fifty-year history, his own publications, where a complex relationship to Europe, among so many other things, is laid out through an argumentative strategy that never simply aims at a definitive, binary decision in the form of a "yes" *or* "no" but that attempts each time to take a position, to be decisive, in a thoughtful, reflective manner, with a "yes . . . but," a "no . . . and yet," and so on— gestures that are so easily dismissed today as wanting to have it both ways, as lacking core beliefs, as wavering, indeed, to cite one of the slogans of the 2004 U.S. presidential campaign, as *flipflopping*.

Derrida says in relation to Ignacio Ramonet's editorial:

> I subscribe as much to the thirty-six "nos" as to the eighteen "yeses." This represents for me not a decalogue but something like a set of commandments, the credo or act of faith for ethics, law, and justice, for the politics of our time and for the future of our world. In a moment, I will say why, on this anniversary, I would be tempted to privilege, in the political urgency of the hour, at least one of these "yeses." I, if I may say so, who one day declared my old love for the word *resistance*, to the point of choosing it, and in the plural, for the title of a book; I, who, for decades, and most explicitly in *Specters of Marx* in 1993 and in "On Cosmopolitanism" in 1997, and in so many other places, spoke not against the cosmopolitanism of world citizens, which I have nothing against, on the contrary, even if it still belongs to an era of the political theology of

sovereignty and of the territorialized State; I, who have criticized the improper, excessive, and "instrumentalizing" use, the ideological and economic misuse of the vocabulary of *mondialisation* or globalization, in truth, the notion of a single global market; I, who made a case for a new International, which I defined at some length, after having denounced all the evils that must be resisted, as "not only that which is seeking a new international law . . . [but] a link of affinity, suffering, and hope, a still discreet, almost secret link . . . but more and more visible . . . an untimely link, without status, without title, and without name, barely public even if it is not clandestine, without contract . . . without party, without a country, without national community (International before, across, and beyond any national determination), without co-citizenship, without common belonging to a class" [*SM* 85].

In 1993 Derrida called for this new International and now, more than ten years later, he reads the continuing existence of *Le Monde diplomatique* and the growth of certain international movements, anti- or counter-globalization movements, as signs, fragile and discreet but unmistakable signs, of its realization or its promise. He continues:

> The one who wrote these lines more than ten years ago can only rejoice at seeing *Le Monde diplomatique* become more and more a major point of reference for these burgeoning *altermondialist* movements. No matter how heterogeneous and at times confused they might still appear, these new *altermondialist* gatherings are to my eyes the only reliable force and the only one worthy of the future. For all this is in opposition to the G8, the consensus of Washington, the totalitarian market, unrestricted free trade, and the "four aces of evil" [*le poker du mal*]: the World Bank, the International Monetary Fund (IMF), the Organization for Economic Cooperation and Development (OECD), and the World Trade Organization (WTO), in opposition to what is happening today, and could not but be happening, in Iraq, according to the disastrous plans laid by Mr. Wolfowitz, Mr. Cheney, and Mr. Rumsfeld, well before September 11.

Derrida then goes on to speak of Europe's role in all of this, the fact that after fifty years *Le Monde diplomatique* is still based in Paris, is still published in French, even though it is translated into many other languages throughout the world, the fact that it is "still visibly anchored in Paris, in France, and so is still undeniably rooted in Europe." Indeed, he declares,

> I know of no country in the world, no other continent, I cannot imagine any other place, where such a newspaper could be born,

could live, and could survive with this freedom, these standards, and these qualities.

We are thus called to assume, in the world as it is and as it announces itself, an irreplaceably French and European responsibility in the *altermondialist* movement, between American hegemony, the growing power of China, and Arab and Muslim theocracies.

Derrida thus *situates* Europe in general and France in particular in a unique position geographically but, more importantly, politically, intellectually, and philosophically between the superpower of the United States and the growing powers of China and certain Muslim or Arab theocracies. Europe appears to offer something of an alternative not only to the Far East and the Middle East but to a United States whose model of government, or at least whose current political regime, is even more tied than Europe's to a theological model of religious authority and sovereignty. In the interview given just after 9/11, Derrida—once again invoking hope—suggests even more clearly this unique opportunity and role for Europe in the world.

What would give me the most *hope* in the wake of all these upheavals is a potential difference between a new figure of Europe and the United States. I say this without any Eurocentrism. Which is why I am speaking of a *new* figure of Europe. Without forsaking its own memory, by drawing upon it, in fact, as an indispensable resource, Europe could make an essential contribution to the future of the international law we have been discussing . . . Such a philosophical "deconstruction" would have to operate not against something we would call the "United States" but against what today constitutes a certain American hegemony, one that actually dominates or marginalizes something in the United States's own history, something that is also related to that strange "Europe" of the more or less incomplete Enlightenment I was talking about ["AI" 116–17; my emphasis on *hope*].

One can perhaps hear the critics, despite Derrida's explicit denials, claiming to detect in these words a creeping Eurocentrism or Eurochauvinism coupled with a veiled anti-Americanism. But, notice, Derrida suggests that there is in the United States' own history a certain "United States" that runs counter to American hegemony, one that entails, we might speculate, such values as religious tolerance and freedom, a separation of church and state, the welcoming of foreigners to its shores, and so on.

And against the charge of Eurocentrism, it is perhaps enough to recall that Derrida really became known, indeed infamous, for his relentless critique of Eurocentrism in philosophy, his critique, for example, of the seemingly innocent use European thinkers have regularly made of Europe as an *example*, as a putatively mere example of what culture, or language, or philosophy is and/or should be. Derrida was in fact relentless in demonstrating the way in which such "mere examples" inevitably become in these European, Eurocentric discourses the good example if not the exemplar of all language, culture, or philosophy. Even a cursory reading of Derrida's earlier works would suggest that he has more than earned the right to say the following in "A Europe of Hope":

> It would be hard to consider me a Eurocentric philosopher. In fact, for more than forty years I have been accused of being exactly the opposite. But I believe, without Eurocentric illusions or pretensions, without the slightest European nationalism, indeed without even much confidence in Europe as it now is or seems in the process of becoming, that we must fight for what this name represents today, with the memory of the Enlightenment, to be sure, but also with a complete awareness and a full admission of the totalitarian, genocidal, and colonialist crimes of the past. We must thus fight for what of Europe remains irreplaceable for the world to come, so that it might become more than just a single market or single currency, more than a neo-nationalist conglomerate, more than a new armed force. Though on this last point, I am tempted to think that it needs a military force and a foreign policy capable of supporting a transformed United Nations, one headquartered in Europe and equipped with the means to implement its resolutions without having to yield to the interests or unilateral opportunism of the techno-economic-military power of the United States.
>
> From this point of view, I would privilege and vigorously underscore the thirteenth "yes" of those resistances proposed by Ignacio Ramonet. Yes, he says, to a more social and less market-oriented Europe. A "yes" that I would develop into a "yes" to a Europe that, without being content simply to compete with the superpowers, and without giving them free rein either, becomes, at least in the spirit of its constitution and in its political practice, an engine for *alter-mondialisation*, its laboratory, even its force of intervention, for example, in Iraq or in the Israeli-Palestinian conflict.

As he moves toward a conclusion, Derrida begins working with yet another form or convention more common to the newspaper than the academic journal or book—the declaration or manifesto, a certain call to arms. With a series of short paragraphs beginning "A Europe that . . . ," Derrida gives us some indication of what "A Europe of Hope" might look like, a Europe, it seems, of endless critical reflection, of analysis and discussion, a Europe that might in fact serve as an "example" of such reflection and analysis, an "example"—for Derrida here no longer shies away from the word—not of what a culture or a language could or should be, but of a mode of inquiry and reflection that requires us to interrogate the very notions of Europe, reflection, and hope, along with the dangers of just such a *logic of exemplarity*. Here, then, is the first of these short passages beginning with "A Europe that"—passages that can all be heard as being preceded by a silent but unmistakable "I subscribe to," "I endorse," "I affirm," "I say yes to," indeed, "I am putting my hope in":

> A Europe that serves as an example of what a politics, a reflection, and an ethics might be, the heirs of a past Enlightenment that bear an Enlightenment to come, a Europe capable of nonbinary forms of discernment.

And Derrida then gives us examples of such nonbinary forms of discernment, where one is not content with simply saying yes or no, good or evil, you are either with us or against us, but, rather, yes . . . but, no . . . and yet, on the one hand . . . and yet on the other, and so on. Instead of giving in to easy slogans and caricatures, Derrida invites us to accept the challenge, which is much more difficult but much more noble, and, I am tempted to think with Derrida, the only real solution for the future, of actually thinking through and reflecting upon Europe today not in order to say "yes" or "no" to it but so as to criticize what has to be criticized within it and realize the best of what it has promised. In the passages that follow, these nonbinary forms of discernment take the form of being able to level a critique against something *without* being labeled the enemy of that something or the friend of that something's enemies—that is, forms of thought that leave room for serious reflection and critique *without* ceding to or being subjected to hasty, binary evaluations and identifications.[5]

Derrida thus continues his "manifesto" or, better, his litany of affirmations and hopes for a Europe to come—and I shall cite here straight through to the end of the essay in order not to break the rhythm and momentum of what was probably, let me recall this one last time, Derrida's final declaration, plea, or appeal for "Europe."

> A Europe where one can criticize Israeli politics, especially those of Sharon and Bush, *without* being accused of anti-Semitism or Judeophobia.

A Europe where one can support the legitimate aspirations of the Palestinian people to recover its rights, its land, and a state, *without*, however, condoning the suicide attacks or the anti-Semitic propaganda that often—all too often—tend in the Arab world to give credence to the monstrous *Protocols of the Elders of Zion*.

A Europe where one can express concerns about the rise of both anti-Semitism and Islamophobia. Mr. Sharon and his policies are clearly neither directly responsible nor accountable for the intolerable return of anti-Semitism in Europe; but one must also claim the right to think that this return is not completely unrelated to him, and that he has been able to take advantage of the situation in order to call upon European Jews to return to Israel.

A Europe, finally, where one can criticize the agendas of Mr. Bush, Mr. Cheney, Mr. Wolfowitz, and Mr. Rumsfeld, *without* countenancing in the least the horrors of the regime of Saddam Hussein. A Europe where, *without* anti-Americanism, *without* anti-Israeliism, *without* anti-Palestinian Islamophobia, one can ally oneself with those who, whether American, Israeli, or Palestinian, bravely criticize, and often with more vigilance than we do, the governments or the dominant forces of their own countries, and thus say "yes" to all the "yeses" I have recalled.

That is my dream. I thank you not only for helping me to dream this dream, to dream, as Ramonet said, that "an other world is possible," but for giving us the strength to do everything we can to make this world become a reality. Millions and millions of men and women throughout the world share this dream. Slowly, with the pains and labors of birth, they will, one fine day, bring it to the light of day. [My emphasis on *without*.]

So ends Derrida's brief essay from *Le Monde diplomatique*, an essay written in French, I recall, delivered in French, addressed in a first instance essentially to the French, then published in French, and yet, clearly, from everything Derrida says here and elsewhere, addressed perhaps also *to us*. "Europe" is the name of a call, and "Europeans" the name of those who, throughout the world, are attempting to answer this call. Derrida is thus perhaps addressing *us here today*, calling upon us to study, to reflect, to reject easy slogans and identifications, to do our homework, to learn history and languages, to challenge our provincialism and our prejudices in the name of "Europe." It is of this "Europe" that we must be the guardians, since this "Europe" is perhaps what is best and most noble *in us*, something "related to that strange 'Europe' of the more or less incomplete Enlightenment" Derrida spoke of just after 9/11. It is this "Europe" that is perhaps also related to a certain "United States," that is, to *our hope*, to a "United States" that will resist the Americanism—the globalization—to which the United States might think it is beholden or destined but that is in the end merely the slogan for a program that will be global in only the worst ways, that will actually concentrate wealth and power in unprecedented ways, that will, in the end, be a betrayal of that other "United States," of what is best about our American past in relation to the promise of this Europe. We can only hope—though, clearly, for Derrida, hope is something more than just wishful thinking. It is the very draw or *aspiration* of the future.

ॐ

I wish to conclude this brief reading of "A Europe of Hope"—Derrida's final reflections on a "Europe to come"—with a personal anecdote or a personal memory about Derrida and the future. This memory dates back just a couple of years, to what seems like only yesterday, the summer of 2002, when I was fortunate enough to hear Derrida present at a ten-day conference at Cerisy-la-Salle in Normandy the majority of what would become *Rogues*. Now that summer, the summer of 2002, marked the hundred-year anniversary of conferences at Cerisy, or, to be precise, first at Pontigny, France, then, interestingly, for a brief period during the Second World War, in the United States, at Mount Holyoke College in Massachusetts, and then at Cerisy-la-Salle. For the centennial celebration of this exquisite tradition of European thought, a magnificent document and photo exhibit was organized by IMEC (Institut Mémoires de l'Édition Contemporaine) in the city of Caen in Normandy, and the participants of the Cerisy conference were all invited on a particular day to attend. There were dozens of pictures, letters, and documents from so many of the intellectuals—mostly European—who had marked Cerisy by their presence over the course of the last century. All of us—including Derrida—spent over an hour looking at the extraordinary collection of artifacts documenting the passage through Cerisy of André Gide, François Mauriac, Gabriel Marcel, Raymond Aron, Martin Buber, Vladimir Jankélévitch, Martin Heidegger, and, more recently, Roland Barthes, Philippe Sollers, Gilles Deleuze, Jean-François Lyotard, and, of course, Derrida himself—an entire pantheon of French and European intellectuals who had converged at some point upon this one chateau in northwestern France. Displayed there all together was an entire century of intellectual life, a picture of Heidegger lecturing in the library at Cerisy, a group photo outside the chateau of Derrida, Lyotard, and Deleuze during the famous 1972 conference on Nietzsche, and so on.

At the conclusion of the exhibit, Derrida was asked if he would like to say a couple of words. A master at such improvisation, even if he always denied it, Derrida thanked his hosts and the organizers of the exhibit, and then recalled in some detail his own experience at Cerisy, enumerating the colloquia he had attended and those devoted to his work, coloring his words with anecdotes and humor and a genuine affection for the place and its people. And then he spoke of the exhibit itself. He said that when you enter the exhibit room and see all those photographs of the past you cannot help but gasp, you cannot help but have your breath taken away, and this feeling of being breathless, he said, this suspension of breath, this gasp before the past, is—and I will never forget these words because they were for me so striking and unexpected—"the very experience of the future."

Today, in the wake of Derrida's death, as I look through the archives of my own memory, as I continue to see him, here in the United States, before me there at Cerisy, I am still trying to understand these words—still trying to grasp exactly why he would describe this relation to the past, this gasp in face of the past, as the experience of the future, as an opening onto the future. The best I can do for the moment is to reflect upon the reason why I recount this story today, why I remember and feel compelled to repeat it, why it no doubt secretly animated my entire reading of this little text of Derrida on Europe, and why and how this *memory* of the past compels me to read Derrida again today, a memory of the past that makes me feel responsible not simply for the past as past but for what it enjoins us for the future, a memory, a responsible memory, I hope, for the thought and person of Derrida, for the one who now joins all those other European intellectuals in the archives of a bygone Europe and who speaks to us here today of a "Europe" to come.

Perhaps that is what he *meant* on that day in July, 2002. Perhaps that is what he *means* when he says today in the language that was his: *C'est l'expérience même de l'avenir.*

Derrida's America

We have been edging ever closer to this theme from the beginning. It is now time to make the crossing and tackle it head on. This chapter thus looks not at Derrida's Algeria, Derrida's France, or Derrida's Europe, but at "Derrida's America," that is, at the history of Derrida and deconstruction in America, as well as Derrida's evolving relationship to and thinking about America from the early 1960s up through 2004. Though this might be seen as yet another imposition of American cultural hegemony, yet another claim to American privilege in the reception, interpretation, dissemination, and, now, the inheritance of Derrida's thought, it is, as I will try to show, simply an acknowledgement of the unique role America played in Derrida's life and work. For if, as Derrida himself once put it, "no theoretical work, no literary work, no philosophical work, can receive a worldwide legitimation without crossing the [United] States, without being first legitimized in the States" (*EIRP* 29),[1] then we are simply acknowledging the facts when we observe that, while Derrida lived the first eighteen years of his life in colonial Algeria, while he attended university in France and subsequently taught for over forty years in Paris, it was really only in America, or only through his success in America, that Jacques Derrida, professor at the École Normale Supérieure and École des Hautes Études in Paris, came to be known, indeed renowned throughout the world, as "Jacques Derrida, the founder of deconstruction."

In what follows I would like to remember Derrida by recalling his time in America so as, first, to confirm the importance of his thought and work in and for America but then, also, so as to question some of the myths with regard to that importance. I will thus try to consider in the most straightforward way possible the impact or influence of Derrida's thought on or in America, the fate, therefore, of "deconstruction in America," but then, also, America's influence on Derrida, the way in which Derrida marked but was himself also marked by American friends, thinkers, institutions, and issues. Finally, I will take up Derrida's reading *of* America, his thoughts about America, and, in the very end, his way of relaunching the promise of "America," his unique way of reinscribing "America"— and "America," as we will see, always in relation to a certain "Europe"—as the name of a promise.

As a certain kind of American, then, I shall try to address the question of "Derrida's America," or "Derrida's American Question,"[2] by answering in what I would call a singularly "American" mode, that is, with a series of unequivocal, unilateral, if not preemptive affirmations, a series of firm and unwavering "yeses." But then, each time, and in a second moment, I will, as a certain kind of American, try to temper my affirmation and enthusiasm with one of those more "European" "yes, buts" or "no, and yets" that we discussed in the previous chapter—a form of bilateral thinking that I think Derrida believed to be the only way of thinking responsibly today, the only way of thinking responsibly whether in Europe *or* in America.

Derrida in America

Let me begin, then, with what are widely acknowledged to be the facts regarding Derrida in America, by which I mean, in this context, Derrida in the United States. Like many middle-class boys growing up in the 1930s and 1940s in colonial Algeria, Derrida was no doubt exposed early on and often to American culture, and particularly American movies. Indeed, his real or given name was, in fact, not Jacques but "Jackie," after the California-born child actor of the 1920s "Jackie Coogan." Like many young Algerians, then, he was familiar with a certain America or a certain image of America, and he would have no doubt come into contact with Americans in the early 1940s, during the North African Campaign to free Algeria from Vichy France.

But what Derrida once called his own *débarquement*, that is, his own "landing" in America, did not take place until 1956–57, when at the age of twenty-six, having just passed the *agrégation* exam in France, he boarded a ship named the *Liberté* for his first trip to America.[3] Having been granted a fellowship to Harvard University on the—as Geoff Bennington puts it—"somewhat fictitious pretext of consulting microfilms of unpublished work by Husserl," Derrida traveled to New York and then made his way to Cambridge, Massachusetts, where he would spend the year reading philosophy and literature, particularly Joyce (*JD* 329).[4] Though he would remain virtually unknown in the United States for another decade, this year appears to have been decisive in the personal life and professional or intellectual development of Jacques Derrida.[5] For this year abroad no doubt made it easier for Derrida to accept an invitation some ten years later that would mark his grand entry onto the American intellectual scene. The story, now legendary, is that in 1966 Derrida was invited by René Girard to participate alongside other important French intellectuals, such as Roland Barthes, Jacques Lacan, Jean Hyppolite, and Jean-Pierre Vernant, in a conference at Johns Hopkins University in Baltimore entitled "The Structuralist Controversy: The Languages of Criticism and the Sciences of Man." Derrida there delivered a paper, later published as "Structure, Sign, and Play in the Discourse of the Human Sciences," that at once leveled a devastating critique against structuralism, the reigning thought of the time, and laid out much of what would come to be known as Derridean "deconstruction."[6] Within this star-studded field of French theorists, Derrida's star shone bright, and his reputation quickly spread. When he published the following year no fewer than three major books—*Of Grammatology*, *Speech and Phenomena*, and *Writing and Difference*—that reputation was solidified within the American academy and his work began to be widely disseminated throughout the United States. Not long thereafter, Derrida was invited to teach a couple of weeks a year at Johns Hopkins and, in 1975, alongside J. Hillis Miller and Paul de Man at Yale. By the mid-1970s one thus began to speak of a "Yale School" of literary criticism,[7] a school that would find itself, and Derrida most prominently, at the center of intense and often very polemical debates surrounding the so-called "invasion" of "deconstruction in America."[8]

Derrida in the late 1970s and throughout the 1980s thus became the most visible and arguably the most influential figure in a wave of French theorists that included Barthes, Foucault, Lyotard, Deleuze, Levinas, Lacan, Kristeva, and others. By all the most obvious measures—publications, colloquia, curricular and institutional influence, and, though more difficult to measure, just sheer enthusiasm—this would prove to be the heyday of "post-structuralism," "postmodernism," or, more generally, "French theory" in America. Though Derrida remained popular and significant throughout the 1990s, continuing to publish widely and to teach part of the year on both coasts, it is fair to say that the end of the "golden age" of French theory in America was already on the horizon, with several of its leading figures, from Levinas to Lyotard to Deleuze, dying in the course of the decade. When Derrida himself died in October 2004, his death was thus perceived by many in the United States and elsewhere as something like the end of a celebrated generation of post-structuralist or postmodern thought.[9]

Derrida's Influence in America

These, then, are, to the best of my knowledge, the barest essential facts, on the basis of which I will put forward my first unwavering affirmation concerning "Derrida's America": as a result of the series of events just described, Derrida came to have as much notoriety and influence in the American academic scene as any single intellectual, whether American or not, from the mid-1970s through the 1990s. From the mid-1970s onward, a steady stream of translations kept his thought in circulation throughout the English-speaking world, where it would have an enormous influence not only on philosophy and modern language and literature departments, but on disciplines as different as feminism, critical legal studies, critical race studies, art, architecture, theology, and many others. Through his more than seventy books, through innumerable colloquia and public speaking engagements, through his many academic appointments in the United States, from Johns Hopkins, Yale, and New York University to the University of California at Irvine, through his honorary degrees from places like Williams College, Columbia University, and the New School for Social Research, through at least two films,[10] one of which made its debut in 2002 at the Sundance Film Festival, Derrida became an intellectual celebrity throughout the United States and the one word with which he was most often associated, *deconstruction*, something of a household word. Even if the word tends to mean in America little more than "to analyze" or "pick apart," or else to "negate" or "destroy"—all very inadequate ways of describing the work of deconstruction—the word has entered our common parlance, and so shows up fairly regularly in the press and even in the occasional movie (like Woody Allen's *Deconstructing Harry*). All this seems to support the view, the tale or legend, that Derrida became an American intellectual "superstar," that is, a French intellectual made into a superstar in America—the most famous, most celebrated, most widely read and disseminated figure in a famous and celebrated generation of French theorists in the United States.

This reception of French theory in general and Derrida in particular did not, of course, occur in an intellectual and institutional vacuum. Among the many factors that no doubt contributed to Derrida and deconstruction finding a fertile ground in the United States are, surely, a growing institutional flexibility and interdisciplinarity in the American academy during this time, America's strong, but in the 1970s often forgotten or neglected, religious and theological tradition, particularly in the university,[11] certain movements, such as phenomenology, in American continental philosophy during the 1960s and 1970s, the importance of New Criticism in literary theory and a concurrent interest in German romanticism,[12] a diverse but well-connected college and university system,[13] university-related and -supported journals such as *Glyph*, *SubStance*, *boundary 2*, and *Critical Inquiry*, along with relatively well-supported and well-distributed university presses, beginning with the University of Chicago Press, which published many of Derrida's early texts. All these factors contributed to the growth and prominence of Derrida and deconstruction in America—making the latter a household name and the former an intellectual superstar.

But now it's time for my first "yes, but," time for a bit of "European reserve" or bilateral thinking to temper my American, unilateralist enthusiasm. For the tale I just told, while not without a certain truth, is misleading on many fronts, beginning with my rather glib and unthinking repetition of that journalistic phrase "American intellectual superstar." A first caveat would thus have to be raised concerning the extent to which Derrida's work has been disseminated and read in the United States. Though Derrida is indeed well known in certain academic circles, I sometimes have to tell European friends, who often have greater misconceptions about Derrida's fame in America than Americans do, that one does not and did not during the 1980s ever see people on television discussing Derrida's analyses of Heidegger or his theory of metaphor, or beachgoers in Fort Lauderdale or Laguna Beach reading *Of Grammatology*, or people commuting to work in Chicago listening to book on tape versions of *Glas* or *Specters of Marx*. In fact, from what I know, Derrida's books, published almost exclusively with academic or university presses, rarely sell more than between five and thirty thousand copies in the United States, that is, in a country of three hundred million people where not only works of fiction but works of nonfiction can often sell over a million copies. While the average academic book in the United States sells no more than about four hundred copies, so that five to thirty thousand copies qualifies as an unqualified academic bestseller, it is difficult to characterize such sales figures as a mass phenomenon.

A second reason to be skeptical of this tale of American superstardom is that Derrida was just as well if not better received in many places outside the United States, from Canada to Japan, Brazil to Romania, Portugal to Australia, indeed, even in France, where he was admired and read by many, even if it was often outside the university system. Though Derrida once declared, with a bit of humor, the "state of theory" to be California, and "theory"—which would include "deconstruction"—an essentially American or "purely North American artifact" ("SST" 71), he flatly rejected the notion that the United States was the "country of deconstruction" (*PM* 114).

Third, if Derrida's success and status are to be attributed to America, we must reckon with the fact that nowhere else in the world was Derrida subject to more violent or more virulent critique than in the United States. Nowhere more than in the United States did influential academic authorities try to discredit Derrida and those who read him with insinuation and insult rather than, as one might have hoped for in the university, thoughtful and engaged critique. And such campaigns were often carried out in well-known publications, such as *The New York Review of Books*, with a much wider distribution than Derrida's own work, the result being that many more people were probably exposed to Derrida through the critique of him and the intense debates surrounding him than through actually reading his work.[14] One thinks here of the so-called culture wars of the 1970s and '80s, of what came to be known as the de Man affair,[15] of the Heidegger controversy,[16] or of the role played by certain American academics in the protest at Cambridge University over Derrida being awarded an honorary degree.[17]

If deconstruction was thus widely welcomed, praised, and ardently defended by many in the United States, it was also terribly feared, reviled, and viciously attacked by many others. If Derrida's work received an enthusiastic reception in some quarters of the American academy, it was greeted with outrage, skepticism, or simple, persistent, or willful misunderstanding in many others. For example, the tendency to understand deconstruction as a kind of linguistics, when it in fact mounted a critique of the reign of structural linguistics and its logocentrism, was nowhere more widespread than in the United States, as was the tendency to hypostasize and capitalize "Deconstruction" despite Derrida's regular insistence that deconstruction is not a monolithic entity and that there are, in fact, only deconstruction*s*.[18]

Finally, Derrida was suspicious, and so should we be, of the interests and motives of those in the United States and, perhaps especially, in France who wished to promote this label or image of Derrida as an

"American intellectual superstar" as a way of disparaging or discrediting his work. What is often implied by this French attribution of American superstardom is the notion that only in America could someone like Derrida make it big, only in America could a flashy, flamboyant, but ultimately shallow thinker like Derrida be taken seriously, only in America could the glib simulacrum of genuine knowledge and erudition be taken for the real thing. Old Europe, according to the premise of the argument, had known better from the start and had sent the imposter abroad. By presenting Derrida as something of a pop star or cultural icon in the United States, the French could at once snicker at a naïve America taken in by the merry prankster of deconstruction and write off the prankster himself as "America's Derrida."[19]

If the word *deconstruction* thus did or does enjoy mass notoriety in the United States, used by everyone from hipsters and advertisers to right-wingers who want to talk about the deconstruction—that is, for them, the destruction or undermining—of American values and American cultural identity, I think it is fair to say that the person and thought of Jacques Derrida did not and do not hold such a place of prominence. If the word *deconstruction* and the name "Jacques Derrida" are known to a certain cultural milieu, if, as I have argued, no single thinker has had more of an impact on the academy and even beyond than Jacques Derrida, it is difficult to characterize this as a mass phenomenon.[20] There are many admirers, students, faithful readers, and teachers of Derrida's work, to be sure, but no mass appeal, and, for here is yet another prejudice, no cult followers.[21] As someone who, I think, would know about a cult if there was one, I have often reassured people both in France and the United States that I've never heard of any Derridean dissemination rituals, never participated in any breaking of the holy pharmakon, never learned any secret deconstructionist handshake.

America's Influence on Derrida

Derrida marked America, to be sure, but perhaps not in the way we like to think, perhaps in ways that cannot even immediately be identified with him, that is, in more secret, subterranean, but perhaps all the more powerful and transformative ways. But then what about the mark left by America on Derrida? It's time for another big, bold American assertion: Derrida was marked and transformed by the American scene in a way that few European intellectuals have ever been. Each year Derrida spent several weeks teaching and lecturing in the United States, so that America, and certain place names and personal names to begin with, came to mark his corpus and inflect his interests. At the very least, America came to be for Jacques Derrida an open series of proper names, of friends and colleagues and place names, that is, a vast network of intersecting singularities from New York, New Haven, and Ithaca, on the East Coast, to Santa Monica, Laguna Beach, and Irvine, on the West.[22] From the late 1960s on, innumerable conferences and texts are marked by American contexts and the places and names associated with them. The relatively recent text "The University Without Condition," for example, is marked from beginning to end by Derrida's experience in the American university system and by the original context for this text, its delivery in 1999 as part of a lecture series at Stanford University; *Specters of Marx* was written for a colloquium at the University of California, Riverside, and cannot be read without some understanding of its American context and audience; and then there is Derrida's piece on the American "Declaration of Independence," a text Derrida would no doubt have never written were it not for an invitation to speak at the University of Virginia during a conference marking America's bicentennial in 1976.[23] One could cite a long list of texts that were either first delivered in the United States or else written for and within an American academic context. So, yes, Derrida was profoundly marked by America, by *his* America, and Derridean deconstruction was marked, translated, transformed by the American context, often taking forms that Derrida could not have predicted and might even have had difficulty recognizing.[24]

And yet, and here's my more measured, European counterpoint, Derrida remained through it all, and despite this American influence, *profoundly European*. Though he marked and was marked by America, he remained a European intellectual, though, as always, in his own way, that is, as a European who claimed to be European by *not* being European *through and through*. Near the end of *The Other Heading* in 1991, Derrida himself declared: "I am European, I am no doubt a European intellectual, and I like to recall this, I like to recall this to myself, and why would I deny it? In the name of what? But I am not, nor do I feel, European *in every part*, that is, European through and through."[25] For all our talk of Derrida's America, or of Derrida in America, Derrida's corpus bears witness to a European provenance and orientation, to elective affinities that are essentially European in name even if Derrida used them to rethink and critique Eurocentrism. We have seen these affinities throughout, from some of my introductory remarks on Derrida's love of the French language to my brief look in the last chapter at Derrida's *hope* for Europe. In an interview in 1991, Derrida says it so happens that he was "*born* . . . in the European *preference*, in the preference of the French language, nation, or citizenship, . . . and then in the preference of this time, of those I love, of my family, of my friends—of my enemies also, of course, and so on" (*P* 362–63). Hence Derrida taught regularly in the United States, indeed every year, but it is important to recall that he never emigrated to America or took up a full-time position there and continued throughout his career to give regular seminars in France.[26] Equally revealing, perhaps, is the fact that, while certain English phrases such as *double bind* or *speech act* entered Derrida's vocabulary quite early on, French remained the only language in which Derrida wrote. This was more than just a question of comfort or competence, for Derrida spoke excellent English and was at ease answering questions and even giving seminars in the United States in English,[27] but a matter of responsibility and, indeed, of passion—of a preference and passion for European languages, German, Latin, Greek, but, especially, French. In literature, too, Derrida's tastes and interests were largely European, indeed Western European: French, Artaud, Baudelaire, Blanchot, Genet, Mallarmé, Ponge, Sollers; or Germanic, Celan, Hölderlin, Kafka; or English, Shakespeare, Defoe, Swift, Blake, Shelley, Joyce, Hopkins, but scarcely American. Beyond a couple of short stories by Poe, most notably "The Purloined Letter," already analyzed by Lacan, and Melville's "Bartleby the Scrivener," along with passing references to Faulkner or Stein, Wallace Stevens or William Carlos Williams, Derrida remained rather unmarked, it would seem, by the American literary tradition.[28] This is not terribly surprising for an Algerian-born, French-speaking and -writing thinker, but it does need to be pointed out to temper any hyperbole concerning the fate of Derrida or deconstruction in America.[29]

In terms of philosophers, there is the same decidedly European inclination; there are several references to Peirce in *Of Grammatology*[30] and allusions here and there to Thoreau and Emerson; there is the debate with John Searle over a reading of J. L. Austin,[31] then, much later, a critique of Francis Fukuyama's book on the end of history, and then punctual references to recent works of Noam Chomsky or Jeremy Rifkin.[32] But Derrida was, in the end, a European thinker, whose preferred philosophical texts ran from Plato and Aristotle to Descartes, Kant, Leibniz, Rousseau, Hegel, Husserl, Heidegger, Benjamin, Bataille, Levinas, and so on. In other words, his interests coincided in large part not with the dominant philosophy of the English-speaking world but with various concerns in the history of philosophy and in what is called contemporary continental philosophy in the United States, a philosophy that is rather peripheral to the predominately analytic scene. Indeed, as Derrida himself once observed, the hegemony of so-called analytic, Anglo-American philosophy in the United States, Britain, and many other places throughout the world is perhaps not unrelated to the growing, global hegemony of the Anglo-American language.[33] It is thus perhaps not surprising that Derrida's work first entered America not through philosophy departments but through French and Comparative Literature departments. Even though today more and more thinkers are attempting to bridge the so-called analytic and continental divide, Derrida is still not a particularly popular or widely read figure in American philosophy departments, despite the fact that the vast majority of his books are original, rigorous, and provocative readings of canonical figures in the history of philosophy and that for almost forty years he taught *philosophy* in Paris.[34]

Derrida on America

A colonial Algerian living in France, a French speaker within an Anglo-American idiom, a European within the American state, a continental thinker within an essentially analytic profession, Derrida—and here's another bold, American assertion—brought a certain Europe to America more than he brought America back to Europe.[35] Though he visited the United States regularly for almost forty years, he did not follow the French tradition, what he once called that "French specialty," which runs from Alexis de Tocqueville to Jean Baudrillard, of writing a book about or entitled "America."[36]

And yet, one might counter, though Derrida did not write a book about America, examples from America, the issues and problems raised by America, mark his discourse from as early as "The Ends of Man" in 1968, with its pointed reference to the Vietnam peace talks and the assassination of Martin Luther King, Jr.[37] Moreover, the contexts, tones, and growing frequency of Derrida's remarks about America over the last two decades mark a certain trajectory and, I think it is fair to say, demonstrate a growing dissatisfaction not with America *as such* but with certain tendencies and governmental policies within the United States. In 1982, for example, in "Of an Apocalyptic Tone Recently Adopted in Philosophy," Derrida remarked upon America's sensitivity to "phenomena of prophetism, messianism, eschatology, and apocalypse," to its use of religious language in political discourse ("AT" 30).[38] Two years later, in "No Apocalypse, Not Now," a text written in French but with a title in English, he analyzed the Reagan administration's rhetoric regarding nuclear proliferation, deterrence, and war. In *Specters of Marx*, he again returned to this apocalyptic aspect of American political culture and philosophy in a reading of Francis Fukuyama's *The End of History and the Last Man*, a work Derrida characterized as "neo-testamentary" or "neo-evangelistic" in its rhetoric (*SM* 56–60).

In the 1990s, references to American hegemony and to the predominantly Americanizing process known as "globalization" became more and more frequent and explicit.[39] Derrida thus spoke of American hegemony in academics,[40] in the culture and information industries,[41] and, especially, in the global dissemination and domination of the Anglo-American language.[42] Because of the time he spent in America, the growing number of Americans he counted as his friends, colleagues, and students, and, of course, because America is not just one country among others on the global stage, American examples and issues became more and more common in his work. Thus, in an analysis of television and media, Derrida turned to the Rodney King case;[43] in an analysis of perjury and lying in politics, he was drawn to the Bill Clinton / Monica Lewinski affair and everything it teaches us about the American obsession with truth-telling and public confession.[44] And in the final decade of his life, Derrida spoke often in his teaching and publications about the death penalty in America, "the only Western-style democracy," as he once put it, "with a dominant Christian culture, to maintain the death penalty and to remain inflexible about its own sovereignty."[45] In aligning the United States with other states that maintain the death penalty, that is, with China and certain Arab-Muslim states, and opposing these to European states, his critique was clear and even led to an open letter in 1996 to Bill and Hillary Clinton protesting the death sentence of Mumia Abu-Jamal. Derrida thus became a vocal critic of the death penalty in America, as well as of the obvious racism involved in its application and in the American penal system more generally.[46]

Finally, during his last few years, Derrida spoke very critically of American hegemony and of the imposition of American sovereignty throughout the world. This criticism became most explicit in *Rogues* (2003), which contains Derrida's most sustained analysis and critique of American foreign policy, particularly as concerns the U.S. government's use and abuse over the last two decades of the demonizing expression "rogue state" to further its own sovereign interests at home and abroad.[47] It is not hard in this and other works to make out a growing distance from and dissatisfaction with certain tendencies within American political culture and discourse, for example, the privileging of clear binary distinctions and decisions, of unwavering and unreflective resolve, as opposed to more nuanced, more balanced, and more difficult analyses.

Deconstruction is/in America

But what, then, of deconstruction not *in* America but *as* America? What of that now infamous claim or, really, hypothesis that "Deconstruction *is* America"? Back in 1984, during a series of lectures at Irvine, Derrida confessed to being tempted by the idea of addressing the theme that I have broached here, namely, the theme of "Deconstruction in America." He ultimately resisted this temptation, he says, for several reasons. First, "Deconstruction in America" is, he argued, a work or a phenomenon in progress, and so is still radically undecided, something that, let me add, is still true today, even after the death of Jacques Derrida. Second, one cannot just assume that deconstruction was something that once existed in Europe and was then simply transplanted or translated into America, since there were "original configurations" of deconstruction in America well before his work and multiple and sometimes ambivalent forms after the arrival of his work.[48] Third, since deconstruction has done nothing if not question the "classical assurances of history, the genealogical narrative, and periodizations of all sorts," it makes little philosophical sense to speak of a clearly delimited and isolatable epoch of deconstruction in America. Fourth, and finally, as we've already said, there is no one, single, monolithic thing called "Deconstruction."[49] Any responsible analysis of something like "deconstruction in America" would thus have to confront such objections before going on to take account of all the political, technological, religious, ethical,[50] and academic dimensions of deconstruction's place or work in America—for example, to take just this last, the way in which "deconstruction has accompanied a critical transformation in the conditions of entry into the academic professions [in the U.S.] from the 1960s to the 1980s" (*MPD* 16), along with a flexibility and permeability of disciplinary boundaries and a change in the constitution, scope, and role of the canon in education.[51]

It is thus in the context of all these objections, hesitations, warnings, and reminders that Derrida offered, back in 1984, not a claim about America, not even a hypothesis regarding it, but, you will notice, a hypothesis concerning a hypothesis. Derrida wrote:

> Were I not so frequently associated with this adventure of deconstruction, I would risk, with a smile, the following hypothesis: America *is* deconstruction [*l'Amérique, mais c'est la deconstruction*].

In this hypothesis, America would be the proper name of deconstruction in progress, its family name, its toponymy, its language and its place, its principal residence. And how could we define the United States today without integrating the following into the description: It is that historical space which today, in all its dimensions and through all its power plays, reveals itself as being undeniably the most sensitive, receptive, or responsive space of all to the themes and effects of deconstruction. (*MPD* 18)

But just a couple of lines later, Derrida withdraws this hypothetical hypothesis, recalling that "we have learned from 'Deconstruction' to suspect these always hasty attributions of proper names." He then continues: "My *hypothesis* must thus be abandoned. No, 'deconstruction' is not a proper name, nor is America the proper name of deconstruction. Let us say instead: deconstruction and America are two open sets which intersect partially according to an allegorico-metonymic figure. . . . This is why I have decided not to talk to you about 'deconstruction in America'" (*MPD* 18–19).

Derrida thus offers a hypothesis but then quickly withdraws it; he offers it all the while knowing he is going to withdraw it. He does so because, in addition to all the aforementioned objections and hesitations, and perhaps before all else, it is not clear what exactly is being identified with the name "America." Just before the passage cited above, Derrida writes: "In order to speak of 'deconstruction in America,' one would have to claim to know what one is talking about, and first of all what is meant or defined by the word 'America.' Just what is America in this context?" (*MPD* 17–18). If Derrida complained that, in America, deconstruction was often taken to be a single, monolithic enterprise, Deconstruction with a capital *D*, he himself was circumspect with regard to the name "America" itself, with regard to the American thing, careful not to hypostasize it or use it as a slogan with which to conceal a whole series of internal differences. In the interview he gave just weeks after 9/11, Derrida warns us once again, just as he did in 1984, against an unthinking conflation of the name "America" or the "United States" with some single reality. Speaking no doubt in part in reaction to growing anti-American sentiments in France and elsewhere, Derrida advocates a "philosophical 'deconstruction' [that] would have to operate not against something we would call the 'United States' but against what today constitutes a certain American hegemony, one that actually dominates or marginalizes something in the U.S.'s own history, something that is also related to that strange 'Europe' of the more or less incomplete Enlightenment I was talking about" ("AI" 116–17).[52] Seventeen years after the hypothetical hypothesis "Deconstruction *is* America," Derrida cautions us against the same thoughtless repetition of a name. And yet, seventeen years later, not everything will have remained the same—including, and perhaps especially, a certain America. For it is important to underscore that in the passage I just cited Derrida speaks of that "strange 'Europe' of [a] more or less incomplete Enlightenment"; he does not speak—as I think he might have been tempted to speak a couple of decades ago—of that "strange 'America.'" Indeed, I suspect that Derrida would today hesitate even to offer, so as then to withdraw, this hypothesis of a hypothesis regarding America as deconstruction. He would hesitate, I think, because of the more and more serious reservations he came to have about a certain America, reservations about its internal and foreign policies, about its jealously guarded sovereignty and its apparent disdain for international law and institutions, reservations about an America that, as Peggy Kamuf so aptly puts it in her introduction to *Without Alibi*, has become but "the effective or practical name for the theological-political myth we call sovereignty" (*WA* 14).[53]

Derrida's "America," Derrida's "Europe"

Derrida continued to speak and would today continue to speak, I believe, of a certain United States or of something within the United States' own history and tradition that would resist the theological-political myth we call sovereignty; he spoke, and would continue today to speak, of a certain American tradition of "civil disobedience,"[54] and of resistance to and within the dominant American order. But he would not, it seems to me, risk any misunderstanding about America as the "most sensitive, receptive, or responsive space of all to the themes . . . of deconstruction." America might well be the most receptive place in the world to the *effects* of deconstruction, the most vulnerable to certain autoimmune or self-deconstructive processes, but I think it would be hard to argue that it is *today*—though this may well change—the most receptive to deconstructive themes or to their *thoughtful* engagement.

That is why Derrida, for good geopolitical and strategic reasons, it seems to me, tended in the last few years of his life to situate not America but a certain "Europe" in the place of this resistance to the hegemonic order, "Europe" in its unique political, ideological, and philosophical position between the superpower of the United States and its others. It is perhaps more than a mere stroke of chance that, as we saw in the previous chapter, one of Derrida's very last pieces, written in May and published in November of 2004, was entitled "A Europe of Hope," not "An America of Hope." Indeed, in several texts over the past couple of decades, beginning perhaps with *The Other Heading*, Derrida continued to use the name "Europe," often in quotation marks, to signal a promise that was born in what is called Europe but that nonetheless exceeds every geographical designation or current political formation of ten, fifteen, twenty-five, or twenty-seven member nations. Fully aware of the way in which Heidegger once situated Germany between the two superpowers of the United States and the Soviet Union, Derrida recognizes that Europe, despite its numerous problems and inadequacies, despite the inadequation between its reality and its promise, nonetheless offers something of an alternative not only to the Far East and Middle East but to a United States whose model of government, or at least whose current political regime, is even more tied than Europe's to a theological model of religious authority. We saw in the last chapter just what the promise of "Europe" means to Derrida, the reasons for his *hope* in it, and his growing skepticism with regard to the United States. For how could one deny that there is in the United States today, as Derrida put it already back in 1985, a certain "resistance to theory. Resistance to things European. Not only to individuals from Europe, but even to Americans who are more 'European' than others"?[55] This twenty-year-old rhetorical question could not be more current or more pressing for us today. It goes far beyond the simplistic, binary acceptance or rejection of Europe or America, far beyond Eurocentrism or American chauvinism, far beyond anti-Americanism or Francophobia, for—as we saw—Derrida suggests that America's resistance to a certain Europe signals a resistance to something essential about America itself.

My conclusion thus surely is not, or is not quite, that Derrida left or turned away from America and turned back to Europe during the final years of his life. What Derrida taught us, whether we are talking about that strange "Europe" of the Enlightenment to come or about a certain "America," is that it can never simply be a question of saying "yes" to Europe or "no" to America, of unilaterally affirming the one while eschewing the other. Near the end of "A Europe of Hope," Derrida says he dreams of "A Europe that serves as an example of what a politics, a reflection, and an ethics might be, the heirs of a past Enlightenment that bear an Enlightenment to come, a Europe capable of nonbinary forms of discernment," that is, I think, a Europe capable of forms of reflection where one can criticize a certain America without being anti-American and speak in the name of a certain "Europe" without being Eurocentric.[56]

Though no country or continent could possibly have a monopoly on such a way of thinking, "European" is today, Derrida suggests, the best name for it—though it might well be otherwise tomorrow. It is a way of thinking that does not force us into believing that moral clarity always requires saying simply yes or no, a way of thinking that allows one the freedom of critique and honest interpretation to say "yes, but," "no, and yet," a way of thinking that keeps us from acceding to the belief, during politically divisive times, that nuance, measure, and honest self-critique are signs of a lack of moral purpose or resolve.

It is this form of reflection that allows one to say that, *no*, Derrida was not American, *and yet* he was a friend to a certain "America" and, I can attest, to certain extremely privileged Americans; *yes*, he was European, *but not* European through and through, European, then, always in his own way; *yes*, he was North African, *but* only in a certain way,[57] one that could not be thought without taking into account the whole history of the Jewish diaspora and of modern colonization. He was thus a foreigner to America, but also to France and even to Algeria, but, again, always in his own way, a foreigner who brought a certain European tradition—as well as what exceeds it, since he taught us that the tradition always exceeds itself—to America, and a certain America—one that exceeds our common images of it and the predominant culture within it—back to Europe. It was, it is, it will remain, an extraordinary itinerary, an inimitable, singular, quite literally impossible itinerary, even if it took place, over here *and* over there, in Europe and in America, an itinerary and a life for which, to speak not out of American enthusiasm but with a form of affirmation we have learned from Jacques Derrida, we cannot but say "yes" to—this time, this one time, without the slightest "yes, but."

Derrida at the Wheel

(Ah, the wheel [*le tour*]! Let me confide in you here . . .

On the threshold, on the cusp, on the lip of what I had *hoped* to be a singular, incomparable testimony, a unique offering—though I now have no illusions, for the lid is already ajar, the gift inexorably doubled and doomed—I too would like to begin by offering a parenthetical word of confidence or confession: Jacques Derrida has been so many things to so many of us—instructor and inspiration, master and mentor, philosopher and friend—and he has written so much on so many subjects (I won't even begin to enumerate) that it seems ill advised, even indecent, to try to reduce him here to any one of these figures or to focus on any one of these subjects. My sole consolation in what follows will thus be that the single figure or conceit—the single analogy—I have chosen, the single representation of Jacques Derrida to which I shall limit myself, is one for which Derrida himself expressed an avowed preference in one of his very last works. Near the beginning of *Rogues*, Derrida confides this image to us in an aside: "(Ah, the wheel [*le tour*]! Let me confide in you here how much I love this image of the potter, his art, the turns of someone who . . .)" (*R* 13).

Derrida the potter, then, Derrida "at the wheel," not driving along by turning the wheel, as he also loved to do, but more or less immobile, "at his wheel" as one would speak of a philosopher "at his desk," a philosopher *à son tour* or, rather, philosopher and potter *tour à tour*, that is, *by turns* philosopher *and* potter, or finally, philosopher *as* potter. Throughout *Rogues*, Derrida likens himself to someone who has been bound, stretched, tortured on the wheel by being pulled in opposite directions by contrary imperatives, and while that image fits that context, a more appropriate image is, for me today at least, Derrida not *on* but *at* the wheel, driven rather than driving, driven but immobile at the center of a spinning disk, a master craftsman at his wheel, spinning his materials at the center of a turning machine: "(how much I love this image of the potter, his art, the turns of someone who, on his wheel, makes a piece of pottery rise up like a tower by sculpting it, molding it, but without subjecting himself, or herself, to the automatic, rotating movement, by remaining as free as possible with regard to the rotation, putting his or her entire body, feet and hands alike, to work on the machine)." Derrida at the wheel, then, a creator or demiurge moving and shaping the four elements, molding and fashioning bits of earthen clay by spinning them through the air, mixing in water to make them smooth and pliant, and then firing and vitrifying the sculpted pots, jugs, and urns to be exported to the four corners of the globe. Imagine him, then, Derrida at the wheel . . .

I am thinking, for example, of the writing desk in the sunroom in Ris-Orangis, Derrida surrounded by his materials, books and articles, dictionaries and lexicons, the Apple at the center of the wheel being worked on, manipulated with both hands, a text molded and shaped over the course of a morning. Or, better, I think of him at the École des Hautes Études on the Boulevard Raspail, teaching, educating, exercising, in truth, the craft of a master potter before a couple of hundred students or apprentices, who have come not to sit at the master's feet but to learn at his hands "(putting his or her entire body . . . cultivating the art of a sculptor but also that of an architect and composer who imposes on or rather grants to matter differences in height, changes in color and tone, variations in rhythm, accelerations or decelerations [*allegro* or *presto*, *adagio* or *lento*], in a space as sonorous in the end as a sort of musical transposition or discreet word)." And I think of him especially—for it was there that I first met him, there that he once turned to me and said, as I recounted in the first chapter, *Alors, qui êtes-vous?*—at the École Normale Supérieure on the rue d'Ulm, seated at a desk on that slightly elevated stage or platform of the Salle Dussane, Wednesday afternoons, 5 to 7, turning his materials with mastery and care, speeding up and slowing down as the work dictated, the point being not simply to produce a beautiful pot, jar, or urn by the end of the session but to instruct the apprentice potters fortunate enough to attend how to make or "throw" pots of their own. Both a performance and an invitation, it is absolutely fitting that the published works of Derrida that bear the most visible traces of these seminars are *On Hospitality* and *Politics of Friendship,* works whose subjects are one with the tone and atmosphere in which they were presented.

Demiurge, sculptor, architect, composer, host, *master potter.* Derrida as a professor and philosopher was all of these things. Rather than simply passing on some preformed and prepackaged knowledge or doctrine to passive disciples, Derrida taught his students how to fashion thought, how to spin or turn words, and how to *receive* the tradition, how to welcome it so as to transform it, how to give it form so as to underscore or reactivate the void or aporias that give form always from within it.

Were Derrida himself, then, to have read these words comparing him and his work to a potter at his wheel, he would no doubt have submitted such images, such *turns of phrase,* such analogies, to an interminable critique—to a long and patient "ceramitology," perhaps even a "crematology"—examining everything from the creation of the ceramist to the ashes of the funeral urn. Though one could have expected this master potter to begin in some unexpected, unforeseen fashion, one could also have counted on him to convoke, indeed to "throw" together, turn together, great pots and potters, famous urns and jars, from around the world and throughout the ages. He would have thus no doubt analyzed the trope of the potter in various religious, literary, and, especially, philosophical discourses in order to question a whole series of assumptions about, say, the activity of the potter as creator, demiurge, or prime mover, the nature of what is produced as artifact, object, or commodity, the jar as a figure of the body, the soul, or the void, and the presumed nature and stable identity of the goods or doctrines preserved therein. Beginning, perhaps, at the beginning . . .

He might thus have had us recall that in Genesis man is himself formed out of earth or clay, which is then infused by God with "the breath of life,"[1] an analogy developed by Isaiah, who warns against confusing the maker with what is made, the potter with the earthen vessels he has fashioned: "O Lord, you are our Father; we are the clay, and you are our potter."[2]

At the beginning of Western literature as well, pots, urns, or jars—artifacts, receptacles of the potter—play a crucial role not quite in creating man but in securing his future. From Homer on, jars and jugs, often associated with Zeus Ktesios, "Zeus of Household Property,"[3] ward off hunger and allow one to offer hospitality to the visiting stranger or the returning friend: such are the wine jars closely guarded by Telemachus in anticipation of his father's return.[4] These receptacles of baked clay open up time and secure man a future; in some cases, they even determine that future: Achilles says to Priam in one of the final scenes of the *Iliad*, "two urns [*pithoi*] are set upon the floor of Zeus of gifts that he giveth, the one of ills, the other of blessings" (24.527–28).[5]

It is this Homeric and, indeed, ultimately *tragic* vision of life, where the best one can hope for is a "mixed lot" and not a life full only of "ills," that Plato will attempt to overcome by means of a philosophy that invokes its own series of urns and jars. In the *Republic*, for example, Socrates proposes censoring any poet who presents Zeus as "dispenser alike of good and evil to mortals."[6] If God or the Demiurge is a potter, he must be absolved of all responsibility for the creation of evil in the world, the fault lying not in his creative activity but in our mortal, sensible clay, which must be molded, fashioned, educated by a potter who, in Plato, begins looking a lot like a philosopher. ("For as sculptor or architect, the potter in his turn is by turns poet and musician, rhetorician and political orator, *perhaps even a philosopher*"; my emphasis.)

A favorite example in Plato of a craft that requires a certain technical knowledge combined with apprenticeship and practice, the potter's craft will provide an image of the activity of education and, ultimately, of the philosopher.[7] Socrates thus defends the idea that the children of the military class must learn by watching their parents in action by referring to the way "the sons of potters [*tōn kerameōn*] look on as helpers a long time before they put their hands to the clay."[8] Educators and philosophers must follow this example, it seems, the ascent out of the cave being a long and patient apprenticeship at the hands of a master craftsman. One must not, therefore, says Socrates in the *Laches*, "try to learn pottery by starting on a wine-jar," that is, one must not begin with the biggest or most valuable things without first training on smaller, less valuable ones. Socrates uses this proverbial expression to caution the generals Laches and Nicias against experimenting with the education of their own sons before knowing what they are doing, before having honed their craft and learned how to instill virtue in others—that is, he cautions them against trying to learn pottery on the "big jars" of their sons' souls.[9]

The soul is thus itself fashioned by Plato (*plattein* means, after all, "to mold or fashion"), and it is itself depicted as a jar. Malleable, impressionable, open to corruption, the receptacle of the soul is always in danger of being ruined by the doctrines it takes in and preserves. When a young friend of Socrates expresses his desire to hear the great Protagoras, Socrates warns him that when purchasing a doctrine or belief, as opposed to food or drink, one cannot carry it away from the marketplace in a "separate vessel" but must instead "when one has handed over the price, take the doctrine in one's very soul by learning it, and so depart either an injured or a benefited man."[10] Without a proper education or "formation," the impressionable soul risks becoming a leaky jar. Trying thus to convince or persuade the excitable Callicles in the *Gorgias* that the orderly life is preferable to the insatiate, licentious one, Socrates cites the Pythagorian "fable in which—by a play of words—[someone] named this part, as being so impressionable [*pithanon*] and persuadable [*peistikon*], a jar [*pithon*]." In the insatiate or thoughtless, then, the part of the soul with licentious and unruly desires is like "a leaky jar" or "sieve," "unable to hold anything by reason of its unbelief and forgetfulness."[11] The soul of the moderate and wise man, on the contrary, is sound and airtight, solid and abiding, just like the goods it contains. Socrates thus contests elsewhere not only a Heraclitean theory of names but a Heraclitean ontology when he says that "no man of sense" can say that "all things are flowing like leaky pots [*panta hōsper keramia rhei*]."[12] Only a crackpot, in short, only a soul that has never experienced an abiding good, an unchanging form, would think that all things flow. The life of a full and sound jar that never or rarely flows is thus far preferable to that lived as a leaky one in constant need of being refilled, and the person best able to secure his jar and perhaps those of others is the genuine potter, that is, the philosopher, the one whose soul and thoughts will be not only well turned but airtight, sound, stable, and abiding.

Though Socrates argues in the *Republic* that potters and philosophers must be kept apart, that neither must meddle in the other's affairs, that only the worst could come from a potter coming to rule by mistake in place of a philosopher, though he argues that one cannot be "by turns" potter and philosopher, it appears that the *true* or *genuine* potter, the one who forms not simply pots and jars but good and virtuous souls, the receptacles of learning and truth, is none other than the philosopher.[13] If Plato's philosopher or philosopher-king is by turns the true statesman, true physician, true guardian, true shepherd, true midwife, true musician, and so on, should it be at all surprising that he turns out to be the only true or real potter as well?

When Derrida writes in *Rogues* that "the potter in his turn [or at his wheel] is by turns poet and musician, rhetorician and political orator, *perhaps even a philosopher*," he is thus conjuring up a long tradition, one that begins in Plato and runs right up through Heidegger. Taking issue, at least implicitly, with the notion of a soul as a jar containing doctrines and, quite explicitly, with the notion of a receptacle as an object that simply holds its contents, such as water or wine, Heidegger in "*Das Ding*" has the daring and genius to ask the seemingly banal and quintessentially unphilosophical *ti esti* question: "What is the jug?" In that essay, the jug is not simply *a* thing but *the* thing par excellence, something molded by a potter who shapes not only, or not essentially, the clay, says Heidegger, but "the void" that will contain what is poured into and out of it. "From start to finish the potter takes hold of the impalpable void and brings it forth as the container in the shape of a containing vessel." It is the void that gives the vessel its form and its function. It is the void of the jug, not its contents or its container, that allows one to fulfill the jug's vocation of making offerings and sacrifices. "In the gift of the outpouring earth and sky, divinities and mortals dwell *together all at once*."[14] The gift is thus not essentially what is given, whether wine or doctrine, and comes not essentially from what gives, whether potter or jug, but proceeds instead from the "impalpable void." The jug is thus less an object than a "thing," less an object within the world than the "thing" around which the world gathers, around which the fourfold of earth and sky, mortals and divinities, comes to dwell.

One cannot help but think here of Wallace Stevens's famous "Anecdote of the Jar," with its smooth, alliterative play on a jar that is round and when set upon a hill gathers round by causing nature to surround it. ("I placed a jar in Tennessee, / And round it was, upon a hill. / It made the slovenly wilderness / Surround that hill"). But to this jar that gathers and brings order to the careless nature around it, this jar that "took dominion every where," Derrida would have perhaps preferred a more aporetic or more jarring formulation, one that does not gather space but leaves it unsealed, cracked open, out of harmony or out of joint, in a word, *a-jar*. In *Works and Days*, we might recall, it is Pandora's opening of a jar, the duplicitous gift of Zeus fashioned by Hephaestus and accepted by Epimetheus in disregard of his brother Prometheus's advice, that opens time for mortals and brings upon them "countless plagues," diseases, and sorrows, such that "only Hope remained . . . under the rim of the great jar."[15]

Hope remained within the jar but was destined to return in another form and within another register to help define the jar itself. In a certain Christianity we ourselves are said *to be* the jar and there is *hope* only to the extent that we are the receptacles of something greater and more valuable than we are. "We have this treasure in clay jars, so that it may be made clear that this extraordinary power [*hē hyperbolē tēs dynameōs*] belongs to God and does not come from us. We are afflicted in every way, but not crushed . . . always carrying in the body the death of Jesus, so that the life of Jesus may be made visible in our bodies" (2 Corinthians 4:7–10). Man himself is thus a clay jar, an earthen vessel, the container of what comes before and is infinitely greater and more valuable than he. If God is the potter who made man, He put within that earthen vessel an idea that no vessel can contain. Paul interprets this as the death and resurrection of Christ. But one can also interpret it—precisely by refusing to interpret it, by refraining to project some image into or onto that earthen receptacle—as the idea of God, or the idea of infinity, or the idea of the infinite Other. Charles Du Bos once wrote—and I recall his memory here because of a memory (yet another form of grace) that I have of Derrida recalling how, as an adolescent in Algeria, he would regularly go to a newsstand to buy recently published essays of literary criticism by Du Bos: "I've come to realize, with an odd sort of horror mingled with tenderness, that at this very moment at least I have no life of my own worth mentioning; I am now but the *receptacle of the life of the other*—in other words (and this is no small consolation), the hearth wherein the life of the other throws up its highest and liveliest flames."[16]

Derrida the master potter never ceased thinking such aporias of reception, the aporias of a container that contains what comes before and is greater than it, a container that is absolutely sealed, airtight, and yet open from within to what infinitely exceeds or overflows it—call it the other, the idea of the infinite, justice, or the event. In this sense, Derrida the philosopher never ceased thinking about what it means to *receive,* whether it be in relation to the *khōra* of Plato's *Timaeus,* the place that gives space to all things, or the funeral urn containing remains and ashes, taking within it—like a person in mourning—that which can never be incorporated or interiorized. I recall here not only *Glas, Cinders,* or *The Work of Mourning* but a short essay by Derrida on the Kerameikos, the ancient cemetery of Athens, so named because it was located near the potters' district.[17] Were we to dig around elsewhere (I am tempted to think almost everywhere), we would be certain to find in Derrida's corpus all kinds of pots, urns, jars, and jugs—so many crypts—essential, as we have seen, to philosophy, literature, and religion, but also to art, commerce, hospitality, writing, politics (from the balloting urns to the practice of ostracism), and so on. And we might find not only references to these crypts but images of them, texts containing crypts and texts well turned like them. (The little aside or parenthesis of *Rogues* that I have done little more than turn round here might thus itself be read—or seen—as forming, with its beautifully turned phrases, a little receptacle or urn of its own, bordered, rounded off, by the curved lines that begin and end it:

> (Ah, the wheel [*le tour*]! Let me confide in you here . . .
> . . . End of this little confidence.)

a mini-crypt with some "discreet word," I would be tempted to say some "secret word," sealed up within it.)

Places of storage and secrecy, Derrida's receptacles offer hospitality but never security to the secret. They are hermetically sealed from without and yet opened up from within to a future that exceeds them, a future that would be either salutary or destructive, a saving remedy or a deadly poison (like the hemlock, the *pharmakon*, that Socrates once drank from a small ceramic cup or *kylix*). It is in this sense that deconstruction is always a deconstruction of the container, of what it means to welcome and receive, of our pretensions to unequivocally identify and master what it is that we receive. If Derrida was, as I have suggested, a master potter, his oeuvre is in some sense a vast storehouse of jars, urns, and pots, a Kerameikos of its own, where each text, each jar, each receptacle, contains a problem or question—an aporia or undecidability—that opens the inside out or, rather, lets the outside well up or haunt it from within: sealed jars that open onto crypts and call for reading. If Derrida thus has "disciples," it is only to the extent that they have undergone an apprenticeship in the craft of "throwing pots" or "turning words," of finding within each airtight jar the "aporia" that turns the inside out and opens the past to the future, the self to the other, one pot to all the others, and that gives a chance to the "discreet word" that may one day *visit* or *call* us anew, that may one day call out to be reread.

It is thus worth recalling that jars are not only contained and preserved within texts throughout the tradition but were often privileged means of preserving texts, of passing them on to the future. Were it not for the work of skilled potters, we would not have, for example (but what an example!), the Dead Sea Scrolls, preserved in jars until 1947, when they were first discovered. Sealed with wax or animal fat, such jars were among the first time capsules, preserving valuables, preserving perishables—canning texts—for the future and, thus, opening that future to us.

If only those jars could talk! we might be tempted to say. If only they could not just preserve the voices in those texts but could themselves speak! And yet, throughout the tradition, not even this is unheard of: for urns are not only contained in texts and themselves sometimes contain texts, or can be read as texts (not just their letters, of course, but their shapes, colors, geometric patterns, figures, and so on), but they themselves sometimes address us so as actually to *produce* texts. In Keats's "Ode on a Grecian Urn," for example, the poet, after addressing the antique urn throughout the poem, lends his voice to the urn itself for the poem's most memorable couplet, spoken to us or to the future from out of its ruinous

Derrida at the Wheel ■ *119*

form or poetic void: "Beauty is truth, truth beauty,—that is all / Ye know on earth, and all ye need to know."

And then there is the popular story—another "anecdote of the jar" (for anecdote means precisely unpublished, not yet publicly revealed or unsealed)—of a potter who was throwing a pot at the Last Supper and who would have thus preserved the memorable words spoken there in the clay he was fashioning, words such as "Do this in memory of me." More miraculous than any Holy Grail, the pot needs only to be spun at the right speed for Christ's words to echo forth from out of it so as to transform anew bread and wine into flesh and blood . . .

And then there is, let me recall—though at the risk of mixing the sacred with the profane—an episode of the *X-Files* in which the Last Supper chalice is turned into "The Lazarus Bowl." The story goes "that when Jesus raised Lazarus from the dead, there was an old woman . . . spinning a clay bowl on her wheel nearby and that Christ's words, the actual incantation to raise the dead, were recorded into the clay grooves of the pottery, kind of like music is recorded onto vinyl. . . . [such] that the words in the ceramic still had the power to raise the dead, just like Jesus raised Lazarus."[18]

Imagine words that could retain, in the absence of any animating intention, any living presence, the performative power to resuscitate, resurrect, or reanimate. Imagine such a performative "power" attached to *no one*, to no living presence or origin . . .

Though it might seem to be little more than a pipe dream, is this not precisely the "power"—the "weak force"—of writing? Lazarus came out of his tomb, out of his jar, still wrapped in cloth after Christ had called him out by calling out "Come!" "Come forth!" (John 11:43). Lazarus came forth, just like a Dead Sea scroll, wrapped in linen and deposited in a crypt, just waiting for the day . . . Is that not precisely the "living" power of the "dead" word? The power *not* to live forever, *not* even to live again or come back to life, but, simply, to *sur-vive* or *out-live* or *live on for a time*?

In the hands of Derrida, every text became—every text remains, and as a remains—a kind of Lazarus Bowl. What is in each case resurrected or reactivated is *not*, however, some once living body, Plato or Hegel, Heidegger or Blanchot, Celan or Benjamin, but precisely a certain "Come forth!" or, better, "Come!" the "Come!" and the "to come," the *à-venir* of a Husserl, Nietzsche, or Joyce, a unique, inimitable, unrepeatable call that is then immediately "written, quoted, repeated, archived, recorded, grammophoned," "the subject of translation or transfer" ("UG" 266), a call that resonates from the thing itself, so to speak, from out of the jar of the other, to Derrida and then to those who, having heard him, will themselves echo and say, repeating him and yet doing so on their own and from out of themselves, from out of the jar that they will have become, "Come! come!" For what they will have learned from Derrida is that this is the only way of opening oneself up, of being hospitable, of taking the other within oneself without reducing the other to oneself, the only way, perhaps, of ever offering to anyone, including the master potter himself, anything on one's own, anything of one's own, and so the only way of thanking him in all modesty by offering him a little jar, pot, or memorial urn of one's own, or—in his absence, which is today still so painful and so difficult to encrypt—simply a shard of what might have been, just a bit of baked clay, a single ceramic tile to be added to the mosaic. For such an apprentice, it would be the only real chance he now has to receive Derrida's words, to take them in hand, to mix them with his own, and to return them as an offering, in gratitude, in memory, and, alas, in recognition that, as he once spun it so beautifully in *Cinders*:

> "*the urn of language is so fragile*" (*C* 53)
> . . . End of this little confidence.)

7

"One Nation . . . Indivisible"

Of Autoimmunity, Democracy, and the Nation-State

Pledge of Allegiance I

To bring the work of Derrida into even closer proximity to the American context, I would like to begin this chapter with a personal and quintessentially American memory. It is a rather old memory for me, but one that I suspect many readers of this work may share. It is the memory of a speech act, a sort of originary profession of faith, the memory of a pledge that I, like most other American schoolchildren, recited by heart, that is, in my case, thoughtlessly, mechanically, irresponsibly, with the regularity of a tape recording played back in an endless loop, at the beginning of every single school day. So as to try to bring it all back for some of you, and simply to inform the rest, imagine a young schoolchild—he could be any child in an American public school—standing beside his desk some morning, any morning, putting his hand over his heart and reciting by memory so as not to have to put his heart into it, this inaugural pledge: "I pledge allegiance to the Flag of the United States of America, and to the Republic for which it stands: one Nation indivisible, with Liberty and Justice for all." There it is, the United States Pledge of Allegiance, more or less as it was originally penned by Francis Bellamy in 1892, more or less as I myself recited it every school day for twelve long years, more or less as it welled up within me as I began to reflect on Derrida's work on the nation-state, sovereignty, and democracy. In beginning, then, with this Pledge of Allegiance, I wish to draw attention to the way in which Derrida in some of his last works linked the "I" of the "I pledge" not only to the sovereignty and indivisibility of the autonomous subject or nation-state but to a kind of profession of faith or pledge of *allegiance*, a kind of originary fidelity—as we saw in Chapter 3—before the bond of any nation-state or religion,[1] a faith that opens up the nation-state and every national context to something that exceeds it, call it the democracy to come, or the *khōra* of the political, or, more provocatively still, a god to come. I will thus attempt in this chapter to retrace just some of Derrida's recent thought with regard to the political, theological, and philosophical heritage of the concept of sovereignty and the ways in which this heritage is being transformed today, the way in which it is subject, in truth, to what Derrida calls a terrifying and suicidal autoimmunity.

In the United States, and I know the same has been true in many other places throughout the world, just about everyone—and not just inside the academy—has spent the past few years speaking about sovereignty. While those, for example, who supported the American intervention in Iraq often appealed to perceived threats against United States national sovereignty post–9/11, those who opposed such actions argued that the United States had no right to attack another sovereign nation-state or that it should do so only under the auspices of a more sovereign international body, such as the United Nations. Something is clearly happening today not just to sovereign nations but to the very notion of sovereignty itself, as the sovereignty of nation-states continues to be threatened by other nation-states, to be sure, but also by the transnational sovereignty of international organizations, multinational corporations, and nonstate terrorist networks. Old sovereignties are thus threatened by new ones, and sometimes in the name of the oldest sovereignty of them all, that is, in the name of the Sovereign Himself, the One God who, as we will see, is thought to protect and bind the United States into "one nation indivisible."

These are some of the central issues in Derrida's interview on 9/11 and, even more poignantly, in *Rogues*. Written between the winter and summer of 2002, in the wake, therefore, of 9/11 and in anticipation of the U.S. invasion of Iraq, *Rogues* treats the themes of sovereignty, democracy, freedom, and the relationship between politics and theology within the context of the Unites States' use and abuse during the past two decades of the demonizing expression *rogue state*. This timely political analysis is embedded by Derrida within a rich and provocative reading of several canonical texts on democracy (from Plato and Aristotle to Rousseau and Tocqueville), as well as some less canonical ones (from Schmitt and Benjamin to Nancy). Demonstrating the aporetic nature of concepts like sovereignty, freedom, and democracy within these classic philosophical discourses, Derrida argues that such aporias will and must remain irreducible, due to a "constitutive autoimmunity" that at once threatens them and allows them to be perpetually rethought and reinscribed.

What 9/11 confirmed beyond all doubt, Derrida argues, is that the cold-war logic that located the enemy within identifiable, self-identical, sovereign nation-states is itself under attack. Today the threat is located not primarily in "outlaw regimes," "pariah nations," or "rogue states" (though this has not prevented the United States from continuing to use these terms as an alibi), but in non-state or trans-state entities that do not declare war like nation-states once did but work instead by turning the resources of a state (from its freedoms to its airplanes) against the state itself. Today the enemy is no longer within foreign nation-states but within non-state networks *and* within the immune system of the nation-state itself.

True to the "method" of deconstruction or, better, true to the "autoimmune processes" he finds already at work, Derrida attempts to show that our traditional notion of sovereignty always harbors within it or always in fact produces, secretes, so to speak, the very forces that threaten to compromise or undermine it. Though Derrida began using the term *autoimmunity* already back in the mid-1990s, particularly in the essay "Faith and Knowledge," it became more prominent and got developed in a more accelerated fashion after 9/11. "Autoimmunity," the "illogical logic," as Derrida put it, that turns something against its own defenses, would appear to be yet another name, in some sense the last, for what for close to forty years Derrida called "deconstruction." But whereas "deconstruction" often lent itself to being (mis)understood as a "method" or "textual strategy" aimed at disrupting the self-identity of a text or concept, the organization of discourses in the shape of what we assumed to be well-formed organic bodies, "autoimmunity" appears to name a process that is inevitably and irreducibly at work more or less everywhere, at the heart of every sovereign identity. Not simply a method or strategy of reading, "autoimmunity" appears to be more akin to what Freud called the "death-drive," a death drive that, I will ultimately conclude, comes to affect not only the bodies we call discourses or texts but psychic systems and political institutions, nation-states and national contexts, and perhaps even, though this is the most contentious, God himself, God in his sovereign self, or God in his phantasmatic, theologico-political body.

This shift to "autoimmunity" enjoins us to rethink what is meant by self-identity in general, as well as automaticity, spontaneity, the event, and finally, "life." With "autoimmunity," deconstruction has to be thought *as that which happens*, like a certain death-drive, to "life" itself. As a "weak force," a force that turns on and disables force or power, autoimmunity at once destroys or compromises the integrity and identity of sovereign forms and opens them up to their future—that is, to the unconditionality of the event (*R* xiv).

In *Rogues*, then, Derrida calls for an "unconditional renunciation of sovereignty" in an exposure to the event, that is, through the separation of sovereignty and unconditionality, a renunciation of sovereign identity in an exposure to the unconditionality of what or who comes, in an openness to what he calls elsewhere an "other heading" or a messianicity without messianism (*R* xiv). *Rogues* is, therefore, not only an extremely important work for thinking Derrida's later thought on ethics and politics but, I will argue, a seminal text for thinking the relationship between the political and the theological.[2] For if we follow Derrida in "this unconditional renunciation of sovereignty," we will have to ask what this means for thinking the Sovereign Himself, a Supreme Sovereign who is typically thought to unite us—whether as humans or members of a nation-state— only insofar as He has the supreme or sovereign *power* to unite in Himself sovereignty and unconditionality.

Autos and Autonomy

To understand the valence or rhetorical force of the trope of "*auto*immunity" in Derrida's work, one must first understand the value of the *autos*. In *Rogues*, autoimmunity appears alongside a whole series of other *auto*-prefixed words and seems at once to complete the series and begin its undoing, that is, its deconstruction. While all the other *autos* words, without exception, express the power, independence, and stability of an enduring self, *autoimmunity* evokes the powerlessness, vulnerability, dependence, and instability of every self or *autos*.

As the last and by far most extensive treatment of the phrase "democracy to come,"[3] *Rogues* takes up concepts at the heart of the philosophical tradition on democracy since Plato and Aristotle, concepts such as freedom, equality, the people, sovereignty, and so on. One cannot think democracy without thinking these notions in relationship to one another and, Derrida argues, in relationship to the *autos* that sustains them. Hence *freedom*, an essential attribute of democracy since Plato and Aristotle, is traditionally grounded upon a notion of sovereignty that is itself grounded in the *autos*, that is, in the self or the selfsame, in the sovereignty of a self-positioning, self-asserting, and deciding self that has the capacity in and of itself to choose something for itself, to vote one way or another by itself, to affirm or deny from out of itself in order to sustain itself and assert its sovereignty as a self. There would be no freedom, no freedom to choose, to vote, to assemble, to speak, to pledge allegiance, without the notion of a selfsame self that does the choosing, the voting, or the speaking, that is, without the authority or capacity of some *sovereign* self. In *Rogues* Derrida names this conjunction of self and sovereignty *ipseity*—from the Latin *ipse*, a word often used to translate the Greek *autos* (*R* 11–12). Insofar as freedom is grounded in ipseity, it cannot be thought apart from a whole series of *auto-* terms that define the self's or the subject's ability to return to and assert itself in its freedom. The self is thus *auto*nomous only to the extent that it is *auto*mobilic and *auto*telic, that is, only to the extent that it can of itself, by itself, give itself its own law with its own self in view (*R* 10–11). Sovereignty, power, autonomy, automobility, autotely: these words form the system or matrix that Derrida names *ipseity*.

Hence freedom, grounded in ipseity, is never exercised without a certain power or ability, a *kratos* or *cracy*, a certain "I can" or "I am able."[4] Force or power is thus posed or presupposed in every self- or auto-positioning of the *autos* as a selfsame self, as a self or a oneself that is one and indivisible (*R* 12). Freedom as it has been traditionally interpreted is thus always founded upon the ipseity of the One. Democracy has been unthinkable, Derrida claims, without this ipseity, without this return to self, without "the *autos* of autonomy, symmetry, homogeneity, the same, the like, the semblable or the similar, and even, finally, God, in other words, everything that remains incompatible with, even clashes with, another truth of the democratic, namely, the truth of the other, heterogeneity, the heteronomic and the dissymmetric, disseminal multiplicity, the anonymous 'anyone,' the 'no matter who,' the indeterminate 'each one'" (*R* 14–15). Democracy, then, and the freedom it requires, has thus been unthinkable apart from a *sovereign* subjectivity, a subjectivity that is, in the end, not only powerful but, as we shall see, incontestable and beyond appeal.

Autos and Autoimmunity

It is in this context of a deconstruction of democracy and of the *autos*—and deconstruction has perhaps never been anything but a deconstruction of the *autos*—that we must try to understand Derrida's recent emphasis on autoimmunity and his more general claims about the autoimmunity of sovereignty itself. How is it that sovereignty immunizes or tries always to immunize itself against the other, that is, against time, space, and language? Derrida writes early on in *Rogues*:

> In its very institution, and in the instant proper to it, the act of sovereignty must and can, by force, put an end in a single, indivisible stroke to the endless discussion. This act is an event, as silent as it is instantaneous, without any thickness of time, even if it seems to come by way of a shared language and even a performative language that it just as soon exceeds. (*R* 10)

Derrida agrees with thinkers of sovereignty from Plato and Bodin to Carl Schmitt who argue that sovereignty is essentially *indivisible* and *unspeakable*. In its essence without essence, sovereignty must be unshareable, untransferrable, undeferrable, and silent, or it "is" not at all. Sovereignty can thus never be parceled out or distributed in space, deferred or spread out over time, or submitted to the temporality and spatiality of language. As soon as sovereignty tries to extend its empire in space, to maintain itself over time, to protect itself by justifying and providing reasons for itself, it opens itself up to law and to language, to the counter-sovereignty of the other, and so begins to undo itself, to compromise or autoimmunize itself. That is the aporetic—indeed the autoimmune—essence of sovereignty. Derrida writes:

> Sovereignty neither gives nor gives itself the time; it does not take time. Here is where the cruel autoimmunity with which sovereignty is affected begins, the autoimmunity with which sovereignty at once sovereignly affects and cruelly infects itself. Autoimmunity is always, in the same time without duration, cruelty itself, the autoinfection of all autoaffection. It is not some particular thing that is affected in autoimmunity but the self, the *ipse*, the *autos* that finds itself infected. As soon as it needs heteronomy, the event, time and the other. (*R* 109)

Time, space, language, and the other: this is the fourfold over which sovereignty in its essence, in its unspeakable, unavowable, unapparent, essence, has no authority. Sovereignty "goes without saying," and that is at once its supreme power and the source of its autoimmune vulnerability, the reason why even supreme sovereignty dare not speak its name.[5]

> To confer sense or meaning on sovereignty, to justify it, to find a reason for it, is already to compromise its deciding exceptionality, to subject it to rules, to a code of law, to some general law, to concepts. [It is] . . . to compromise its immunity. This happens as soon

as one speaks of it in order to give it or find it some sense or meaning. But since this happens all the time, pure sovereignty does not exist; it is always in the process of positing itself by refuting itself, by denying or disavowing itself; it is always in the process of autoimmunizing itself, of betraying itself by betraying the democracy that nonetheless can never do without it. (*R* 101)

The autoimmunity of sovereignty can thus be translated into a sort of double bind: sovereignty must remain silent and yet must go on speaking endlessly about its silence—protecting itself and so compromising itself, compromising itself by protecting itself, expressing and justifying itself by introducing within itself counter-sovereignties that threaten to destroy it.[6] While sovereignty must be beyond question and justification, indivisible and unspeakable, it must continually assert itself and meet the challenges posed to it by justifying and dividing itself. The autoimmunity of sovereignty is thus indeed a kind of double bind or aporia, even an exemplary case for the logic of the supplement. For the supplement too appears to add to, support, and protect the origin but begins already to compromise it, and to show that the origin (e.g., speech or presence) was already from the beginning compromised (by writing or absence). The logic of the supplement was thus, in some sense, "already" a logic of autoimmunization, even if, it must be emphasized, it took the supplement of autoimmunity in Derrida's later texts—and, thus, a certain autoimmunity in the concept of the supplement—for this "already" to make any sense.

Autoimmunity Before *Rogues*

In *Rogues*, then, it is first sovereignty, and essentially the sovereignty of the *autos*, that is autoimmune. But what is autoimmunity in general, if there is such a thing, for Derrida? Where and how did this trope enter Derrida's vocabulary?[7] It is worth recalling that while Derrida, in *Rogues*, relates autoimmunity to the way in which the *autos* in general, that is, ipseity or self-identity in general, is open to its undoing, it is in the context of more explicitly political works such as *Specters of Marx* and *Politics of Friendship* that the term first emerged in Derrida's discourse.[8] In 1993 in *Specters of Marx*, Derrida thus wrote, speaking of Karl Marx and Max Stirner:

They both share, apparently like you and me, an unconditional preference for the living body. But precisely because of that, they wage an endless war against whatever represents it, whatever is not the body but belongs to it: prosthesis and delegation, repetition, dif-férance. The living ego is autoimmune [*Le moi vivant est auto-immune*], which is what they do not want to know. To protect its life, to constitute itself as unique living ego, to relate, as the same, to itself, it is necessarily led to welcome the other within (so many figures of death: différance of the technical apparatus, iterability, non-uniqueness, prosthesis, synthetic image, simulacrum, all of which begins with language, before language), it must therefore take the immune defenses apparently meant for the non-ego, the enemy, the opposite, the adversary and direct them at once *for itself and against itself.* (*SM* 141)[9]

We see here how the introduction of this "biologistic" term, this concept from the life sciences, gets related straightaway, almost automatically, to the insertion of the technical or the machinelike, the iterable and non-unique, within life itself.[10] The autoimmune has to do not only with com-promising the immunity of some *autos*, with the way in which the life of the ego or the *autos* gets compromised or threatened in its life, but with the way in which *life itself*, almost automatically, with the regularity, re-peatability, and predictability of a machine, admits nonlife—the "techni-cal apparatus," the "prosthesis," the "simulacrum," and so on, the way in which life itself, in order to sustain itself, in order to *live on*, requires the introduction of the nonliving and the foreign body. What is compro-mised in autoimmunity is thus not only, as Derrida makes clear in *Rogues*, the life of some self-identical being but the very being or unity of self-identity and, perhaps more provocatively, the notion of life as something opposed to the machine, life as opposed to death and absence. We are, in some sense, right back at the beginning of deconstruction, back to a cri-tique of the integrity and self-identity of the living present. Derrida af-firms in *Rogues*: "what I call the autoimmune consists not only in harming or ruining oneself, indeed in destroying one's own protections, . . . com-mitting suicide or threatening to do so, but, more seriously still, . . . in compromising the self, the *autos*—and thus ipseity. It consists not only in committing suicide but in compromising *sui*- or *self*-referentiality, the *self* or *sui*- of suicide itself" (*R* 45). Autoimmunity thus begins, to put it in a different register, with the first specter's haunting of the self, that is to say, from the very beginning. "'I am' would mean 'I am haunted'" (*SM* 133), writes Derrida in *Specters of Marx*. Our being is thus ontologically, haunt-ologically, autoimmune. The I cannot do without the specter; life cannot do without nonlife; identity without difference; or the uniqueness of a living *autos* without repetition, iteration, and, thus, death. Hence Derrida's claim that autoimmunity compromises not the life of some identifiable *autos* but the *autos* itself as the foundation and guarantor of identity.

Now, it is around this time, in 1994 in "Faith and Knowledge," that Derrida brings together all these elements in his most sustained analysis of autoimmunity before *Rogues*. In this long, important essay, Derrida uses the concepts of immunity and autoimmunity to demonstrate the way in which any attempt to immunize or indemnify religion against technoscience ultimately leads to science and knowledge becoming the necessary supplement of faith or religion and an originary faith the precondition of all science and knowledge. This autoimmune logic explains, for Derrida, contemporary religion's use of tele-technoscience to vilify and condemn science; it explains why both religious groups and terrorist networks, organized via the satellite transmission of cell phones and the Internet, must wage "war against that which protects [them] only by threatening [them], according to this double and contradictory structure: immunitary and autoimmunitary" ("FK" 46).

Moreover, as we saw in Chapter 3 in an analysis of Derrida's notion of *laïcité*, religion and science appear autoimmune inasmuch as they share an origin in the performative of an elementary faith—a sort of pledge of allegiance not to this or that god, nation, scientific fact, or revelation but to the irreducible relation to the other. Hence religion—which always has two sources, a specific historical revelation and the revealability of that revelation—cannot be thought apart from science, and religion and science, which often oppose one another, share a common source in a faith that precedes all historically determined revelations. Autoimmunity, then, says Derrida in a long footnote where he tries to justify his lexical choice, helps explain the relationship between faith and science in particular and the "duplicity of sources in general." In that note, Derrida acknowledges the development of "immunity" in political, diplomatic, and ecclesiastical contexts, before going on to discuss the biological origins of the term.

> It is especially in the domain of biology that the lexical resources of immunity have developed their authority. The immunitary reaction protects the "indemn-ity" of the body proper in producing anti-bodies against foreign antigens. As for the process of autoimmunization, . . . it consists for a living organism . . . of protecting itself against its self-protection by destroying its own immune system. As the phenomenon of these antibodies is extended to a broader zone of pathology and as one resorts increasingly to the positive virtues of immuno-depressants destined to limit the mechanisms of rejection and to facilitate the tolerance of certain organ

transplants, we feel ourselves authorized to speak of a sort of *general logic of auto-immunization*. It seems indispensable to us today for thinking the relations between faith and knowledge, religion and science, as well as the duplicity of sources in general. ("FK" 72–73, n. 27; my emphasis)

Though I cannot even begin to do justice here to this extremely rich and difficult text where autoimmunity is first fully elaborated, let me simply note four characteristics of this development.

First, it is in the context of a discourse on *religion*, and religion in relation to politics and the community, that the trope of autoimmunity is first fully developed. As I will argue at the end of this chapter, this will hardly be a coincidence.

Second, the notion of autoimmunity, taken, as Derrida says, largely from the "domain of biology," gets deployed in a text on *life*, on living on and salvation, on religion's sacrifice of life for something greater than life, and thus on the spectral, phantasmatic character of sovereignty and the spectralizing messianicity that interrupts that phantasm. Derrida writes in "Faith and Knowledge":

no community [is possible] that would not cultivate its own autoimmunity, a principle of sacrificial self-destruction ruining the principle of self-protection . . . and this in view of some sort of invisible and spectral sur-vival. This self-contesting attestation keeps the autoimmune community alive, which is to say, open to something other and more than itself: the other, the future, death, freedom, the coming or the love of the other, the space and time of a spectralizing messianicity beyond all messianism. ("FK" 50–51)

Third, already in "Faith and Knowledge" autoimmunity is presented not only as a threat but as a chance for any living organism: a threat insofar as it compromises the immune system that protects the organism from external aggression, but as in the case of immuno-depressants, a chance for an organism to open itself up to and accept something that is not properly its own, the transplanted organ, the graft, in a word, the other, which is but the cutting edge, the living edge, of the self. Without certain forces of autoimmunity, we would reject organs and others essential to "our" survival—whether we are talking about an individual body, a community, or a nation-state.[11] Hence there can be no community without autoimmunity, no protection of the safe and sound without a perilous opening of borders.

Fourth, and finally, in "Faith and Knowledge," in the course of developing what Derrida calls "a general logic of autoimmunity," a logic to which all kinds of beings, from discourses to institutions, seem vulnerable, something gets named that remains immune, so to speak, to the processes of autoimmunity, immune not because of a sovereign or omnipotent immune system that would protect it from all external aggression—indeed there can be no such thing for *structural* reasons—but immune because it has no identity, no *autos*, to protect. That something that is clearly not a thing is *khōra*, as it is found in Plato's *Timaeus*. Unlike religion, which, in immunizing itself against its other infects itself with its other, *khōra*, says Derrida, remains foreign to all indemnification or self-immunization, and, thus, to all notions of the sacred and the Good. Hence *khōra* remains:

> absolutely impassible and heterogeneous to all the processes of historical revelation or of anthropo-theological experience. . . . It will never have entered religion and will never permit itself to be sacralized, sanctified, humanized, theologized, cultivated, historicized. Radically heterogeneous to the safe and sound, to the holy and the sacred, it [*khōra*] never admits of any *indemnification*. . . . It is neither Being, nor the Good, nor God, nor Man, nor History. It will always resist them, will have always been . . . the very place of an infinite resistance, of an infinitely impassible persistence [*restance*]: an utterly faceless other. ("FK" 20–21)

We will want to keep this passage in mind when we turn later to Derrida's claim in *Rogues* that the "democracy to come would be like the *khōra* of the political" (*R* 82), a phrase we already looked at in Chapter 2 in the context of Derrida's work on Plato.

Autoimmunity and Democracy

Having seen how autoimmunity is characterized in the mid-1990s in *Specters of Marx* and especially "Faith and Knowledge," I would now like to return to *Rogues* to see how Derrida incorporates, so to speak, the notion of autoimmunity in order to help him at once reread and remark his own corpus and develop a critique of democracy as autoimmune. In *Rogues* Derrida quite explicitly inscribes autoimmunity into a series of other terms, from *undecidability* and *aporia* to *double bind* and *différance*, in order, I would argue, *not* to relativize or neutralize this term but to make it comprehensible *and* give it a force of rupture. Derrida writes, for example, in *Rogues* that he could "without much difficulty . . . inscribe the category of the autoimmune into the series of both older and more recent discourses on the *double bind* and the aporia." While "*aporia, double bind*, and *autoimmune process* are not exactly synonyms," he goes on to say, "what they have in common, what they are all, precisely, charged with, is, more than an internal contradiction, an undecidability, that is, an internal-external, nondialectizable antinomy that risks paralyzing and thus calls for the event of the interruptive decision" (*R* 35). While thus denying any equivalence between these terms, while presenting them as nonsynonymous substitutes or supplements, Derrida will develop a discourse on autoimmunity by inscribing this term from the life sciences into this series of previously elaborated terms within his corpus.

Democracy is thus "autoimmune," first of all, because its concept or quasi-concept is "undecidable." Like any other concept or quasi-concept, democracy is essentially void of any content or meaning in and of itself, that is, outside the linguistic matrix in which it is located; it is thus always open to iteration and reinscription, its meaning in some sense always still to come. But, unlike other political regimes such as monarchy, timocracy, or plutocracy, democracy is, we might say, structurally or constitutionally undecidable or autoimmune. As Derrida puts it, there is "an autoimmune necessity inscribed *right onto* [à même] democracy, right onto the concept of a democracy without concept, a democracy devoid of sameness and ipseity, a democracy whose concept remains free . . . in the free play of its indetermination" (*R* 36–37). Through a reading of various attempts to *define* democracy within the history of Western philosophy and an analysis of some of the fundamental aporias of democracy—for example, the aporia or internal contradiction between equality and freedom—Derrida traces an undecidability, a semantic void, indeed a kind of *freedom*, within the very "concept" of democracy itself. Though Derrida will not follow Jean-Luc Nancy in *The Experience of Freedom* and attempt to submit to deconstruction the notion of political freedom as the power of a subject, he *will* identify such a radical freedom with the essence without essence, that is, with the autoimmune or auto-deconstructive essence of democracy. It is not the decentered subject that is radically free but, for Derrida, the quasi-concept of democracy. This is no doubt one of the reasons why Derrida will reinscribe the word *democracy*, and not *freedom*, within his quasi-political discourse, why he will speak not of a radical "freedom to come" but of a "democracy to come," a democracy that remains to come to the extent that there is radical freedom or free play in its concept: "The feeling of aporetic difficulty affects not only some supposedly endless approach of democracy *itself*, of the democratic thing, if one can still say this. . . . This aporia-affect affects the very use of the word *democracy* in the syntagma 'democracy to come'" (*R* 82). This aporia-affect is the very chance and threat of democracy, of the word and concept of *democracy*, whose ineffaceably Greek origins are never immune to reinscription and, even in Greek, are never fully present and adequate to themselves. Already in Greek, says Derrida, democracy is "a concept that is inadequate to itself, a word hollowed out at its center by a vertiginous semantic abyss that compromises all translations and opens onto all kinds of autoimmune ambivalences and antinomies" (*R* 72)—for example, that between freedom, the unconditionality and incalculability of freedom, and the measure and calculability of equality. Derrida thus declares that there is, "in the final analysis, no democratic ideal. For even if there were one, and wherever there would be one, this 'there is' would remain aporetic, under a double or autoimmune constraint" (*R* 37).

Autoimmunity stems not simply from the fact that we can never know whether we have chosen well or ill, whether something will turn out good or bad, whether it will have shown itself to be a threat *or* an opportunity, but, rather, from the fact that the opportunity *is* the threat, and the threat the chance. The chance or opportunity of democracy—law, for example, or calculating technique—is thus "always given as an autoimmune threat" insofar as it "destroys or neutralizes the incommensurable singularity to which it gives effective access" (*R* 53). That is why, for Derrida, one must continue to negotiate between the calculable and the incalculable, invent new ways of calculating or reasoning between them. Hence individual autonomy, which tends to immunize itself against infection by the other, has as its only chance an autoimmunity that opens it up to its others, even if this autoimmunity threatens to destroy the autonomy of the self through this chance, that is, even if it threatens to destroy the power of an autonomous individual, indeed right down to the power to welcome and receive the absolute singularity of an other.

What Derrida calls democracy's "constitutive autoimmunity" can thus be seen, for example, in the *aporias* or *double injunctions* of hospitality, in its desire for two *incompatible* things: "on the one hand, to welcome only men, and on the condition that they be citizens, brothers, and compeers . . . on the other hand, at the same time or by turns, . . . to open itself up, to offer hospitality, to all those excluded" (*R* 63). With the graft of autoimmunity onto the Derridean corpus, what was characterized in a series of books and essays in the 1990s as the antinomies or aporias of hospitality can now be described as the autoimmunity of hospitality, the necessity within limited or conditional hospitality of welcoming a guest who threatens to turn the host's immune system against itself, right up to and including the host's very capacity to receive or invite a guest, that is, right up to and including the sovereign power or ipseity of the host. The host thus needs the guest, or the parasite, to be himself, and yet the parasite also threatens not only the life but the very self-identity or ipseity of the host. This does not mean that the host cannot or should not choose and select, decide who is to be received and who not; it's just that this choice must be made with the recognition, first, that such a reception is always self-affirming and self-serving, and thus "hospitable" only in the conditional sense, and that, second, it too is always a risk to the extent that the other who is received is never completely identifiable or known.

Undecidability, aporia, antinomy, double bind: autoimmunity is explicitly inscribed in *Rogues* into a veritable "best of collection" of Derrideophemes or deconstructo-nyms. This is done, I would argue, both because the graft of autoimmunity "breathes new life," so to speak, into these earlier terms and because these earlier terms, while appropriate for describing or understanding the constraints and perverse effects of canonical *discourses* about democracy and the double injunctions of democracy, are less appropriate than *autoimmunity* for describing the ways in which the *practices* or the *putting into practice* of the democratic ideal are susceptible to auto-deconstruction, less appropriate for describing what happens within the *bios politikos* if not within the very *life* of the polis.

Hence Derrida relates the autoimmunity of democracy not only to the concept of and discourses on democracy but to the *practices* or *mise en oeuvre* of democracy by adding two more Derrideo-phemes to the list, *espacement* as the becoming-time of space or the becoming-space of time and *différance* as irreducible spatial differing and temporal deferring. These additions accomplish at least two things. First, the association of différance with the autoimmunity of democracy allows Derrida to argue contra his critics that différance was already, even in the 1960s, in some sense political. Derrida declares: "The thinking of the political has always been a thinking of différance and the thinking of différance always a thinking *of* the political, of the contour and limits of the political, especially around the enigma or the autoimmune *double bind* of the democratic" (*R* 39). The grafting of autoimmunity onto différance allows Derrida to argue not just that différance can now be interpreted retrospectively as political but that it *always already was* political, that différance was from the beginning a deferring of the relationship to the other (whence its immunity) and a referral or deference to the other (whence its autoimmunity).[12]

The second, more essential reason for introducing notions of spacing and différance into discussions of the autoimmunity of democracy is that these allow Derrida to take better account of the irreducible differing and deferring of democracy as it is and, in effect, cannot but be *practiced*. As

Derrida analyzes it in *Rogues*, democracy always involves both a spatial referral or sending off, a *renvoi*, and a temporal deferral or putting off. Wherever it is practiced, democracy, in the name of democracy, in the name of its own protection and immunization, always excludes some of the *dēmos* from its practices, whether this be in the right to securing citizenship, in voting, or in serving in government, and it always, again in the name of protecting democracy, defers or adjourns democracy "itself" to another day (*R* 35).

Democracy thus "protects itself and maintains itself precisely by limiting and threatening itself" (*R* 36). Derrida offers a stunning example of this autoimmunity in the suspension of elections in 1992 in his native Algeria. In this paradigmatic case, a democratically elected government suspended democratic elections when it became evident that a majority was about to elect a party that had as its objective the end of democratic rule and the installation of a theocratic regime. In the name of democracy, then, the democratic leaders in Algeria suspended the democratic process *temporarily* so that the opposing party would not, once elected, put an end to it *permanently*. For Derrida such an "autoimmune suicide" of democracy is not some aberration or mere accident that befell Algeria but a constitutive or intrinsic possibility of its democratic regime.[13] While a monarchic, aristocratic, or plutocratic regime *may* change over time, may improve or may be destroyed—the monarch may be overthrown or may die, the aristocracy may become corrupted and lead to a plutocracy, the members of the wealthy class may shift—such changes are not *intrinsic* possibilities of these regimes. Understood as rule by a *dēmos* that cannot, as Aristotle reminds us, rule all *at once* (one reason why, let me add parenthetically, a *dēmos* is not exactly "a people"), democracy must devise ways for one part of the people to rule and another part to be ruled *in turn*, *in alternation*, in *rotation*, one part followed by another. Because a transfer of power from one part of the *dēmos* to another is an intrinsic possibility for democracy, there is always the possibility that, through the most democratic of elections, a part of the *dēmos* will come to rule that, whether wittingly or unwittingly, puts an end to democracy itself. (Hence the more recent U.S. worries that elections in Iraq might lead to the victory of a Shiite majority that would not only exclude Sunnis from the political process but turn the democratically elected government into an Islamic theocracy.)

If the suspension of elections in Algeria provided Derrida with his first privileged example of autoimmunity in democracy, the reaction to 9/11 in America, or rather, the response of the Bush administration to 9/11, provided Derrida with his second example. We here see, as Derrida analyzed it, a "democratically elected" American administration—or at least that's what the Supreme Court said—taking measures to restrict certain democratic freedoms in the wake of 9/11 in the name of, or under the pretext of, protecting those same freedoms, or else taking measures to suppress information about its intentions in Iraq under the pretext of spreading freedom and openness throughout the Middle East (*R* 39–40).

This autoimmunity of democratic practices stems *not* from the fact, let me underscore, that democratic practices can never "live up to" the true, democratic ideal, but from the fact that these practices must put to work an "ideal" that, as we have seen, has nothing proper about it. Derrida writes: "there is no absolute paradigm, whether constitutive or constitutional, no absolutely intelligible idea, no *eidos*, no *idea* of democracy. And thus, in the final analysis, no democratic ideal. For even if there were one, and wherever there would be one, this 'there is' would remain aporetic, under a double or autoimmune constraint" (*R* 36–37).

Autoimmunity, Messianicity, and Democracy to Come

Because the very name, concept, and practices of democracy are often what are at issue in democracy, there is an intrinsic perfectibility in democracy that always allows one faction to replace another because it promises to be more democratic, more inclusive in its definition of the people, more just in its distribution of powers or its extension of rights, more liberal in its understanding of equality or freedom, and so on. Or else—since this openness to the future and to transformation can never be determined a priori—to the opposite of these, to a pervertibility within this perfectibility, to a restriction of rights and freedoms, to a more unjust and unequal concentration and accumulation of power and wealth—all under the guise or, perhaps, in the name of protecting democracy from its enemies.

One sign or symptom of this fundamental undecidability within democracy can be seen, Derrida suggests, in the way canonical discourses of democracy from Plato and Aristotle on have had difficulty distinguishing between the goods and evils of democracy, difficulty distinguishing, say, freedom from license or democracy from demagogy.[14] The perfectibility of democracy is thus related to what Derrida calls the "hyperbolic essence," the "autoimmune" essence, of democracy (*R* 41), or, as in the case of Algeria in 1992, to an "autoimmune pervertibility" (*R* 34). It is the essence without essence of democracy that makes it possible to claim that certain perfections of democracy are also perversions of it, that, for example, in Aristotle, every extension of political equality or equality according to number levels or renders insignificant equality according to worth, or that every perversion of democracy is being carried out in the name of democracy's perfection or preservation.

Hence Derrida relates the autoimmune not only, as we have seen, to undecidability, double bind, aporia, antinomy, espacement, and différance, but to more "futurally oriented" notions like "perfectibility/pervertibility," and, finally, to what might appear to be more "positively" inflected notions like memory, promise, and messianicity without messianism.[15] Near the end of the first part of *Rogues* Derrida speaks of "the semantic void at the heart of the concept [of democracy], its rather ordinary insignificance or its disseminal spacing, memory, promise, the event to come, messianicity that at once interrupts and accomplishes intrinsic historicity, perfectibility, the right to autoimmune self-critique, and an indefinite number of aporias" (*R* 91).

Democracy is, for Derrida, the only political regime or quasi-regime open to its own historicity in the form of political transformation and open to its own reconceptualization through self critique, right up to and including the idea and name of "democracy." Derrida argues that we must think the "right to self-critique—another form of autoimmunity—as an essential, original, constitutive and specific possibility of the democratic, indeed as its very historicity, an intrinsic historicity that it shares with no other regime" (*R* 72). Autoimmune self-critique is what gives the quasi-concept of democracy an intrinsic historicity within Western political institutions, though also, and perhaps first of all, within Western political philosophy, which suggests that philosophy is itself an autoimmune discipline par excellence. The phrase "democracy to come" thus names not some as yet unheard-of form of democracy but the autoimmunity of democracy itself, its openness to change and reinscription—though always, let me underscore, for good *or* ill:

> the expression "democracy to come" takes into account the absolute and intrinsic historicity of the only system that welcomes in itself, in its very concept, that expression of autoimmunity called the right to self-critique and perfectibility. Democracy is the only system, the only constitutional paradigm, in which, in principle, one has or assumes the right to criticize everything publicly, including the idea of democracy, its concept, its history, and its name. Including the idea of the constitutional paradigm and the absolute authority of law. It is thus the only paradigm that is *universalizable*, whence its chance and its fragility. (*R* 187; my emphasis)

The essential perfectibility/pervertibility of democracy is what made it such a good candidate for reinscription within the Derridean lexicon as "democracy to come," another nonsynonymous substitute for what Derrida in "Force of Law" and elsewhere calls *messianicity*: "The 'to-come' [in the expression "democracy to come"] not only points to the promise but suggests that democracy will never exist, in the sense of a present existence: not because it will be deferred but because it will always remain aporetic in its structure (force *without* force, incalculable singularity *and* calculable equality, commensurability *and* incommensurability, heteronomy *and* autonomy, indivisible sovereignty *and* divisible or shared sovereignty, an empty name, a despairing messianicity or a messianicity in despair, and so on)" (*R* 86). What is thus perhaps most surprising about this rhetoric of autoimmunity—a rhetoric that became widespread in popular parlance in the 1980s and 1990s because of particularly destructive viruses such as HIV—is that Derrida makes autoimmunity the condition of the event.[16] The event, as that which cannot be foreseen or seen on the horizon, as that which comes down upon one always from above, in a vertical fashion, is possible only on the condition that the *autos* does not close itself off to what is outside it: "there is no absolutely reliable prophylaxis against the autoimmune. By definition. An always perilous transaction must thus invent, each time, in a singular situation, its own law and norm, that is, a maxim that welcomes each time the event to come" (*R* 150–51). Hence "autoimmunity is not an absolute ill or evil. It enables an exposure to the other, to *what* and to *who* comes—which means that it must remain incalculable. Without autoimmunity, with absolute immunity, nothing would ever happen or arrive; we would no longer wait, await, or expect, no longer expect one another, or expect any event" (*R* 152). Autoimmunity is the very condition of the unconditionality of the event; it is what opens the *autos*, what opens *us*, to time, space, language, and the other. Without autoimmunity, without some compromise in the forces of identity that form and sustain—that *seem* to form and sustain—the *autos*, there would be no relation to anything beyond the self. And since the self cannot return to itself and thus be itself without this openness, without some alterity, autoimmunity—like deconstruction—is the case.[17]

Autoimmunity as Force, as What Happens

What autoimmunity underscores perhaps better than any other Derridean trope or nonsynonymous substitute, better than any other supplement in the open series of supplements, is, as Derrida tried to affirm in many essays and interviews over the past couple of decades, the way in which deconstruction is not a "method" of reading but simply "the case," the way it is "at work"—and practically everywhere. In an interview in 1994 Derrida said:

> For me, deconstruction does not limit itself to a discourse on the theme of deconstruction; for me, deconstruction is to be found at work [*il y a la deconstruction à l'oeuvre*]. It is at work in Plato, it is at work in the American and Soviet military commands, it is at work in the economic crisis. Thus deconstruction does not need deconstruction, it does not need a theory or a word. ("SA" 32)

Deconstruction is at work in texts and discourses, but also, as becomes clear in texts such as *Rogues*, in structures and organizations, in nation-states and international institutions, in every *autos* that tries to maintain its sovereignty, its autonomy and power, by immunizing itself against the other. Hence autoimmunity is not *opposed* to immunity but is, as it were, secreted by it; it is a self-destructive "force" produced by the immunizing gesture itself, a weak force that undoes the force or power of sovereignty.

This thinking of deconstruction as auto-destructive force is surely not new in Derrida's work, but it does seem to gain greater momentum in later texts and perhaps helps explain Derrida's shift in terminology from self- or auto-destruction to autoimmunity. For autoimmunity appears to describe the *automaticity* of this self-destructive force, a logic at once "terrifying" and, in both senses of the French word, *fatal*—at once deadly and inevitable, fatal and ineluctable ("FK" 44). Derridean deconstruction would thus itself be but a sign or symptom of this more general autoimmunity that is today at work in texts, discourses, and debates, as well as individual bodies and nation-states. It is surely no coincidence that such an emphasis on "suicidal" autoimmunity comes at a time when many feel threatened not only by the violence originating in seemingly rational nation-states out to protect their national sovereignty, identity, and interests but by the violence of suicide attacks on the part of nonstate individuals or groups. With the end of the Cold War, Derrida argues, terror has become delocalized, deterritorialized, no longer controlled by some rational game theory that would exclude the possibility of the worst through what used to be called, with some assurance, "mutually assured destruction." This delocalization makes "terrorism" at once a very real and destabilizing threat *and* an easily manipulable specter in the hands of any government wishing to frighten or motivate its people with the threat of an attack that might come "anytime, anywhere."

In *Rogues*, Derrida asks himself the very question I have been implicitly asking him here. He asks himself why he thought it necessary to give auto-immunity, a trope from the life sciences, such pride of place in his work. He asks himself why he ceded to the temptation of what "might look like a generalization, without any *external* limit, of a biological or physiological model" (*R* 109), why he thought it legitimate to extend the notion of autoimmunity "far beyond the circumscribed biological processes by which an organism tends to destroy, in a quasi-spontaneous and more than suicidal fashion, some organ or other, one or another of its own immunitary protections" (*R* 124). He proceeds to give two answers.

First, he says, autoimmunity allows him to try to rethink the notion of *physis* "before the separation of *physis* from its others, such as *technē*, *nomos*, and *thesis*" and the notion of *life* "before any opposition between life (*bios* or *zōē*) and its others (spirit, culture, the symbolic, the specter, or death)" (*R* 109). In other words, the generalization and reinscription of autoimmunity allows him to pose questions of nature and life otherwise.[18]

The second reason he gives is that an emphasis on autoimmunity allows him to consider "all these processes of, so to speak, normal or normative perversion quite apart from the authority of representative consciousness, of the I, the self, and ipseity." This was the only way, he says, "of taking into account within politics what psychoanalysis once called the unconscious" (*R* 109–10). Inasmuch as it expresses the "implacable law of the self-destructive conservation of the 'subject' or of egological ipseity" (*R* 55), autoimmunity allows the work of deconstruction to be reinscribed back into a psychic economy that includes the unconscious and the *death drive*. Near the very end of *Rogues* Derrida argues that the Enlightenment to come would have to "enjoin us to reckon with the logic of the unconscious" and, thus, with "this poisoned medicine, this *pharmakon* of an inflexible and cruel autoimmunity that is sometimes called the 'death drive' and that does not limit the living being to its conscious and representative form" (*R* 157; see 123). As a term that came to be known to most of us through the emergence or discovery of viruses that can be considered either dead or alive, or neither dead nor alive, as either nano-machines or micro-organisms, autoimmunity makes us rethink both life and death. If the term thus came to prominence in a biological discourse or register, it will have attacked in an autoimmune fashion the disciplinary boundaries of that discourse in order now to question the very meaning of *bios* and the limits of life and death.

Autoimmunity and God

Deconstruction is at work: in us, through us, and quite beyond the sovereignty of our conscious, egological ipseity. Deconstruction is what happens; it is at work; it has a life of its own; or it is life on its own, in discourses, bodies, institutions, and states. Every *autos* is autoimmune, every sovereignty—and the Enlightenment to come would call us to recognize this—suicidal. But what about the sovereignty of the Sovereign Himself? What about the sovereignty of God—God who has been, up until now, conspicuously absent from my analysis though not, curiously, conspicuously, from *Rogues*? What does God have to do with sovereignty, and particularly political sovereignty, today? What does God have to do with democracy?

Near the very end of the first part of *Rogues*, Derrida makes a rather surprising, provocative, if not downright roguish, gesture. Having given his most complete explication to date of the phrase "democracy to come," having developed perhaps his most trenchant critique of American foreign policy pre– and post–9/11, having demonstrated in great detail the autoimmune logic of sovereignty in general and of democracy in particular, Derrida pauses, shifts tone, and avows somewhat dramatically:

> In preparing for this lecture, I often asked myself whether everything that seems to link the democracy to come to the specter, or to the coming back or *revenance* of a messianicity without messianism, might not lead back or be reducible to some unavowed theologism. Not to the One God of the Abrahamic religions, and not to the One God in the political and monarchic figure spoken of by Plato in the *Statesman* and Aristotle in the *Politics*, and not even to the plural gods who are the citizens of that impossible democracy evoked by Rousseau when he longs for a "people of gods" who, if they existed, would govern democratically.
>
> No, but on account of the to-come, I asked myself whether this did not resemble what someone in whom we have never suspected the slightest hint of democratism said one day of the god who alone could still save us. (*R* 110)

Derrida will go on, as those who have read *Rogues* know and those who have not could anticipate, to discuss Heidegger's famous and much discussed line in the *Der Spiegel* interview about a god who can save us and his less famous and less discussed words about democracy in the same interview. Without getting led into the details of that discussion, I would like to conclude this chapter by asking why Derrida thought it necessary to end in this way. Why, at the end of a book on democracy, that is, on a regime where the *dēmos* or the people rules by popular consent, and not a cleric or monarch by divine right—why would Derrida turn yet again to Heidegger, and not to Heidegger on, say, *Mitsein*, but to Heidegger on democracy and the Hölderlinian-Heideggerian rhetoric surrounding "a god who can save us"? Why, at the end of a long analysis of the auto-immunity of sovereignty, and even more particularly, American uses and abuses of U.S. sovereignty in recent years, does Derrida turn to Heidegger and onto-theology? It is not, or not only, I would argue, because in 2002 phrases such as the "axis of evil" and strains of "God Bless America" were still very much in the air, but because, for Derrida, as we already saw in our chapter on *laïcité*, the most sovereign Sovereign, the guarantor of all identity and all sovereignty, is always, and even in democracies, God. If other sovereignties, whether political or otherwise, can, at least in appearance, be divided up, shared, distributed in time and space, the sovereignty of God is the exceptional case that defines the very essence and exceptionality of sovereignty.

For Derrida as for Carl Schmitt, sovereignty is always related to the sovereign exception to suspend rights and laws, and this exceptionality still today, and even in democracies, is what makes sovereignty inextricable from onto-theology. Let me cite again a crucial passage from *For What Tomorrow*:

> Without this category of exception, we cannot understand the concept of sovereignty. Today, the great question is indeed, everywhere, that of sovereignty. Omnipresent in our discourses and in our axioms, under its own name or another, literally or figuratively, this concept has a theological origin: the true sovereign is God. The concept of this authority or of this power was transferred to the monarch, said to have a "divine right." Sovereignty was then delegated to the people, in the form of democracy, or to the nation, with the same theological attributes as those attributed to the king and to God. (*FWT* 91–92)

It is because of the theological filiation of sovereignty, and even in democracy in the figure of "the people,"[19] that Derrida ultimately questions, at the end of *Rogues*, whether the democracy to come might be understood as, or translated into, a god to come. It is thus necessary, says Derrida in the same interview, "to deconstruct the concept of sovereignty, never to forget its theological filiation and to be ready to call this filiation into question wherever we discern its effects. This supposes an inflexible critique of the logic of the state and of the nation-state."[20]

As I argued in Chapter 3, regardless of whether one agrees or not with Derrida's interpretation of sovereignty, it is indisputable that, in order to understand Derrida's itinerary over the past couple of decades, one must take into account what *he* considered to be this still irreducible theological heritage within Western political thought. While readers of Derrida have spent a great deal of time debating Derrida's "turn to the political" in the 1980s and 1990s, what has been less discussed is the fact that Derrida's more *explicit* engagement with political issues was always accompanied by, or carried out under the aegis of, a thoroughgoing deconstruction of the politico-theological. This represents anything but—let me be clear—a "theological turn" in Derrida's work. It is, rather, what might be called, in the language of Jean-Luc Nancy, a "deconstruction of Christianity" or, better, a "deconstruction of the Abrahamic filiation."

The premises for this deconstruction of the theologico-political are already evident in Derrida's 1976 essay on the U.S. "Declaration of Independence," where it is shown how God functions in that founding political document as the final instance or authority, the "Supreme Judge and Sovereign," able to unite constative and performative, statement and prescription, so as to guarantee that "these united Colonies are *and* of right ought to be free and independent states" (see *N* 51–52; my emphasis). Derrida's reading of sovereignty as essentially theologico-political is central to that text, and it is a constant refrain in *Rogues*, both in Derrida's analysis of the philosophical tradition's treatment of democracy and in what he takes to be the uniquely American alliance of democracy and religion, particularly in the recent rhetoric of the Bush administration. This emphasis on the theologico-political is somewhat less obvious, though is none the less crucial, as we have already seen, in Derrida's more recent analyses of hospitality, forgiveness, the death penalty, globalization, and so on. It thus indeed appears that Derrida was in many ways carrying out the task he once called for, that of a "prudent, patient, differentiated, strategically complex deconstruction of political onto-theology" ("PMS" 14).

But if the essence of sovereignty is, as Derrida puts it, "phantasmatico-theological" ("PMS" 18), what kind of *essence* can that be? I said earlier that sovereignty is, for Derrida, indivisible, unshareable, and unspeakable, *or it is not at all*. Well, if sovereignty is autoimmune, if it cannot but be divided, shared out, spoken, presented and represented, then it "is" precisely—as phantasmatic—*not at all*. This does not mean, of course, that the *effects* of sovereignty are any less real, but it does mean that sovereignty is sustained only by a certain faith, credit, or belief in—or a certain pledge of allegiance to—the phantasmatic-theological source of these effects.

This helps explain Derrida's concern at the end of *Rogues* with an una-vowed relation between democracy and the Judeo-Christian idea of salva-tion, a salvation that, Derrida argues, needs to be distinguished from the unconditionality of the other or the event, that is, from an unconditional that is neither sovereign nor sacred, an unconditional that, in *Rogues* and elsewhere, would go by the name of *khōra*.

In "Faith and Knowledge," let me recall, Derrida spoke of *khōra* as "radically heterogeneous to the safe and sound, to the holy and the sa-cred," as never admitting "of any *indemnification*," as "neither Being, nor the Good, nor God, nor Man, nor History," as "the very place of an infi-nite resistance . . . an utterly faceless other" ("FK" 20–21). This "specter" of an "infinite resistance" helps explain, I believe, why Derrida in *Rogues* will wonder aloud about "some unavowed theologism" in his reading of "democracy to come" and why he will reserve the name *khōra* for one of the most provocative formulations of the book: "the democracy to come," he writes, "would be like the *khōra* of the political" (*R* 82). Derrida risks this formulation, this reinscription, this conditional comparative, because *khōra*, unlike God, unlike the One God or God as One, is not subject to autoimmunity. *Khōra*, unlike God, does not immunize or indemnify itself or others because it has no capacity to act and no sovereignty to protect, because in its unconditionality *without* sovereignty it undoes sovereignty rather than guarantees it, because in its infinite resistance to theological and anthropological appropriation it neither unifies humankind or the nation-state nor is itself united like God.[21]

Pledge of Allegiance II

We are back, finally, to my inaugural gesture, my pledge of allegiance, and the possibility of an originary pledge or profession of faith that elides every trace of the theologico-political within it. As you may have noticed, what I recited by what seemed to be rote, mechanical memory in my introduc-tion as the United States Pledge of Allegiance was indeed the pledge more or less as it was originally written by Francis Bellamy in 1892, but it was not quite the pledge that I recited or that school children in the United States today recite. Let me recall, since this has become the subject of controversy and many court cases in the United States in recent years, that in addition to more minor changes in the Pledge of Allegiance in 1923 and 1924, the words *under God* were added to the pledge only in 1954, after a campaign organized by the Knights of Columbus convinced Congress and President Eisenhower to make this change. No doubt against the original intent of Francis Bellamy,[22] cousin of the utopian novelist Edward Bellamy, author of *Looking Backward*, the Pledge of Allegiance was changed to read: "I pledge allegiance to the Flag of the United States of America, and to the Republic for which it stands: one Nation *under God*, indivisible, with Liberty and Justice for all." The sovereignty that dare not speak its name under pain of deconstruction or autoimmunity, a sovereignty that did not mark the pledge, at least not explicitly, for more than half a century, thus came, near the beginning of the Cold War—and this is surely no coincidence—to mark the pledge and assure the unity and indivisibility of the nation and its many states: not "one Nation indivisible" but "one Nation under God, indivisible," one Nation, or a Nation that is One and indivisible, only insofar as it is gathered and protected by the One God.

What Jacques Derrida would perhaps tell us today is that even if, someday, the words *under God* are ultimately stricken from the pledge, "under God" someday put under erasure, the task of a deconstruction of the theologico-political will remain, a deconstruction carried out in the name of the other and of a "justice without power." That is the task with which Derrida leaves us at the end of *Rogues*, where it is salvation, or a certain Abrahamic lineage of salvation, that is being questioned in the relationship between health, holiness, salvation, sovereignty, and the national context. Rogue that he was, rogue that he is, Derrida is not suggesting, it seems to me, that we try to think a purely godless sovereignty, a purely secular, human sovereignty, since sovereignty is itself a theologico-political concept, but rather that we negotiate with a god without sovereignty, a god that, like *khōra*, would be not only under erasure but compromised in its very sovereignty, not only suffering or withdrawn but vulnerable in its very ipseity, not a god that may come in the future to save us but a god that is essentially autoimmune, that is, a god that one day might not even be called one—and to which we might then, though never without trembling, pledge our allegiance.

8

Autonomy, Autoimmunity, and the Stretch Limo

From Derrida's Rogue State *to DeLillo's* Cosmopolis

> Things inside were distant and still, where he was supposed to be.
> —**Don DeLillo,** *Falling Man*

It may strike the reader as somewhat retrograde to be coming out *at just this time* with another book on Derrida, especially one with the implicitly optimistic title *Derrida From Now On*. For we are living at a time when "literary theory" or "cultural theory," or, as it has simply come to be known, "Theory," is no longer being reviled or criticized (those were perhaps the good old days) but has been declared simply dead or irrelevant, its time come and gone, a mere cultural relic "from now on." And the death certificate of the late-great-Theory has been signed and certified not just by its critics but by some considered to be its leading voices. Terry Eagleton, for example, begins his 2003 book *After Theory* with the unambiguous pronouncement, "The golden age of cultural theory is long past."[1] It is not simply past, says Eagleton, but *long* past, and those who today lay claim to the mantle of cultural theory bear little resemblance to the giants of that golden yesteryear. Cultural theory too had its "greatest generation," and it is now long gone.

But what exactly does Eagleton mean here by "cultural theory"? It would, it seems, be a general name under which to gather a whole series of movements of the 1960s through the 1990s, movements ranging from structuralism, critical theory, deconstruction, and postmodernism to psychoanalysis, feminism, postcolonialism, cultural studies, and so on. But as

Eagleton goes on to argue, and this is really the critical point of his book, these different movements did not live up to the true vocation of cultural theory in the same way or to the same degree. For what we witness during this forty-year period, and what ends up bringing about the demise of cultural theory in the best sense, is a progressive depoliticization of theory, a turn away from critical theory and class analysis to what Eagleton considers more apolitical forms of theory such as postmodernism and cultural studies. Eagleton thus begins the chapter entitled "The Path to Postmodernism": "As the countercultural 1960s and 70s turned into the postmodern 80s and 90s, the sheer irrelevance of Marxism seemed all the more striking."[2] Eagleton clearly deplores this irrelevance and displays a good deal of nostalgia for those countercultural 1960s and 1970s, a time—a golden age—when cultural theory was not, according to him, as insular and narcissistically self-absorbed as it is today but was still concerned with the social and political realities of the day. Thus while theorists of the 1960s and 1970s once wrote about important questions of class and poverty, today's generation of postmodernists and hipster theorists write "reverential essays on [the TV show] *Friends*."[3] As Eagleton puts it in one of those pithy phrases that always spice his prose, "an interest in French philosophy has given way to a fascination with French kissing."[4]

Yet Eagleton's opening salvo, "The golden age of cultural theory is long past," is not only a lament for a bygone critical theory tied to political practice and activism but a sort of promise of, or hope for, something new on the horizon. Now that the "golden age" is *long* past, now that cultural theory has turned so completely away from a world of staggering inequalities and injustices to concern itself with bourgeois popular culture, with such things as navel-piercing and cyborgs, now that the bankruptcy of cultural theory has been so completely exposed, something new is perhaps—just perhaps—in the offing. Eagleton writes: "A new and ominous phase of global politics has now opened, which *not even* the most cloistered of academics will be able to ignore. Even so, what has proved most damaging, *at least before* the emergence of the anti-capitalist movement, is the absence of collective, and effective, political action. It is this which has warped so many contemporary cultural ideas out of shape."[5] Something is happening, Eagleton seems to be suggesting, that will make a new, repoliticized cultural theory not only possible but perhaps even inevitable. Whereas the postmodern 1980s and 1990s were typified by an absence of collective and effective political action, the anticapitalist or what might be called the antiglobalization movement has made such action possible once again. The future is thus already here, and it may be giving rise to a new "golden age," or at least an age where theory is no longer politically irrelevant but can contribute to a new counterculture to address the causes of inequality and injustice.

Though there is much to contest in Eagleton's account of cultural theory over the past forty years and in his diagnosis of the contemporary situation, there is, I think, something to be said for it. I say this as someone whose academic life will have begun some time after those countercultural 1960s and 1970s and will have been lived for the most part during those irresponsible, postmodern 1980s and 1990s. Trying to avoid, then, both an unproductive nostalgia about that earlier time and an over-defensiveness about my own, I would want to affirm Eagleton's call for a repoliticization of theory and yet argue that postmodernism—or certain forms of critique commonly identified with it—has much to teach us about how best to heed that call. For the form of critique called deconstruction, often conflated with postmodernism and often criticized for being apolitical, not only gives us the tools for this repoliticization but has been in its own way rethinking the political throughout the 1980s and 1990s and now into the new millennium.

Identified largely with Derrida, deconstruction has always had, I would maintain, a political edge, one that has become even more trenchant during the past couple of decades. As practiced at least by Derrida, deconstruction has always been concerned with questions of justice, with a whole series of ethical questions that cannot be reduced to but cannot be thought apart from the social and political questions and realities of the day. In my view, then, deconstruction escapes the kind of critique Eagleton levels against the depoliticization of theory during the 1980s and 1990s. If I agree in the end that the "golden age of cultural theory is long past," that the days are gone when English, French, and Comparative Literature departments across the United States were abuzz with the newest import of the theory industry, this is perhaps less an indication of the death or irrelevance of deconstruction than a sign of the need for it or the possibility of its renewal and transformation. If the golden age of Theory is indeed long past, then perhaps we can begin to read again, and to read without having to buy into the opposition between theory and practice, to begin to read again—and, yes, perhaps even a novel—as a way of posing and analyzing the most pressing philosophical *and* political questions of our time.

What if, then, in the wake of what is called globalization, and in the wake of 9/11, in a world where sovereignty and power appear to have shifted away from such identifiable units as the nation-state and gravitated toward, on the one hand, multi- or trans-national corporations and supernational entities such as the UN, and, on the other, non-state or counter-state entities such as terrorist networks and protest movements, what if deconstruction were no longer some theory nicely cloistered away in our university classrooms but that which is happening today in our bodies, our culture, our cities, and our states? What if, in a world "after theory," deconstruction hovered somewhere between a theory that is practiced and a process that is undergone—an "autoimmune" process that can be read in our art, our theory, and our politics, in what we read, how we think, what we do, and what we undergo? What if the very claim that we live in a world "after theory" were the best proof that this theory is alive and well, that a certain death drive continues to live on?

In what follows, I would like to explore these provocations not just through the works of Derrida but through a recent work of popular fiction—Don DeLillo's *Cosmopolis*.[6] Though this may seem to invite precisely the kind of criticism Eagleton levels against those who turn away from social and political realities toward a fascination with popular culture, I will argue that this brief two-hundred-page novel can teach us a great deal about what is happening today in the United States—and thus, as we saw in Chapter 5, a great deal about deconstruction in or as America.

If DeLillo's writing has not often been read in relationship to deconstruction, it has regularly been identified with postmodernism, and *Cosmopolis* is a perfect example. The novel was thus characterized by James Wood, for example, in a rather unfavorable review in *The New Republic*, as "postmodern flâneur fiction"—a clever jibe, to be sure, but one that I think misses what is most thought provoking about the book.[7] *Cosmopolis* is indeed an exemplary book for thinking through postmodernism—or, as I would prefer, deconstruction—since its main protagonist is not really, I would argue, twenty-eight-year-old billionaire Eric Packer but his limousine, his automobile. Even more precisely, the subject of the novel is the *autos* itself, *autos* being, of course, the Greek word for "self" or "same," the word that stands at the very beginning of Western philosophy in the form of the Delphic inscription that Socrates took as his motto or credo, *Gnōthi se auton*, "Know thyself." If deconstruction is a critique, though not a rejection, of that credo, then it cannot but be a critique of the *autos*, that is, a calling into question of every claim to the naturalness or self-evidence of the *autos*—of the self or the selfsame.

Indeed, if deconstruction is or brings about, as I would want to claim, a thoroughgoing critique of every putatively natural, stable, and self-same identity—every formation of a self that would remain intact and self-same—then *Cosmopolis* would be something of a primer for a world, a cosmos, and a city—and not just any city—in deconstruction. I thus propose to read here *Cosmopolis*, and at the same time say something about deconstruction, and perhaps also postmodernism, by organizing my remarks around nine different *autos* or *auto*-concepts: here's the whole lot of them, the nine used *autos* in my lot: autochthony, automobility, autonomy, autobiography, autarky, auto-body, autopsy, auto-destruction, and, finally, the last term in the series, at once continuous and discontinuous with the rest, autoimmunity. My thesis will thus be that *Cosmopolis* is something of a postmodern fable of the *auto* in the breakdown lane, a fable of deconstruction as autoimmunity.[8]

The plot of *Cosmopolis* is strikingly simple, even classical, and can be summed up in a couple of sentences. It is the story of the precipitous and spectacular downfall of Eric Packer on a single day in April 2000. A twenty-eight-year-old billionaire currency trader, Packer begins the day in his 104-million-dollar triplex atop a nine-hundred-foot, eighty-nine-story residential tower on 1st Avenue and 47th Street in New York City, and he ends that day on the other side of Manhattan, on 47th and 11th Avenue, in an abandoned building that is being squatted by a disgruntled employee—a former college professor—who will eventually kill him. Between morning and night, Packer drives down 47th Street in his white stretch limo and will do, undergo, and witness a whole series of odd events: he will get caught in a bizarre antiglobalization protest and will have his limousine graffitied and attacked; he will lose not only his own fortune but that of his wife as he borrows huge amounts of yen he will be unable to pay back because of the yen's dramatic rise throughout the day; he will lose his wife, to whom he has been married for all of two weeks; he will attend a techno rave in an abandoned theater, as well as the funeral of a Sufi rapper; he will kill one of his bodyguards in a playground and sleep with another, as well as with his mistress, his financial advisor, and his wife. He will eat several meals, drink a few vodkas, have a full physical inside his limo—including a prostate exam—and dream of immortality while looking at his watch. It will make for a pretty full day. It is as if all the ills and desires of self and state were telescoped into a single day to highlight both the literally ephemeral nature of human existence and, perhaps, the speeding up of time and events in a postmodern world where fortunes can be made and lost in hours, and events on one side of the world can ripple across to the other side in minutes. For it did not take the events of 9/11 to prove to us—though they were surely the spectacular confirmation of this law—that much can change in a day and that even the tall and mighty can, unthinkably, come tumbling to the ground.

First auto, then, *autochthony*: from the Greek for "ground" or "earth" and *auto*, meaning, again, "self" or "same," *autochthony* suggests being indigenous, native born, indeed born from out of the earth itself. As I understand it, deconstruction is perhaps first and foremost a thoroughgoing critique of all claims to autochthony, all claims to a natural relation to some part of the earth, and, by extension, all political claims based upon a natural relation to soil or blood. In works such as the *Politics of Friendship* and *Of Hospitality*, Derrida tries to expose the uncriticized philosophical assumptions upon which all claims to autochthony are based, all claims to an enclosed, self-same community that must protect itself from external threats and aggression.

Set in New York City in April 2000, DeLillo's *Cosmopolis* clearly has something similar in mind. Set in a "cosmo-polis," a world-city with citizens from all over the world, the novel is peopled with Greeks, Sikhs, Chinese, Czechs, Italians—almost everything but true-blue, native-born, dyed-in-the-wool Americans.[9] As the quintessential cosmopolitan city, New York would be less an exception than the best example of what many cities are becoming today or, perhaps, have always been to a greater or lesser extent. For has there ever been a completely autochthonous city, one where the inhabitants came out of the earth without mixing and matching, without intermarriage and cultural exchange?

The only exception to this cosmopolitanism might seem to be the New York City–born protagonist, Eric Packer. Though he is surrounded by foreigners in his business and personal life, married to a Swiss wife (or at least he thinks she's Swiss), though he makes his living trading in foreign currencies, there is a part of Packer that is thoroughly American, thoroughly New York. "I'm a world citizen," he says, "with a New York pair of balls" (26). But the drama of *Cosmopolis* is, on one level, triggered by the fact that Packer is not a world citizen, not someone connected to the outside world and its citizens in any more than an abstract monetary way. He is in fact isolated from that world, indeed, isolated even from his native New York City, which he experiences more through television screens and the darkened glass of his limousine than through his own eyes and ears. Unless, of course, this is precisely what cosmopolitanism has become today.

This brings us to our second auto, the automobile, *automobility*: I said that the subject of *Cosmopolis* is as much Packer's stretch limo as "Packer" himself—a name that sounds very much like Packard, one of the first manufacturers of limousines in the United States, the limousine actually being defined by the fact that the passengers are covered, their bodies enclosed.[10] From the moment he emerges from his penthouse on 1st Avenue to the time he goes to meet the disgruntled employee out to kill him, Packer is in or around his limo. And what a limo it is: indistinguishable from all the other white stretch limos on the outside, the limo is equipped on the inside with TV monitors, computers, and video displays, a built-in bar, of course, and toilet,[11] all the necessities and amenities, but also all the aesthetic excesses, a Carrara marble floor, a marble from "the quarries where Michelangelo stood half a millennium ago" (22), and on the ceiling a semi-abstract painting depicting "the arrangement of the planets at the time of [Packer's] birth, calculated to the hour, minute, and second" (179). In the course of this day in April, Packer will do everything from conduct business, watch TV, have a medical exam, have sex, drink vodka, and relieve himself in his auto-mobile, in this seemingly self-enclosed, self-sufficient little world. The name "Cosmopolis" thus suggests not only a world-city, a cosmopolitan city like New York, but a microcosmos, a city that, like the limo, can bring the whole world within.

To top it all off, the limo was, as Packer puts it in a nice, compact neologism, "prousted," that is, corklined, soundproofed, in imitation of Marcel Proust's room on the Boulevard Haussmann in Paris, where he wrote much of *Remembrance of Things Past* (70). Like Proust, Packer, who suffers from insomnia, will be motivated throughout the novel by a memory of things past, the smells and sounds of a barbershop in his father's old neighborhood. Unlike Proust, however, who remained immobile and brought the outside in through writing—Combray, Balbec, Paris, Venice, Odette, Swann, Charlus, the Princess of Guermantes—Packer will move through the city, taking characters into his limo as he travels west. The limo is "prousted" and, of course, armored; as Packer says, "It's a gesture. It's a thing a man does" (71). If to be "prousted" is to be protected from the outside, soundproofed and bulletproofed, then Packer's vulnerability will coincide with his extraction from the limo, his extrusion from this mobile bunker. Packer will thus end up shedding the limo altogether by the end of the novel, his crosstown adventure ultimately being a journey not *in* but *out of* the limo, out of the *auto* and all the *autos* it embodies or carries with it.

What makes Packer's limo exemplary and not just some billionaire's eccentricity is the fact that *Cosmopolis* is the very comic story of many limos—including that of the President of the United States and those in the funeral procession of Sufi rapper Brutha Fez—inching across the city, bumper to bumper, intersecting, interrupting, and impeding one another, turning what would normally be an hour walk across Manhattan into an all-day odyssey. What Eric Packer thus sheds, what *Cosmopolis*, dare I say, "deconstructs," is a certain quintessentially American dream or ideology of autonomy and independence, of self-determination, individualism, freedom, and self-sufficiency, all the values conveyed by the American automobile. We read in *Cosmopolis*, "He wanted the car because it was not only oversized but aggressively and contemptuously so, metastasizingly so, a tremendous mutant thing that stood astride every argument against it" (10). Though the car will be attacked and graffitied during the antiglobalization demonstration, it will indeed resist every assault and argument against it. Which is why Eric Packer must ultimately leave it behind. For if the auto, the automobile, is what protects us, gives us a sense of identity and fullness, of autonomy and independence, it is also what prevents us from experiencing anything like an event—and it is the event, I will argue, something that breaks the circuit of the same, that Eric Packer is ultimately after.

So, third auto, *autonomy*—that is, self-rule, self-governing behavior, self-directed, independent movement and action. To be autonomous is to give oneself one's own law, to be independent of other laws or the laws of others. Though Packer is driven around in his limo and does not himself do the driving, he is the one who calls all the shots, he is the Decider and Chief, the one who pilots the ship and determines the course to be taken. His autonomy is supreme, his rule, his empire, invulnerable—or so it seems at the beginning of the novel, at the beginning of this day in April.

Though *Cosmopolis* is set in the year 2000, in pre–9/11 New York City, at the end of the millennium and the market boom of the 1990s, it is hard not to see the cloud of 9/11 already hanging over it. I have no idea whether the book was started or perhaps even mostly written by DeLillo before 9/11, but it is difficult not to hear 9/11 behind the story of a man who begins his day atop an eighty-nine-story tower, "a tower that soars to heaven and goes unpunished by God" (103), and ends with the same man stretched out naked on a street in Hell's Kitchen as the cameras roll to tape his demise. The title of DeLillo's 2007 novel explicitly about 9/11, *Falling Man*, could really have been the title or subtitle of this one. What is called into question in *Cosmopolis* is thus precisely Packer's autonomy—to say nothing of that of New York or the United States—Packer's sense of independence and self-determination, his sense of invulnerability. How can one not hear the ghost of 9/11 haunting an exchange like this one between Packer and his security analyst? "Our system's secure. We're impenetrable. There's no rogue program. . . . There's no vulnerable point of entry. Our insurer did a threat analysis. We're buffered from attack." "Everywhere," asks Packer. "Yes." "Including the car." "Including, absolutely, yes" (12).

What drives the novel, what drives Eric Packer in some obscure way from 1st Avenue to 11th, is not only the fact that he wants something over on 11th that he cannot get anywhere else, anywhere else in the world, in fact, a haircut from his childhood barber, but a threat, what is called a "credible threat," against his life. The threat level, we might say, has been raised to red by Packer's department of homeland or hometown security, and everything from Packer's bodyguards' actions to Packer's own movements will be determined by this threat. What we have here is the end of autonomy or, rather, the end of the ideology or even the illusion of autonomy. For what deconstruction shows us, I believe, is that autonomy, self-identity, and self-determination are formed only through a relationship to others, from the moment they give us our name to the time they pronounce and give meaning to our death.

Fourth auto, then, *autobiography* and the linear narrative form that is usually assumed to go alone with it, that is, a narrative writing, the *-graphy*, that follows the life, the *bios*, the same or self-same life—that's the *autos*—from birth to death: *auto-bio-graphy*.[12] If postmodernity is supposed to challenge this linear notion of time, then *Cosmopolis* would appear thoroughly modern inasmuch as it follows one day in the life of Eric Packer from early morning to late at night. The action, too, appears to be more or less linear, beginning on 1st and 47th in Manhattan and following 47th Street west to 11th Avenue and 47th, with just a couple of detours down toward Times Square in between.

Yet the telling of this linear narrative is not without interruption or detour, for embedded within it, like the foci of an ellipsis, are two sequences of what are called "The Confessions of Benno Levin," the first, entitled "Night," recounting events *after* the death of Eric Packer, that is, *after* the events recounted at the end of the book, and the second, "Morning," giving us the events that led up to the day, that is, what happened *before* the beginning of the book.[13] Hence the linear narrative is interrupted by a second narrative that inscribes or enfolds within it in chiasmatic fashion the limits of the first narrative, the first sequence enlightening the reader about the fated end of Eric Packer and the second giving us background into what led to that end.

Very postmodern, it might be said, but also quite classical. In ancient Greek tragedy, for example, the use of already-known myths and the incorporation of foreshadowing techniques such as prophecy meant that an audience already knew at the outset of the play what was going to happen, that Oedipus, for example, would come to know himself to be the murderer of his father and the lover of his mother, that he was going to lose his wife, his vision if not quite his life, and his place in the polis. DeLillo's *Cosmopolis* appears to use the "Confessions of Benno Levin" in a similar way, to interrupt the linear narrative but also to provide a kind of foreshadowing within it. And DeLillo achieves this by telescoping, by packing, the downfall of Eric Packer and the collapse of his financial empire into a single day, that is, as Aristotle recommends in the *Poetics*, into "a single revolution of the sun."[14]

This reference to tragedy perhaps tells us something else about the postmodern if not about deconstruction: instead of simply rejecting traditional models of literature or interpretation, postmodern music, architecture, and literature often work with these models, either citing them—sometimes respectfully or reverently, sometimes with detachment or irony—or juxtaposing them, combining them in an eclectic mélange. This eclecticism can be seen throughout *Cosmopolis*, vividly illustrated by the two elevators that lead to and from Packer's penthouse, the one always playing Erik Satie and the other Brutha Fez. Like postmodernity itself, like *New* York City itself, Eric Packer brings old and new together, high and low culture, even old and new money, his marital union with Elise Shifrin being the merger of an old-world banking fortune with twentieth-century cyber-capital.[15]

Money and capital buy us our fifth auto, auto-arky or *autarky*, from the Greek *autarkeia*, meaning auto- or self-sufficiency. If money can't buy you love, the least it can do is bring you independence and self-sufficiency. But self-sufficiency will not quite suffice for Eric Packer. One of the clues as to why this is so is contained in a single Greek word uttered by Vija Kinski, Packer's "chief of theory," his postmodern guru, a sort of Jean Baudrillard with an Eastern European accent. The word is *chrimatis-tikos*, which, DeLillo probably knows, gets its first full philosophical treatment in Aristotle's *Politics*, where a distinction is drawn between *oikonomikē*, the art of household economy, the art of meeting the limited needs of the household, and *chrematistikē*, an art of commerce and exchange driven not by need and use but by unlimited desire.[16] Aristotle's *Politics* in fact anticipates the Marxist distinction between use value and exchange value, product and commodity, and the properly fantastic or phantasmatic character of the latter.[17] All this helps explain Packer's unlimited desire for wealth or money, his desire, or, rather, since DeLillo probably wants us to hear the pun—indeed the etymology—his *yen* (a Chinese word meaning "addition") for more and more yen on this spring day in NYC.

Being a currency trader, Packer is the ultimate chrematistic overlord. He deals not in goods, not even in stocks vaguely related to goods, but in the units of exchange themselves.[18] As Kinski understands, "Money has taken a turn. All wealth has become wealth for its own sake. . . . Money has lost its narrative quality the way painting did once upon a time. Money is talking to itself" (77). Kinski is suggesting that the meta-narrative of money, whether it be that of capitalism or communism, has come to an end. Money talks only to and about itself, creating its own laws, inflating itself, growing from out of itself, quasi-automatically, an image of either superabundant growth and generosity or absolute and uncontrollable monstrosity.

In the end, however, it is not a desire for unlimited capitalist accumulation that drives Packer through the novel but the simplicity of a haircut. Not just any haircut, of course, but a haircut from a barber in Hell's Kitchen who once knew his father. As Packer tells an associate, "We're in the car because I need a haircut. . . . A haircut has what. Associations. Calendar on the wall. Mirrors everywhere. There's no barber chair here [in the car]. Nothing swivels but the spycam" (15).[19]

It is perhaps this realization, a hope or a dream, that something still exists beyond the marketplace that also drives the bizarre antiglobalization protest near the middle of the book, where anarchists / terrorists / street performers dressed in gray spandex release hundreds of rats into the New York City streets and float an enormous styrofoam rat down the street as if part of a rogue Macy's Thanksgiving Day parade, in which Willard replaces Mickey in the Magic Kingdom (86). In the middle of it all, the protestors manage to hack into the ticker tapes of Times Square to post this message: "A specter is haunting the world—the specter of capitalism" (96). This is, of course, an ironic and inverted citation of the first line of Marx's *Communist Manifesto* of 1848, with the word *world* replacing *Europe* and *Capitalism* replacing *Communism*. But the inversion of this Marxist slogan in the end supports the Marxist spirit of the original: both are critiques of capital's omnipresent specularity, its emphasis on profit and speculation rather than the values of human labor and community. Packer, the ultimate cyber-capitalist, finds himself spellbound in his limousine by the demonstration, by both the high-tech hacking job and the low-tech rats, by both the message conveyed and the incantational, "ancient and formulaic" way it is delivered (74).

Finally, a second ticker tape is taken over by the cyber-radicals, who post the phrase "a rat became the unit of currency" (96), a phrase of Polish poet Zbigniew Herbert, author of, among other works, *Report from the Besieged City* and *Mr. Cogito*. "A rat became the unit of currency": the phrase could be analyzed endlessly for all the ways it wreaks havoc on both exchange and use value, the most fluid and disembodied of currencies, cyber-capital, becoming the most fully embodied, the most fully recalcitrant to symbolic conversion—the rat.[20]

Sixth auto, the *autobody*, by which I mean—pardon my abuse of the term—the body as one's own, as individual and, as we learned to spell it in grade school, "sep-*a rat*-e" from other bodies. We've already seen how

Packer's limousine becomes a kind of pod or second skin, a second city or second self, a moving cogito that must ultimately be shed if Packer is to confront something that exceeds his knowledge and his expectations. But Packer's body itself goes through a similar process of expropriation; well-dressed, sunglassed, and girded for business in the beginning of the novel, Packer will end up naked on the New York streets, wondering about the connection between human bodies. It is, curiously, Benno Levin, a kind of failed Packer, a homeless double or doppelgänger of Packer, who gives us both the principle of the body—that is, its totality—and the clearest critique of that principle. "World is supposed to mean something that's self-contained. But nothing is self-contained. Everything enters something else. My small days spill into light-years. This is why I can only pretend to be someone" (60). In short, we are the world, or we are like a world, pretending to be total, self-contained, but, as Whitman put it, we contain contradictions, multitudes—other totalities.

The auto-body, the totality and integrity of the self, is thus explored both figuratively and literally throughout *Cosmopolis*. In some sense, the entire novel is about a certain obsession with and a repression of the body.[21] One of the oddest moments in the novel occurs when Packer's body is penetrated by a latex glove during a prostate examination in his limo. As the doctor "examined the prostate for signs," like a latter-day soothsayer reading the signs of the future off the internal organs of some sacrificed animal, Packer can no longer forget his body (47). "He [Doctor *In*gram; my emphasis] was here in his body, the structure he wanted to dismiss in theory even when he was shaping it under the measured effect of barbells and weights" (48). With his body penetrated, with the doctor detecting signs of an asymmetrical prostate, Packer, in a rather extraordinary parody of philosophical introspection, begins asking the really "big questions": "What are the questions he asks himself from this position in the world? Large questions maybe. . . . *Why something and not nothing. Why music and not noise?* . . . He did not think he was speaking for effect. These were serious questions" (50–51). Proctology thus recapitulates ontology—as well as aesthetics—from Heidegger to John Cage. It is the materiality of the body rather than the immateriality of the mind or soul, the body's anomalies rather than its symmetries, that provoke questions about the Good, the Beautiful, and the True.

In many of their guises, both postmodernism and deconstruction place emphasis not on interiors and depths but on surfaces, since even the most internal of organs, a prostate, a heart, can—especially today—be turned into a surface. The body can be not only penetrated but exposed, unfolded, pictured, x-rayed, opened up on the operating table, or digitalized on monitors and computer screens, even supplemented through grafts and transplants, whether organic, metallic, or synthetic. Let me recall here Jean-Luc Nancy's magnificent essay "The Intruder," which recounts and analyzes in probing detail Nancy's own heart transplant, the strange incorporation of all that is other into what we would like to think of as the "natural" human body, everything from the hands and instruments of the surgeon to the heart of another human being, with its own DNA, antibodies, and immune system.[22] If the modern is concerned with depths and interiors, whether of society, the family, or the self, postmodernity would try to expose those interiors, to lay them bare, to expose, for example, how the putatively natural interior is already culturally marked, how the supposedly secret, inviolable interior is not only violable but already violated, inhabited, invaded. *Cosmopolis* is one long unfolding of the interior into the exterior, an unfolding of the secret, inviolable, natural interior into a series of coded, readable, exterior surfaces.

Perhaps Packer's most striking rediscovery of his own body occurs when he finds himself at the intersection of 11th Avenue and 47th Street in the middle of a movie shoot, where some "three hundred naked people [were] sprawled in the street . . . flattened, fetal . . . a city of stunned flesh" (172). Without hesitation, Packer undresses and joins the huddled masses, a man-child lying naked in fetal position on a New York City street. How far the mighty have fallen, we might think—how far his body will have come from its separation from everything and everyone atop the eighty-nine-story tower where his day began.[23]

This reference to film brings us to our seventh auto; after the autobody, the *autopsy*. From *autos* and *opsis*, the Greek word for "vision," *autopsy* or *autoscopy* suggests a seeing into the body and by extension a reproduction of the body as it is filmed, digitalized, and projected. *Cosmopolis* is chock full of reflections, mirror images, video feeds, and TV screens through which characters learn about others and themselves. Packer understands his own body through its reflection on his glass building (9), through movies he saw with his mother as a child (183), through car video cameras, and through the mirrors in the barbershop of his childhood. He thus learns about himself not through introspection, not by following the Socratic dictum *Gnōthi se auton*, "Know thyself," not, like Descartes, by turning within so as to discover his own Mr. Cogito, but by looking at the image of himself produced by the "spycam" in his limo: "The car stopped and moved and he realized queerly that he'd just placed his thumb on his chinline, a second or two after he'd seen it on-screen" (22). When his limo is later surrounded by protesters during the antiglobalization demonstration, Packer ducks back inside to see what's going on. "It made more sense on TV. He poured two vodkas and they watched, trusting what they saw. It was a protest all right" (89).

The events of everyday life—and even everyday death—all enter in through images in this age of what Walter Benjamin called "mechanical reproduction." It is thus through a live news report on the Money Channel that Packer learns—indeed witnesses, and then witnesses over and over through the replays—the assassination in North Korea of Arthur Rapp, managing director of the International Monetary Fund. The narrative structure I spoke of earlier, in which one narrative time is set alongside or juxtaposed with another, is perhaps best achieved in such a video age: "Eric watched [Arthur Rapp] sign a document on one screen and prepare to die on another" (33).

The reproducibility, iterability, and reproduction, the obsessive replaying, of the moment, of the event, is thus essential to *Cosmopolis*, to the contemporary city or the techno-global village: "Eric wanted them to show [the assassination] again. *Show it again.* They did this, of course, and he knew they would do it repeatedly into the night, our night, until the sensation drained out of it" (34).[24] When the body, the "real" body, of Sufi rapper Brutha Fez goes by in a funeral cortege, Packer wants "to see the hearse pass by again, the body tilted, for viewing, a digital corpse, a loop, a replication. It did not seem right that the hearse had come and gone" (139).

The repetition or reproducibility of the event is thus inseparable from the event itself.[25] What, for example, would 9/11 have been without its repetition, without its worldwide transmission and iteration?[26] Would anyone seriously claim that the repetition was simply extrinsic to, merely a representation of, what we call "the events of September 11?" What provoked us to yell out, especially during the first forty-eight hours, "show it again!"? Show the crumbling towers again, show the event again, show it again so we can look and turn away again, but also show the spectral images of the two towers *before* they fell, the images that now outlive the things and are haunted by their collapse. Postmodernity is thus the time of specters, of images, sounds, and digital imprints that all outlive, or at least potentially outlive, the things they purport to represent. In postmodernity, the image is no longer three removes from the real, to paraphrase book 10 of the *Republic*, the fallen simulacrum of the realm, but something more powerful and in some sense more real than the real itself.

Eighth auto, and I'm now accelerating, self- or *auto-destruction*, the turning of a hand against oneself, sometimes out of despair, sometimes in the name of some other good. The most spectacular example of this, the one that most impresses Packer, is the act of *auto-da-fé* or self-immolation that he witnesses during the antiglobalization protest. *Auto-da-fé* is yet another *auto*-word, though it comes not from the Greek *autos* but from the Portuguese, meaning "act of faith." Even if the antiglobalization demonstration might itself be understood as "a fantasy generated by the market," a bit of negativity to be recuperated and capitalized upon by the market, the self-immolation of one of the protestors suggests to Packer that "the market was not total. It could not claim this man or assimilate his act. . . . This was a thing outside its reach" (90, 99–100).[27] Though Packer's mistress, Didi Francher, had earlier given him a glimpse of an economy where expenditures cannot be recuperated, an erotic economy beyond the marketplace, telling him that "talent is more erotic when it's wasted" (31), it takes Packer some time to get a knack for wasting his talent and himself so completely.

Yet *Cosmopolis* is about more than just the self-destructive behavior of a single arrogant or hubristic individual; it is about the implosion or auto-destruction of an entire system or structure. Packer's precipitous demise is occasioned by the fact that the yen's sudden rise cannot be understood by any of Packer's prior models of analysis. With his system, or perhaps *the* system, in meltdown, Packer ignores the prudent counsel of all his advisors and leverages his position beyond all reason. He confesses, "I don't know what money is anymore" (29). This loss of confidence in a rational order, and in himself, coincides with the "credible threat" against his life and with a growing sense that some other unpredictable, undecipherable law—some inscrutable fate—is ultimately leading him on. With the loss of his wealth and confidence in a rational order goes Packer's autonomy. Instead of moving and shaking others, he has the sense that he is being moved and shaken—a dispossession that will give him an odd jubilation, as if his empire and his autonomy had to be given up in order for him to get down to the "business of living."

With the IMF director being assassinated earlier in the day, with markets becoming unpredictable, perhaps even, as a former Federal Reserve chairman would have put it, "irrationally exuberant," Packer's fall portends not just a revolution, not just a new countercultural movement justified and motivated by an antiglobalist ideology, but a much more general apocalypse, a "whole system . . . in danger" (116), a sense of "a species in peril" (81). It appears as the end of an era, the end of an era of security for some and not for others, the end, perhaps, of an era of immunity. From now on, it would appear, *no one is immune.*

Ninth and final auto, then, *autoimmunity*, which does not mean immunization or protection of the *autos* but, precisely, the *auto*'s destruction, an immunization not *of* but *against* the self. Unlike all the other *autos*, therefore, the notion of autoimmunity does not sustain or support but actually attacks and compromises the *autos* itself. Whereas claims to autochthony are usually made to bolster a sense of sameness and community, whereas autobiography is usually written to confirm the self-identity of the one writing, and so on, autoimmunity, which we all know best from diseases such as AIDS, entails an attack not simply on the self through some kind of self-destructive behavior but an attack on those things that protect and defend the self, leaving it open, vulnerable, hospitable to outside forces, be they good or bad. *Cosmopolis* is, in many ways, a postmodern tale of autoimmunity, a sort of death drive down 47th Street that ultimately threatens to ruin the self or else open it up to a genuine event.

The first manifestation of autoimmunity in the novel is nothing more sophisticated than self-doubt or self-critique, putting oneself in question, which would seem to suggest that philosophy as self-questioning is already a kind of autoimmunity.[28] Already at the beginning of Western philosophy, self-critique, Socratic self-questioning, seems to go hand in hand with the *Gnōthi se auton*. In addition to being a rational animal, or an animal endowed with speech, or a political animal, as Aristotle calls him, perhaps even a cosmopolitical animal in the wake of Kant, the human animal may well be an autoimmune animal, that is, an animal who acts and then questions why it has acted, even who it is who did the acting. That would be a first autoimmunity.

But, even more dangerous and disastrous, the human animal is perhaps also that rational, autoimmune animal who, precisely through its rationality, creates the very conditions for destroying itself—weapons of unimaginable destructive force, systems of staggering inequality—so that perhaps, just perhaps, the task must be to combat this second autoimmunity by means of the first. As the Tiresiaslike Vija Kinski says to Packer, "What is the flaw of human rationality? . . . It pretends not to see the horror and death at the end of the schemes it builds. This is a protest against the future. They want to hold off the future. They want to normalize it, keep it from overwhelming the present" (90–91). By the end of the novel, Packer has perhaps gained a glimpse of that horror, and so appears driven to seek out—in an autoimmune fashion—the "credible threat" that will destroy him. How else can we explain the fact that Packer dies not simply by turning a hand against himself, in a suicide that would have given his action some meaning or purpose, that would be for some cause, but by turning against his bodyguards, against his own immune system, so to speak, so as to leave himself vulnerable to whatever might happen? Packer thus takes out one bodyguard, Kendra Hays, by sleeping with her and sending her home for the rest of the day, and he then lures his chief of security, Torval—Tor, as in the German word for door or gateway[29]—into a playground, where Packer shoots him with his, Torval's, own voice-activated gun.[30] Packer kills his own bodyguard, disables his own immune system, we might say, because "Torval's passing cleared the night for deeper confrontation" (148). With "his bodyguards gone," he was "mortally alone now" (158).

Cosmopolis does indeed appear to be a fable of autoimmunity. Just a couple of pages before the death of Torval, Packer himself actually contemplates the immune system in what must surely be read as something more than just a bit of postmodern irony. "He felt a sneeze begin to develop in his immune system. . . . He realized that he always sneezed twice, or so it seemed in retrospect. He waited and it came, rewardingly, the second sneeze. What causes people to sneeze? A protective reflex of the nasal mucous membranes, to expel invasive materials" (140).

To "begin the business of living" (107), as the novel puts it, Packer had to dispatch those who had been protecting him, who had separated him from others, who had enabled his cool, postmodern detachment. Packer's killing of Torval seems ordered by an implacable—autoimmune—necessity: to open himself up and make himself vulnerable to what might either save or destroy him, to open his auto—indeed his whole fleet of autos, from autonomy to autarky—to a life-transforming event. How else are we to explain the fact that Packer not only does not avoid the credible threat but walks right into it? He leaves Anthony's barbershop in mid-haircut, with an asymmetrical head of hair to match his asymmetrical prostate (169), and has his driver "cut off all means of communication with the complex" (170), thinking, "Something had to happen soon" (171). As the limousine crosses 11th Avenue and enters what is called "the car barrens," a place of "old junked-up garages and ratty storefronts. . . . Stripped cars ranked on the sidewalk," we know that the novel is in the home stretch (179). Leaving his driver to park the limo in an underground garage, Packer is finally alone, de-limoed, extruded, as it were, from his cogito by the jaws of life—"reborn," we might go so far as to say, since it is at that very moment that Benno Levin, his future assassin, calls out his name, his full name—"Eric *Michael* Packer"—for the first time in the novel, "Michael" being, as we learned from Anthony the barber, Eric's father's name.[31] Packer then walks right into the abandoned building in which Levin is squatting to confront his inverted mirror image, his failed double. "Think how surprised I was," writes Levin, "that I did not have to track him and stalk him, which I was unfitted to do . . . haunted by opposing forces concerning does he die or not" (59). Like a single, autonomous self now split in two, Packer and Levin—who are both thinking about time, fate, and immortality, who both, as they learn, have asymmetrical prostates—engage in a conversation that will lead, first, to Packer blowing a hole in his own hand, and then to Levin finishing Packer off in a kind of murder/suicide, in the ultimate destruction, it might be argued, of the *autos* itself.[32] We have gone from the wasteful *auto*, the pretentious, metastacized limousine, to the *autos itself* that is wasted, done in, shot.

In Derrida's *Rogues*, this law of autoimmunity is given a definition that helps explain, I believe, not only the ending of *Cosmopolis* but what is happening to us today, to our bodies, our communities, our states, our notions of sovereignty, democracy, even homeland security. Derrida there writes:

> What I call the autoimmune consists not only in harming or ruining oneself . . . [but] in threatening the I [*moi*] or the self [*soi*], the *ego* or the *autos*, . . . compromising the immunity of the *autos* itself. . . . It consists not only in committing suicide but in compromising *sui*- or *self*-referentiality, the *self* or *sui*- of suicide itself. Auto-immunity is more or less suicidal, but, more seriously, it threatens always to rob suicide itself of its meaning and supposed integrity. (*R* 45)

Though Levin initially tries to justify his killing of Packer, and Packer himself wants to see a reason for Levin's violence—"Violence needs a cause, a truth," he says (194)—the death of Packer seems motivated by another necessity. Levin himself perhaps comes pretty close when he says: "I have my syndromes, you have your complex. Icarus falling. You did it to yourself. Meltdown in the sun" (202). Or as he says earlier: "Your whole waking life is a self-contradiction. That's why you're engineering your own downfall" (190). Having been delimited and de-limoed, Packer wants to be demolished, more than that, *auto-da-fé-ed*, with a jet plane substituting for the prousted limo. "He wanted to be buried in his nuclear bomber. . . . Not buried but cremated, conflagrated, but buried as well. He wanted to be solarized" (208–9).

When Packer blows a hole in his own left hand, he blows a hole in the wholeness and continuity of time and space. For the shot activates the electron camera inside his watch, which begins filming and projecting images on the watch face, images of Packer, his surroundings, a beetle on a wire in the room, but then images that appear to come from the future, Packer's own body in an ambulance, in a morgue, the miracle of the electron watch allowing him—just for a moment—to see himself dead, to be able to pronounce the impossible speech act from Poe that Derrida cites as an epigraph to *Speech and Phenomena*, namely, "I am dead," or rather, as Packer transcribes it, "Oh shit I'm dead" (206).

"Whose body and when?" he asks himself. "Have all the worlds conflated, all possible states become present at once?" (205).One signs a document on one screen and is assassinated on another—at the same time—all times and worlds conflated. For the first time, Packer looks back, looks back on his life, even if it is from the future anterior. He used to think: "To crush and cut. To eviscerate. Power works best when there's no memory attached" (184), but now that the power of memory, of digitalized immortality, is overtaking him, he begins to think otherwise.

In the end, however, something resists this digitalized archive; something resists the market and all its mechanisms of reproduction. "The things that made him who he was could hardly be identified much less converted to data. . . . the stuff he sneezes when he sneezes. . . . He'd come to know himself, untranslatably, through his pain. . . . the vague malaise of winter twilights, untransferable. . . . the click in his knee when he bends it, all him, and so much else that's not convertible to some high sublime, the technology of mind-without-end" (207–8). Something resists that is initially identified with pain, with *his* pain ("his pain interfered with his immortality"; 207), something that cannot, however, ultimately be reduced to an *autos*, to the self-sameness of a being who is autochthonous or autonomous, who could deliver his self-sameness in an autobiography. As Packer himself understood, "the things that made him who he was could *hardly be identified* much less converted to data" (207; my emphasis). Something resists autoimmunity that is not an *autos* or a self; something survives that goes beyond the self, beyond an identifiable *autos*, something unique and yet hardly identifiable—a singularity that eludes all our models of analysis and yet provides the only reason to get up one day and drive across town.

For Derrida, autoimmunity announces at once a threat and an opportunity. The threat or danger is that in compromising the self, in allowing the self to be breached, whether that self be an individual, a city, or a state, the self—the *autos*—may allow within it something that will eventually destroy it, a virus, a would-be assassin, a terrorist cell. But the opportunity consists in the fact that by compromising the *autos* in this way, by opening the self to what is other than and outside it, beyond its borders, it has the chance of welcoming something that may help it go beyond itself, beyond the self, a lover to assist it in its freedom, an immigrant to hold it to its own ideals of justice and democracy, an other to accompany it in its death.

If deconstruction as autoimmunity is indeed what's happening today, then the best way to protect ourselves against the worst is not, as Packer does before this day in April, to close ourselves off to questioning and to critique, to enforce the borders of our thinking and our theory, to show ourselves intolerant to everything that threatens our dogmas, beliefs, and patriotisms, but to embrace such questioning and critique as the best way of warding off the worst, to embrace an active and vigilant questioning of what it is that is happening to and through us. If deconstruction as autoimmunity is what's happening today, happening in our bodies, our cities, and our states, then the task must be not simply to evaluate and then say yes or no to postmodernity or to deconstruction but to negotiate between these better and worse forms of autoimmunity, to find the right limit, or at least the right speed limit, in any given situation. For to stop the *autos*, to remain in neutral, is in the end to perish, and to go too fast, to open it up on what may look like the open road, is to risk crashing in an autoimmune fashion into the oncoming *autos* that will always resemble our own. We must thus learn to drive by coming to terms with what drives us.

So please, please drive safely.

9

History's Remains

Of Memory, Mourning, and the Event(s) of 9/11

In early September 2001 Jacques Derrida published in English a collection of essays written over the span of about two decades on the theme of mourning. Though many had been published before, some even in English translation, they had never been gathered together into a single volume before Derrida allowed Pascale-Anne Brault, Kas Saghafi, and myself to publish them under the title *The Work of Mourning*. The book was thus released in early September but was, as one might expect, quickly forgotten in the wake of what came to called the "events" of September 11th.

Yet as the initial shock of those events, along with the pain, anguish, and mourning that immediately followed, began to give way to reflection and to questioning, the book began to attract more and more attention as many began to wonder whether Derrida's work might not speak in some way about how we should best respond to what had happened in New York City and in Washington, D.C., though also, albeit in a different way, in the rest of the United States and throughout the world. When in early October Derrida did a book signing at Labyrinth Books in New York City, over four hundred people turned out—coming, I think, to hear Derrida speak of mourning and to learn from his writing something about how to mourn but also, no doubt, by coming together and partaking in this commercial ritual actually to participate in the work of mourning in one of the first in what would prove to be a long series of public or collective gatherings of mourning in New York City and elsewhere. Though

The Work of Mourning is essentially a book about what we might call private mourning, individual mourning, here Derrida's mourning of some fourteen close friends and colleagues, there are clues throughout that volume about how to relate these reflections to public mourning, to better and worse ways of remembering the dead through ritual and memorialization, better and worse ways of speaking about, recalling, or understanding death—or, perhaps, the "event."

In this chapter I propose to take up some of these clues from Derrida's *The Work of Mourning* in order to ask about collective or communal mourning in America, about how we mourned and remembered, how we should have mourned and remembered, in the wake of the event—or the events—of September 11. How is it that we mourn together—as a family, a community, or a state? Why do we do it, and is it a good thing? Is it really mourning or are all the rituals and ceremonies of public mourning designed to assure us that death has not really taken place and that there is no real need to mourn?

But rather than enter the debate or polemic surrounding the proper response to 9/11 at ground zero, whether to rebuild or not, whether to build a monument to celebrate freedom or a memorial to honor the victims, I wish instead to develop these questions of collective or communal mourning by looking at two very different examples, one from each end of the Western tradition, so to speak, the first, the role mourning plays in the constitution of the state in Plato, particularly in his *Laws*, and then, closer to home, the controversy surrounding another relatively recent attempt in the United States to remember and memorialize, a controversy with its roots in the Vietnam conflict but one whose effects are still with us today, post–9/11 and right up to the current conflict in Iraq. In the spirit of repatriating the very concept of communal mourning, I will focus here on the *uniquely twentieth-century* ritual of collective mourning known as the dedication or consecration of the Tomb of the Unknown Soldier in Arlington National Cemetery, a story of haunting and a story itself haunted, as we shall see, by many of the ethical and philosophical issues that have been pressed upon us in large part by 9/11. Ignoring here all the differences between a memorial erected to soldiers fallen in combat during wartime and one commemorating civilians killed in an attack outside conventional warfare, I will suggest that we can learn a great deal about mourning—and perhaps about how to mourn the event, *these events*—by looking at this controversy and at the way in which it marks a certain epoch of mourning in the West and most particularly in America. My trajectory will thus be from Derrida's *The Work of Mourning*, through the "beautiful death" of ancient Athens, to what might be called in the wake of recent events "mourning in America."

❧

The Work of Mourning comprises fourteen remarkable texts written by Derrida over a period of two decades after the deaths of friends and colleagues, namely, Louis Althusser, Roland Barthes, Jean-Marie Benoist, Gilles Deleuze, Paul de Man, Michel Foucault, Edmond Jabès, Sarah Kofman, Emmanuel Levinas, Max Loreau, Jean-François Lyotard, Louis Marin, Joseph Riddel, and Michel Servière.[1] Though these texts vary in form, with some being words or letters of condolence, and others memorial essays, eulogies, or funeral orations, they nonetheless share certain traits that make them identifiable as belonging, if not to a clearly defined genre, at least to a delimitable mini-corpus within the corpus of Derrida. In each of these texts, Derrida attempts to continue his decades-long meditation on the structures and ethical implications of death and mourning at the same time as he is undergoing, in a very personal way but also in public, in the public light, the death and mourning of a friend. Though Derrida had argued from quite early on, indeed already in his work on Husserl in the 1950s and 1960s, that the very structure of the trace implies death, and though he had written more recently about how friendship is structured from the very beginning by the possibility at least that one of two friends will see the other die, and so, surviving, will be left to bury, to commemorate, and to mourn, that is, though Derrida had formalized these laws of death and of mourning in numerous texts over the last few decades, he also had to undergo or bear witness to these laws as friends—and there were many of them—went before him, making explicit or effective the structural laws that will have determined all his relationships and friendships from the very beginning.

From the very first of these essays, "The Death*s* of Roland Barthes" (my emphasis), written in 1981, up to the very last, "Lyotard and *Us*," written in 1999, Derrida was concerned with the relationship between the singularity of death and its inevitable repetition, with what it means to reckon with death, or with the dead, with all those who were once close to us but who are now either only "in us" or infinitely other. *The Work of Mourning* thus gathers together into a single volume a series of until then singular responses to singular deaths. It brings together not those texts that speak of the work of mourning, of phantoms and specters, in a more or less theoretical fashion, but those that enact this work of mourning—and of friendship—in a more explicit way, texts written after the deaths of friends and colleagues to remember their words and deeds, their works and days, and so bear witness to a living relationship with them. It is a volume, then, not simply of Derrida's words or works on the *theme* of mourning, but his own *work* or *labor* of mourning, still legible—and so still at work—in these texts.

In this collection, Derrida continues his long meditation on the alterity and the gaze of the other from Husserl to Levinas by suggesting that mourning has to do with incorporating not exactly the deceased but their gaze, a gaze that makes us responsible before the deceased and that can be responded to only as a kind of absolute imperative. It is this gaze that makes all mourning, according to Derrida, at once necessary and impossible, necessary insofar as the work of mourning involves incorporating the friend, coming to terms with his or her death within ourselves, and impossible insofar as the singularity of the friend, that which must be incorporated, the gaze that first calls us to be responsible, always exceeds our subjectivity and our capacity to make the other our own. Hence mourning is always related to the impossible incorporation of a gaze that constitutes for us an infinite demand, a gaze that always hovers between someone and something, the completely identified and the unidentifiable, the knowable and the unknown. Throughout the essays gathered in *The Work of Mourning*, Derrida thus evokes the possibility of an interiorization of what can never be interiorized, of what is always before and beyond us as the source of our responsibility. This is, Derrida writes, the "unbearable paradox of fidelity" (*WM* 159). The look that is "in us" is not ours, as the images within us might seem to be. We look at the dead, who have been reduced to images "in us," and we are looked at by them, but there is no symmetry between these gazes. In other words, writes Derrida, "Ghosts: the concept of the other in the same . . . the completely other, dead, living in me" (*WM* 41–42).

In all these texts Derrida at once thematizes and undergoes this work of mourning, this individual or personal work of mourning, and he does so in each case in a more or less public way, participating in public rituals and using a form if not a genre that is recognizable and repeatable. Indeed, it is only on the basis of this form or genre that all these texts can be delimited within the Derridean corpus and assigned a particular and unique place within it, separate from all the other texts of Derrida that speak of death and of mourning. *The Work of Mourning* is thus a collection of texts that belong to the same "genre"—call it the eulogy, the funeral oration, the memorial essay, or simply "the work of mourning." And yet such "work" is surely not one genre among others but the very one that, it could be argued, opens up the possibility of a social or political space to accommodate all the others. Though Derrida does not try to show in *The Work of Mourning* how politics or the political is related to or perhaps even arises *out of* mourning, out of the rites and rituals of mourning, he has written of these larger stakes in many other places, from *Glas* to *Specters of Marx* to *Aporias*. In the last, for example, he writes: "In an economic, elliptic, hence dogmatic way, I would say that there is no politics without an organization of the time and space of mourning, without a topolitology of the sepulcher, without an anamnesic and thematic relation to the spirit as ghost" (*AP* 61–62). And in the long essay in *The Work of Mourning* devoted to Jean-François Lyotard, Derrida speaks of Lyotard's own analyses, in *The Differend* and elsewhere, of the political dimensions of the funeral oration. Since Plato's *Menexenus*, or since the funeral oration of Pericles that Plato parodies in this dialogue, politics would seem to be related to, or founded in, mourning. In the Athenian context, for example, it is related to a rhetoric of mourning that, for Lyotard, tries to complete or else foreclose mourning by lifting death up, sublating it in the fulfillment and glory of the "beautiful death."

The genre of the funeral oration is thus more than a powerful genre within an already constituted social and political context; it is the genre that helps consolidate if not constitute the power of that context, with all the promises and risks this entails. In his 1999 essay "Lyotard and *Us*," written for a conference commemorating the one-year anniversary of Lyotard's death, Derrida analyzes in detail an enigmatic phrase about mourning that Lyotard wrote in 1990 in an issue of a journal dedicated to the work of Derrida. The phrase consists of seven words in French, *il n'y aura pas de deuil*, shortened to just five in English, "there shall be no mourning." Derrida spends much of the essay turning round this phrase in a way that resembles Lyotard's own analyses of phrase regimens. In the wake of Lyotard's death, this elliptical phrase could be heard either as a description or perhaps as a prediction of what *will* happen or what was bound to happen after the death of Lyotard or some other, "there shall be no mourning," in other words, "wait and see, there will be no mourning, no one will mourn," or else as a wish, desire, or prescription, "there shall be no mourning," "I would prefer that there be no mourning," or even as a prohibition or order, "there shall be no mourning," "I forbid you to mourn." Derrida then goes on in the essay to argue through a reading of Lyotard's 1983 book *The Differend* that there are two other instances in which Lyotard, without explicitly uttering the word *mourning*, in effect tells us that there is or shall be no mourning. The first is the instance of the "beautiful death," the death extolled by Pericles in his funeral oration, or else by Socrates in his pastiche of that oration in the *Menexenus*. The second, around which so much of Lyotard's work in general and *The Differend* in particular revolves, is "Auschwitz"—the exact opposite of the beautiful death, that is, the opposite of a death undergone for the sake of the city or some higher good. As Lyotard put it in *The Differend*, " 'Auschwitz' is the forbiddance of the beautiful death."[2] Though opposites with regard to the meaning of death, or meaning in death, the one assigning an ultimate meaning to death and the other evacuating all meaning from it, both the beautiful death and Auschwitz give us no reason to mourn; both at once describe and prescribe that "there shall be no mourning."

But rather than follow here Lyotard's brilliant analyses of the Greek beautiful death and of "Auschwitz," or Derrida's rereading of these in *The Work of Mourning*, I would like to turn instead, as I announced earlier, to two different though related examples, one from the same Greek period Lyotard discusses and one from the twentieth century, two examples of collective mourning, two inscriptions, I will argue, of "there shall be no mourning," namely, the regulation of mourning in Plato's *Laws* and, closer to us, the consecration of history's remains in the Tomb of the Unknown Soldier in Arlington National Cemetery.

༄

Like the *Republic*, Plato's *Laws* attempts to think nothing less than the social organizations, arrangements, practices, rituals and, of course, *laws* by which the members of a *polis* should lead their lives from the cradle to the grave—or, actually, since the Athenian prescribes both a gymnastic regimen for pregnant women and ways of treating ghosts—from the womb to well beyond the tomb. The *Laws* is thus an exemplary text for demonstrating Derrida's claim that "there is no politics without an organization of the time and space of mourning, without a topolitology of the sepulcher." Numerous passages in the *Laws* are thus devoted to regulating the form, appearance, size, and duration of the rites or rituals of mourning. Most of these are grouped together near the end of the twelfth and final book of the dialogue—a book devoted, we might say, to last things, to the night synod that will preserve and maintain the polis and to the burial of the dead who, as we shall see, will serve as the polis's ultimate sanction or guarantor. My hypothesis in reading the *Laws* will thus be that, for Plato, the banner under which the well-regulated individual and polis must live is always, to cite Derrida citing Lyotard: "There shall be no mourning." Because mourning is a threat to both the individual and the state, to the individual because it convinces us that the body is more important than the soul and to the state because it puts private or family interests above the interests of the state, the rites of mourning must be tightly regulated and controlled. For both political and philosophical reasons, the city and its citizens must be convinced or taught to get over death and, thus, to get over mourning. This will be done not by prohibiting rites of mourning altogether but by controlling, converting, or transforming these rites, or, since Derrida uses the word in his analysis of Lyotard, *sublating* them into the beautiful death or, indeed, into the philosophical death.

In the *Laws*, mourning is limited or transformed in at least four ways. First, because the right or privilege to mourn or to be mourned is tacitly granted by the state, certain actions on the part of an individual can lead to that privilege being revoked. Those convicted of the willful murder of a parent, child, or sibling are thus, argues the Athenian stranger, to be executed and cast out of the city "naked" on a "crossroad," their corpse left unburied (*ataphon*; 873b).[3] The suicide, though allowed to be buried in a tomb, will have no headstone to mark the name, the "nameless" body being buried on the borders of the city, in a kind of barren no-man's-land (873d; see also 909c), as if the limits to mourning or to the rituals of mourning were already being thought in conjunction with the limits or borders of the polis.[4] For some, then, for the worst kinds of criminals, such as those who kill someone of their own blood, there shall be no mourning, no rituals of mourning, not on the part of the city and not on the part of individuals in the city.

If rituals of mourning are limited or prohibited in the case of individuals whose conduct is unbecoming to the city, it makes sense that the converse should be granted and even proscribed in the case of individuals who have performed heroic or admirable deeds for the city. In the final book of the *Laws*, we are given prescriptions for how the examiners or inspectors of the state, those most important to maintaining and overseeing its laws, are to be buried. Adorned all in white, the only color appropriate to the gods, these leaders are to be buried in an underground tomb of long-lasting stone whereupon a grove of trees is to be planted in memory of their service (947e; see 956a). They are to be given a full military funeral, with everyone dressed in military garb and young boys singing the "national anthem [*to patrion melos*]" (947c), hymns of praise and celebration being the only sanctioned musical accompaniment for such occasions. Competitions in music, gymnastics, and horse racing are then to be held every year in honor of these men (947e).

Clearly, Plato envisions using the rites of mourning—or, really, the rites of remembering the dead, ceremonies commemorating and celebrating the service of the dead to the city—as ways of consolidating the body politic, techniques for unifying it around the ghosts of leaders past. The burials of public men are thus celebrated and recalled yearly in an attempt to set before the citizens models of virtuous conduct, particularly with regard to death and the dead. At the same time, then, as they provide explicit models of virtue, they also provide implicit models of the proper way of treating the dead; instead of mourning the deaths of the virtuous in the city, citizens are to celebrate their lives. So even here, even in the case of those who deserve the citizens' honor and thus, it seems, deserve to be mourned, their deaths lamented, there shall be no lamentation and no mourning.

For the worst citizens, the worst criminals, there shall be no rituals of mourning, no burial, while for the best citizens, the leaders of the polis, there shall be celebration rather than mourning. For those in between these two extremes of virtue, those who die neither criminals nor heroes, mourning will be allowed—or tolerated—but it will be limited, the ideal still being, it seems, the vanishing point at which there shall be *no* mourning. Because, as the Athenian says, for all who have grown up and grown old in a law-abiding life an "end" will come "in the course of nature [*kata physin*]," the death of the body, as a natural event, must not be given undue importance (958d-e). A series of regulations is thus implemented to minimize the potentially harmful effects of the dead on the living. Rule number one: get rid of the body as quickly as possible; the body of the deceased, the lifeless body, a site for potential mourning, should thus remain in the house only long enough for one to be *certain* it is dead, with the burial usually taking place three days later (959a). Second, tombs, whether great or small, are not to be put on tillable land but on land suitable "to receive and hide [*dekhomena kryptein*] the bodies of the dead with the least hurt to the living" (958d-e). In addition, the memorial mound erected over the dead is to be limited in size to what can be accomplished by five men in five days, and the stone pillars shall not be "more than is required to hold . . . a eulogy of the dead man's life consisting of not more than four heroic lines" (958e).[5]

Though it is "unseemly," as the lawmaker admits—but probably also almost impossible and counterproductive—to prohibit weeping for the dead, the state can and must nonetheless control its *appearance* in public. Hence loud mourning and lamentation *outside* the house is forbidden, and the dead cannot be carried on open roads and lamented in the streets. The funeral party must thus meet *outside* the city before daybreak (960a). Though citizens will no doubt mourn—and little save education can prevent this—either inside the house or outside the city, there shall be no mourning *outside* the house *inside* the city. Though we are not at the point of completely prohibiting mourning, its scope and public display are severely limited—or else displaced. There can be mourning, but only outside the city, or only by proxy, with mourners hired from abroad, the implication of the Athenian being that it would be unseemly for a citizen to do the mourning himself (see 800e).

Mourning is thus always done within the limits set by the city and for the good of the city. The people of the city, says the Athenian, must be constantly reminded that they are but "creatures of a day [ephēmeroi]" and that both they themselves and their property belong not to them but to their "family line [genous]," both past and future, while their "family and its property belong to the state" (923a). Hence the laws will not allow a dying man to make a will that is contrary to what is best for his state or his family. The limits of mourning and the terms of succession are thus established by the state for the good of the state and the good of generations past and future.

All these limits and conditions to mourning proposed by the Athenian meet with the general approval of his Cretan and Spartan interlocutors, both of whom come from timocratic states with customs, if not laws, already resembling these, and sometimes in stark contrast to more extravagant Athenian ways. Indeed, these three ways of promoting, if not instituting, that there shall be no mourning—prohibiting burial for certain crimes, celebrating rather than lamenting the deaths of state leaders, and, finally, minimizing the deaths of members of the state for the ultimate good of the state—are hardly unique to Plato. One could cite any number of passages from Xenophon or others extolling, say, a belief in the glorious or beautiful death as a sacrifice for the polis that should be celebrated rather than lamented (see, e.g., Xenophon's *Hellenica* 6.4.16). But what is rather unique and new, I believe, is the ultimate philosophical justification Plato gives for such sacrifice—the fourth and final inscription in the *Laws* of "there shall be no mourning."

In Plato, or at least in a certain Plato, there is the belief that in giving oneself over to death, and even when doing so for the state, one is not merely sacrificing one's individual life for the continuance and survival of the state itself, or for one's own individual *kleos* or glory in the state for generations to come—though these too may be true—but simply recognizing the proper, natural relationship between the body and the soul. For those who understand the true relationship between the body and the soul, for those who understand that the soul is immortal and that, as the *Laws* puts it, the things of the soul are to be honored above those of the body, there is no need to prohibit mourning because there simply shall be—there simply *will be*—no mourning. As the Athenian succinctly puts it in the *Laws*, in a formulation that recalls Socrates' rebuke of those beginning to mourn him in the *Phaedo* (see 63b) and his seeming indifference to the fate of his own body after his death, the corpse is but a "soulless altar [*apsychon . . . bōmon*]" to the gods of the underworld, on which one must spend in moderation (959d). In other words—and this is the great reversal we call Platonism—the body is but an appearance, an image or *eidōlon* of the soul, in the end, little more than a ghost. The Athenian says on behalf of his lawgiver in the *Laws*:

> As in other matters it is right to trust the lawgiver, so too must we believe him when he asserts that the soul is wholly superior to the body, and that in actual life what makes each of us to be what he is is nothing else than the soul, while the body is a semblance which attends on each of us, it being well said that the bodily corpses are images [*eidōla*] of the dead, but that which is the real self of each of us [*ton de onta hēmōn hekaston ontōs*], [is what] we term the immortal soul [*athanaton . . . psychēn*]. (959a-b)

For Plato, then, giving up the ghost means not, as it seems to have for Homer, releasing or breathing out the spirit or soul, a kind of ghost, from the body but, rather, leaving behind the ghost that *is* the body. It thus follows that one should not spend extravagantly on burials, for the "flesh [*sarkōn*]" one is burying, the Athenian affirms, is but the image of the friend or relative who has departed in fulfillment of his "destiny [*moiran*]" (959c). This would seem to be the final justification, beyond or in addition to any political expediency, for transforming mourning into celebration, the result, I would argue, of subordinating an ethics of mourning to, and organizing the politics of mourning around, an ontology and epistemology marked by a rigorous opposition between being and becoming, the soul and the body. For once one *knows* the difference between being and becoming, the soul and the body, once one *knows* this on the ontological level and is not simply persuaded of it by the guardians of the state, then there can be no mourning, there *will be* no mourning, while for those who do not yet know this the prescription must always remain—for the good of the state but also for what is beyond the state—"there *shall be* no mourning." To put it in the terms of Derrida's final interview, once one *learns how to live* and, thus, learns how to die, that is to say, learns what dying means, then one knows why there is no longer any real reason to mourn and why "there shall be no mourning."

ॐ

I turn now to my second example, more current and closer to home, so as to "bring closure," as we in the United States are so fond of saying, to this analysis of the politics of mourning. There are many examples I could have chosen to try to say something about how we in the United States, as families, as communities, and as a nation try to come to terms with death and the dead, how we try to forgo mourning by ritualizing it, but few are as striking as the dedication of a Tomb of the Unknown Soldier—where all Americans, at least theoretically, are asked to collaborate or labor together in mourning the death of someone who has died, we tell ourselves, protecting our freedoms and liberties, someone particular whose name we do not know, someone nameless who stands as a symbol for all those we have lost.

I have also chosen this example because of a personal memory—one of the strongest and strangest memories I have of collective mourning, a memory of the televised ceremony on Memorial Day 1984 of the dedication of the Tomb of the Unknown Soldier for the War in Vietnam. I still recall very vividly sitting in a small tavern in Boston around noontime with just a couple of other patrons and a bartender in the room, all strangers to me and, I think, to one another, watching on TV without comment the ceremony at Arlington National Ceremony during which the unidentified remains of a U.S. serviceman were consecrated as part of the Tomb of the Unknowns, containing the unidentified remains of soldiers from three previous American wars, the first two World Wars and the Korean War. The setting was something right out of the *Laws*, flags everywhere, officers decked out in full military regalia, a single coffin with an American flag draped over it, and, to top it all off, presiding over it all, the American Pericles, President Ronald Reagan, larger than life in this ceremony of death, secular leader of the free world, at once president and priest and intercessor for us, all of us watching him on TV, with the Judeo-Christian God. With one hand outstretched toward this God and the other turned downward toward the casket, Reagan concluded his speech by speaking in our name, or in the name of our nation, to this nameless soldier, speaking to him in the second person without a proper name, appealing to God to take him in glory from this mortal realm. Presenting the Medal of Honor to this unknown soldier, Reagan concluded: "Let us, if we must, debate the lessons learned [from this war] at some other time: Today we simply say with pride, 'Thank you, dear son. May God cradle you in His loving arms. We present to you our nation's highest award, the Medal of Honor, for service above and beyond the call of duty in action with the enemy during the Vietnam Era.'"[6]

Part of the reason I can still hear the echo of these words, the ghost of Ronald Reagan, more than twenty years later is, I think, that I heard them in public, that I had to check my emotions as I heard them because I was in public, and because I could tell by the attention and the silence in the tavern that my emotions were shared, profoundly shared. And shared, no doubt, by millions like us across the nation, a collective mourning filmed before a live audience but staged and scripted for satellite transmission to TV screens from coast to coast. Though my fellow patrons and patriots there in Boston were probably just as cynical as I was about these kinds of ritual events, and especially about the Vietnam War, though we all saw the flags and pomp for what they were, though we were all well aware that the great communicator before us was no intercessor or priest for our nation but simply someone who knew how to play one on TV, we were all deeply moved. Though I had yet to read any of Kathleen Hall Jamieson's brilliant work on Reagan's rhetoric, I think I already knew some of its guiding principles.[7] And yet, despite this knowledge, I was moved, moved by the ceremony, moved by the death of a young man, and yet also—because this second thought came quickly on the heels of the first—moved and deeply disturbed by the terrifying thought that with this one ceremony all the horror and uncertainty, all the lies and deceptions of Vietnam, had been recuperated, lifted up, transformed into a beautiful or glorious death. As if—and this was clearly its intention—all the protests, all the soul-searching, all the criticisms, all the anxiety of all our *Apocalypse Nows* had been put into the service of our national interest, the remains of the unidentified victim of the Vietnam War joining those of three other wars in the American pantheon called Arlington National Cemetery. Though I did not put it in these terms at the time, I remember thinking that, from now on, when it comes to Vietnam, *there shall be no mourning.* Assuming that there was ever a time for mourning Vietnam, it had been proclaimed over by presidential decree. From now on, I thought, it would do no good mourning Vietnam, for with the burial of those unidentified remains everything in us that could not be identified, all our doubts and all our fears, all our anxieties and uncertainties, would be memorialized, glorified, and, thereby, forgotten—sublated by presidential decree and a Medal of Honor.

(Let me add here parenthetically that I felt a similar clash of emotions, and there is no coincidence in this, during the 2002 Super Bowl pregame and half-time shows as images of the falling towers and ground zero—images that, after their endless repetition, had been removed for several weeks from our collective image screens—were juxtaposed with shots of former presidents, the statue commemorating Iwo Jima, and a tombstone bearing the name "unknown" at Gettysburg. We were even treated to a reconstitution of the signing of the Declaration of Independence, complete with costumes from the period, and to a reading of the Declaration by former presidents and, yes, present football stars. Watching that spectacle, I felt the same mixed emotions, the same fascination and the same horror, as one of the two remaining Beatles and the Irish U2 played tributes to freedom American style and as the names of those killed on September 11 were projected onto two enormous panels behind U2, which were raised slowly up to the roof of the Super Dome and then allowed to collapse quickly down to the ground like the crumbling towers. And I said to myself that in a few short months we had done such a fine job remembering these events, such a good job drawing or fabricating parallels between these events and others that have marked our nation—World War II, the Civil War, the War of Independence—that we were well on our way to forgetting them, to transforming our collective dirge of mourning into that triumphant chant that made its debut, I believe, during the U.S. victory in hockey over the Soviet Union in the 1980 Olympics, that collective chant "U-S-A, U-S-A, U-S-A." And I told myself that, despite the many declarations of its imminent demise, the nation-state still remains pretty effective at glorifying, recuperating, lifting up, and putting to work the blood that is spilled or the bones that are buried in its soil. So good had we become at remembering, so wrapped up had we become in it, that we were clearly well on our way to forgetting. As Lyotard once put it, memorial history *nous emballe*—it wraps us up and gets us wrapped up, wraps us up in a flag and gets us wrapped up in a national ideology—like the one I saw being staged and orchestrated during that 2002 Superbowl half-time show and during that Memorial Day ceremony at Arlington National Cemetery some eighteen years before.)

And yet, over the years, I have continued to think back on this extraordinary event in my own life and in the life of our nation. I have often thought that, despite my concerns that the Reagan rhetoric of mourning overcame in a single gesture all the uncertainties that surfaced during what Reagan euphemistically called the "Vietnam Era," the fact that a tomb exists in our national cemetery commemorating the *remains* of *unidentified* or *unknown* soldiers leaves open a gaping wound at the very heart of the glorious death. Though they are buried as symbols of other unknown soldiers buried elsewhere, and so represent to some extent the sacrifices of all those killed in war, whether identified or unidentified, these unclaimed pieces of matter, these bones without a proper name, remain—an unidentifiable specter, somewhere between a who and a what, which haunts our collective mourning and, by resisting our knowledge and our narratives, makes it interminable. These remains remain to claim us, I believe, in some very powerful way, reminding us that the separation of the dead from everything that remains for us the living, and so the separation of the dead from their very *name* and *history* remains for us more palpable here, the absence more present and more pressing.

Though there have no doubt always been soldiers missing in action, soldiers never found, or soldiers whose remains were found months or years later and so could not be identified, it is only since the beginning of the last century, after World War I, that the United States has had an official Tomb of the Unknowns (though there were similar tombs of the unknown for soldiers killed during the Civil War).[8] Due in part to advances in technology during the First World War, which could so ravage the human body as to make identification almost immediately impossible, the first unknown soldier was laid in the Tomb of the Unknowns in 1921, the remains of that soldier being chosen from among more than 1,600 other unidentified remains. In May 1958, when the remains of an unknown soldier from the Second World War and one from the Korean War were buried, there were more than 8,500 sets of unidentifiable remains to choose from for World War II, and for the Korean War, a war with far fewer American casualties, still more than 800 sets of unidentified remains. And choose the Department of Defense did, using as its criterion the standard of so-called "best remains," those where at least 80 percent of the body was recovered, the idea being, it seems, to choose remains that were as intact as possible, as identifiable as possible, without being positively identifiable as someone in particular.

But then came Vietnam, where advances in technology that could so mutilate the body as to render it unidentifiable were countered by other technologies that made it easier to retrieve and identify human remains. And so, according to the website of Arlington National Cemetery, due to the "prompt evacuation of the dead and wounded by helicopter, improved military record-keeping, and scientific advances in identification, there had never been more than four Vietnam unknowns at the Central Identification Laboratory in Hawaii at any one time." The technology that made victims unidentifiable in the first place now contributed to making them more and more easily identifiable, and not only just after death but many months and years later. Thus the work of identification continued long after the war, so that by 1982 there were but two unidentified sets of remains from the Vietnam War, and the question was raised whether to place one of these into the Tomb of the Unknowns. With the political stakes so high, interests weighed in on both sides. While groups like the Veterans of Foreign Wars and the American Legion wished, along with the Reagan administration, to commemorate one of these sets of remains and so symbolically include the Vietnam War in the twentieth century's list of honorable or glorious war efforts, other groups, like the

National League of POW-MIA Families fought against such a selection, fearing that the United States would be less committed in its efforts to locate and identify those still missing in action. (One need only recall, I mention again parenthetically, Plato's and Xenophon's accounts of how Socrates almost got himself killed over his unwillingness to participate in the unjust prosecution and putting to death of the generals held responsible for not recovering the Athenian war dead from the waters of the Aegean Sea after the battle of Arginusae.[9] When bodies are not recovered, when the state cannot manage and organize mourning well, one can be sure that heads will roll.) Though the Department of Defense had followed the orders of Congress in 1973 to construct a Tomb for the Vietnam Unknown, the tomb had remained empty. And so the pressure mounted to identify one of the two unidentifiable remains as being those of the Unknown Soldier of Vietnam.

With just two to choose from, and with techniques for identification constantly improving, the decision over which one to bury was made in large part on the basis of which one appeared *least* likely to be identified in the future. This meant that the previous standard of "best remains" had to be ignored or, actually, reversed, the search for the best remains turning into a search for the worst, that is, for those in the worst shape. Because the then-new technique of photo superimposition gave hope that one of the two sets of remains would one day be identified,[10] the remaining set of remains, those referred to as X-26, came to be designated. They consisted of only six bones—four ribs, a pelvis, and a humerus, a mere 3 percent of the body—unidentifiable, and thus appropriate for inclusion in the Tomb of the Unknowns, and yet identifiable enough to ensure that these were indeed the bones of an American serviceman, the other necessary condition for the Tomb. Unknown, then, in terms of name, rank, and serial number, these remains were not completely without a profile. Though they held the least promise of ever being identifiable and attached to a proper name, it was nonetheless determined at the Central Identification Laboratory that they were the remains of a "Caucasoid man of average muscularity, whose height had been approximately 68.4 inches and who had been between 26 and 33 years old."

Not completely identifiable, though identified like the other remains in the Tomb of the Unknowns as belonging to a man, a soldier, an American soldier, these remains without any proper name were designated those of the unknown soldier of Vietnam. To ensure that the remains would remain unidentified in perpetuity, that is, as an Army spokesperson said, "To preserve the casualty's anonymity," the "Army ordered all records pertaining to the case destroyed." A spokesperson would say only: "He's an American. We know he died in the conflict, but we just don't know who he is. We used every trick, but we cannot match him to any known missing soldier. We think we can safely say this is a true Unknown from the Vietnam War."

And so they were entombed, those six bones, laid in the tomb amidst the controversy I have recalled, during the ceremony I spoke of and still recall so vividly today in its televised version on May 28, 1984. They were entombed on Memorial Day 1984, and there they would remain, it was thought, forever, unidentified and unknown. As the inscription on the Tomb of the Unknowns in Arlington National Cemetery reads, "Here rests in honored glory an American soldier known but to God." Unknown to us, then, but not to God—who, according to this happy hypothesis, is able to recognize, identify, lift up, and glorify any unknown and who, in His omnipotence and omniscience, is alone in this ability. Hence these remains were entombed and subsequently visited by hundreds of thousands of people a year, visited, honored, and respected in their anonymity for some fourteen years—up until the moment, that is, when God's knowledge became our own, that is, when these remains were overtaken in their eternal repose by the powerful technologies of identification that emerged at the end of the last century and that are in the process of transforming just about everything having to do with our human condition, including the meaning of life and death and the possibilities for mourning, in this new century and millennium.

Many Americans can no doubt still recall "the rest of the story," which received a good deal of U.S. media attention at the time, while many others, living in the genome age, could easily anticipate it: because of where the remains designated X-26 were found and when it was thought the death took place, hypotheses had long been formed about the possible identity of X-26, hypotheses that could be neither adequately proved nor disproved until the development of mitochondrial DNA testing in the mid-1990s, which would allow comparison between the DNA of the remains and that of the presumed relatives of the deceased, particularly those in the matrilineal line. In May 1998, therefore, at the behest of the Blassie family from St. Louis, which had long suspected the remains in the Tomb of the Unknown Soldier to be those of their son and sibling, Michael Joseph Blassie, missing in Vietnam since 1972, the remains of the unknown soldier were disinterred, the "hallowed ground" disturbed, as Defense Secretary William Cohen put it, "with deep reluctance."[11] DNA testing proved that the remains of X-26 were indeed those of Blassie, and so they were sent to St. Louis and buried there in July 1998, on the banks of the Mississippi, beneath a simple white tombstone—limited in size, I should add, by cemetery regulations—that included the inscription, "Michael Joseph Blassie, Killed in Action; Unknown Soldier, May 28, 1984, May 14, 1998."[12]

So ended, it would seem, the epoch of the unknown soldier, which, as I have tried to suggest and will try to spell out more clearly to conclude, is not one epoch or one ritual among others. The Department of Defense has decided that remains will never again be designated those of an unknown soldier unless "it can be unequivocally assured, in perpetuity, that the remains of the American serviceman would be forever unidentifiable." But "given the advances in DNA analysis techniques," a Defense Department spokesperson has conceded, "I don't think we will be able to have complete confidence that any set of remains . . . would remain unknown forever." As long as there are remains, it seems, we will eventually be able to identify, to put a name to the body, or to a piece of body, however small. From now on, there will be no remains unaccounted for. There will no doubt continue to be men and women missing in action, bodies lost or vaporized right down to the last strand of DNA, but there will no longer be unidentifiable remains, that is, remains any more substantial than ashes.

(Indeed it is now thought that some of the victims killed in the World Trade Towers will never be identified, every trace of DNA having been destroyed by temperatures that exceeded those of a crematorium. It is thus difficult to call these "unidentifiable remains," which is why, in an article in *The New Yorker* from October 1, 2001, Victor Weedn, the founder of the Armed Forces DNA Identification Laboratory, the very lab that identified the remains of Michael Joseph Blassie, says that, in his opinion, there would be no "Tomb of the Unknown New Yorker in lower Manhattan." "I don't believe it would be palatable," he said, "I don't think the government could stand the pressure not to identify everyone."[13] In an attempt to help the families of victims avoid what is called "ambiguous grief" or "ambiguous mourning," extraordinary measures were already being taken in September 2001 to test what may have amounted to hundreds of thousands of tissue samples found in the rubble. But as of May 30, 2002, the day when the clean-up operation at ground zero was officially declared finished, there were still some 1,700 unidentified victims. And so analyses continue to this day, like the work of mourning itself. One thing, however, is certain: politics and mourning can no longer be thought without these new technologies of life and death, technologies that provide the only means of distinguishing one victim from another, or, indeed, a friend from an enemy, which is why, as a *New York Times* article reported,[14] victims' families had to scour their homes for microscopic pieces of their loved ones left on tooth- and hairbrushes or on old clothing, and it is why federal authorities have tried to obtain DNA samples from the family of Bin Laden so that, one day, a bone fragment or piece of burned or decomposed flesh might find a match in these samples and prove to us that Bin Laden is indeed finally and officially dead.)

Between the identifiable, the single strand of DNA to which a name can, in principle, be attached, and unidentifiable ashes, there can be no remains—there *shall be* no remains. What remains beyond ashes will always, it seems, be identified, in some sense named, understood, repatriated, incorporated into our history and our narratives; there will be no remains known but to God. If mourning is an attempt, as Derrida has argued, to dialectize the undialectizable, to incorporate what cannot be incorporated, if mourning always negotiates between the infidelity of not mourning insofar as we leave the dead outside us, leave them to their alterity with no attempt to recognize, identify, remember, and incorporate them, and the infidelity of not mourning insofar as we have identified too much, understood too much, taken in and comprehended an alterity or remains that cannot and should not become part of us or our history, then mourning remains always somewhere between these two "there shall be no mournings." If mourning must always endure the aporias of knowing and not knowing, of identifying and not being able to identify, of getting at what cannot and can never be identified through what can, then the Tomb of the Unknowns in Arlington National Cemetery may have been a good symbol of mourning—or perhaps something much less, and thus much more, than a symbol—despite Ronald Reagan's attempt to recover this symbol and so dissolve these aporias. This Tomb of the Unknowns, which recalls so many atrocities of the twentieth century, has the special merit of marking a site between two epochs of collective mourning, two different epochs, one where the body retained a certain opacity and resistance to knowledge and science, even if it remained vulnerable in its very namelessness to the strategies of glorification and of the beautiful death, and one where the body is readable and thus identifiable, nameable, recuperable, or so we believe, by our narratives and our history, right down to a single strand of DNA. Though the two epochs of mourning can be differentiated by the advances in technology that have so radically changed our relationship to life and death, both will have provided strategies for the identification and incorporation of the dead into the body politic, whether through narratives of the beautiful death or through the simple inscription of a name on a headstone. For both, the political injunction will have always been "there shall be no mourning"—certainly no interminable mourning. There may be memory and remembrance, or what we call memory and remembrance, and perhaps rituals of celebration and recognition, but if mourning is, as Derrida argues, related to the incorporation of something that can never be completely identified or incorporated, there shall be no mourning as such. Though this is hardly a plea for "ambiguous mourning," hardly a suggestion that every step *not* be taken to identify the remains of those killed in war or in any other kind of atrocity, I do wish to suggest, as a reader of Derrida, that every mourning is and should remain "ambiguous," that every mourning that succeeds too well is doomed to fail, while the mourning given over to failure—like the mourning of an unknown—is exemplary of a certain kind of success. In matters of mourning, it might just be necessary that we, as Americans, learn just a bit better how not to do it so well.

The Tomb of the Unknowns thus stands at a kind of crossroad, a very literal no-man's-land, between identification and nonidentification, the technologies of life and those of death, between the interests of the family and those of the state, materiality and the symbolic, the corpse and the corpus, as Plato would say in the *Gorgias*, the *sōma* and the *sēma*. Between two different epochs where the political injunction is always "there shall be no mourning," something about the Tomb of the Unknowns *resists*, something that remains buried in the past century and will remain unknown even to God, something that resists our technologies and our knowledge: an absolute remains, *the* absolute remains, inaccessible to our gaze even as it calls us to attention and to respect, a tomb even more inaccessible and more unknown within the space opened up by the Tomb of the Unknowns. And that leaves me with the odd thought, the perplexing conclusion, that, from the perspective at least of this exemplary collective ritual of remembrance called the consecration of the Tomb of the Unknown Soldier, the twentieth century, this time of the unknowns, would lie at a critical crossroad between two epochs of state or collective mourning. Insofar as the twentieth century still has remains that cannot be identified, and insofar as it will have memorialized those unknown remains if not all that must remain unknown in them, it still holds open a gap between the name and the body, between someone and something, the corpus of history and the corpse. In other words, the twentieth century will have posed for us *the question of remains as such*, a question of what exceeds our history and our science, of what resists all our attempts to cut our losses, a question that, I believe, still remains to be thought even if we today in the twenty-first century are in danger of forgetting it. The question of remains—*that* is what remains, what *shall* remain, and remain for mourning—assuming that we can still identify it.

As Derrida himself once wrote in a most economic and penetrating fashion back during that same "Vietnam era," *L'autre—laisse tomber le reste*, that is, "The other—leave(s) the remains," "The other—lets the remains fall," and then, once again in *Glas*, in two words engraved on that text like an inscription on the tomb of the Tomb of the Unknowns: *Tombe, reste*.[15]

10

Comme si, comme ça

Following Derrida on the Phantasms
of the Self, the State, and a Sovereign God

Those of us today still *following* Derrida, either in the sense of coming after him, following after him, or continuing to read and study him, have no doubt all asked ourselves on occasion over the past few years what Jacques Derrida would have done or thought about this or that, how he would have responded to some discourse or event. Though we speculate and, I think, should continue to speculate, since that is part of following him, we will never know—and must not claim to know. How, for example, would Jacques Derrida have responded to a subtitle that begins "Following Derrida"? We simply cannot know, though were I to speculate, and I think we must speculate, I believe he would have tried to turn us away from thinking of ourselves as simply the heirs of a bygone past, or else as those who simply come along after him as his followers or, worse, his disciples. He would have turned us instead, I would like to believe, toward a promise of the future that we would in fact be following or trying to follow after, a promise that goes by the name "Derrida" even if he, Jacques Derrida, was himself always following after it. In short, he would have turned us toward the future as the best way of warning us against making of him a father or a master or an icon, the best way of preventing us from thinking that he himself *embodied* the promise that he himself was following, the best way, in the end, of dispelling any *phantasm* about him.[1]

In this chapter I would like to pull together many of the conclusions of the previous few chapters in order to ask about the nature of the phantasm in general in Derrida's work and, as I conclude, the dangers of turning Derrida or his memory into a phantasm. For if we must continue to honor the thought and memory of Derrida by reading him, by following him, we surely must not do so by submitting everything we say and do to his authority or his sovereign gaze, by treating him *as if* he were here, watching and judging us, passing judgment in advance over what we say and do. To treat the memory of Derrida in this way would run the risk of turning him into that which his entire work, from beginning to end, attempted to interrupt, namely, a phantasm, an *as if*, a *comme si*, that tries always to pass itself off as an *as so* or an *as such*, a *comme ça*. From *comme si* to *comme ça*, from the *comme si* of a speculative fiction to the *comme ça* of an inflexible law—that, as we shall see, is the nature, the conventional but seemingly natural nature, of a phantasm, the kind that Jacques Derrida spent so much of his work warning us against by calling into question and submitting to vigilant critique.

I will concentrate in this penultimate chapter on three such phantasms, which are also three forms of sovereignty—those of the self, the nation-state, and God. We have already seen these three forms of sovereignty in several earlier chapters, but I return to them here in order to explore Derrida's insistence, especially in some of his later texts, that we must ultimately relinquish sovereignty, the phantasm of sovereignty and the sovereignty of the phantasm, in the name of the very thing that has traditionally been identified with it, that is, in the name of the *unconditional*. The fictions and phantasmatic powers of sovereignty must be given up, Derrida suggests, in the name of the unconditionality of the event or the unconditional coming of the other, since without such a renunciation there *can* be no ethics and there *will* be no future. Though sovereignty—be it the sovereignty of a self-determining or self-legislating individual, of a self-sufficient or self-founding nation-state, or of a single, all-powerful God—is today undergoing critique or deconstruction of its own accord or in accordance with what Derrida has called, as we saw in Chapter 7, an ineluctable "autoimmune process," this deconstruction of the phantasm nonetheless remains for us an essential task. Following Derrida's thinking about the phantasms of self, state, and a sovereign God, I will conclude that at a time such as ours, when the power of the phantasm shows no signs of abating, a thought like Derrida's—the haunting thought of Derrida—becomes all the more vital. Though the 1970s and 1980s will continue to be characterized by the theory textbooks as the "heyday of deconstruction," I would like to suggest that now may really be the time to be "following Derrida." I say this, I hope, I wager, without phantasm or illusion, even if, in the end, the ruses of the phantasm are such that we can never really *know* this for sure.

Specter, ghost, phantom, spectrality, fantomaticity, hauntology, phantasm: these words are, as we know, at the center of Derrida's work, and already from the beginning, even if they have the appearance of becoming more explicit and central in the final two decades of his life.[2] I will not rehearse here the relationship between what Derrida calls dissemination, différance, or iterability and spectrality or hauntology. Others, such as Kas Saghafi, have already done this work, and done it in an exemplary fashion.[3] It thus no longer needs to be shown how Derrida, almost from the beginning, spoke of the "spectral errancy of words," of the "ineluctable originarity of the specter," of a *revenance* of the mark that "does not befall words by accident" but conditions them "from their first emergence," of the trace as being related from its first inscription to an originary mourning and a certain kind of living on (*SQ* 53).

While the notion of the phantasm undoubtably belongs to this same set of words or quasi-concepts, I would like to try to reserve for it a rather special use and status in Derrida's work. I will try to situate this status by asking, first, just what a phantasm is, what contexts it emerges in, what problems—of individual identity formation, nation-station identification, or religious understanding—it helps us to diagnose, and, finally, what promises a critique of the phantasm at the level of the individual, the nation-state, and religion can hold for us today.[4]

Though the notion of the "phantasm" appears in many earlier works, from *Speech and Phenomena* to *Glas*, to name just two, I would like to begin this reading of the phantasm in one of Derrida's most autobiographical works, *Monolingualism of the Other*. Appearing, then, in a genre of writing that typically assumes a coincidence or identity between the one writing and the one being written about, this text introduces, it seems, a certain noncoincidence, nonsimultaneity, or deidentification between the self and itself, the self that is writing and the self being written about. This should come as little surprise, of course, since one of the very first lessons of deconstruction is that a certain difference or distance is necessary to the production of what would seem to come before it, the living presence of a self in absolute proximity to itself, the immediate presence of a self hearing itself speak and so assuming within itself the meaning of a *vouloir dire*. But in *Monolingualism of the Other*, this classic Derridean theme is cast in a slightly different light, that is, in the light of the phantasm. Speaking of the fact that the language one speaks is always the other's and that there is, thus, an inalienable alienation within one's own speech, Derrida writes:

This structure of alienation without alienation, this inalienable alienation, is not only the origin of our responsibility, it also structures the peculiarity and property of language. It institutes the *phenomenon* of hearing-oneself-speak in order to mean-to-say [*pour vouloir dire*]. But here, we must say the *phenomenon* as *phantasm*. Let us refer for the moment to the semantic and etymological affinity that associates the phantasm to the *phainesthai*, to phenomenality, but also to the spectrality of the phenomenon. *Phantasma* is also the phantom, the double, or the ghost. (*MO* 25)

We have here, bundled into one tight paragraph, many of the words I mentioned a moment ago: *phantasm, phantom, ghost, spectrality.* But are these all quasi-synonyms or nonsubstitutable synonyms for the same phenomenon? Derrida ends this passage by speaking of the spectrality of the phenomenon, which is, I take it, the intrinsic possibility of doubling and iteration that makes any phenomenal appearance possible. Spectrality would be one of those nonsynonymous substitutes for what was once called iterability or différance. As for *phantasm*, it comes, as Derrida points out, from the same semantic "family" as *phenomenon*, namely *phainesthai*, meaning "to appear, become apparent or phenomenal." The point would seem to be that iterability or spectrality is the condition of every coming to appear, including the coming to appear of oneself to oneself or the coming to hear oneself speak in a meaning-to-say, or a *vouloir dire*. But this spectrality or "inalienable alienation" then "institutes," Derrida says, "the *phenomenon* of hearing-oneself-speak in order to mean-to-say [*pour vouloir dire*]," that is, it institutes "the *phenomenon* as *phantasm.*" Spectrality would thus seem to be the condition of phenomenality as well as of the particular kind of phenomenon called the *phantasm*. Without having at this point to circumscribe the field of the phantasm in relation to other kinds of phenomena, we can see coming to light one defining characteristic of the phantasm: the phantasm suggests or leads us to believe in a nonalienation of the self from itself in language; it leads us to believe in a coincidence of the self that speaks and the self that hears itself speak in a *vouloir dire*, the immediate apprehension of a self by itself in a *vouloir dire*. The very first phenomenon as phantasm would thus seem to be the phantasm of hearing-oneself-speak in order to mean-to-say. Though the phantasm as phenomenon, as an appearing to the self, always introduces appearance, iterability, and, thus, difference into every self-relation, the phenomenon of the phantasm suggests an expulsion, repression, or purification of this iterability and this difference, that is, in short, of the very phenomenality of the phenomenon. The phantasm is thus both the phenomenon of the phantasm and the suppression or repression of the phantasm *as* phenomenon, the lure of a phantasm, then, beyond the phenomenon—the lure of a phantasm purified of the phenomenon and, as we shall see in a moment, the lure of a phantasm of purity.

Just a few pages later in *Monolingualism of the Other*, Derrida explicitly relates the phantasm to purity and to deconstruction. In the midst of those pages, where Derrida avows that the only purity he ever loved and sought was the purity of the French language, he writes: "I have never ceased calling into question the motif of 'purity' in all its forms," and he then opens a parenthesis to add, "the first impulse of what is called 'deconstruction' carries it toward this 'critique' of the phantasm or of the axiom of purity, or toward the analytical decomposition of a purification that would lead back to the indecomposable simplicity of the origin" (*MO* 46).[5] Deconstruction would thus be, first and foremost, a deconstruction of the phantasm, a deconstruction of any putatively pure origin, indeed, of any phantasm of purity and of any simple, seemingly self-evident or axiomatic, origin, any indivisible, inviolable center.[6]

Now, if one returns to *Speech and Phenomena* and to the critique of pure auto-affection in a meaning-to-say, one will find, I think, all the premises for Derrida's later thinking about the phantasm. While Derrida is careful to point out that Husserl himself distinguishes the transcendental ego from the "formal or metaphysical phantom [*fantôme*] of the empirical ego," Derrida will, through an analysis of language and expression in Husserl, displace the transcendental ego within a more general structure of différance or of what will later come to be known as spectrality.[7] The purity and indivisibility of self-presence will be compromised *not* by the phantom of an empirical ego within the transcendental ego but by a transcendental ego that is shown to be the effect of the phenomenon of expression. By demonstrating, in effect, that the purity of auto-affection, the purity of a self speaking to itself in a *vouloir dire*, is compromised both by the relation to others who first give me my language and by a structure of différance that opens the purity of meaning to repetition and difference, Derrida can argue that "this movement of difference is not something that happens to a transcendental subject; it produces a subject. Auto-affection is not a modality of experience that characterizes a being that would already be itself (*autos*). It produces sameness as self-relation within self-difference; it produces sameness as the nonidentical" (*SP* 82).

The critique or deconstruction of auto-affection, of the putative purity of auto-affection, is thus, one would be tempted to say using a later language, a critique of the phantasm of auto-affection by means of a general theory of spectrality or iterability. But what produces this phantasm, exactly? Derrida gives us some clue in a passage right before the one I just cited:

> *Even while repressing* [*tout en refoulant*] difference by assigning it to the exteriority of the signifiers, Husserl could not fail to recognize its work at the origin of sense and presence. Taking auto-affection as the exercise of the voice, auto-affection supposed that a pure difference comes to divide self-presence. In this pure difference is rooted the possibility of everything *we think we can exclude* [*tout ce qu'on croit pouvoir exclure*] from auto-affection: space, the outside, the world, the body, etc. (*SP* 82; my emphasis)

I have underscored two phrases here: *even while repressing* and *everything we think (or believe) we can exclude*. Repression and belief—we will want to follow the relationship between these and the phantasm in everything that follows. For only these—and especially the latter—will allow us to take into account the force and tenacity of a phantasm that, metaphysically speaking, does not exist but that we *believe* exists, a phantasm that would be nothing other than our belief in a phenomenon that transcends itself, that spontaneously gives rise to itself—like an Immaculate Conception. For any consideration of the phantasm one must emphasize less the ontological status of the phantasm than its staying power, its returning power, I would be tempted to say its *regenerative* power. In a word, one must emphasize the fact that the phantasm lives on, the fact that, to cite an English idiom, it seems always to have "legs."

Auto-affection is thus an effect of difference, not that which precedes and commands it. As Derrida puts it in *Speech and Phenomena*: "Hearing oneself speak is not the inwardness of an inside that is closed in upon itself; it is the irreducible openness in the inside; it is the eye and the world within speech" (*SP* 86). The eye and the world—and, I would add, the possibility of the phantasm—are thus now displaced or inscribed within language. The "phenomenon of language" is, hence, the starting point for Derrida to question, critique, or deconstruct the phenomenon of the phantasm, the phenomenon of a phantasm that makes us believe in a phenomenon that can do without phenomenality, iterability, or spectrality. Just after invoking, on the final page of *Speech and Phenomena*, the flight of Icarus, who, like the *phonē*, rises up toward the "sun of presence" and is, thus, fated to fall, Derrida writes: "And contrary to what phenomenology—which is always phenomenology of perception—has tried to make us believe, *contrary to what our desire cannot fail to be tempted into believing*, the thing itself always escapes" (*SP* 104; my emphasis). As Derrida here suggests, however, even if the thing always escapes, the phenomenon of the phantasm cannot fail to be sustained by the desire, by the temptation, to *believe*.

The first phantasm would thus appear to be the phantasm of a self purely present to itself, a self able to hear and coincide with itself in the immediacy of a *vouloir dire*, through signs that are understood immediately and without delay—that is, through signs that go beyond the sign, signs that appear so natural that we treat them as a kind of second skin. In *Of Hospitality* Derrida once again relates the *phantasm* of auto-affection to language, to hearing-oneself-speak, indeed, this time, to hearing-oneself-speak one's mother tongue. A sort of "second skin" or "mobile home," says Derrida, the mother tongue would *seem to resist* all the dislocations and expropriations from the home brought about by tele-technology (*H* 89). Accompanying me wherever I go, the mother tongue would appear to be the very figure of "the proper or property, at least the *phantasm* [*phantasme*] of property . . . as close as could be to our bodies" (*H* 91). This "supposed mobility of our mother tongue" is related, for Derrida—and notice here the appearance of so many of the terms we followed in Chapter 8—to the supposed "auto-mobility of the living thing [*du vivant*] in general," that is, to "the phantasm of this auto-nomy" and to the "auto-mobile auto-affection of which language's hearing-oneself-speak is the privileged figure" (*H* 137). Automobility, autonomy, auto-affection—a mother tongue, my mother tongue: it is this that Derrida calls "the most unbreakable of phantasms [*le plus increvable des phantasmes*]" (*H* 91). Even though language is also, indeed, "*in reality, in necessity*, beyond the phantasm [*au-delà du phantasme*]," even though "language only works *from* me" and is always, and even as a mother tongue, the "language of the other," the phantasm of it *belonging* to me remains—*increvable*, says Derrida, that is, unbreakable, unpuncturable, undeflatable, inexhaustible, indefatigable, unflappable, and undefeatable. One's mother tongue, one's home, or else, as we saw in the preceding chapter, the burial place of one's ancestors—these are the phantasms of all those who have been exiled or uprooted. Derrida writes in *Of Hospitality*: "two nostalgias: their dead ones and their language" (*H* 87).

Beyond or just beyond this first phantasm of a self that believes it can speak and hear itself in a natural language, in a mother tongue, would be a self that believes—that desires—that it can bring what it engenders back into its orbit. In "Passions"—a text written three years before *Monolingualism of the Other*—Derrida argues:

> The infinite paradoxes of what is so calmly called narcissism are outlined here: suppose that X, something or someone (a trace, a work,

an institution, a child) bears your name, that is to say your title. The naïve rendering or common phantasm [*fantasme courant*: common illusion] is that you have given your name to X, thus all that returns to X, in a direct or indirect way, in a straight or an oblique line, *returns* to you, as a profit for your narcissism. ("P" 11–12)

Though such narcissism, such a "common phantasm" or "illusion," is, in the end, always frustrated by the paradoxes of narcissism, it nonetheless remains. Though "narcissism is frustrated a priori by that from which it profits or hopes to profit" ("P" 12), though it is forever and a priori frustrated by the *phenomenon* of narcissism, since we *are not* our name or our title or our children, it remains a common phantasm—and a common *theoretical* phantasm, as Pleshette DeArmitt has shown in some of her recent work.[8] Though there are a million signs every day to counter this narcissism and this naïve theory, they nonetheless resist, and resist even the most sober and vigilant denegation of this phantasm. Indeed what interests me here is the persistence of a "common phantasm" despite its frustration, critique, or denegation, the effects, affects, and attachments of a phantasm that is "in truth" always frustrated and yet always at work. Derrida makes this perfectly clear in *Paper Machine*. In the context of a passage on our *nostalgia* for biblio-culture, for the book, for paper, for the putative intimacy and self-proximity of handwriting, Derrida speaks of the "*phantasms* [*phantasmes*] of contact, of caress, of intimacy, proximity, resistance, or promise." He then continues, giving us in a single sentence one of the most condensed and yet complete definitions of the phantasm in his work: "These are certainly *phantasms* [*phantasmes*]. The word condenses all together image, spectrality, and simulacrum—and the weight of desire, the libidinal investment of affect, the motions of an appropriation extended toward that which remains inappropriable, called forth by the inappropriable itself, the desperate attempt to turn affection into auto-affection. These phantasms and affects *are* effectiveness itself" (*PM* 63).

The phenomenon of the phantasm thus first arises in the self's phantasmatic coincidence with itself and its affective appropriation of everything it engenders or *believes* it engenders. But in the work of Derrida, it is perhaps most powerfully in the form of the political that the phantasm holds our fascination and accounts for our attachment. In an address delivered in Athens in 1999 under the title *Unconditionality or Sovereignty*, Derrida makes several enlightening remarks about the phantasm. He argues in this work, as he did in several others in the following five years, that one must oppose "two close but heterogeneous representations of freedom"—namely, sovereignty and unconditionality (*IS* 44). While sovereignty would name the freedom or seeming freedom of a sovereign or sovereign state to act and exercise its power, unconditionality would have to do with the unlimited freedom to pursue the truth and to question, to deconstruct, in a word, every form of sovereign power—for example, "the *sovereignty* of a state, people, monarch, or God" (*IS* 46–48), the "phantasm of sovereignty that inspires the politics of all state-nationalisms" (*IS* 48). Though this second freedom, this unconditional freedom to critique, runs the risk of looking like the sovereign power of another sovereign subject, the counter-sovereignty of, say, a critical subject who can contest the sovereignty of the nation-state, the unconditional is, properly speaking, powerless, not a counter-sovereignty with its own power but a *weak force* that can disrupt the power of any sovereign phantasm, including its own. (It was no doubt this risk of unconditional freedom looking like a counter-sovereignty that, let me add in passing, eventually led Derrida to relate this unconditionality not to the power of a critical performative but to an event that undoes the power of any kind of subject, even that of a critical or deconstructive subject.)

Every form of sovereignty thus appears to be a phantasm, and every phantasm a phantasm of sovereignty, the phantasm, for example, of a nation-state that has power, that is in possession of an origin that is self-grounding, and so on. As Derrida puts it in *Paper Machine*:

> As regards humanity at least, sovereignty has only ever run on fantasy, whether we are talking about the nation-state, its leader, the king or the people, the man or the woman, or the father or the mother. It has never had any other theme or motive, this thing called sovereignty, than that old fantasy [*fantasme*] that sets it going. An omnipotent fantasy, of course, because it is a fantasy of omnipotence [*Fantasme tout-puissant, certes, car fantasme de toute-puissance*]. For those who prefer more refined or scholarly languages, the word *sovereignty* has only ever translated the performative violence that institutes in law a fiction or a simulacrum. Who wants to create belief in sovereignty, and in whom? In the sovereignty of anything or anyone, the Nation-State, the People, the King, the Queen, the Father, or the Mother. For example. (*PM* 106)

The principle of sovereignty is thus a principle of the phantasm, what Derrida calls an "archaic principle-phantasm of sovereignty," archaic, as we will see, because it is an *arche* and because it comes in response to the most archaic impulses or desires for identification and exclusion, the most primitive or archaic expressions of violence. This principle of sovereignty is an archaic phantasm, and it is, Derrida adds, of "theological origin." "Religion, ethnicity, and the nation-state are bound together," he writes, "in the same *sovereignist* discourse" (*IS* 50). Hence Derrida in "Fichus" can say that we must "begin by 'deconstructing' both the onto-theologico-political fantasies [*phantasmes*] of an indivisible sovereignty and pro-nation-state metaphysics" (*PM* 172), that is, carry out a "deconstructive critique that is sober, wide awake, vigilant, and attentive to everything that solders the political to the metaphysical, to capitalist speculating, to the perversions of religious or nationalist feeling, or to the fantasy of sovereignty" (*PM* 179). Hence the "political task" is to find the best "legislative" transactions or "juridical" conditions by changing "laws, habits, phantasms [*phantasmes*]—a whole 'culture'" (*PM* 131)—in other words, by changing the fantasies or phantasms that lead to various forms of xenophobia and nationalism. What thus distinguishes "in *principle* an unconditional freedom of thought" as it is found, for example, at least in principle, in the university, and the sovereignty of the nation-state is ultimately, Derrida argues, the ideological origin of the concept of sovereignty and the "theologico-political history of power" (*IS* 58), a history that—as we saw in Chapter 3—always conjoins sovereign power and the notion of an indivisible and all-powerful God. As Derrida writes in "Ulysses Gramophone," "omnipotence remains phantasmatic, it opens and defines the dimensions of phantasm" ("UG" 293).

From the self to the state to a sovereign God: it appears that we are moving up levels on the totem pole (or the divided line) of the phantasm. And yet, as we have seen in previous chapters, the theological principle of sovereignty is, for Derrida, at work already in the phantasm of the nation-state, if not already in the self. For the principle or phantasm of sovereignty is, in the end, always haunted by the phantasm of a divine sovereignty at the heart of political power, not only as it once was found in the monarch but in modern democracies in the form of the people—which is held, like every sovereign, to be inviolable and indivisible. Derrida writes: "I continue to believe that the theological filiation of sovereignty remains even there where one speaks of popular freedom and self-determination" (*IS* 60). All "bellicose state-nationalisms" are the result of this filiation (*IS* 62).

Derrida's prescriptive message in *Unconditionality or Sovereignty* and many similar texts, including *Rogues*, is pretty clear: we must continue the "*deconstruction* in progress of sovereignism, of the phantasms of political theology" (*IS* 52). We must continue—through what looks like a kind of sovereignty, a kind of power and freedom—to help with the deconstruction in progress, a deconstruction that is happening in spite of or through us and thus beyond all sovereignty (*IS* 52). New forms of shared or limited sovereignty must thus be invented at the same time as we try to think an unconditionality without sovereignty and, thus, without power or phantasm. The counter-sovereignty of the university must then, through an appeal to the unconditional and therefore powerless freedom of thought, question the phantasm of sovereignty and, first of all, the phantasm of sovereignty's *indivisibility*. Derrida writes in "The University Without Condition": "It would be necessary to dissociate a certain *unconditional* independence of thought, of deconstruction, of justice, of the Humanities, of the University, and so forth, from any phantasm of *indivisible sovereignty* and sovereign mastery" (*WA* 235). The phantasm needs to be exposed and denounced not because it is untrue, false, or merely apparent but because it is so powerful it threatens the very freedom that makes it possible. Derrida writes, again in *Unconditionality or Sovereignty*: "The unconditionality of thought must put into question, in the name of freedom itself, the principle of sovereignty as a principle of power" (*IS* 62). Hence Derrida opposes the power of sovereignty to an "unconditionality without sovereignty," to a "freedom without power" but *not* without "force" (*IS* 64). Only such a force, such a "weak force," will allow one to resist, says Derrida, the "laws of the city," the phantasm, we might say, of the city's sovereignty, as well as the temptation to turn this critical force into a new power and, thus, a new phantasm of sovereignty. The weak, unconditional force of the university must thus not be transformed into or allow itself to be taken for a new power; it must organize its resistance to sovereign power without becoming itself just one more reactive, sovereign power. Hence the university must not, writes Derrida, "enclose itself and reconstitute the abstract phantasm of sovereignty, whose theological or humanist heritage it will perhaps have begun to deconstruct"; it must instead ally itself "with extra-academic forces, in order to organize an inventive resistance . . . to all attempts at reappropriation . . . to all the other figures of sovereignty" (*WA* 236).

But here is perhaps another trait of the phantasm. In resisting different kinds of sovereign power both inside and outside the university, the weak force of thought must not become another *reactive* sovereign power, or, rather, must not become another power in general since *all* power is, it seems, reactive. To return to our reading of *Speech and Phenomena*, the phenomenon of the *phantasm* was, in some sense, a *reaction* to the phantasm *as phenomenon*, to the fact that différance, iterability—indeed spectrality—is the condition of all hearing-oneself-speak. The phantasm is not simply conditioned by spectrality but is a reaction to it, a reaction to an original disappropriation, to an original nonidentity to self, which happens first of all through the giving of language to the self by the other. Speaking in his last published interview, *Learning to Live Finally*, of his own history as he tells it in *Monolingualism of the Other*, Derrida says: "I have only one language, and, at the same time, in an at once singular and exemplary fashion, this language does not belong to me. I explain this better in *Monolingualism of the Other*. A singular history has exacerbated in me this universal law: a language is not something that belongs. Not naturally and in its essence. Whence the phantasms of property, appropriation, and colonialist imposition" (*LLF* 38). The phantasm would thus be a *reaction*, a phenomenological reaction, to an originary spectrality. It should thus come as no surprise that an originary contamination of presence or impurity of roots would lead to the reactive phantasms of purity at the level of ethnicity or the nation-state. Indeed, as Derrida demonstrated in many texts and in his seminars of the 1980s on "Philosophical Nationality and Nationalism," phantasms of the nation-state often involve claims about purity, health, or salvation, along with related calls to purge, heal, or save the state from an offending or dangerous invasion. To give just a single example, Derrida spoke in 1993 of the way in which Jean-Marie Le Pen, as head of the right-wing party Le Front National, frequently evoked the "quasi-biological image of the health of the nation's body" in order to raise the specter of certain threats posed to the French nation by immigration. As Derrida remarks, "the nationalist *phantasm*, as with its politicking rhetoric, often passes by way of these organicist analogies" (*N* 102; my emphasis).[9]

As a critique "of the phantasm or of the axiom of purity," deconstruction would call into question such organicist analogies, such attempts to purify the body politic by purging it of what threatens its putatively natural health and integrity. In his preface to Alain David's *Racisme et antisémitisme*, Derrida argues that the very origins of racism and anti-Semitism are related to the phantasms of purity and, thus, contamination, an inviolable identity and, thus, threats to that identity: "There where, beyond the artifact, there is no race in and of itself, no '*the* Semite' or '*the* Jew,' how can one speak of racism or anti-Semitism without taking seriously *the effects* of the artifact, of the phantasm, of the imaginary—and, before all else, of affect?" ("FF" 24).[10] Anti-Semitism would thus be born of a phantasm, of an artifact—with its accompanying fascination—that has "real" effects and undeniably powerful affects.

But in this preface Derrida goes even further, relating a fascination with form not simply to the phantasm of race but to nothing less than the fascination with an organizing form in general, with an *eidos*, and thus to the very motivation behind a metaphysics of presence. Derrida speaks of a "fascination with form, that is, with the *visibility* of a certain organic or organizing contour, an *eidos*, if you will, and thus an idealization, an *idealism* as that which institutes philosophy itself, philosophy or metaphysics as such"("FF" 10). It is as if metaphysics itself, then, were a reaction to an original deformation of form, quite literally a *reactive formation*, which transforms an original spectrality, where presence is determined by absence and difference, into what is assumed to be an original and uncontaminated presence. Metaphysics would be a reactive formation whose entire work would be the production of phantasms of form, and a fascination with these phantasms. The phantasm *as such*, then, would be the phantasm of the "as such" of form.

Though Derrida does not state it in precisely this way, it would seem from what he has argued that deconstruction is always a deconstruction of the phantasm of form. While the phantasm is continuous with other terms in Derrida's work, such as the phantom, the ghost, and the specter, it appears to be a particularly powerful or tenacious form of metaphysical phenomenality, that is, a phenomenality that attempts to conceal or repress the iterability of the phenomenon in order to give rise to a "phenomenon" that goes beyond the phenomena, a *vouloir dire* that would precede and exceed all phenomenal expression, that would even exceed, as we will see, all life. Though the deconstruction of a metaphysics of the phantasm demonstrates that the phantasm does not, metaphysically speaking, *exist* or exist beyond its appearance, it is perpetually resurrected because of this nonexistence, because of its promise of a life beyond the phenomenon of life, a beyond of immanence, perhaps, in the sense that Len Lawlor has been developing this notion in some of his recent work.[11]

This tendency of the phantasm to promise a beyond of the phenomenon and a beyond of life can be seen in an exemplary fashion in "Faith and Knowledge," one of Derrida's most important and challenging texts of the 1990s. The phantasm there plays a role on a number of levels in Derrida's investigation of the relationship between religion and science—a relationship that is arguably even more crucial to our geopolitical situation today than it was a decade ago, insofar as the phantasms produced by it are as widespread, as powerful, and as ominous as they have ever been. But before turning to this essential text, let me briefly review the characteristics we've already seen attached to the phantasm.

First, the phantasm involves the coincidence or the assumed coincidence of the self with itself, a self that would be indivisible and inviolable. Second, this self-coincidence or self-identity, what Derrida called in several later texts "ipseity," leads to the phantasm of a self-same self that can act, that has power—in a word, that is sovereign. The phantasm is thus always a phantasm of power, and power—as opposed to force—is always a phantasm. Third, the phantasm of sovereignty tends to present itself as natural or as organic, as excluding the machine or the artifact, even if, as Derrida shows, it is always the effect of an artifact. It thus always presents itself as pure or as a call to purity. Fourth, the phantasm, though always historically conditioned and linguistically coded, appears as ahistorical and nonlinguistic, as having a nonconventional origin. The phantasm thus tends—a fifth characteristic—to try to pass off what is always a historically conditioned performative fiction as a constative or objective observation. The power of sovereignty lies precisely in this elision of a fictional origin and its real effects, the elision of a performative fiction (an "as if," a *comme si*) and a constative observation (an "as such" or a "like that," a *comme ça*). From *comme si* to *comme ça*: that is the movement of every sovereign fiction and the constitution of every sovereign power. It is in the nature of the phantasm that it not appear as what it "is," that what is but a projection appear natural or in nature, that the *comme si* of the phantasm be conflated with a *comme ça*.[12]

Though not all fictions become sovereign, all sovereignties are fictions or phantasms. This is, I think, the central lesson of Derrida's essay on the Declaration of Independence, where a performative or prescriptive *ought* is shown to be conflated or elided with a constative *is* or *are* in the crucial phrase "these United Colonies are *and* of right ought to be free and independent states" (my emphasis).[13] That a fiction, fable, or phantasm is at the origin of political power is also the central lesson of an essay such as "Force of Law"—a phrase, "force of law," that in and of itself gives voice to this conflation or elision of *nomos* and *physis*, the speech act or, as Derrida liked to put it, the juridical performative of law and the illocutionary and perlocutionary effects of that law.[14] Sixth and finally, the phantasm as artifact cannot be confused with a fallen, inferior, or mimetic image of the truth; it is not to be understood simply in terms of truth and falsity, or image and reality, but in terms of power and affect. Even more, the power of the phantasm comes precisely from the way in which the "subjective" projection of a putatively pure, original, or preoriginal sovereign is seen, read, or understood as an "objective" reality, as a kind of truth. While the phantasm is not true, it is not enough to say that it is simply false, for it presents to us not the way things are or are not but, a bit like a Freudian illusion, the way we would wish them to be and, thus, the way we then assume them to be. The phantasm thus cannot be dispelled simply by pointing out the truth, since this notion of truth as objectively determined and independent of me is precisely one of the *effects* of the phantasm.[15]

In "Faith and Knowledge," a couple more important traits are added to this list. First, the phantasm—the result, as always, of the machine and the artifact—promises a surplus or abundance of life, a life beyond both life and death, beyond the mechanisms of life and beyond the machine. In this respect the phantasm will be something like the metaphysical shadow of Derrida's concept of *living on*, one of the reasons, I would suggest, why Derrida retained it, since by never shaking completely free of its metaphysical double Derridean living on or survival exerts a *critical force* against this powerful metaphysical phantasm. While the phantasm promises a life beyond life, a pure life without technique or the machine, a life beyond history and time, the concept of living on or of survival acknowledges history and convention and promises an intensification of life, a life in death, but never any immortality. Finally, in "Faith and Knowledge" the phantasm appears to be a decidedly "masculine" formation, even if, obviously, it is not simply the phantasm of men. The phantasm helps explain both violence against women, according to Derrida, and—through this violence or through the exclusion of women—their phantasmatic and symptomatic return through phantasms of purity, inviolability, and superabundant life.

Hence Derrida argues in "Faith and Knowledge" that an absolute respect for life, a respect nurtured by religion for the safe and sound, the immune, for a life that goes beyond life, is not unrelated to the mechanisms of death and, thus, to repetition, iterability, virtuality, and teletechnology. Indeed, such an absolute respect for life is actually pursued through virtuality and teletechnology, that is, through the very things that threaten the purity, sanctity, and indemnity of life. Hence religion is, as Derrida puts it, *autoimmune*, the pursuit of an indemnified life by means of the very things that compromise such a life. Today's religious "manifestations" of the pope or of religious fundamentalists or other groups would be impossible without an appropriation of *teletechnoscience*, which is then eschewed in the name, precisely, of life. While such an autoimmune appropriation of digital culture and cyberspace appears new and is most certainly taking place at an unprecedented rate today, religion has never done without it. As Derrida succinctly puts it, "the ether of religion will have always been hospitable to a certain spectral virtuality," a spectral virtuality, he will go on to show, that is put in the service of a hyperbolization of the value of life ("FK" 70, n. 17). That is why religion appears always related to questions of health and salvation, to a restoration of health, a healing of the sick, and a reconstitution of the healthy body—to what might be characterized as a *phantasmatic* immunity, a self or state that appears and wishes itself to be indemnified, safe and sound, but that is in fact always open to a *spectral* autoimmunity.

Now, at the same time as Derrida's text speaks clearly and forcefully about this autoimmunity, it also *enacts* it, for in the midst of a discussion between Derrida and other European men on the subject of religion, in a discussion of religion that has—and this was surely not Derrida's choice—excluded women, Derrida will let two phantasmatic figures of the feminine appear in his text, as if to demonstrate that when women are excluded they tend to return—but precisely *as phantasms*. These two figures, one Greek and one Roman, Persephone and Gradiva, would need to be read in conjunction with a third figure, that is, with *Khōra*, whom Derrida treats explicitly and in some detail in this text because *Khōra* is precisely that which or she who, while opening up the space for all phantasm, for the phenomena of the phantasm, constantly eludes and interrupts the phantasm of phenomena, including every anthropomorphic or theological phantasm.

It is in the context, then, of religion's attempt to indemnify life through the teletechnological machine that Derrida first uses the word *phantasm* in "Faith and Knowledge"—and uses it, as in *Speech and Phenomena*, in reference to a certain repression. Speaking of how the stakes of today's "cyberspatialized or cyberspaced wars of religion" have been repressed, "dissimulated, or displaced," Derrida claims that this repression "never occurs without symptoms and fantasies [*phantasmes*], without specters *(phantasmata)* to be investigated" ("FK" 24). This is perhaps the first clue about how we are to interpret the later appearance of Gradiva in Derrida's text, Gradiva, who is not only explicitly called a phantasm or illusion and a symptom in Freud's famous text but whose name in psychoanalysis is almost synonymous with repressed desire that surfaces as phantasm and symptom—as the male delusion that results from a repression of women or, perhaps, from the transformation of sexual difference into sexual opposition. For as we know from Freud, repression leads not to effacement but to displacement, to the transformation of desire into dreams, into art, into religion, or into delusions or phantasms to be read as symptoms—as *reactions*—to desire.

A second clue to understanding the appearance of Gradiva in "Faith and Knowledge" can be found in section 39, where Derrida continues his argument about the double origin or source of religion, namely, faith *and* belief, revealability *and* revelation, along with the originary faith that is at the origin of *both* religion *and* science. Derrida marshals all his arguments together in this section in order to explain an ultimate phantasm in religion, what he calls the *phallus effect*—at once the phenomenality, the *phainesthai*, of the phallus and, because of the law of iterability, its *detachment* from its own pure, proper presence. The phallus is thus in essence detachable, its own *phantasm*, double, specter, or fetish, a supplement or artifact that comes after the original but *presents itself as coming before*, as having greater value, greater power, as having—as we will see with Gradiva—a surplus of life, a capacity to live on after life and in defiance of death. The phallus, as opposed to the penis, thus brings together life and the machine; it is the technical supplement or detachable marionette that presents itself as that which is most productive of life and most able to protect or indemnify life. It is that which, through the *colossal automaticity* of erection, promises a maximum of life through an automatic reflexivity that runs counter to that life.

The phallus is a virtuality that appears to bring together the calculable and the incalculable, putting the calculability of teletechnoscience into relation with the incalculable source of religion in a life beyond life. Derrida thus speaks of "faith in the most living as dead and automatically *surviving*, resuscitated in its spectral *phantasma*, the holy, safe and sound, unscathed, the immune, sacred . . . the spectral fantasy [*phantasme spectral*] of the dead as the principle of life and of sur-vival [*sur-vie*]. This mechanical principle is apparently very simple: life has absolute value only if it is worth *more than* life" ("FK" 48, 50). Everything Derrida goes on to say about sacrifice and circumcision can be related to this movement: the penis is transformed, resuscitated, automatically raised up, into the phallus through the circumcisional cut, the undetachable organ being thereby transformed into the detachable fetish, a respect for life transformed into a call to sacrifice. While this vocation for sacrifice, this "principle of sacrificial self-destruction," this autoimmunity that opens the community to contamination and to a compromising of its self-protection, is always carried out "in view of some sort of invisible and spectral sur-vival," this survival wavers between an openness to "something other and more than itself: the other, the future, death, freedom, the coming or the love of the other, the space and time of a spectralizing messianicity beyond all messianism," and, I would like to emphasize, all that *and more*, namely, the hyperbolic phantasm—the absolute phantasm—of an absolute life or a pure life, the phantasm of a life beyond life ("FK" 50–51).

Now, it is just after this invocation of the phallus as phantasm or fetish, this invocation of what we might call a "masculine" phantasm, that Derrida turns, almost automatically, to what might be called a "feminine" phantasm or a phantasm of the feminine. Derrida argues, in effect, that the force of life, the *swelling* of life, the automaticity that is transformed into a fetish, has to be thought in relation to the spontaneity not just of *erection* but of *pregnancy*. Derrida then appends at precisely this point a long footnote on Benveniste, who relates the Greek *kurios*—usually translated as "sovereign"—to the sacred and to its origin in the word *kuien*, meaning to grow or "to swell." The identification we have seen from the beginning between the phantasm and sovereignty is thus here confirmed, but this time on the side of the mother *as well as* the father. The sacred or the holy is related not just to sovereign power but to an exuberant, fecund force capable of bringing to life in a spontaneous and automatic way. The phallus effect or the fecund belly rises up of its own accord, self-seeding and self-bearing—like an Immaculate Conception.

Just after this note, which follows the reference to the phantasm and the fetish, to the supplemental *cut* that attempts to restore the original indemnified state, Derrida asks why the "privileged" victims of ethno-religious violence are so often women—and often by rape or mutilation. Derrida's answer to this question becomes clear in what follows: violence against women *and* the sacralization and protection, the indemnification, of them go hand in hand. When "real women" are forgotten or excluded, their phantoms emerge—their purity made into the object of fetishized desire. When life or life-death is forgotten, when the relationship between life and the technical supplement is forgotten or repressed, life or life-death becomes replaced by a hyperbolization of life, the colossal phallus or the spontaneously swollen, pregnant belly. In an autoimmune reaction to the uprooting or deracination of the phallus effect, to the move beyond life into living on through media and technology, one turns against this deracination by turning against the living, proper body. Hence Derrida, in section 42, argues that today's "religious wars"—and Derrida was no doubt thinking of what was going on in the former Yugoslavia at the time—have two ages, and thus two forms of violence, one *contemporary*, which makes use of hyper-sophisticated military teletechnology and digital culture, and the other a *new archaic* violence. This second, archaic violence takes revenge on the first violence through the teletechnological means of the first—an archaic violence that, as Derrida analyzed the destruction of the World Trade Center on 9/11, feeds on the technoscience it turns against. Derrida thus speaks in his interview on 9/11 of the "phantasms—both conscious and unconscious—of those who decided and then put into action, in their heads and in their airplanes, right up to suicide, the slashing open and collapse of this double tower": "Archaic and forever puerile, terribly childish, these masculine *phantasms* were in fact fed by an entire techno-cinematographic culture, and not only the genre of science fiction" ("AI" 187 n. 6, my emphasis).

In an autoimmune reaction, the second, archaic violence turns against the first in order to return, says Derrida in "Faith and Knowledge," to the *living, proper* body—or, rather, he says, to its *phantasm* ("FK" 52). By turning against the expropriating, decorporealizing machine, one thus turns back to the *bare hand*—to decapitation, to the mutilation of both women and men, to rape, to the exposure of bodies—and all this, and even when it is recorded, filmed, and distributed by teletechnology, in order to return to the *phantasm* of the living body. When the relationship between the proper body and the machine—another name for death—is forgotten, the living body tends to return as *phantasm*, as a body that offers a surplus of life, a phenomenon of the phantasm that promises a beyond of the phenomenon.

Now, I said above that it is not only Gradiva who is invoked in "Faith and Knowledge" but also Persephone, the figure who is so central to "Tympan," or so central, at least, to the right-hand column of that text, though also, as Tom Dutoit has argued, to many other Derrida texts.[16] A symbol of violence against women because of her rape by Hades, a symbol of both life and death, fertility and barrenness, insofar as she divides her time between Hades and earth, Persephone is evoked by Derrida without being explicitly named in at least two places in "Faith and Knowledge." In both cases, a single word raises her specter, a word that is almost a synecdoche for her: that word is "pomegranates." In the final lines of section 51, the next to last section of this great text on religion, Derrida writes: "Ontotheology encrypts faith and destines it to the condition of a sort of Spanish Marrano who would have lost—in truth, dispersed, multiplied—everything up to and including the memory of his unique secret. Emblem of a still life [*nature morte*]: an opened pomegranate [*la grenade entamée*], one Passover evening, on a tray" ("FK" 66). With almost nothing to contextualize this line, the secret of what seems to be a memory for Jacques Derrida risks being, after his death, forever forgotten, definitively lost. And yet this word *pomegranate* or, in French, *grenade*, can still be read, its semantic kernel split open, both in the passage I just read and, some 15 sections earlier in "Faith and Knowledge," between sections 37 and 38, where Derrida once again drops this word without context and without warning in order to introduce the remaining sections of the text. After section 37 Derrida thus writes in French *et grenades* and then comments: "(Having posed these premises or general definitions, and given the diminishing space available, we shall cast [*satellisons*] the fifteen final propositions in a form that is even more granulated [*égrenée*], grainy [*grenadée*], disseminated, aphoristic, discontinuous, juxtapositional, dogmatic, indicative or virtual, economic; in a word, more than ever telegraphic)" ("FK" 47). While the latter context justifies the translation of *grenades* by "pomegranates," its context here, in the midst of a text on religion *and* science, faith *and* violence, is not so determined as to exclude the other meaning of *grenades* in French, namely, "grenades." Indeed, Derrida appears to have lobbed this word into the middle of the fifty-two sections of "Faith and Knowledge" in order to gather or, rather, disperse many of the themes of the phantasm we have been following throughout this essay, in order to evoke all the tensions between, precisely, faith and knowledge, nature and culture, the pomegranate of religion and the grenade of technoscience, a symbol of female fertility, of life-giving seed, on the one hand, and an image of masculine violence, of shrapnel-casting death, on the other, the blood-red pomegranate of Persephone, on the one hand, and the army-green hand-held machine of technoscience, on the other.[17] *Et grenades*—the perfect still life or *nature morte*, it seems, for a life that is always already opened, compromised, exposed, *entamée*. If the phantasm is always the reaction of form and meaning to a deformation of form and an ambivalence that exceeds controllable meaning, then it just might be that the first form of the phantasm in "Faith and Knowledge" is the belief that we can handle this word *grenade*, this techno-religious pharmakon, so as to turn it in one direction or another, disarm its ambivalence by reducing it to polysemy, and turn its fundamental difference into a system of oppositions (male-female, death-life, *technē-physis*, and so on).[18]

It is in this context, with these values in the background, that I would like to read the phantasmatic appearance of Gradiva in "Faith and Knowledge," a figure who is much more explicitly evoked than Persephone and so is less liable to be the object of my own hermeneutic phantasms. Gradiva is, of course, the delusion or phantasm of Wilhelm Jensen's archaeologist in the novella "Gradiva: A Pompeiian Fancy," to which Freud devotes a close reading in *Delusion and Dream*.[19] The reason for Gradiva's appearance in "Faith and Knowledge" ("FK" 38, 66) is in some sense strictly determined by the context, namely, a meeting in February 1994 on the island of Capri, not far from Pompeii, indeed within eyeshot of it, which brought together a number of thinkers, all European, or at least all Judeo-Christian, and all men, to discuss religion. Derrida thus recalls, in section 5 of "Faith and Knowledge," "not a single woman!" just after remarking "No Muslim is among us, alas," and just before recalling that one of the reasons for the meeting in the first place was everything "that is hastily grouped under the reference to 'Islam,'" which seems "today to retain some sort of geopolitical or global prerogative, as a result of the nature of its physical violences, of certain of its declared violations of the democratic model and of international law" ("FK" 5). No Muslims and no women, then, in a dialogue about religion. It is as if Derrida wished to remind us that when women are forgotten in the context of religion or when, in religion, they are exalted beyond life, they tend to return—like Gradiva—as symptoms, as delusions or phantasms to replace living women. That is why, I would like to believe, Derrida refers to *Khōra*, to Persephone, to Gradiva, and, perhaps especially, to the unnamed women who are, says Derrida, the privileged victims of religious violence. What is repressed, to use the word we've been tracking since *Speech and Phenomena*, pushed into the unconscious or into the underworld, returns—as phantom, as delusion, as symptom. With no women present in Capri, what Derrida makes place for in his discourse are not the voices of absent women, *as if* he could speak for them—since that would be the worst phantasm—but, instead, female figures of male phantasm, Gradiva being first among these as the phantasm of a life in excess of life, the phantasm of a *life* resurrected from the ashes of Vesuvius.

Yes, life: for in the story of Gradiva it is life in the form of Zoë Bertgang that is forgotten, abandoned, or repressed by the protagonist archaeologist, so that what takes its or her place in this repression, through this repression, is the dangerous delusion or phantasm of a woman who would seem to go beyond life, beyond Zoë, in the figure of the once ashen and dead but now ivory-cheeked and resurrected Gradiva. Overcoming death and time, this phantasm holds us in its power, in its spell, and risks destroying us with the illusion of an exuberance and a life purely present to itself, a proper body that goes beyond life and death, endlessly resuscitated or resurrected, immaculately conceived at midday from the ashes of Pompeii. Though there is no reading of Freud's Gradiva essay in "Faith and Knowledge," everything Derrida writes about violence and women in relation to the phantasm seems to support this view.[20] It is thus hardly by accident, hardly out of a mere rhetorical flourish, that Gradiva appears in the final paragraph of the essay, as Derrida writes: "*This, perhaps, is what I would have liked to say of a certain Mount Moriah—while going to Capri, last year, close by the Vesuvius of Gradiva*" ("FK" 66).

Again, the phantasm is not an error to be measured in relation to truth; it is not some imitation, image, or representation to be measured against the real but is akin to what Freud, in *The Future of an Illusion* and elsewhere, terms an "illusion." Not a representation or misrepresentation of the way things are but a projection on the part of a subject or nation-state of the way one would wish them to be—and, thus, in some sense, the way they become, with all their real, attendant effects.[21]

From *Speech and Phenomena* to *Learning to Live Finally*, a certain figure of the phantasm comes to light: the phantasm is what always presents itself as emanating from a self coincident with itself, an ipseity with power, that is supported through metaphors of the natural and the organic, that, in its sovereignty, offers a life beyond life, a conflation of the technical and the natural, a spontaneous and automatic growth and abundance in the form of either the phallus or the swollen belly, and so, in the end, the phantasm of either a father or a mother who can generate all by itself through an Immaculate Conception. It is time, since I am close to the end, to deploy what has been for me an almost failsafe hermeneutic principle when trying to check any hypothesis or thesis regarding the work of Jacques Derrida. The principle runs something like this: make your case by ranging widely throughout Derrida's corpus, from early to later texts, for example, in trying to understand the nature of the phantasm, piece together remarks in texts as different as *Speech and Phenomena*, *Monolingualism of the Other*, "Faith and Knowledge," "Ulysses Gramophone," and so on, but *then* turn at the end of the day to *Glas* to see whether the whole thing was not already laid out for you, from start to finish, in 1974.

Once again, this principle will not have failed me. Though it is impossible to do justice here to the development of the phantasm in that work, it is equally impossible to ignore the way Derrida's reading of the phantasm in relation to Hegel confirms each and every one of the moves we have followed. Let me take just a moment to demonstrate this rather remarkable prolepsis.

As we have seen, the phantasm is related to a self-coincidence or self-possession, to what Derrida calls "ipseity." We read in *Glas* "that"—*ça*, a little word that is written like the *ça* of *comme ça* but is pronounced like *Sa*, as in *Savoir Absolu*, or absolute knowledge—"That (*ça*) is called a colossal compensation. The absolute phantasm as an absolute self-having [*s'avoir absolu*]" (*GL* 198bi). So much for self-possession or self-coincidence. As for this self-possession or self-identity being not originary but, as we have seen, already a reaction, Derrida in *Glas* relates the phantasm to the formation and reaction of a system of oppositions to an original difference. "As soon as the difference is determined as opposition, no longer can the phantasm (a word to be determined) of the *IC* be avoided: to wit, a phantasm of infinite mastery of the two sides of the oppositional relation" (*GL* 223a). This mastery is nothing less, as we saw, than the history of metaphysics as the reduction of all ambivalence to polysemy, all deformation to form and figure, all differences to oppositions, oppositions that "have as cause and effect the immaculate maintenance of each of the terms, their independence, and consequently their absolute mastery. Absolute mastery that they see conferred on themselves phantasmatically the very moment they are reversed and subordinated" (*GL* 223a).

This determination of difference as opposition then appears to give rise, as the reference to the Immaculate Conception makes clear, to phantasms of purity and to the opposition—as opposed to the difference—between the sexes, that is, to the opposition between two sexes that can now generate on their own, spontaneously, automatically, like the erect phallus or the swollen belly. "The virgin-mother does without the actual father, both in order to come and to conceive" (*GL* 223a). And then: "phantasmatic would be the effect of mastery produced by the determination of difference as opposition (and up to the value of mastery itself), of sexual difference as sexual opposition in which each term would secure itself the domination and absolute autonomy in the *IC*: the effect—the son (rather than the daughter) comes back to me all by myself" (*GL* 224a).

This, recall, was already the phantasm of narcissism, the phantasm of a narcissism that is always undone by its phenomenon, the phantasm, as we saw in Chapter 2, of a Father who can beget a son on his own and keep that son within his orbit. As we have seen throughout, it is precisely this phantasm *as phenomenon* that checks the power of the phenomenon of the phantasm—and so it is in *Glas*. "The *check* of such a desire of the return to self, or the circle of double virginity, that would be the limit of the phantasm. . . . The phantasm is the phenomenon. The names indicate this" (*GL* 224a). And yet, as we have also seen, it is the nature of the sovereign phantasm to tend toward hyperbole, that is, toward the absolute phantasm—and, in *Glas*, toward the phantasm of the absolute. Once the phantasm is thus seen in terms not simply of truth and reality but of power and affect, indeed as that which produces truth, it is difficult to see what could possibly check it. Derrida asks in *Glas*: "In front of what would the phantasm of the *IC* have failed? In front of 'reality'? . . . Who would dare say that the phantasm of the *IC* has not succeeded? Two thousand years, at least, of Europe, from Christ to *Sa*" (*GL* 224a). Yes, from Christ to Sa, from Christ to *savoir absolu* or absolute knowledge: in Derrida's reading of Hegel in *Glas* the phantasm moves not just from *comme si* to *comme ça* but from *ça* to *Sa*, an absolute phantasm that would risk having no check at all were it not for the fact, perhaps, that *ça* and *Sa*, homophones differently written, are enough to suggest—as we saw in our earlier reading of "Plato's Pharmacy"—that expression, that writing, will always come to compromise the self-possession of a *vouloir dire*: "Will it be said, to determine the *IC* as phantasm, that the *IC* is not *true*, that that [*ça*] does not happen like that [*comme ça*], that this is only a myth? That would indeed be silly. . . . the (absolute) phantasm of the *IC* as (absolute) phantasm is (absolute) truth. Truth is the phantasm itself" (*GL* 224a).[22]

The phantasm is indeed produced in the move from *comme si* to *comme ça*, from the performative fiction of writing to the phantasm of hearing oneself speak *like that*. From *comme si* to *comme ça* and then ultimately to *Sa* as *savoir absolu*: "*Sa* is the final accomplishment of the phantasm . . . the absolute phantasm: *Sa*. But do not conclude from this: *Sa*, that is nothing but—the phantasm. . . . No longer can it be said of an infinite phantasm that it is *nothing but*. *Sa*'s discourse disqualifies the *nothing-but*" (*GL* 225a).

ᴣ

If deconstruction is always a deconstruction of the phantasm, then it must take on both the father and the mother without opposition; it must tender the hypothesis that not only the father but the mother—the seemingly natural, organic mother, the one who conceives and gives birth beyond phenomena and beyond every speech act—is also a legal fiction, the result of a *comme si* that always tends toward a *comme ça*. The phantasm of the mother after the father, the phantasm of an Immaculate Conception— that would be, in the end, something like the ultimate phantasm.

It is worth recalling in this regard, as a way of concluding this chapter, Derrida's preface to Jacques Trilling's book *James Joyce ou l'écriture matri-cide*, where Derrida recalls yet again Joyce's famous line concerning pater-nity as a legal fiction, paternity, we might say, as a phantasm, in order, this time, to apply it to the mother. Derrida argues in this preface that we must go beyond the "commonplace" view, shared by Joyce, Freud, and others, that, while the father is always the result of inference, speculation, calculation, and so on, the mother is not, since we can see the mother give birth with our own eyes. That is, we must go beyond the evidence fur-nished to us by a phenomenality of birth that leads us to believe that the mother is an object of knowledge beyond all speculation and belief. In an age of frozen embryos, in vitro fertilization, and surrogate motherhood, we must today acknowledge, argues Derrida, what has in fact always been the case: the mother, like the father, is subject to "substitution, rational inference, phantasmatic or symbolic construction, speculation, and so on." In a word, the mother, like the father, is a legal fiction that risks becoming a sovereign phantasm, a legitimate or legitimated phantasm and a phantasm of legitimation. Arguing, in effect, that this evidence of the eyes has never been trustworthy, that, to cite the end of *Speech and Phe-nomena*, "the eye and the world [are] within language," Derrida writes in the preface to Trilling's book on Joyce:

> If today the unicity of the mother is no longer the sensible object of
> a perceptual certitude, if maternities can no longer be reduced to,

indeed if they carry us beyond, the carrying mother, if there can be, in a word, more than one mother, if "the" mother is the object of calculation and supposition, of projection and phantasm, if the "womb" is no longer outside all phantasm, the assured place of birth, this "new" situation simply illuminates in return an ageless truth. The mother was never only, never uniquely, never indubitably the one who gives birth—and whom one sees, with one's own eyes, give birth. . . . The mother is also a speculative object and even a "legal fiction." ("NW")[23]

Subject to phantasm, then, the mother is not natural but inscribed in history, in conventions, subject to symbolization, speculation, and replacement. Once again, the mother as phenomenon compromises the phenomenon of the mother as phantasm, that is, as an essentially "masculine" phantasm, the mother as unique, natural, organic, beyond history, the source of a life beyond life, a divinity, the source of a priceless dignity of life, of a life to be sacrificed in the name of what goes beyond life, and so on. It is this phantasm that deconstruction calls into question so as to think not exactly the mother but, perhaps, maternity—another name, here, for the event—anew, maternity without sovereignty and thus without phantasm, if there is such a thing . . .

※

I would like to believe that this is, in fact, what Derrida was suggesting in the movie *Derrida*, by Amy Kofman and Kirby Dick, when he refused to name a philosopher who would have been his mother. The question is asked by a male voice off-screen: "If you had a choice, what philosopher would you like to be your mother?" Obviously amused and intrigued by the question, Derrida says, after a long pause, that he could not have a philosopher as a mother because, for him, philosophy, the philosophy he has tried to deconstruct, is a phallogocentric enterprise whose figures are always masculine and paternal—an enterprise, I think we could say, of phantasmatic fathers whose phantasms Derrida tried always and everywhere to expose. As we saw in Plato, philosophy would be an affair between the Father and his son. Were he to have a mother, says Derrida, she would not be a philosopher but—since he distinguishes between these—a *thinker*, and she would come not from the past but from the future, a postdeconstructive thinker—his son, he first suggests, or else his *granddaughter*. Turning us toward the future of thought rather than toward some phantasm of the past, he says, finally, "my mother as philosopher would be my granddaughter." It is, I believe, in this direction that we must turn in following Derrida today, though it is hard not to wonder whether we will ever be able to do so completely without phantasm, without some silhouette—whether his or hers—casting its shadow over us, that is, without even the "phantasm of a signature" ("UG" 304).

11

Lifelines

> Whatever one might say about it, and this can be drawn out *ad infinitum,*
> *there is a line.*
>
> **—Jacques Derrida, *SQ* 95**

In order to bear witness to the extraordinary intersection of life and work
that goes by the name of "Jacques Derrida," I shall limit myself here to
an analysis of what is no doubt Derrida's shortest published work, a one-
line poem published in a somewhat obscure collection of poems more
than two decades ago and then republished more recently in the *Cahier
de l'Herne* devoted to Derrida.[1] It is a text that fits on a single line and
one that speaks, precisely, of the line and of life, and of the intersection
of work and life, an exemplary text for thinking questions of living presence and its repetition, living speech and the dead letter, life and living
on, the living being and its specters. I am tempted to say that the entire
oeuvre, the entire "life," of Jacques Derrida is sealed in this single line
published more than two decades ago, a line that, it must be said, sounds
so very different today now that that life and that lifeline have run their
course. Here is the text in its entirety, along with its title and signature,
which I cite here in French before venturing a translation in what will
follow:

Petite fuite alexandrine (vers toi)

Prière à desceller d'une ligne de vie

Jacques Derrida[2]

For a long time, this little verse, published in 1986 as a "Monostiche" or "One-Line Poem," remained for me more or less inaudible, incomprehensible, indecipherable, whatever is sealed within it unreadable and inaccessible. But more recently I have had the impression that something has come loose within it, something unsealed, something that has put me on the path to an even more profound and irremediable inaccessibility—not simply another, more cryptic gift but, perhaps, the gift of its crypt. For what I had first taken for a *fuite*, a flight, an evasion, a verse itself in flight and perhaps even written on the fly, what I had first taken for a loss (*fuite*) of meaning, has come little by little to reveal itself as a revelation, a "leak" (*fuite*) of information or a kind of teaching on the subject of "life" itself.[3]

Prière à desceller d'une *ligne* de vie

We must begin reading this line of poetry as if it were, precisely, a *ligne de vie*, a lifeline—taking into account the length, duration, and continuity of the line, that is to say, the number of letters or syllables, along with the cuts or interruptions, the caesuras, between them. It is indeed, as the title suggests, an alexandrine, a classic and traditional form of French verse of twelve syllables with a caesura in the middle. Hence the line of poetry, like the lifeline, is destined by convention to have a certain length, a caesura foreseen or prescribed somewhere near the middle, here between *desceller* and *de*, even if no one could have foreseen or prescribed this so singular verse.[4] This *petite fuite*—this little line, this little flight—thus begins already to blur the line between form (the line of poetry) and content (the lifeline). One line leads already to the other, the lifeline spilling over into a line of poetry, which is then itself aligned with the lifeline.

First question, then, apparently biographical—though, as we will see, life and work, life and line, seem to cross in this one-line poem: With what did Jacques Derrida write this little verse, this little leak? On a single page, undated and reproduced in the *Cahier de l'Herne*, it would appear (though I cannot be absolutely certain of this) that the "original" iteration was written along with several others on a typewriter, but then chosen as the "original," decided upon and elected, circled, and then repeated as the chosen "original" with a pen, a verse first written, then, on a machine but then chosen and reinscribed *by hand*, with that elegant but barely decipherable handwriting that was his. And I would like to imagine that the line was written not with a fountain pen but with a kind of pen called a "Pilot Fineliner," of which he once said in an interview in 1986—the same year this one-line poem was published: "It's the only instrument that really suits me, that is, with which I have the impression that my

spontaneous gesture is not hindered by the instrument. And where I recognize my writing and can read it."[5]

I thus imagine Jacques Derrida in the process of writing this little line
of flight, in the process of piloting this Pilot Fineliner, the pen held between the thumb and index finger, almost a prolongation of the lifeline,
as if the writing flowed of itself from this line that seals the secret of a
destiny, as if the lifeline simply extended itself into a line of poetry, a
flowing of the hand into verse, a flight, a loss, a leak that runs through
the hand in order to become speech—and the speech, prayer. For let me
recall in anticipation that the speech of prayer is often joined to the hand,
indeed to the two hands, as two lifelines are pressed together in order to
become word, supplication, psalm, verse (*vers*) . . .[6]

But is there ever such a continuity between life and work, between a
so-called "natural" line like a lifeline and a "conventional," for example,
"poetic" line? Isn't it one of the lessons of the entire work of Jacques Derrida that there is always a difference, if not a caesura, a "line," between
the natural line and the conventional one, and that this "line between"
actually *precedes*, in some sense, the terms it separates?

Prière à desceller d'*une ligne de vie*

What is a *ligne de vie*, a lifeline, this curved line on the palm of the
hand that is supposed to mark out a future or a destiny? In an interview
of 1983 entitled "Unsealing ('the old new language'),"[7] Derrida is asked
the question of his "destiny as a philosopher" and he speaks, pointedly,
of the "lifeline":

> Do you seriously want to get me to speak about my "destiny" under
> these conditions? No. But if by destiny one means a singular manner
> of not being free, then what interests me is especially that, precisely
> and everywhere: this intersection of chance and necessity, the *life-
> line*, the proper language of a life, even if it is never pure. . . . I feel
> myself to be engaged, for the last twenty years, in a long detour that
> would lead me back to this thing, this idiomatic writing whose pu-
> rity, I realize, is inaccessible, but about which I continue to dream.
> (*P* 118)[8]

The lifeline does not trace, according to Derrida, a destiny that would be
determined and accessible, a sort of pre-text, a writing *avant la lettre*, a
line of writing before speech and conventions. "This intersection of
chance and necessity" would be, rather, "the proper language of a life,"
the idiomatic writing of which he dreams. The lifeline would be a sort
of idiomatic writing, so proper, so unique, that it would remain forever

unappropriable. If the lifeline is thus readable, accessible, it is because it is already in the process of becoming detached from itself, in a line of poetry, for example—or else in a prayer, a prayer that can thus no longer be the vain attempt to rewrite a destiny that is already fixed and determined.

Just after this idiomatic reinterpretation of the lifeline, the interviewer goes on to ask Derrida: "What do you mean by 'idiomatic'?" He answers:

A property that one cannot appropriate; it signs you without belonging to you; it only appears to the other and it never comes back to you except in flashes of madness that bring together life and death, that bring you together dead and alive at the same time. You dream, it's unavoidable, about the invention of a language or of a song that would be yours, not the attributes of a 'self,' rather the accentuated paraph, that is, the musical signature, of your most unreadable history. I am not talking about a *style* but an intersection of singularities, habitat, voices, graphism, what moves with you and what your body never leaves. In my memory, what I write resembles a dotted-line drawing that would be circling around a book to be written in what I call for myself the "old new language," the most archaic and the most novel, therefore unheard-of, unreadable at present. (In Prague, you know, the oldest synagogue is called the Old-New Synagogue.) This book would be something completely different from the path that it nevertheless still resembles. . . . an interminable anamnesis whose form is being sought; not only *my* history, but culture, languages, families, Algeria first of all. (*P* 118–19)

If the lifeline marks a point of pure singularity, "the proper language of a life," it would seal a destiny and render it, in some sense, unreadable, inaccessible, unappropriable. In order, then, to become readable, in order to leave its trace, in order to open itself up to interpretation, the lifeline must begin to get detached from itself. That is the real necessity, the real fatality or destiny, of a lifeline: it can never remain pure, and so is never absolutely "itself." The lifeline, like the "old new language," must be repeated, inscribed in a coded and iterable language. In order to be read, appropriated, interpreted, the lifeline must be signed, the line that opens and first gives time itself marked and inscribed *in* time. In "Shibboleth," a great work on the poem, first delivered in 1984 but then published—it too—in 1986, Derrida writes: "Wherever a signature has cut into an idiom, leaving in language the trace of an incision, the memory of an incision *at once* unique and iterable, cryptic and readable, there is date"

(*SQ* 48).[9] The lifeline dates and dates itself; it is itself dated and read. It is linked to the line of poetry to the extent that it lends itself to repetition. It is indeed the inscription of Necessity, but Necessity no longer dictates some particular event to come—death, for example, on some predetermined day—but repetition itself: "It is necessary that this repeat itself. It is Necessity itself, *Anankē*. The One, as self-repetition, can only repeat and recall this instituting violence" (*AF* 79). If the lifeline is indeed this intersection of chance and necessity, if it is what is most idiomatic, most "our own," it does not belong to us. As Derrida says in an interview on Paul Celan, "language is not something that belongs, that is, something that belongs to someone [*la langue n'appartient pas*]" (*SQ* 97–107). Like the proper language of a life, then, the lifeline would have no proper meaning before becoming nonproper.

The poem would thus be the unsealing of a lifeline, of an idiomatic and unreadable writing. The poem would tear open the seal placed on an unreadable idiom; it would lead the "old new language" into the language of the poem. It would thus be necessary to undo the seal of a singular or unique destiny in order to read it, that is, in order to sign and seal it in turn: *that* is necessity. The line of poetry would thus be like the memory of an "event sealed with an indecipherable signature, a set of initials, a line [*dessin*] before the letter" ("SN" 60); it would be like the specter of a lifeline: "And each time, at the same date, what one commemorates will be the date *of* that which could never come back. This date will have signed or sealed the unique, the unrepeatable, but to do so, it must have given itself to be read in a form sufficiently coded, readable, and decipherable for the indecipherable to *appear* . . . even if it appears *as* indecipherable" (*SQ* 18–19). Where to draw the line, then, between the lifeline and the line of poetry? Let us begin again at the intersection of *desceller* and *de*, at the caesura that cuts the verse in two, that detaches or loosens one part from the other.

Prière à *desceller* d'une ligne de vie

According to Littré, the verb *desceller* means to open up what is sealed, to break or lift off the seal of an act or document. But the word also means to undo or detach, to loosen, to "tear out what was sealed in," in the sense that one speaks of loosening or working loose a stone (*pierre*)—Littré's example—from a wall.

How, then, is one to hear "prière à desceller d'une ligne de vie"? In at least three ways: First, if the *de* suggests possession, then there would be a prayer to be unsealed or loosened *in* or *on* the lifeline; the prayer would belong, so to speak, to the lifeline—as if the lifeline sealed up within its pure idiom, within its unbroachable singularity, a prayer to be unsealed. But, second, *de* can also suggest that the lifeline is the *means* by which the prayer is unsealed. The lifeline would not be or would not contain the prayer to be unsealed but would be that which helps in its unsealing. Third, the *de* can suggest separation or differentiation; the prayer must be unsealed—that is, loosened, torn away, separated, or differentiated—from a lifeline.

In the interview where Derrida speaks of the lifeline, he evokes—is this an accident?—unsealing. He is essentially asked the question that I am asking here: How are we to read Derrida today? "To read you," says the interviewer, "one has to have read Derrida," and Derrida replies: "But that's true for everyone! Is it so wrong to take account of a past trajectory, of a writing that has in part sealed itself, little by little? But it is also interesting to undo, to unseal. I also try to begin over again in proximity to the simplest things, which is sometimes difficult and dangerous" (*P* 117). In order to read someone, no matter whom, it is necessary to reckon with a writing that is sealed, signed, identifiable, and coded. It is necessary to read by means of all the more or less traditional protocols of reading. But Derrida says that it is also interesting to undo, to unseal, to open the seal of a signature, to begin again as close as possible to the most simple—as close as possible to "the old new language," a language even more "sealed," so idiomatic that it would no longer even belong to the one who uses it—a remainder that shall remain forever indecipherable.

The word *desceller* thus unseals or undoes itself: it means at once opening the singular to the multiple, the most idiomatic to light and readability ("What desingularizes, unseals, desiglums, opens the eyes by blinding"; *GL* 171b), as well as opening, lifting off, or undoing the seal of the signature in order to seek out the idiom that does not come to light, that cannot be read, and does not belong even to the author.

There would be a prayer (a silence) to unseal, to open, in the lifeline. But such a prayer can be loosed or unsealed only by opening the seal on the surface of the lifeline, only by opening the lifeline as prayer to readability. Against the well-known line of Wittgenstein, Derrida says, "What cannot be said above all must not be silenced, but written" (*PC* 194).

The interview entitled "Unsealing" continues:

Q: Are you going to write it [this book in the "old new language"]?
JD: You must be joking . . . But the accumulation of dreams, projects, or notes no doubt weighs on what is written in the present. One day, some piece of the book may fall out like a stone [*pierre*] that keeps the memory of a *hallucinatory architecture* to which it

might have belonged. The stone still resonates and vibrates, it emits a kind of painful and indecipherable bliss, one no longer knows whose or for whom . . . (*P* 119; my emphasis)

Derrida dreams of a language that would be like the invention to come of the oldest of languages, the invention of an archaic language of prayer, the invention of a hallucinatory architecture—as I will suggest in conclusion, a kind of temple, where each stone would retain the memory of this unreadable language, where each stone, *chaque pierre*, would be like the promise or the prayer, the *prière*, of a language to come. The "prayer to be unsealed [*prière à desceller*]" is thus situated right near the "old new language" (to unseal), right near the oldest and newest of languages, still to come.[10] One must thus learn how to read between the lines.

Prière à desceller d'une ligne de vie

The line blurs or, rather, gets drawn out, between the reading of the poem (the unsealing of the meaning of the poem) and the reading in the poem (the prayer to be unsealed), between chance (the line of poetry) and destiny (the lifeline), between the constative ("there is a prayer to be unsealed . . .") and the performative (the verse as prayer). By working with the multiple meanings and interpretations of the poem, notably of "line," "unseal [*desceller*]," and, in a moment, *vers*, we begin to unseal or work loose not so much a "thesis" on the prayer as an idiomatic writing about it, perhaps even a prayer right on the poem. I say "perhaps" here because, for Derrida, prayer never presents itself as such in a present but remains always "to come." If Aristotle speaks true when he suggests in *On Interpretation* (3.17a4) that the prayer is an enunciation that is "neither true nor false," it is because the vocation of prayer is not to make some claim or other but to call for or to affirm the *to come* itself: "The affirmation of the *to come*: this is not a positive thesis. It is nothing other than affirmation itself, the 'yes' insofar as it is the condition of all promises and all hope, of all awaiting, of all performativity, of all opening toward the future, whatever it may be, for science or for religion" (*AF* 67–68). For Derrida, prayer is nothing other than an affirmation of the to come, a prayer for another voice to come, a prayer for the origin of prayer, an origin to be found not in one's own voice but always in the voice of the other. Derrida writes in *Cinders*: "The words 'another voice' recall not only the complex multiplicity of people, they *call*, they *ask for* another voice: 'another voice, again, yet another voice.' It is a desire, an order, a prayer or a promise, as you wish: 'another voice, may it come soon now, again, another voice . . .' An order or a promise, the desire of a prayer, I don't know, not yet" (*C* 27). To unseal the prayer means to make it readable, to de-singularize it, in a sense, to betray or annul it; but it is only in making it readable, audible, multiple that there is the possibility of a prayer that can be opened or that can open itself up to the vocation of prayer, to this other prayer in prayer, to this call for another voice. In "How to Avoid Speaking: Denials," a conference first delivered—it too in 1986—in Jerusalem, Derrida writes:

> In every prayer there must be an address to the other as other, and I will add, at the risk of shocking you, *God, for example.* In the act of addressing oneself to the other as other one must, of course, pray, that is, ask, implore, summon. It does not matter what one is asking for; pure prayer asks only that the other hear the prayer, receive it, be present to it, be the other as such, gift, call, and the very cause of the prayer. (*PSY II* 176)

But just as the lifeline or the proper language of a life can never remain proper, prayer itself can never itself remain prayer. At the end of "How to Avoid Speaking: Denials" Derrida asks himself with regard to prayer: "Does one have the right to think that, as pure address, on the edge of silence, foreign to every code and to every rite, hence to every repetition, prayer should never be turned away from its present by a notation or by the movement of an apostrophe, by a multiplication of addresses? That each time it takes place only once and should never be recorded [*consignée*]?" (*PSY II* 194).

It might be thought that prayer can or must remain pure, that its inscription in a coded, repeatable language represents a betrayal or a failure, a fall, if you will, in the very vocation of prayer. But Derrida continues by asking if a coded language, if rites—in short, if religion, if writing—are not the only chance for prayer, just as the line of poetry, the poem, a writing and a reading, would be the only chance for a lifeline: "But perhaps the contrary is the case. Perhaps there would be no prayer, no pure possibility of prayer, without what we make out as a threat or a contamination: writing, the code, repetition, analogy or the (at least apparent) multiplicity of addresses, initiation. If there were a purely pure experience of prayer, would one need religion and affirmative or negative theologies? Would one need a supplement of prayer?" (*PSY II* 195). Prayer must supplement, must supplement itself, in order to supplicate (see *PSY II* 145). Prayer, like the lifeline, must become contaminated by repetition, by writing—for example, by poetry; the palm opens up into psalm, the life into a line. It is thus only by opening prayer, by reading or reciting it, by unsealing our lips, that prayer can be left to its silent vocation. Can we thus unseal the prayer, the desire, the dream of an old new language through this little verse published in 1986?

Petite fuite alexandrine (*vers toi*)

Prière à desceller d'une ligne de vie

If there is indeed prayer here, to or toward whom is it addressed? The title tells us "toward you," *vers toi*? But who is "you"? How is one to read or unseal "you"?

It may be that there is in fact a single addressee of this one-line poem (a hypothesis Derrida himself continually entertains in his readings of Celan), a single he or she for whom this little *fuite* was destined; it may be that this individual, a name or identity, is encrypted in the poem itself and that this individual marks the very event of the poem. With the death of Derrida, and in the absence of any other testimony, this singular addressee may remain forever unreadable, forever unknown, lost at the bottom of the crypt. But since "I" too can read the poem, since "I" too can unseal a meaning or meanings within it, "I" too am *toi*, "I" too am "you." Derrida writes in "Shibboleth":

> The crypt takes place (it is a passion, not an action, of the poet) wherever a singular incision marks language. . . . But the voice of the poem carries beyond the singular cut. I mean by this that the cut becomes readable for certain of those who have no part in the event or the constellation of events consigned to it, for those excluded from partaking, yet who may thus partake and impart. (*SQ* 48)

A reader can read the poem, this poem, without being its singular addressee; he or she can decipher, unseal, interpret, or read without having taken part in the singular event that is consigned to the poem and sealed up within it. Derrida cites in "Shibboleth" Celan's poem "With Letter and Clock" (*SQ* 19):

> Wax,
> to seal the unwritten
> that guessed
> your name,
> that enciphers
> your name.

Just as the lifeline marks the poem with its idiomatic writing, the "you" marks the poem with its unrepeatable singularity; but just as the lifeline becomes ineluctably the line of poetry, the encrypted "you" opens up to reading and is repeated in the reader. The sealed unwritten becomes unsealed in writing, the unique and unreadable accessible to another, to another "you" still to come, a "you" that would be like the very opening to the future.

The "you" is thus at once singular and plural, a multiplicity of singularities. In the interview entitled "Unsealing," Derrida asks: "Are the signatories and addressees identifiable in advance or produced and divided by the text? Do the sentences describe something or are they doing something? For example, when I say, in an undecided tone: 'You come [*Tu viens*].' Do we have sure criteria for deciding it?" (*P* 117).

The example is hardly fortuitous. The "you" to whom the poem is addressed comes not after the poem but before it; it is the "you" that in some sense animates the poem that comes toward "you." The envois of *The Post Card* are in this sense a great love poem written to "you," toward a "you" that precedes and calls the addressor, that destines him, but that is also always to come, a you that might be approached only in "prayer" and whose name is perhaps not yet even known. Here is what the addressor of *The Post Card* will have received one day from "you" on the subject of prayer—and I here faithfully transcribe not only the words but the fifty-two blanks, the silence, that would be in *The Post Card* like the very respiration or respect, the aspiration or attention, of all prayer . . .

> One day, years ago, you wrote me this that I, the amnesiac, know by heart, or almost: ". . . are we delirious, each alone, for ourselves? Are we waiting for an answer or something else? No, since at bottom we are asking for nothing, no, we are asking no question. The prayer."   Okay, I'll call you right away. You know everything, before me
>   you will always precede me. (*PC* 19)

Everything begins with "you." The *vers*, the verse, that goes *vers*, that goes toward, you, that goes *vers toi*, begins with *toi*, with you. As another line of *The Post Card* puts it: "You are my Destiny, my Destined One" (*PC* 163).

But, as we have already seen, everything also begins with this idiomatic writing that is the lifeline, this idiomatic writing that opens to "you." The poem, the prayer of the poem, if prayer there is, would thus be like a line stretched between two singular, inaccessible, and undecipherable points, between the lifeline and you: to cite the subtitle of a recent text, "between two infinites, the poem."[11]

The prayer to be unsealed of a lifeline would be nothing, at the limit, but the pure line or ellipsis of an apostrophe, an apostrophe *to* or *toward* (*vers*) . . . Within each and every work of Jacques Derrida there is, I believe, just such an apostrophe, *une prière à insérer*, or, as one also says in French, *un prière d'insérer*. (Derrida speaks in another recent book of this "exquisite tradition" of the *prière d'insérer*, this tradition of placing or inserting a little summary text within the book itself, a supplement that advertises, stands in for, or represents the book, a little text that, as Derrida writes, is "not an intrinsic part of the work it introduces" [*GG* 60] and so is often more idiomatic and elliptical than others, more fragile, more vulnerable, more detachable, more exposed to chance, to accident, to loss, in short, to some kind of *fuite*.[12])

Prière à desceller d'une ligne de *vie*

Finally, the question of life. As Shelley poses the question in *The Triumph of Life*, a poem to which Derrida will have devoted a long and important reading in *Parages* (another text from 1986!): "Then, what is life?" If there is a response to this question, it would be found not *in* life "itself," and not *outside* life either, but in what Derrida calls a tension within the tradition or within our heritage, within what holds us to life by giving a future to this heritage, by giving us to think and rethink, for example, what the old word *vie*, what "life," first means.

> Life—being-alive—is perhaps defined at bottom by this tension internal to a heritage, by this reinterpretation of what is given in the gift, and even what is given in filiation. . . . But I will not use any of these words without placing quotation marks and precautions around them. It would be necessary to think life on the basis of heritage, and not the other way around. (*FWT* 3–4)

"Life"—just like the "lifeline"—is stretched between two shores and two dreams, between *deux rives* and *deux rêves*. In an interview in *Paper Machine*, Derrida sketches out these two dreams in the following way: on the one hand, the dream of "an absolute memory" where everything is kept or saved, where everything survives in memory, where "after the keeping of everything, really (it's my very respiration)—my imagination continues to project this archive *on paper*," and, on the other hand, the dream "of living paperless," that is to say, without machines, conventions, or repetition, without writing, a dream that sometimes sounds to Derrida's ears, he confides, "like a definition of 'real life,' of the living part of life" (*PM* 65).

But here is already the sur-vival of "life" itself: "true life" is always elsewhere; it comes already, as we know, from our heritage or tradition, from a line of poetry, and it is taken up, as we also know, by one of the great thinkers of filiation at the beginning of *Totality and Infinity*.[13] "Life" lends itself already to citation, to repetition—a "true life" already, originally, between quotation marks. "Life" between quotation marks—*now that's truly living*.

The "true life" that resists reproduction and repetition, that cannot be reduced to paper, that defies all translation, inevitably calls for translation and iteration, the arrival of another language, that is, the future and the survival of "life" itself. "True life," as close as possible to the proper language of a life, to a line of life, resists translation and, in this very resistance, calls for the advent of the other, of the foreigner: "The resistance to translation *is* translation itself, it is the experience of translation but [also] the experience of the other language . . . the non-said of my own idiom must be at the same time the opening to the language of the other, to the other language" (*MAR* 121).

And so, finally, after a long detour, a first translation:

Prayer to be unsealed from a lifeline

The chance of English here, the chance of translation, is that *lifeline*— unlike *ligne de vie*—suggests not only the curved line of the hand that would trace one's life span or the major events in one's life but that which saves our life, or, better, that which keeps us alive, allows us to live on for a time. A *lifeline* is a safety line, a cord or rope thrown out to save us from disaster or death, from drowning, for example, a link or line that comes to our aid at a critical moment, attaching us to life and keeping us alive.

Prayer to be worked loose from a lifeline.

Jacques Derrida

This singular poem, this verse, this *vers*, this *line* between two singularities, is, in the end, neither a *ligne de vie* nor a *ligne de poésie* but, simply, a *lifeline*—yet another *lifeline* signed "Jacques Derrida." There thus cannot be, there must not be, any definitive translation of this line, just as there cannot be, there must not be, any definitive interpretation of Derrida's life and work. We must at once read this line, interpret and translate it, and yet also—and precisely through this—leave it intact. We must renounce ever knowing definitively what this line tells us, what the life and work of Jacques Derrida will have given us. It is only on this condition that we will continue to read, interpret, and translate him:

Prayer to be worked free by a lifeline

For me, as for so many others, in France and abroad, "Jacques Derrida"—at the intersection of life and work—will have been just such a *lifeline*. He will have saved us not from death but from our dogmatisms and prejudices with regard to life and death, with regard to what living, living on, and saving all mean. He will have saved us from a moribund repetition by giving us a future for writing, for philosophy, for thought, and for "life." Each book, each line, attaches us to life by giving us the chance for a counter-signature, for a joyous affirmation, for a way of scanning our very breathing otherwise—like a prayer or a promise, a lifeline thrown out to and from another shore. For Derrida will have always said *Oui, à l'étranger*, that is, "Yes, to the stranger. Yes, in foreign parts," yes to being taken abroad (*PSY II* 231). In each case, he will have signed with his first name, as he himself says in *The Post Card*, "*J'accepte* [I accept, with *J'ac* being a homophone of *Jacques*], this will be my signature henceforth . . . *de toi j'accepte tout* [from you I accept everything]" (*PC* 26).

How many times did Jacques Derrida say in his lifetime, *Oui, j'accepte*? How many times did he sign with such an affirmation, and how many of these affirmations, how many of these crypts, are out there waiting to be read, reaffirmed, and countersigned? How many lines, how many affirmations, how many prayers are there? How many gifts and how many benedictions? How many "traces in the history of the French language"? And now, though very differently, in ours?

⟁

I spoke at the outset of this chapter of having rediscovered Derrida's one-line poem in the *Cahier de l'Herne* devoted to his work—a volume I received in the mail, I must now add, only two days before Derrida's death. It was an unexpected and most welcome gift, but it was not the only one I received that day in October 2004. For in paging through that volume a couple of lines from another text jumped off the page and caught my eye, lines I had both read and heard before but had forgotten or never really paid sufficient attention to.[14] Like a crypt within a crypt, these lines, cited by Derrida in a text entitled "'*Le parjure*,' Perhaps," are taken from Henri Thomas's novel *Le parjure*. Spoken by the main character of Thomas's novel, Stéphane Chalier, as he looks at the hand of Judith, his wife to be, the lines come from a poem by Hölderlin entitled, precisely, "Lifelines." Gazing at Judith's hand, Chalier recalls and cites these lines from "Lifelines" as a kind of prayer, but one, I believe, with neither redemption nor salvation in view, a prayer that speaks not of the one and only God, and not of a plurality of gods, but of *a* god, a god to come, perhaps, who will complete us, or complete our lifelines.[15] The lines run: "The lines of life [or "Lifelines"] are different, / What we are here below, only a god can there complete."

Now it turns out that these two lines, cited by Derrida citing Thomas, whose character Stéphane Chalier is citing Hölderlin, are in fact but the first and third lines of a four-line poem by Hölderlin. According to a letter written by Hölderlin's friend Ernst Zimmer in 1812, Hölderlin would have written these lines in pencil on a plank of wood upon seeing in Zimmer's home the sketch (the outline or contour) of a temple. The full poem reads:

> Lifelines are different,
> Like paths and the contours of mountains.
> What we are here, a god can there complete,
> With harmonies and eternal recompense and repose.[16]

I shall leave these lines, these lifelines, without comment, except to say that I hear them today as expressing the infinite sadness of an epitaph, as lines that come to us from the future and that call us to complete them, or, rather, to respond to them, as only Jacques Derrida could have done. Perhaps we can thus read or receive them today as the gift or benediction of the life and work of a man who wrote one day in 1986:

> Prière à desceller d'une ligne de vie.

But also, in the only language he says he ever learned to cultivate:

> Désir ou don du poème, la date se porte, en un mouvement de bénédiction, vers la cendre.[17]

Conclusion

The World Over

How could one not think the world of him—especially here, at this gathering, so soon after his death, at the annual meeting of an organization, SPEP, where so many of us will have been in one way or another influenced by his thought, educated by his writing, inspired by his presence, touched by his generosity, graced by his hospitality, or blessed by his friendship?[1] How could one not think the world of him, especially here, where almost any one of us could have been honored, as we three have been honored, to speak this evening of his extraordinary life, work, and legacy, where almost any one of us could have borne witness to the genuine chance of reading one of his essays or books at a critical moment in our education, of receiving a gracious or encouraging letter penned by his hand, or of attending one of his seminars at the École Normale Supérieure or École des Hautes Études, where students from around the world came to study with him and to bear away with and within them not simply a teaching but an ethos and a voice, a masterly and yet always inviting, hospitable voice—a voice I once heard say innumerable times during the academic year 1988–89, and many times within me since then, even if, I must confess, it sounds so very different today: *O mes amis, il n'y a nul ami*, that is, O my friends, there is no friend.

How could you not think the world of him, and I say "him" here not just because I no longer know precisely what this proper name refers to today, but because of the heartbreak I feel each time I pronounce the name "Jacques Derrida," heartbreak at the way it now oscillates between the signature of an incomparably rich and varied corpus that will be read and reread long into the future, with more than seventy books, translated into innumerable languages, and many more, we can be sure, to come, a corpus we have genuine cause to celebrate today, a corpus with indisputably seminal texts on Plato, Aristotle, Augustine, Descartes, Rousseau, Kant, Hegel, Kierkegaard, Nietzsche, Freud, Husserl, Heidegger, Benjamin, Levinas, but also Joyce, Ponge, Celan, and Blanchot, and the list goes on and on, a name that oscillates between a signature for all that and the proper name of a mentor and friend we will never see again, a teacher who, as he taught us, speaks now only in us, a name for what has gone irremediably from our lives, from our world, without any hope of resurrection or redemption.

Three weeks after his death, it is still uncertain, and will be for some time, whether the surest sign of fidelity is to praise the person or his work, to speak out of appreciation and celebration or sadness and sorrow, to reread and rethink something in that enormous corpus that remains still so unknown to us or else to recall more private moments, to share among us the memories we each have of him. Since he himself often gave in to the desire or perhaps even need to speak of the dead friend in mourning by recalling not only public deeds but private moments or personal anecdotes, I feel emboldened to recount here just two among so many other possible ones. The first dates back to 1996, to October 7, 1996, to be precise, during a conference organized by my colleague David Krell at DePaul University on the topic mourning and politics in Derrida's work. At an informal luncheon with Derrida during that conference, another friend and colleague, Peg Birmingham, told us all the funny story of how her daughter, then three, had appropriated and made her own the story she had heard from a family member of how they had recently been in a roll-over car accident and found themselves, fortunately unhurt, suspended from above by their seat belts. A couple of days after hearing the story, Peg's daughter said with conviction and insistence, "Mom, remember that time we were in a car accident and I was hanging from the roof of the car in my car seat?" Peg laughed, and we all laughed, at the obvious moral of the story—kids say the darndest things and you better be careful what you say around them. But Jacques, with a bit of a mischievous smile, turned to Peg and asked, "Peg, why do you continue to repress the memory of this accident?"

The second anecdote comes from yet another friend and colleague, Bill Martin, who tells of Derrida back in the 1980s at the University of Nebraska giving one of those long, difficult, though, for so many of us, always riveting lectures, after which a woman from the law school who was supposed to respond to Derrida's talk stood up and began, "Professor Derrida, listening to you I'm reminded of a very famous movie here in the United States about a young girl named Dorothy and her little dog Toto who get taken up by a tornado and transported to another world or magical land where all kinds of strange things happen." And the woman went on like this for several minutes, as Bill tells it, in excruciating detail, giving everyone just a taste of what it must have been like to be Jacques Derrida on a daily basis, before concluding, "So at the very end Toto pulls the curtain aside to reveal that behind the scenes, pulling all the strings, creating all the illusions with smoke and mirrors, was a wizard with *very white hair*, and, well, what I'm wondering, Professor Derrida, is whether you aren't just a little bit like that?" And Derrida, again with a little smile, answered right back. "You mean am I like the dog? Yes, absolutely."

These anecdotes are instructive on so many levels—for Jacques Derrida was a consummate teacher even when he wasn't teaching. Why should we, after all, unquestioningly believe the adult's version of events, or the version offered by conscious life rather than that of the unconscious? Why not, as a hermeneutic principle, listen for voices and meanings beyond the intended one? Why not try to pull the curtain on our metaphysical presumptions or illusions instead of trying to confront them head on? Why not imagine the child's version, why not take the side of the dog, or else, as I heard Derrida do this past spring at the College International de Philosophie in Paris—an institution he himself helped found in 1983—the side of the sacrificed ram in the story of Isaac and Abraham on Mount Moriah?

Now, I recount these stories and not others because it just so happens that the last time I saw Jacques Derrida, this past summer, at the home of his niece and her family in a suburb of Paris not far from Ris-Orangis, the town where Jacques lived for so many years with his wife Marguerite, he began to reminisce about his family and about Algeria as I had never heard him do before. He talked about his younger sister, with whom, Jacques recounted, he never had even the slightest disagreement or argument after the very first days of this sister's life, when he, then four years old, first insisted that his parents send his newborn sister back in the suitcase he had assumed she arrived in and then, once he saw that this was not going to happen, tried to set her crib on fire. A relationship of total and complete peace, Jacques said with that same mischievous smile, just after having recounted these early, violent manifestations of sibling rivalry.

During that same dinner, Jacques also told his own dog story, the story of moving to France, away from his family in Algeria and away from a beloved childhood dog, who had been given away or had somehow gotten lost during Jacques's stay in France, a dog, then, whom he had never seen buried and so roamed about within him more than it otherwise might have. Many years later, during a visit back to Algeria, Jacques said he saw on a beach that same childhood dog, the very same dog, a dog from that lost world, it seemed, since it came running up to him as if it recognized him, even if the lapse of time meant it could not possibly be the same, a dog that trailed him the entire day and even ran after his car for a long time as he left the beach. He told this story with a sort of smile that suggested at once amusement, wonder, and melancholy, melancholy because the past was gone, completely gone, and yet still lived on in him *as irremediably gone*, not only this dog, of course, but his parents, certain siblings and friends, that whole life, that long-lost Algeria, a melancholy he liked to call his "nost-algeria." And he made a couple of remarks that night about his illness and his death, about events planned for his seventy-fifth birthday over a year away, which he doubted he would ever attend, comments we all tried lamely to dismiss so as to convince him—or really ourselves—that he had much more time left.

It was impossible not to think that evening about his death, and about everything he had written in recent years about the deaths of others through a singular thought of mourning that intersected, especially in a couple of final texts, a singular way of thinking the world. In the spring of 2003, after having been diagnosed with pancreatic cancer, Jacques wrote a short preface to the French edition of *The Work of Mourning*, the collection of eulogies and funeral orations that he gave Pascale-Anne Brault, Kas Saghafi, and me the unique privilege to put together. The title he chose for the French edition was *Chaque fois unique, la fin du monde*, "each time unique, the end of the world," one of those brilliant, inventive, aporetic formulations marked by a caesura without a verb to express what we, according to him, experience at the death of a friend (*CFU* 9– 11). In the opening paragraph of his preface to this volume honoring so many lost friends, Jacques wrote:

> Death declares each time *the end of the world entirely*, the end of every possible world, and *each time the end of the world as a unique, and thus singular, and thus infinite, totality.*
> . . . That is what "the world" means. Such a meaning is given to it only by what is called "death."

Those who will have followed Derrida's extraordinary itinerary over the last half century will hear in this reinterpretation of death and the world echoes or elaborations of his early analyses of, for example, Husserlian intersubjectivity, where, as Derrida read it, Husserl came to acknowledge in the famous fifth *Cartesian Meditation* the necessity of an interruption of phenomenology and of its principle of principles, originary intuition, in order to recognize the radical inaccessibility of the *alter ego*, of another world, we might say, except by way of appresentational analogy,[2] or else echoes of Heidegger on being toward death and the falling away of the everyday world, or echoes of Levinas, for whom the other's death, not my own, is the first death, and for whom the other first opens up the world for me.

At the very end of the little preface to *Chaque fois unique, la fin du monde*, Derrida returns to this reinterpretation of death and the world—opposing, this time, a thought of God and resurrection to this reinterpretation of the death of the other as the end of the world. He wrote, and I recall again that this was in the spring of 2003, the ambivalence of his words being even then almost too painful to bear: "This book is a goodbye book [*un livre d'adieu*]. A *salut*, a farewell, more than one farewell. Each time unique." He then proceeds to oppose the *salut*, the greeting and/or the farewell, to every notion of salvation or resurrection, even to Jean-Luc Nancy's version as *anastasis*, which, Jacques writes, "continues to console" by postulating the existence of a God who would ensure that "the end of *a* world would not be . . . the end of *the* world." Implicitly opposing this "God," this "*Dieu*," to the *adieu* or *salut* of death and the world, he continues:

> "God" means that death can put an end to *a* world, but cannot signify the end of *the* world. A world can always live on after another. There is more than one world, more than one possible world. . . . But death, death itself, if there is such a thing, leaves no place, not the least chance, for the replacement or survival of the sole and unique world, of the "sole and unique" that makes each living thing (animal, human, or divine), a sole and unique living being.

Death, death itself, if there is such a thing, thus appears to give us the meaning of the world just as the world comes to an end. Before death has, we might say, touched our lives in the world, we would have no sense of what the world really means, though we might have a sense of multiple worlds or multiple possibilities for opening up and experiencing the world. But with the death of a friend or loved one, these many worlds seem to disappear as the world itself comes to the fore in order to be eclipsed for a first and unique time. Each time unique, each time total, the death of a friend brings us the end of the world. While "God"—by which Derrida means the one and only, unique God—guarantees a horizon for the many possible deaths of many friends and the disappearance of their many worlds, death itself, inasmuch as it comes to us in the death of a friend, falls upon us from above, vertically, from out of the world, beyond any possible world or horizon. Instead, then, of trying to console us by reminding us that the death of the friend, however painful, is not, as we say, "the end of the world," Jacques Derrida teaches us that we must live with a loss that belongs to another order, another economy, a loss not *within* the world but *of* the world.

Hence we will speak, and it will be right to speak, of what we have lost, meaning what the world has lost, with the death of Jacques Derrida. But we owe it to Derrida to try to think with him what he means when he says that with the death of a friend it is not someone or other within the world we lose, but, uniquely, the world itself, the sole and unique world, that with the death of a friend the world itself is irremediably lost, beyond every possibility for mourning, every possibility of salvation or redemption. For there will be "living on" but there will be no resurrection.

Jacques's brief preface to *Chaque fois unique, la fin du monde* thus guides us in our mourning of the lost friend, and thus, and he knew it, in our mourning of him, but it also points the way to living justly with the friend in life. As was often the case with Derrida, this was done in a discreet, oblique gesture, as if merely in passing. At the very end of his short preface, indeed these are its final words, he writes, "Had I dared to propose a real introduction to this book it would be the essay I am publishing simultaneously with Éditions Galilée, *Béliers* [or *Rams*—subtitled *Uninterrupted Dialogue, Between Two Infinites, the Poem*].[3] This little book turns round a line from Celan that has been with me for so many years now: *Die Welt ist fort, ich muß dich tragen* [The world is gone, I must carry you]."

Unable to do justice to this rich and strategically complex text, which pays tribute to the life and work of Hans-Georg Gadamer through a reading of this line of Paul Celan, let me simply read a few lines with you as I move toward a conclusion. Derrida there writes in the context of his analysis of the line in question from Celan:

> According to Freud, mourning consists in carrying the other in the self. There is no longer any world, it's the end of the world, for the other at his death. And so I welcome in me this end of the world, I must carry the other and his world, the world in me. . . . But if *I must* (and this is ethics itself) carry the other in me in order to be faithful to him, in order to respect his singular alterity, a certain

melancholy must still protest against normal mourning. . . . The "norm" is nothing other than the good conscience of amnesia. It allows us to *forget* that to keep the other within the self, *as oneself,* is already to *forget* the other. (*SQ* 160)

Not, then, to idealize or incorporate the other's world into my own, not to make of that world *a* world, but to live with the melancholy of the end of the world, that is what Derrida seems to suggest we do or must do at the death of a friend. The title *Chaque fois unique, la fin du monde* thus appears to be something of a chiasmatic reinscription of *Die Welt is fort, Ich muß dich tragen,* both expressions of the inexorable and irremediable melancholia we undergo at the death of a friend.[4] In both cases, a caesura marks an interruption, that is, nothing less than the loss, withdrawal, or end of the world. "When the world is no more, when it is on the way to being no longer *here* but *over there,* . . . perhaps infinitely inaccessible, then I must carry *you,* you alone, you alone in me or upon me alone" (*SQ* 158). But Derrida also seems to intimate that this is not simply a response to the death of the friend, to what we might call the actual, effective death of the friend, but the origin of ethics itself in the relationship to the friend. Indeed, Derrida suggests that by reversing the order of the propositions in Celan's line *Die Welt ist fort, ich muß dich tragen,* and by inserting an *if . . . then* between them, we have something that resembles the very origin of ethics itself in the interruption of the world and all its ethical codes:

If (where) *I* must, myself, carry you, yourself, well, then, the world tends to disappear. The world is no longer there or no longer here, "Die Welt ist fort." As soon as I am obliged, from the instant when I am obliged *to you,* when I *owe,* when I owe it *to you,* owe it *to myself* to carry *you,* as soon as I speak to you and am responsible for you, or before you, there can no longer, essentially, be any world. There is no longer any world to support us, to serve as mediation, ground, earth, foundation, or alibi. Perhaps there is no longer anything but the abyssal altitude of a sky. I am alone in the world there where there is no longer any world. (*SQ* 158)

Die Welt is fort, Chaque fois unique. Ich muß dich tragen, La fin du monde. Though ethics and responsibility always exceed, for Derrida, political and ethical codes, though they exceed every kind of ritualization or institutionalization of, say, mourning or memory, there can be no ethics or responsibility without them.

Derrida wrote—let me read his words again—that when we are obligated, "There is no longer any world to support us, to serve as mediation, ground, earth, foundation, or alibi. Perhaps there is no longer anything but the abyssal altitude of a sky." This is what Derrida leaves us with today, it seems to me, not burdened by his death, not crushed beneath a world of cares, like Atlas in Heinrich Heine's "Die Heimkehr," where Atlas laments how he must bear or carry—*ich muß tragen*, he says—the whole world of sorrows, *die ganze Welt der Schmerzen*,[5] but elevated to a light though hardly irresponsible altitude, where, perhaps, we are called to act from beyond the world, called to act when the world is gone, from an abyssal height where, just perhaps, we may smile.

This word *smile* was, as many of you know, one of Jacques's last words to us, read by his son Pierre at his funeral three weeks ago. "I am smiling at you," he wrote, before ending with the verb *to be* in that perfectly appropriate subjunctive mood, "I love you and I am smiling at you wherever I may be [*Je vous aime et vous souris d'où que je sois*]."

I see that smile today, perhaps it will be different for me tomorrow, as a melancholic smile, one that reminds me today both not to forget him and not to remember him so well as to forget him. That smile, neither knowing nor condescending, an infinitely gentle and generous smile, a benediction, perhaps, reminds me that we can never prescribe or universalize the injunction and say "the world is gone, we must bear *him*," "we must bear Jacques Derrida or bear his name or memory in such and such a way," for there is no horizon by which to make this judgment, no knowledge to assure it, but, each time anew, each time the first time, trying to respond in a singular, responsible way, with all the risks this entails, "the world is gone, I must bear *you*, wherever *you* may be, whether in me, or us, or in this gathering among friends, among *your* friends—each time unique, the world over."

Notes

Introduction: *Bénédictions*—"traces in the history of the French language"

1. Derrida's original French reads, "Laisser des traces dans l'histoire de la langue française, voilà ce qui m'intéresse [to leave traces in the history of the French language—that's what interests me]" (*LLF* 37).

2. See *C* 21 ff., *AP* 6 ff., *AOA* 39, Hélène Cixous, *Insister: À Jacques Derrida* (Paris: Galilée, 2006), 60–61, and *LLF* 23.

3. On Derrida's love of the French language, see *MO* 51.

4. See "Rams," in *SQ* 135–63.

5. The subtitle of "Rams" is "Uninterrupted Dialogue—Between Two Infinities, the Poem."

6. For other references to "benediction," see *SQ* 32, 33, 34, 41, 42, 43, 55, and 69.

7. Interview with Mireille Calle-Grüber in "Où la philosophie et la poétique, indissociables, font événement d'écriture: Entretien avec Jacques Derrida," *C.E.S.P.R.* (ULB), no. 20 (1996): 156; cited in Myriam Van Der Brempt's excellent essay "Eloge et bénédiction," *Europe*, no. 901 (May 2004): 29–43. Van Der Brempt looks at the theme of benediction in Derrida from *Signsponge* and "Shibboleth" through *Touching Him—Jean-Luc Nancy*. See Derrida's development of the benediction in *HCFL*, where he writes, for example, "an event, like a benediction, can only be a grace, namely, that which happens or arrives just where not expected, when one no longer anticipates or calculates anything" (126). The benediction, like the event, is thus a "leap" out of the calculable or the anticipatable. Derrida forges the word *bondire* in *HCFL* in order to gesture toward this good-word-leap-bond, this "bond of immortality into a benediction" (130), a letter "countersigned by the benediction" (132).

8. I am gesturing here toward Safaa Fathy's very beautiful 2000 film "Derrida's Elsewhere."

9. "When I recall my life, I tend to think that I have had the good fortune to love even the unhappy moments of my life, and to bless them. Almost all of them, with just one exception. When I recall the happy moments, I bless them too, of course, at the same time as they propel me toward the thought of death, toward death, because all that has passed, come to an end" (*LLF* 52).

10. Here are Derrida's words: "Jacques n'a voulu ni rituel ni oraison. Il sait par expérience quelle épreuve c'est pour l'ami qui s'en charge. Il me demande de vous remercier d'être venus, de vous bénir. Il vous supplie de ne pas être triste, de ne penser qu'aux nombreux moments heureux que vous lui avez donné la chance de partager avec lui. Souriez-moi, dit-il, comme je vous aurai souri jusqu'à la fin. Préférez toujours la vie et affirmez dans elle la survie . . . Je vous aime et vous souris d'où que je sois." Translated by Gila Walker in *Critical Inquiry* 33, no. 2 (Winter 2007): 462: "Jacques wanted no rites and no orations. He knows from experience what an ordeal it is for the friend who takes on this task. He asks me to thank you for coming and to bless you. He beseeches you not to be sad, to think only of the many happy moments you gave him the chance to share with him. Smile for me, he says, as I will have smiled for you until the end. Always prefer life and constantly affirm survival . . . I love you and am smiling at you from wherever I am."On deconstruction as affirmation of life, see *LLF* 51.

11. Derrida writes in *Demeure*, "the adverb *désormais* is for me one of the most beautiful, and one of the most untranslatable, words, in a word, in the French language" (*D* 102).

In a postscript to "NW"—yet another text of memory and of mourning, of birth and the future—Derrida writes, dating his words "July 15, 2000," his seventieth birthday:

> [It is] as if I had said to myself, in short, yet one more time but once and for all, for good and forever: *from now on*, no more writing, especially not writing, for writing dreams of sovereignty, writing is *cruel* . . .
>
> Whence my definition of withdrawal [*le retrait*], my nostalgia for retirement [*la retraite*]: *from now on*, before and without the death *toward which*—as I have written elsewhere—*I advance*, begin finally to love life, namely birth. Mine among others—notice I am not saying *beginning* with mine. ("NW"; my emphasis on *from now on*)

In the spring of 2006 I thought both the French and English versions of this title were my own, echoes, perhaps, of Derrida's words from "The Night Watch," but, nevertheless, my own. It was only months later, back in Chicago, as I was rereading a paper Peggy Kamuf had given at DePaul University about a year before, that I realized my mistake. The title of her paper, now published in *Epochē* 10, no. 2 (Spring 2006): 203–20, is none other than "From Now On." Rather than renounce or lament this redundancy, I have decided to let it stand as yet another sign of a loss that, while absolutely unique and incomparable, resistant to repetition in another, was nonetheless profoundly shared. I thank Peggy for allowing me to share this title with her.

1. *Alors, qui êtes-vous?*: Jacques Derrida and the Question of Hospitality

1. *Qui êtes-vous?* is the name of a popular series of books published by La Manufacture that aims to introduce the work and life of important French artists and intellectuals. There is, for example, a volume entitled: *Emmanuel Lévinas: Qui êtes-vous?*

2. Maurice Blanchot, *Friendship*, trans. Elizabeth Rottenberg (Stanford, Calif.: Stanford University Press, 1997), 289–90.

3. Jacques Derrida, "Il n'y a pas de culture ni de lien social sans un principe d'hospitalité," *Le Monde*, December 2, 1997. My translation.

4. The unfortunate title of *The New York Times*'s obituary of October 10, 2004, was "Jacques Derrida, Abstruse Theorist, Dies in Paris at 74."

5. See *AP* 10, 33–34. For an excellent analysis of the notion of hospitality in Derrida's work and of deconstruction as a hospitable form of thought, see the final chapter of Hent de Vries, *Religion and Violence: Philosophical Perspectives from Kant to Derrida* (Baltimore: Johns Hopkins University Press, 2002), 293–398.

6. "Je suis en guerre contre moi-même" was the title of the interview originally published in *Le Monde* on August 19, 2004.

2. Analogy and Anagram: Deconstruction as Deconstruction of the *as*

1. In "The University Without Condition," Derrida writes: "This small word, the 'as' of the 'as if' as well as the 'as' of the 'as such'—whose authority founds and justifies every ontology as well as every phenomenology, every philosophy as science or knowledge—this small word, 'as,' might well be the name of the true problem, not to say the target, of deconstruction" (*WA* 234).

2. "La pharmacie de Platon" ("Plato's Pharmacy") was first published in *Tel Quel*, nos. 32 and 33 (1969), and then republished in *Dissémination* (Paris: Editions du Seuil, 1972), 69–198. The first page reference is to the English translation in *Dissemination* and the second, which is provided where the French is at issue, is to the French edition. "*Khōra*" was first published in 1987 in *Poikilia: Études offertes à Jean-Pierre Vernant* (Paris: Éditions de l'EHESS) and then republished, with some changes, as a small book by Galilée in 1993. The English translation by Ian McLeod is included in *On the Name*, ed. Thomas Dutoit (Stanford, Calif.: Stanford University Press, 1995), 89–127.

3. Barbara Johnson translates the end of this sentence: "the irreducibility of structure and relation, of proportionality, within analogy."

4. Derrida writes: "Différance, the disappearance of any originary presence, is *at once* the condition of possibility *and* the condition of impossibility of the truth" ("PP" 168).

5. A similar reference to Kant can be found in "*K*" 110–111.

6. Derrida remarks on the "as if": "The abyss does not open all at once, at the moment when the general theme of *khōra* receives its name, right in the middle of the book. It all seems to happen just *as if*—and the *as if* is important to us here—the fracture of this abyss were announced in a muted and subterranean way, preparing and propagating in advance its simulacra and *mises en abyme*: a series of mythic fictions embedded mutually in each other" ("*K*" 113).

7. The "*Khōra*" essay concludes by referring, once again, to the notion of a *logos* as a living organism ("*K*" 96–97).

8. Derrida refers in this earlier text to the "*Khōra*" essay as a "work in progress" that will develop much more fully the reading of *Khōra* he is about to give (*PSY II* 170). While the "*Khōra*" essay will indeed read Plato's discourse on the *khōra* more fully and more rigorously, this earlier text is more direct in its opposition of the Good and the *khōra*—which, let me note, is still called throughout this text "the *khōra*" rather than "*Khōra*."

9. Though I cannot treat this here, the relationship between *Khōra* and the Good is at the center of a fascinating debate btween Derrida and John Sallis. See Sallis's *Chorology: On Beginning in Plato's "Timaeus"* (Bloomington: Indiana University Press, 1996), *Platonic Legacies* (Albany: State University of New York Press, 2004), and, most recently, *The Verge of Philosophy* (Chicago: University of Chicago Press, 2008), esp. chap. 3, 53–109.

10. Near the very end of "PP" Derrida speaks of "The irreducible excess, through the play of the supplement, of any self-intimacy of the living, the good, the true" ("PP" 169).

3. Derrida's *Laïcité*

1. The notion of *laïcité* is a nominalization, dating from around 1880, of the adjective *laic* or *laïque*, a notion enshrined in the French Constitution of 1958. Article 1 of the constitution reads: "La France est une République indivisible, laïque, démocratique et sociale. Elle assure l'égalité devant la loi de tous les citoyens sans distinction d'origine, de race ou de religion. Elle respecte toutes les croyances. Son organisation est décentralisée."

2. Though Derrida did not himself, to my knowledge, enter into the debate surrounding the "headscarf ban," at least one of his friends (and former students), Régis Debray, did. A member of the Stasi Commission appointed by French President Jacques Chirac to study the questions raised by the ban, Debray explains his support of the ban in *Ce que nous voile le voile: La République et le sacré* (Paris: Gallimard, 2004). In the summer of 2004, Derrida and Debray appeared together on French television for a lengthy one-on-one interview. The "headscarf ban" was never addressed directly during that program, though many of the premises for the debate were.

3. I am alluding here to Jean-Luc Nancy's long-awaited project, whose first volume has recently appeared under the title *Dis-Enclosure: The Deconstruction of Christianity*, trans. Bettina Bergo, Gabriel Malenfant, and Michael B. Smith (New York: Fordham University Press, 2008).

4. I am referring here, of course, to Dominique Janicaud et al., *Phenomenology and the "Theological Turn"* (New York: Fordham University Press, 2000).

5. There is thus no necessary contradiction between the thesis I am arguing for here and that found in the works of several scholars who have emphasized the undeniably "religious" thrust of Derrida's work—be it in the direction of a certain Christianity or a certain Judaism. To give just two examples, Ted Jennings, in *Reading Derrida / Thinking Paul* (Stanford, Calif.: Stanford University Press, 2006), argues convincingly that Derrida's work (on justice, the gift, hospitality, forgiveness, and so on) helps us not only to rethink and reinterpret Paul but to criticize "a whole theological institution" that, Jennings argues, has systematically overlooked these crucial sociopolitical aspects of Paul. Jennings thus counts himself among those theologians who—he writes citing Derrida from an interview in 1985—"applaud deconstruction, who need deconstruction, not against their faith but in service to their faith, against a certain theology, even against a certain academic theological institution" ("DA" 12). While Jennings thus takes Derrida in the direction of a certain Christianity that goes against the grain of a "certain theology," John D. Caputo, in works such as *The Prayers and Tears of Jacques Derrida* (Bloomington: Indiana University Press, 1997), takes Derrida with equal legitimacy in the direction of a certain "Jewish *alliance*," though one that would be, precisely, "*sans* Judaism" (xxiv–xxv). Caputo can thus acknowledge Derrida as "a secularist and an atheist" (xxiii) and as a thinker of a messianic promise that goes beyond every positive religion and can even act as a critical lever against every concrete messianism, a "religious" thinker, therefore, who is more profitably thought in relation to the prophetic discourses of Judaism than the apophatic discourses of Christianity, and especially those of negative theology. (See, e.g., the sections "God Is Not *différance*" (2–19), and "An Apocalypse *sans* Apocalypse to Jacques of El Biar" (88–101). What Caputo calls a "religion without religion" might thus well be another way of naming what I call here an "originary secularity," so long as that which opens up and drives this original secularity is faith in the very opening to the future rather than in a transcendental, unthinkable, or unknowable God, that is, as Caputo makes clear, so long as this faith is thought in terms of opening and promise and not of a relationship to the hyperessentiality of negative theology. As Caputo succinctly puts it, and as I tried to argue in the previous chapter, "*Différance* is especially not a hidden God, the innermost concealed Godhead of negative theology" (7). And that is precisely why *différance*—as well as *khōra*—is accessible, insofar as it is accessible, not through the thinking of analogy but through the practice of anagrams.

6. Carl Schmitt, *Political Theology: Four Chapters on the Concept of Sovereignty*, trans. George Schwab (Chicago: University of Chicago Press, 2006), 36.

7. See *PM* 118.

8. Derrida uses very similar language in "M" 164–65 and in *PM*, where he says, for example, that the "concepts of the 'political,' the state, and sovereignty especially, . . . are *theological in origin*. And hardly secularized" (116).

9. Derrida says he wanted to think about the death penalty in order, "hopefully, to change things" ("PMS" 38).

10. In *Psyche II* Derrida even speaks of the "ontotheological or metaphysical presuppositions that still underlie psychoanalytic theorems" (*PSY II* 162).

11. See Samuel Weber's excellent essay "God Bless America!" on the theologico-political character of "the people" in the U.S. Constitution, in *Experimenting: Essays with Samuel Weber*, ed. Simon Morgan Wortham and Gary Hall (New York: Fordham University Press, 2007), 13–43.

12. In *PM* Derrida says he is interested in the notion of the "world" (as opposed to the universe or cosmos) and its "religious history" (118).

13. The word *pacs* is an acronym ("Pacte Civil de Solidarité") for the provision adopted into French law in 1999 that allows both heterosexual and same-sex couples to enter into a civil contract or, translated literally, a "Civil Pact of Solidarity."

14. Of course, it is difficult to know at this point what legitimates even the notion of civil union and whether it is not itself informed by a quasi-religious notion of the "family."

15. Originally published in the *Frankfurter Allgemeine Zeitung*, the article was translated from the German by Jeffrey Craig Miller and is available online at http://www.logosjournal.com/issue_4.2/ratzinger.htm.

4. A Last Call for "Europe"

1. Fortunately, much excellent work has recently been done on this subject, from Marc Redfield's recent article "Derrida, Europe, Today" (*South Atlantic Quarterly* 106, no. 2 [Spring 2007]: 373–91) to Dana Hollander's *Exemplarity and Chosenness: Rosenzweig and Derrida on the Nation of Philosophy* (Stanford, Calif.: Stanford University Press, 2008), to Rodolphe Gasché's *Europe, or The Infinite Task: A Study of a Philosophical Concept* (Stanford, Calif.: Stanford University Press, 2008), which puts Derrida's thinking about Europe into dialogue with that of other European philosophers of the last century, from Husserl and Heidegger to Patočka. My preface to *The Other Heading* also looks at Derrida's analysis of European exemplarity in texts as far back as *The Problem of Genesis in the Philosophy of Husserl*, Derrida's master's thesis of 1953–54.

2. Originally published as "Une Europe de l'espoir," *Le Monde diplomatique*, November 2004, p. 3. The translation here is for the most part my own, though it has been revised in light of the excellent translation by Pleshette DeArmitt, Kas Saghafi, and Justine Malle ("A Europe of Hope," in *Epochē* 10, no. 2 [Spring 2006]: 407–12). Because an earlier version of this chapter was written and published well before the *Epochē* translation appeared, it seemed at once undesirable to rewrite the entire chapter to conform to this translation and imprudent not to take advantage of that translation's many clarifications and felicitous word choices.

3. This extension of "Europe" beyond its generally recognized geographical borders is being discussed today even within the European Union as it considers admitting Turkey as a member nation.

4. See, e.g., *POS* 71.

5. In an interview in *PM*, Derrida phrases his support for Europe in an even more subtle way. Though Derrida says he has anxieties about Europe being little more than a large economic bloc in a world of global capital and hesitations about a "demo-Christian hegemony" in Europe, he nonetheless declares himself to be "'against' all those who are 'against' Europe" (*PM* 133).

5. Derrida's America

1. Derrida comments on this subject in "AID" 224–25 and throughout "DA."

2. Derrida himself broaches the question of his own "American Question" in *CP* 27, 29. For an excellent analysis of Derrida's engagement with the U.S. context, see Peggy Kamuf's introduction to *WA*, 1–27.

3. See *TM* 96 and *CP* 25.

4. In the following years Derrida would publish two French translations of English texts, "Les frontières de la théorie logique," by W. V. O. Quine (with R. Martin), in *Les études philosophiques*, no. 2 (1964), and "Le monde-de-la-vie et la tradition de la philosophie américaine," by M. Farber, in *Les études philosophiques*, no. 2 (1964).

5. This was also the year of Derrida's marriage to Marguerite Aucouturier.

6. Derrida recalls this conference in several places. See, e.g., *CP* 274–75, as well as "Structure, Sign, and Play in the Discourse of the Human Sciences," in *WD* 278–93.

7. The publication in 1979 of *Deconstruction and Criticism* (New York: Seabury Press), with essays by Derrida, Harold Bloom, Paul de Man, Geoffrey Hartman, and J. Hillis Miller, did much to draw attention to this "Yale School." See also Jonathan Arac, Wlad Godzich, and Wallace Martin, eds., *The Yale Critics: Deconstruction in America* (Minneapolis: University of Minnesota Press, 1983).

8. See "DA" 1–33.

9. These are, in short, the facts, the kind of facts one would put in what Blanchot, in a text written after the death of Bataille, once called "the worst of histories, literary history" (Maurice Blanchot, *Friendship*, trans. Elizabeth Rottenberg [Stanford, Calif.: Stanford University Press, 1997], 290).

10. *D'ailleurs, Derrida* (1990), by Egyptian-born cineaste Safaa Fathy, and *Derrida* (2002), by Kirby Dick and Amy Ziering Kofman. Parts of both of these were filmed in the United States. The latter premièred at the Sundance Film Festival.

11. See "DA" 11–12.

12. As Derrida said in 1985: "it's in English departments that things are happening more than in departments of French or philosophy" ("DA" 23).

13. Derrida says that because everything in the United States is "concentrated within the academic institution . . . there was right away a greater intensity of reception in the positive sense of the term, and also, just as great an intensity of reaction, of rejection" ("DA" 5, 8).

14. Derrida responds in several places to the attacks made against him in the pages of *The New York Review of Books*, *The Times Literary Supplement*, *The New*

Criterion, Harvard Magazine, and elsewhere. See, e.g.: *N* 58, where Derrida responds to a 1983 article by William Bennett criticizing deconstruction in *The Wall Street Journal*; *MPD* 41–42n.5; *FWT* 17; and an interview from 1981 with Richard Kearney in *Dialogues with Contemporary Continental Thinkers* (Manchester: Manchester University Press), 124. One might have thought these criticisms to be things of the distant past, but many resurfaced, rather shamefully, in several obituaries of Derrida, including the one in *The New York Times.*

15. See the final essay of *MPD*, "Like the Sound of the Sea Deep Within a Shell: Paul de Man's War," 155–263. See also Derrida's comments in *LI* 153–54.

16. This was played out over the course of several weeks in the pages of *The New York Review of Books,* from February to April 1993, with Richard Wolin and Thomas Sheehan. See *P* 422–54.

17. See *"Honoris Causa*: 'This is *also* extremely funny,'" in *P* 399–421.

18. See *MAR* 125.

19. Derrida himself gives just such an interpretation in *CP* 29. On the "enormous prejudice" fostered in France regarding Derrida's superstardom in the United States, see *SUR* 55 and *P* 351.

20. See Derrida's comments on this subject in an interview with Peter Brunette and David Wills, "SA" 30.

21. In an interview in *PM*, Derrida responds with some irritation to the suggestion that the United States is "*the* country of deconstruction" and that deconstruction is there the object of a "cult." Such a reference, says Derrida, has become a cliché in France (114). On the idea of deconstruction as a sect, clique, cult, gang, or "mafia," see *PSY* 157.

22. Derrida writes, in an essay devoted to Michel de Certeau in *Psyche*: "Let me just murmur a few place-names to myself. I remember the California sun, in San Diego and in Irvine. I remember Cornell, Binghamton, New York" (*PSY II* 232). Derrida speaks of his special relation to New York City in *CP* 101, 119–20, and of his relation to California (to Santa Monica, in *JD* 19 and *CP* 230–33, and to Laguna Beach, in *TM* 23 and *CP* 276–78). California also provides the trope of tremors or earthquakes that became so prominent in Derrida's vocabulary. See, e.g., "DA" 18 and "M" 159. As for Derrida's many friends in America, from New York to California, I will not even begin to make a list, both because it would be too long and because I would risk leaving out too many.

23. "Declarations of Independence," in *N* 46–54.

24. See "DA" 29.

25. *OH* 82. Derrida concludes: "If, to conclude, I declared that I feel European *among other things,* would this be, in this very declaration, to be more or less European? Both, no doubt. Let the consequences be drawn from this. It is up to the others, in any case, and up to me *among them,* to decide" (*OH* 83).

26. See *P* 189.

27. Derrida spoke and understood, it should be specified, American rather than British English. In the interview "AID" 215, Derrida confesses, with a certain hyperbole, "English is difficult for me. I understand American to some extent. But, for me, English is a torture. So, sometimes I keep quiet because I feel incompetent."

28. Derrida cites the famous line "I am dead" from Poe's "The Facts in the Case of M. Valdemar" as an exergue to *SP*; Lacan's reading of Poe's "The Purloined Letter" is at the center of "*Le facteur de la vérité*" in *PC* 413–96. See also: "For the Love of Lacan," in *RES* 39–69; "Mes chances," *Confrontation* 19 (Spring 1988): 26ff.; *PC* 43, 104, 148, 151; *P* 21, 81; *GT* 105; *PF* 151. There is also a brief mention of Poe's "The Oval Portrait" in *MB* 36.

Melville's "Bartleby the Scrivener" is also frequently cited. See, e.g., *GD* 74–76 and *TS* 26–27.

There are many other references to American literature or literary figures, a brief mention of Faulkner and Stein in *AL* (55, 59) and of Wallace Stevens and William Carlos Williams in Derrida's homage to Joseph Riddel in *WM* (127–32). American literature is thus not at all absent from Derrida's work. But, for all his time in America, there is no "Double Session" on Whitman's *Leaves of Grass*, no reading of Hawthorne or Faulkner, Bellow or Roth, to match his readings of Blanchot or Mallarmé, Kafka or Celan. This is not to say, of course, that there are not such treatments of American literary figures among Derrida's as yet unpublished seminars. My friend Thomas Dutoit, who has helped catalogue and organize Derrida's archives, tells me, e.g., that in 1991–92 Derrida devoted several sessions of his seminar on the secret to Henry James's *The Aspern Papers*.

29. A good place to see Derrida's "elective affinities" is his interview with Derek Attridge in *AL* 33–75, where Derrida talks about: Sartre, Camus, Rousseau, Gide, Nietzsche, Mallarmé, Joyce, Celan, Bataille, Artaud, Blanchot, Flaubert, Céline, Ponge, Genet, Kafka, the Bible, George Sand, George Eliot, Virginia Woolf, Gertrude Stein, and Hélène Cixous.

30. *G* 44ff.; see also *EU* 138.

31. See *LI*, as well as Derrida's comments in *EU* 125.

32. Derrida cites contemporary American-born authors such as Noam Chomsky (see *R* 96 and *FWT* 132–34) and Jeremy Rifkin (see "The University Without Condition" in *WA* 225–26), but in neither case is there anything like a sustained engagement with such figures.

33. In *PM* Derrida, responding to a question about modern communications, says that there is no doubt some good and some bad in all of them but that what worries him "more than the technology itself in these exchanges is the increasing dominance of one language, and thus of one culture, the Anglo-American" (119). See also *EIRP* 28–29.

34. Derrida's official title at the École Normale Supérieure was *répétiteur* or, in the school's jargon, *caïman*. In this capacity he was responsible for preparing students for the *agrégation* exam in philosophy. At the École des Hautes Études his official title was *directeur d'études*.

35. Catherine Malabou writes, in *CP* 48: "How does Derrida traverse various countries, frontiers, cities, and languages? How does he set about his *experience* of traveling? It is possible to claim in the first place that Derrida has three countries: his native Algeria, France, and the United States. He divides his life, his teaching, his work, and his home(s) between the last two. We should say more

precisely that his way of life in France owes its stability only to the turbulence of a tension, that of the thread tying, by means of a complex network, his country of birth (Algeria) and his chosen country (United States)."

36. See *MAR* 55 and *SM* 70–71, where Derrida expresses skepticism regarding such undertakings.

37. "The Ends of Man" in *MP* 114.

38. "AT" 30. In *CF* 46, Derrida speaks of the use of religious language and oaths in American politics as well as the right of the American "President and governors" to grant clemency.

39. On the topic of globalization, or what Derrida preferred to call *mondialisation*, see *SUR* 120 and "The University Without Condition," *WA* 223.

40. Derrida became an astute observer of the American university system. He speaks, e.g., in *EU* 145 of the many apparently external pressures on the American university system: the economic, cultural, and political constraints, the link between government funding and military programs and university research, etc. See also "The University Without Condition," *WA* 202–37.

41. On the "homohegemonic" power of the American culture industry, see *ET* 47, 54, 86–87. Derrida spoke frequently of the worldwide presence of the American information industry, e.g., of the CNN phenomenon: "In a digitalized 'cyberspace,' prosthesis upon prosthesis, a heavenly glance, monstrous, bestial or divine, something like an eye of CNN, watches permanently" ("FK" 70n.17); see also *ET* 65.

42. The hegemony of the Anglo-American idiom was a common theme in Derrida's work over his last two decades. In *EIRP*, Derrida writes: "the hegemony of the Anglo-American is all over the world, it is irreversible, something we shouldn't even try and resist. It's done. Everyone in the world will have two languages, his own plus Anglo-American. Then without trying to prevent this, we have to handle this differently" (28–29). See also: "FK" 29, 43; "M" 162; *OH* 23; *PM* 117–18; and "AID," 214.

43. *ET* 90–94.

44. *SUR* 110–20.

45. For an extended discussion of the death penalty in America, see *FWT* 155–59: see also *WA* 245, 263; *N* 385–86; and "M" 175–76. In *PM* Derrida speaks of the United States as the only Western democracy that maintains the death penalty and "does not recognize the convention concerning children's rights and proceeds, when they reach the age of majority, to the carrying out of sentences that were pronounced against minors" (126).

46. See Derrida's comments on racism in America in *FWT* 28, 154. See also "For Mumia Abu-Jamal" and "Open Letter to Bill Clinton," *N* 125–29,130–32, and *CP* 325n.7. On apartheid as not just a South African but "an American problem," see "Critical Response II: But, Beyond (Open Letter to Anne McClintock and Rob Nixon)," *Critical Inquiry* 13 (Autumn 1986): 170.

47. Derrida speaks in *WA* of "the principle of nation-state sovereignty, which the United States protects in an inflexible manner when it's a question of their own and limits when it's a question of others," (262).

48. On the unique "translation" or "transference" of deconstruction in and to America, see, once again, "DA" 73 and "The Time Is Out of Joint," in *Deconstruction is/in America: A New Sense of the Political,* ed. Anselm Haverkamp (New York: New York University Press, 1995), 27–38.

49. *MPD* 11–17. The pages cited were written in January and February 1984.

50. I say "ethical" because deconstruction was often condemned for its "corrupting" influence on the academy. Derrida says in an interview given around the same time: "We can't understand the reception that deconstruction has had in the United States without background—historical, political, religious, and so forth. I would say religious above all" ("DA" 2).

51. See *P* 413.

52. The passage begins: "What would give me the most hope in the wake of all these upheavals is a potential difference between a new figure of Europe and the United States. I say this without any Eurocentrism. Which is why I am speaking of a *new* figure of Europe. Without forsaking its own memory, by drawing upon it, in fact, as an indispensable resource, Europe could make an essential contribution to the future of the international law we have been discussing." On this "Europe" that exceeds its present configuration, see *OH*: "Something unique is afoot in Europe, in what is still called Europe even if we no longer know very well *what* or *who* goes by this name" (5). Derrida goes on to ask, "Is there then a completely new 'today' of Europe beyond all the exhausted programs of *Eurocentrism* and *anti-Eurocentrism*" (*OH* 12–13).

53. It should be said that Europe, which often does America's bidding, is not spared the same critique. In *IS*, e.g., Derrida speaks of "Europe et son tuteur américain" (42).

54. Derrida speaks of Thoreau's notion of "civil disobedience" in *WA* 63–64 and defines it in *PM* as transgressing or objecting to a particular law in the name of a superior law (e.g., human rights) or a justice that is not yet *inscribed* in law (116; see also 132).

55. "DA" 10.

56. In the issue of *Le Monde diplomatique* in which "A Europe of Hope" was published, there is an article with the decidedly less nuanced title "Nous sommes tous antiaméricains," "We are all anti-American," meaning, it seems, "we Europeans, or we Europeans of this political leaning, are today all anti-American."

57. In *WAP* Derrida refers to himself as a "sort of uprooted African" (103).

6. Derrida at the Wheel

1. Genesis 2:7; all biblical citations are from *The New Oxford Annotated Bible* (New York: Oxford University Press, 1991).

2. Isaiah 64:8; see also: 29:16, 41:25, 45:9; Job 10.9; Jeremiah 19; and Romans 9.20 ff.

3. Jane Ellen Harrison, *Epilegomena to the Study of Greek Religion and Themis* (New Hyde Park, N.Y.: University Books, 1962), 298.

4. See Homer, *The Odyssey* 2.340, 23.305.

5. Homer, *The Iliad*, trans. A. T. Murray (Cambridge: Harvard University Press, 1978), 24.527–28.

6. Plato, *Republic*, trans. Paul Shorey (Cambridge: Harvard University Press, 1978), 379d-e.

7. See *Republic* 467a, *Statesman* 288a, *Protagoras* 324e–25a, *Euthydemus* 301c–d.

8. *Republic* 467a.

9. *Laches* 187b, *Gorgias* 514e.

10. *Protagoras* 314b, trans. W. R. M. Lamb (Cambridge: Harvard University Press, 1977).

11. *Gorgias* 493a–94a, trans. W R. M. Lamb (Cambridge: Harvard University Press, 1983). For the history of this "leaky" or "perforated jar," see Giulia Sissa, *Le corps virginal* (Paris: Librarie Philosophique J. Vrin, 1987), 156 ff.

12. *Cratylus* 440c-d, trans. H. N. Fowler (Cambridge: Harvard University Press, 1977).

13. *Republic* 420e–21e.

14. Martin Heidegger, "The Thing," in *Poetry, Language, Thought*, trans. Albert Hofstadter (New York: Harper & Row, 1975), 169, 173.

15. Hesiod, *Works and Days*, trans. Hugh G. Evelyn-White (Cambridge: Harvard University Press, 1943), 83–100.

16. From the journal of Du Bos dated July 25, 1924. Cited by Georges Poulet in *Permanence de Charles Du Bos: Colloque de Cerisy* (Paris: Desclée De Brouwer, 1976), 9. My translation.

17. See *AOA*.

18. *X-Files*, episode of April 30, 2000, "The Lazarus Bowl." I thank my colleague and friend Peter Steeves for pointing me toward this reference.

7. "One Nation . . . Indivisible": Of Autoimmunity, Democracy, and the Nation-State

1. It is the Latin verb *ligare*, meaning "to bind or join," that links *religion* to *allegiance*.

2. See, e.g., *OH* (1991), *SM* (1993), and *PF* (1994).

3. Derrida emphasizes in *R* that "democracy to come" is a phrase and not a sentence, and so cannot be translated into or reduced to a sentence like "democracy *is* to come" (90–91).

4. "Freedom is essentially the faculty or power to do as one pleases, to decide, to choose, to determine *oneself*, to have self-determination, to be master, and first of all master of oneself (*autos, ipse*)" (*R* 22–23).

5. Derrida writes in *R*: "But if the constitution of this force is, in principle, supposed to represent and protect this world democracy, it in fact betrays and threatens it from the very outset, in an autoimmune fashion, and in a way that is . . . just as silent as it is unavowable. Silent and unavowable like sovereignty itself. Unavowable silence, denegation: that is the always unapparent essence of

sovereignty" (100). In *HCFL* Derrida speaks of "the law of might [*puissance*] being autoimmune" (108).

6. To give just one example, once sovereignty is defined in a nation-state in terms of certain principles (e.g., freedom, equality, self-determination, and so on), then another sovereignty can always come along to challenge and claim to supercede these principles. Hence the Declaration of Human Rights, Derrida argues, reveals not a principle of nonsovereignty that might oppose the sovereignty of the nation-state but a counter-sovereignty that reveals the autoimmunity of sovereignty in general. See *R* 88.

7. It should be pointed out that Derrida was not the only thinker, and was in fact far from the first, to make use of autoimmunity as a trope. As Donna Haraway puts it in *Simians, Cyborgs, and Women: The Reinvention of Nature* (New York: Routledge, 1991), 149: "by the 1980s, the immune system is unambiguously a postmodern object—symbolically, technically, and politically." See Mark C. Taylor's magnificent chapter "The Betrayal of the Body: Live Not" in *Nots* (Chicago: University of Chicago Press, 1993), esp. 239–54.

8. For an excellent reading of these early references to autoimmunity in relation to Derrida's later works, see Samir Haddad's "Reading Derrida Reading Derrida: Deconstruction as Self-Inheritance," *International Journal of Philosophical Studies* 14, no. 4 (2006): 505–20.

9. Derrida speaks of a "boomerang" effect just before introducing the notion of the autoimmune.

10. The following year, in 1994 in *PF*, Derrida wrote: "The modality of the possible, the unquenchable perhaps, would, implacably, destroy everything, by means of a sort of autoimmunity [*auto-immunité*] from which no region of being, *physis*, or history would be exempt. . . . The imminence of a self-destruction by the infinite development of a madness of autoimmunity [*auto-immunité*]" (75–76).

11. In an interview entitled "The Deconstruction of Actuality," Derrida argues that the national community must also be open in this way. For were one to propose to "ban all biological or cultural grafts . . . this would extend very far—unless it leads nowhere, straight to death" (*N* 100). In other words, without the graft or the prosthesis, there could be only a pure repetition of the same, and that would be death.

12. It is not my intention to get involved here in the debate over whether or to what degree Derrida's work takes a turn toward the political in the late 1980s and 1990s. All I will add is that *Rogues* is an indispensable text for this debate. Whether Derrida's own strong and explicit defense of the political nature of his earlier writing is read as spin control, revisionism, or faithful interpretation will be up to others to decide.

13. "There is something paradigmatic in this autoimmune suicide: fascist and Nazi totalitarianisms came into power or ascended to power through formally normal and formally democratic electoral processes" (*R* 33).

14. Autoimmunity is, writes Derrida, "a *double bind* of threat and chance, not alternatively or by turns promise and/or threat but threat *in* the promise itself" (*R* 82).

15. Derrida writes in *N*: "The openness of the future is worth more; that is the axiom of deconstruction, that on the basis of which it has always set itself in motion and which links it, as with the future itself, to otherness, to the priceless dignity of otherness, that is to say, to justice. It is also democracy as the democracy-to-come" (105).

16. For a discussion of HIV, see Derrida's "The Rhetoric of Drugs," *P* 251–54.

17. As Derrida puts it in "SST," "One assertion, one statement, a true one, would be, and I would subscribe to it: Deconstruction is neither a theory nor a philosophy. It is neither a school nor a method. It is not even a discourse, nor an act, nor a practice. It is what happens, what is happening today in what they call society, politics, diplomacy, economics, historical reality, and so on and so forth. Deconstruction is the case" (85).

18. Derrida in fact follows the relationship between democracy, sovereignty, and life from the opening pages of *R* on: "Democracy has always been suicidal, and if there is a to-come for it, it is only on the condition of thinking life otherwise, life and the force of life. That is why I insisted earlier on the fact that pure Actuality is determined by Aristotle as a life" (33).

19. See again Samuel Weber's essay on the theologico-political character of "the people" in the U.S. Constitution, " 'God Bless America!' " in *Experimenting: Essays with Samuel Weber*, ed. Simon Morgan Wortham and Gary Hall (New York: Fordham University Press, 2007), 13–43.

20. Derrida says we must call into question "the theological and hardly secularized principle of the sovereignty of nation-states" ("M" 165).

21. Indeed, *khōra* comes on the scene in the *Timaeus* only after the (effective) withdrawal of the Demiurge.

22. Bellamy made it quite clear that he wrote the pledge to commemorate the *political* union of the nation, "the One Nation which the Civil War was fought to prove." It is perhaps also worth citing here President Eisenhower's words of 1954 on this change to the pledge: "In this way we are reaffirming the transcendence of religious faith in America's heritage and future." For a history of the pledge, see the website of John W. Baer and his *The Pledge of Allegiance: A Centennial History, 1892–1992* (Annapolis, Md.: Free State Press, 1992).

8. Autonomy, Autoimmunity, and the Stretch Limo: From Derrida's Rogue State to DeLillo's *Cosmopolis*

1. Terry Eagleton, *After Theory* (New York: Basic Books, 2003). For a more comprehensive and nuanced analysis of this situation, see Jeffrey Nealon's "Post-Deconstructive? Negri, Derrida, and the Present State of Theory," *Symplokē* 14, nos. 1–2 (2006): 68–80.

2. Eagleton, *After Theory*, 41.

3. Ibid., 5.

4. Ibid., 2.

5. Ibid. 7, my emphasis.

6. Don DeLillo, *Cosmopolis* (New York: Scribner), 2003. All other references to this work will be given as parenthetical page references in the text.

7. James Wood, *The New Republic*, April 10, 2003. Another reason for choosing this novel is that one of its central events involves a demonstration of the very antiglobalization movement Eagleton speaks of in *After Theory*.

8. Though DeLillo's *Falling Man* (New York: Scribner, 2007) would seem to be a more logical choice for a post-9/11 narrative, since it is explicitly about the days following the attacks on the World Trade Center in New York, *Cosmopolis* is, I will try to show, an even better example of the logic of autoimmunity. Were I to continue this analysis of autoimmunity in the direction of *Falling Man*, I would no doubt begin with the notion of "organic shrapnel" (16, 66) as a clue to the narrative's logic.

9. The phrase *world city* itself appears at *Cosmopolis*, 88.

10. The limo actually gets its name from the region of France called Limousine, made famous by its eponymous mantle or coat. The Packard Motor Car Company became, around the turn of the century, one of the premier manufacturers of limousines or automobiles with a closed body and a roofed seat for the driver.

11. Packer does wonder, however, in a moment of environmental consciousness, where the waste goes. "He didn't know what happened to the waste. Maybe it was tanked up somewhere in the underside of the automobile or possibly dumped directly in the street, violating a hundred statutes" (158; see also 190).

12. As Derrida once wrote in a text on Nietzsche, "all these matters are currently undergoing a reevaluation—all these matters, that is to say, the biographical and the *autos* of the autobiographical" ("O" 5). What is called into question by deconstruction is thus not simply one or another inauthentic or false self as opposed to the real one, but the very idea of a substantial, abiding, homogeneous, independent, and self-identical self.

13. "Benno Levin"—which sounds like an odd condensation of "Bin Laden" and "nine eleven"—is the pseudonym of Richard Sheets, the disgruntled employee who will eventually kill Packer. In *Falling Man*, 73, there is a more explicit homonymy in the name "Bill Lawton."

14. See Aristotle, *Poetics*, trans. W. Hamilton Fyfe (Cambridge: Harvard University Press, 1932), 1449b. Like Oedipus, Packer begins his day a king, married more or less to a queen, and ends it as a murderer with a death-wish. Moreover, Packer's name (Packard), like Oedipus's ("swollen foot"), already says something, perhaps, about the way he is fated to get around in life. For Packer, however, there will be no Antigone to redeem him, no "Packer in Colonus" to sanctify his memory.

15. As his forty-seven-year-old mistress, Didi Francher, puts it: "Two great fortunes. Like one of the great arranged marriages of old empire Europe" (26).

16. Aristotle, *Politics*, trans. H. Rackham (Cambridge: Harvard University Press, 1932), 1.3. While this reference to the term in Aristotle is certainly helpful, we must follow Kinski's advice and "give the word a little leeway. Adapt it to the current situation" (77).

17. Derrida writes in *MJ*: "The Greek word *phantasma*, which means 'specter,' points to this indecision between the real and the fictive, between what is neither real nor fictive, what is neither simply an individual nor a personage nor an actor—and this recalls as well the question of the phantasm in politics" (24; my translation). See also *GT* 158–59.

18. As Packer himself says, "there's only one thing in the world worth pursuing professionally and intellectually. . . . The interaction between technology and capital" (23).

19. The first barber chair Packer sat in as a child was, appropriately, a "toy chair for kids . . . a green roadster with a red steering wheel" (160).

20. This line of poetry, placed by DeLillo as the epigraph to the book, comes from a poem that Packer himself had recently been reading, so that, in an interesting symbiotic convergence, the antiglobalist and the hyper-capitalist, the anarchist "waving looted Nasdaq T-shirts" and the man whose single portfolio moves markets, are reading the same poetry.

21. For example, as Packer says, "that whole sad business of Judeo-Christian jogging" (49).

22. Jean-Luc Nancy, "The Intruder," in Nancy, *Corpus*, trans. Richard Rand (New York: Fordham University Press, 2008).

23. To reinforce the regression: "He took ten baby steps, reaching the limits of the intersection and the border of fallen bodies" (174).

24. Later, as Packer plays an extra in the filming of a disaster movie, he cannot quite put together the event and its reproduction: "It tore his mind apart, trying to see them here and real, independent of the image on a screen in Oslo or Caracas. Or were those places indistinguishable from this one?" (176).

25. The relationship between "life" and its repetition or technical reproduction was central to DeLillo's previous novel, *The Body Artist* (New York: Scribner, 2001).

26. See "AI" 85–136.

27. Packer admires this act and tries "to imagine the man's pain, his choice, the abysmal will he'd had to summon" (98). He responds to Kinski's cynical comment, "It's not original," with the serious claim, "He did a serious thing. He took his life. Isn't this what you have to do to show them that you're serious?" (100)

28. As Didi Francher frankly tells him near the beginning of the novel, "You're beginning to think it's more interesting to doubt than to act. It takes more courage to doubt" (31).

29. Not many pages later, Packer actually asks himself: "What is a door? It's a movable structure, usually swings on hinges, which closes off an entranceway and requires a tremendous and prolonged pounding before it can finally be forced open" (186). Of course a *Tor*, in German, is also a fool.

30. Packer asks Torval: "What's the difference between the protector and the assassin if both men are armed and hate me?" (185).

31. Eric thinks back to the time of his father's death as he closes in on Levin. He recalls going to the movies with his mother: "trying to learn how to be alone together. We were cold and lost and my father's soul was trying to find us, to settle itself in our bodies, not that I want or need your sympathy" (185).

32. Levin tells Packer, "That's where the answer was, in your body, in your prostate" (200). That is, instead of being obsessed with symmetrical patterns, with mathematical beauty, Packer should have considered the skewed, the lop-sided, the little quirk, the mishap or misshape. Levin is, in the life of Packer, just such a quirk or mishap.

9. History's Remains: Of Memory, Mourning, and the Event(s) of 9/11

1. The French edition of *The Work of Mourning*, entitled *Chaque fois unique, la fin du monde*, contains two additional essays, one on Gérard Granel and the other on Maurice Blanchot.

2. Jean-François Lyotard, *The Differend: Phrases in Dispute*, trans. Georges Van Den Abbeele (Minneapolis: University of Minnesota Press, 1988), 100.

3. All passages are from Plato, *Laws*, trans. R. G. Bury (Cambridge: Harvard University Press, 1984).

4. Derrida himself, though with a somewhat different purpose, cites *Laws* 909b-c in "PP" 97.

5. As for the ceremonies, the lawgiver must set moderate amounts for each of the four property classes and the law-warden must act as "overseer" to make sure all the arrangements are carried out in a proper and moderate way (959e).

6. This speech and much of the information to follow concerning the controversy surrounding the Unknown Soldier of Vietnam can be found on the official website of Arlington National Cemetery: www.arlingtoncemetery.com.

7. See, esp., Kathleen Hall Jamieson, *Eloquence in an Electronic Age: The Transformation of Political Speechmaking* (New York: Oxford University Press, 1988).

8. Hannah Arendt writes in *The Human Condition* (Garden City, N.Y.: Doubleday Anchor Books, 1959), 161: "The monuments to the 'Unknown Soldier' after World War I bear testimony to the then still existing need for glorification, for finding a 'who,' an identifiable somebody whom four years of mass slaughter should have revealed. The frustration of this wish and the unwillingness to resign oneself to the brutal fact that the agent of the war was actually nobody inspired the erection of the monuments to the 'unknown,' to all those whom the war had failed to make known and had robbed thereby, not of their achievement, but of their human dignity." For an excellent analysis of such attempts to glorify war and the war dead through the construction of a "Myth of the War Experience," see George L. Mosse, *Fallen Soldiers: Reshaping the Memory of the World Wars* (New York: Oxford University Press, 1990).

9. See Plato, *Apology* 32b, and Xenophon, *Hellenica* 1.7.15–16.

10. This technique uses computer analysis of remains to reconstruct facial features that can then be compared to photographs.

11. Cohen continued: but "if advances in technology can ease the lingering anguish of even one family, then our path is clear." See www.arlington cemetery.com.

12. This was not to be the end of the controversy. Because the Medal of Honor, the nation's highest and most distinguished medal, was awarded to the remains of an unknown soldier who proved to be Michael Joseph Blassie, the question arose whether Blassie had been, or should be, awarded this medal. It was ultimately decided that the Medal of Honor had been awarded to the unknown solider and not to Blassie, and that, as a result, it must not continue to be attached to his name or his remains.

13. *The New Yorker*, October 1, 2001, 39–40.

14. *New York Times*, February 3, 2002, A1, A14.

15. *GL* 2b, 32b. The latter is translated by Leavey and Rand, "Falls (to the tomb), remain(s)."

10. *Comme si, comme ça*: Following Derrida on the Phantasms of the Self, the State, and a Sovereign God

1. See Derrida's comments about a similar situation in "AID" 215–17.

2. In this chapter I treat more or less synonymously the words *fantasme* and *phantasme* in Derrida's work. While the former most often suggests "fantasy" rather than "phantasm," Derrida, it seems to me, often uses them more or less interchangeably. In the first chapter of *PM*, e.g., Derrida speaks of "two fantasies [*fantasmes*]" with regard to the end of the book (*PM* 15), *fantasmes* that sound very much like the *phantasmes* of the book in a subsequent chapter of the same work (*PM* 63). Both are related to desire, to nostalgia, to intimacy and immediacy, to a return to what has been lost or expropriated, or to what one believes oneself to have lost, to an "*onto-theological dream*" that is "perpetually reinvested" (*PM* 15). Rachel Bowlby is thus right, I think, to translate both words by the same word in English. For the purposes of my argument, however, I prefer to translate both by "phantasm" rather than "fantasy."

Another related word in Derrida's lexicon is *leurre*—more prevalent, perhaps, in earlier works, though also present in later ones. In "Signature Event Context," e.g., Derrida says that the desire and quest for a context suffers from an "ethical and teleological discourse of consciousness," that is, from what he calls the "leurre téléogique de la conscience"—"the teleological lure of consciousness" (*MP* 327). In *PM*, again, *phantasme* is related to the simulacrum and the trap—to the bait [*leurre*] that a huntsman gives a dog or birds of prey (*PM* 62).

3. Kas Saghafi, "The Ghost *of* Jacques Derrida," *Epochē* 10, no. 2 (Spring 2006): 263–86.

4. Though I do not believe that the notion of the "phantasm" can be completely separated from its others, from its "doubles," such as phantom, specter, ghost, and so on, I would be tempted to say that while the latter tend to emphasize iterability, otherness, dissemination, difference, and so on, the former

tends—though this tendency is always frustrated—to emphasize uniqueness, sameness, self-generation, and identity, or at least the illusion or appearance of these.

5. In "Fichus" Derrida speaks of Adorno's desire to go on loving the German language—"but without nationalism" (*PM* 172).

6. "But is not the desire for a center, as a function of play itself, the indestructible itself? And in the repetition or return of play, how could the phantom of the center not call to us? ("Ellipsis," in *WD* 297).

7. *SP* 12.

8. Pleshette DeArmitt does this in her as yet unpublished 2006 dissertation at DePaul University, "Echoes of Narcissus."

9. In *PM* Derrida speaks of changing immigration laws "without yielding to phantasms of security or to demagogy or vote seeking" (116).

10. In "AO" Derrida says that in order to speak of the "Jew," of the name "Jew" or "Jewish," one would need "art, or the genius of an archeologist of the phantasm, the courage of childhood, too" (11).

11. See, e.g., Leonard Lawlor, *The Implications of Immanence: Toward a New Concept of Life* (New York: Fordham University Press, 2006).

12. In *Taking on the Tradition: Jacques Derrida and the Legacies of Deconstruction* (Stanford, Calif.: Stanford University Press, 2002), I tried to demonstrate that "the tradition" is always, in fact, the effect of its reception, of a *comme si* that tries to pass itself off as a *comme ça*. Though I did not put it this way at the time, it could be said that the tradition itself, taken as something determined and fixed, inviolable and inalienable, safe and sound in its original presence or intent, is itself always a phantasm—an ineluctable phantasm, no doubt, but a phantasm nonetheless.

13. "Declarations of Independence," in *N* 46–54. In a note in *PM* Derrida imagines the founding of an internet state "without territory" and concludes: "It reveals a *constitutive* imaginary or fiction: the supposedly legitimate occupation of a fixed territory, if not the assumption of autochthonous origin, has up till now been a condition of civic belonging, in reality the very being of politics, its link to the nation-state, if not to the state" (184n.4).

14. Derrida writes in *SQ*: "If I insist so much on the fable and the fabulous, it is no doubt and too evidently because of fables, like those of La Fontaine. . . . But there is another reason for my insistence on the fabulous. It is because, as the fables themselves show, political force or power, in laying down the law, in laying down its own law, in appropriating legitimate violence and legitimating its own arbitrary violence, is in essence such that this unleashing and restraining of power passes by way of the fable, in other words, by way of a language that is both fictional and performative. . . . In the fable, within a narrative that is itself fabulous, power is shown to be an effect of the fable, of fiction and fictive language, of the simulacrum. Just like the law, like the force of law, which Montaigne and Pascal said is, in essence, fictional" (109).

The fiction or phantasm of the sovereign as a "living law," as at once inside and outside the law, as Agamben has demonstrated, would thus be yet another figure for the theologico-political phantasm.

15. This is perhaps the one point of difference between the thesis I am advancing here and that made by Martin Hägglund in *Radical Atheism* (Stanford, Calif.: Stanford University Press, 2008). Though I agree almost entirely with Hägglund's brilliant and very powerful thesis concerning an original autoimmunity at the very heart of Derrida's thought, an autoimmunity that compromises from the beginning every conceptual formation and, of course, every phantasm, I wonder whether the phantasm can be written off as *simply* false, self-contradictory, or autoimmune. That is, I wonder whether we do not need to take into account the *effectiveness* and *affectivity* of such false, self-contradictory, and autoimmune notions as nature, purity, eternity, and so on. Though Hägglund is surely right to point out the way the trace compromises these notions from the beginning, I think we need to give an account of our mistaken *beliefs* about them. Declaring them false or self-contradictory runs the risk of reinscribing them in a regime of truth—as opposed to power or force or affectivity—that the very notion of the phantasm seems to contest.

16. See Thomas Dutoit, "Mythic Derrida," *Mosaic* 39, no. 3 (September 2006): 103–32, and "Upearthing the Field of English Studies: Discoursing *Pensées* in Jacques Derrida," *European Journal of English Studies* 6, no. 3 (2002): 327–42.

17. The pomegranate is an important image for Greek, Christian, and Jewish culture and, perhaps especially, for Sephardic Jews of the Mediterranean during Passover and other religious celebrations. Note that the section of "Faith and Knowledge" entitled "et grenades" was published separately in English translation as "and pomegranates," in *Violence, Identity, and Self-Determination*, ed. Hent de Vries and Samuel Weber (Stanford, Calif.: Stanford University Press, 1997), 326–46.

18. "If one translates 'all-powerfulness' by sovereignty, or rather by the phantasm of sovereignty, one will conclude from this that the denegation of sexual difference is part of the program of sovereignty itself, of sovereignty in general" ("NW").

19. Sigmund Freud, *Delusion and Dream*, trans. Helen M. Downey (New York: New Republic, Inc., 1927).

20. Gradiva's appearance in "FK" is, of course, not her only one in Derrida's corpus. In *AF*, written more or less at the same time as "FK," Derrida looks not only at Freud's analyses of the phantasm in the Gradiva essay and elsewhere but at Freud's own belief in phantasms and his attempt to conjure them away, his belief in his ability to conjure them up so as to conjure them away. Though I cannot do so here, it would be interesting to relate everything argued here about Gradiva as a male phantasm to the phantasm of the archive. See *AF* 95–101. Derrida writes in the opening lines of the Postscript: "For more than twenty years, each time I've returned to Naples, I've thought of her. Who better than Gradiva, I said to myself this time" (*AF* 97).

21. The phantasm can thus be described as a projection on the part of the subject that is then taken to be something external to the subject, a projection that then has real effects in the world, effects and affects that then reinforce the phantasm. In *LLF* Derrida speaks of refusing to give in to the pressures of an intimidating readership—or, rather, to the pressures of the "phantasm" of such a readership—that would require him to simplify his writing, to give up on paradox or aporia in the name of accessibility. For the phantasm of such a readership ends up contributing to its production. As Derrida says of his own writing, "Each book is a pedagogy aimed at forming its reader," but "the mass productions that today inundate the press and publishing houses do not form their readers; they presuppose in a phantasmatic and rudimentary fashion a reader who has already been programmed. They thus end up preformatting this very mediocre addressee whom they had postulated in advance."

22. The passage continues: "Will it be said, to determine the *IC* as phantasm, that the *IC* is not *true*, that that [*ça*] does not happen like that [*comme ça*], that this is only a myth? That would indeed be silly, and the silliness would again claim 'sexual experience' as its authority. But yes, that [*ça*] happens like that [*comme ça*], and what the greater logic impeccably—this is the right word— demonstrates is that not only is this myth true, but it gives the measure of truth itself, the revelation of truth, the truth of truth. Then the (absolute) phantasm of the *IC* as (absolute) phantasm is (absolute) truth. Truth is the phantasm itself" (*GL* 224a).

23. Whereas "maternity" resists replacement insofar as it marks simply the ineluctability of birth, the mother can always be replaced—or killed, giving way to substitution, fiction, and phantasmatic speculation. Such a thought of the mother can also be found in *AF*, the text in which Derrida speaks at such length of Gradiva: Freud "makes a mistake in affirming that there can be no doubt about the identity of the mother, insofar as it depends on the witness of the senses, while the identity of the father always remains doubtful since it depends, and it alone, on a rational inference, as that 'legal fiction' of which Stephen speaks in Joyce's *Ulysses*. However, better than ever today, if only with the possibility of surrogate mothers, prosthetic maternities, sperm banks, and all the artificial inseminations, as they are secured for us already and will be secured still more for us in the future by bio-genetic techno-science, we know that maternity is as inferred, constructed, and interpreted as paternity. And as paternal law. In truth, it has always been thus, for the one and for the other" (47–48).

11. Lifelines

1. *Jacques Derrida*, ed. Marie-Louise Mallet and Ginette Michaud, Cahiers de l'Herne (Paris: Editions de l'Herne, 2004), 451–61. Three facsimiles of Derrida's poem are reproduced in this volume, along with an extraordinary history and reading of the text by Ginette Michaud, one of the volume's editors. As for the precise chronology of the different versions of the poem, there is no way to prove definitively that the typed iterations of the line in Figure 2 precede the

handwritten version in Figure 3. I agree with Michaud's hypothesis that the handwritten version appears to be the "conclusion" of what was selected among the typed versions, not "preparation" for the typed versions (457). But, again, it is impossible to affirm this with any certainty.

2. Emmanuel Hocquard Raquel, *Orange Export Ltd., 1969–1986* (Paris, Flammarion, 1986), 314. The poem was invited for a section of the book entitled "Monostiches / One-Line Poems."

3. While the published poem was entitled "Petite fuite alexandrine," and the two draft versions seen in the Cahier de l'Herne have that title, when Derrida typed the poem into the letter he sent to the volume's editors, he wrote, for whatever reason, "Petite *suite* alexandrine."

4. There are, for the record, a total of 74 characters (not including the parentheses) in the verse, title, and signature.

5. Jacques Derrida, "Je n'écris pas sans lumière artificielle," in *Ils écrivent*: *Où? quand? comment?* ed. André Rollin (Paris: Éditions Mazarine, 1986), 149.

6. Derrida notes in "Geschlecht II: Heidegger's Hand," trans. John P. Leavey, Jr., in *Deconstruction and Philosophy*, ed. John Sallis (Chicago: University of Chicago Press, 1987), 182: "On the one hand, the sole sentence in which Heidegger, to my knowledge, names man's hands in the plural seems to concern precisely the moment of prayer, or in any case the gesture in which the two hands join together to make themselves only one in simplicity."

7. *P* 115–31.

8. Derrida speaks in *PC* of "the line of my drawing, my life line, my line of conduct" (202).

9. It would hardly be an exaggeration to say that my entire reading of Derrida's poem has been animated and motivated by Derrida's reading of Celan in "Shibboleth." Moreover, Derrida's poem is itself a sort of response to or echo of Celan, where the themes of the line, the hand and the seal, destiny, prayer, and benediction, even the "petrified" blessing, are so prominent. Many of these same themes are also at the center of Derrida's reading of Celan in *Rams*, which, along with "Shibboleth," is included in *SQ.*

10. On the French name "Pierre," see "MC" 30–31.

11. Jacques Derrida, "Rams: Uninterrupted Dialogue—Between Two Infinities, the Poem" (*SQ* 135–64).

12. Jacques Derrida has written many *prières d'insérer* for his own books, most of them with Éditions Galilée, which, as he says in *GG*, is "all but alone today" in keeping this tradition alive and not making do with the back cover to advertise or promote their books (60). Yet Derrida has also, according to certain bibliographies, written a *prière d'insérer* for someone else's book: Mathieu Bénézet's *Dits et récits du mortel* (Paris, Flammarion, 1977), along with yet another *prière d'insérer* (or text entitled *prière d'insérer*) for an issue of the journal *Ubacs* (no. 10, 1991) on Mathieu Bénézet. But precisely because the *prière d'insérer* does not form "an intrinsic part of the work it introduces," it is easily lost, misplaced, effaced like a dream language or idiomatic writing. In the two copies of the book

by Bénézet that I have been able to consult, there has been no *prière à insérer*, no prayer to be unsealed, within it. I do not know if Jacques Derrida speaks in this *prière d'insérer* of the *prière d'insérer* or of *prière*, of prayer, in general. I do not know whether he has—and this would hardly be surprising, or the first time— foreseen just about everything I've said here. The mystery thus remains and the story is to be continued . . .

13. Levinas famously begins *Totality and Infinity: An Essay on Exteriority* by citing Rimbaud's *A Season in Hell*: " 'The true life is absent [*La vraie vie est absente*].' But we are in the world." Trans. Alphonso Lingis (Pittsburgh: Duquesne University Press, 1969), 1.

14. In " 'Le Parjure,' Perhaps," *WA* 180.

15. See the final lines of the first part of *R*, where "a god" is again contrasted with both "God" and "a plurality of gods" (114).

16. "Die Linien des Lebens sind verschieden, / Wie Wege sind und wie der Berge Grenzen. / Was hier wir sind, kann dort ein Gott ergänzen / Mit Harmonien und ewigen Lohn und Frieden" (Hölderlin, *Gedichte* [Munich: Wilhelm Goldmann Verlag, 1961], 124). The French translation by G. Roud in the Pléiade edition runs: "Les lignes de la vie sont diverses / Comme les routes et les contours des montagnes. / Ce que nous sommes ici, un Dieu là-bas peut le parfaire / Avec des harmonies et l'éternelle récompense et le repos" (Hölderlin, *Oeuvres* [Paris: Gallimard, 1967], 1247).

17. Jacques Derrida, *Schibboleth: Pour Paul Celan* (Paris: Galilée, 1986), 74; "Desire or gift of the poem, the date is borne, in a movement of blessing, toward ash" (*SQ* 41).

Conclusion: The World Over

1. This essay was first presented on October 28, 2004, at a memorial session for Jacques Derrida at the annual meeting of the Society for Phenomenology and Existential Philosophy in Memphis, Tennessee. The other two presenters were John D. Caputo and John Sallis.

2. See, e.g., Derrida's very early analysis of Husserl in the subchapter of his 1954 Master's thesis entitled "The Ambiguous Sense of the 'World' " (in *The Problem of Genesis in Husserl's Philosophy*, 109) and his reference to Husserl some forty years later in *A* 51–52.

3. *SQ* 135–63.

4. I would like to thank Ginette Michaud for suggesting to me the proximity between this title and the line of Celan.

5. Ursula Sarrazin first pointed out to me the relationship between Celan's poem and Heine's.

Index

Defoe, Daniel, 104
Deleuze, Gilles, 34, 94, 98–99, 169
DeLillo, Don, 14, 147, 150–66,
    249n.6–9, 11, 13, 15, 250n.18–21,
    23–25, 27–29, 251n.30–32
De Man, Paul, 34–35, 98, 101, 169,
    241n.7, 242n.15
Democracy, 12, 14, 32, 42, 63, 65–66, 68,
    72, 78, 83–85, 87, 106, 122–26, 128,
    142–45, 164–65, 196, 206, 244n.45,
    246n.5; and autoimmunity 132–37,
    247n.13, 248n.18; democracy to come,
    39–41, 60–61, 68–71, 123, 125, 132,
    137–39, 142–43, 145, 246n.3,
    248n.15
DePaul University, 34, 228, 236n.11,
    253n.8
Derrida, Jacques, works: *A*, 257n.2; *AF*,
    217, 219, 254n.20, 255n.23; "AI", 66,
    70–73, 79, 85, 90, 109, 204, 250n.26;
    "AID", 241n.1, 242n.27, 244n.42,
    252n.1; *AL*, 243n.28–29; "AO",
    69–70, 253n.10; *AOA*, 3, 235n.2,
    246n.17; *AP*, 3, 22–23, 29, 171,
    235n.2, 237n.5; "AT", 105, 244n.38;
    C, 3, 118, 121, 219–20, 235n.2,
    237n.5; *CF*, 82, 88, 244n.38; *CFU*, 35,
    69, 230–233; *CP*, 241n.2–3, 6,
    242n.19, 22, 243–44n.35, 244n.46; *D*,
    236n.11; "DA", 239n.5, 241n.1, 8,
    11–13, 242n.22, 24, 245n.48, 50, 55;
    "EH", 12, 83–94, 110, 240n.2,
    245n.56; *EIRP*, 13, 96, 243n.33,
    244n.42; *ET*, 244n.41, 43; *EU*,
    243n.30–31, 244n.40; "FF", 198–199;
    "FK", 16, 56, 64, 74–76, 124,
    130–132, 140, 145, 199–208,
    244n.41–42, 254n.20; "FL", 139, 200,
    253; *FWT*, 30–31, 65, 143, 223,
    242n.14, 243n.32, 244n.45–46; *G*, 98,
    100, 104, 243n.30; *GD*, 64, 243n.28;
    GD2, 68; *GG*, 68, 223, 256n.12; *GL*,
    16, 100, 118, 171, 186, 189, 208–10,
    218, 252n.15, 255n.22; *GT*, 243n.28,
    250n.17; *H*, 20–21, 25, 114, 152, 193;
    HCFL, 235n.7, 247n.5; "HI", 21, 26,
    237n.3; *IS*, 194–197, 245n.53; *JD*, 64,
    98, 242n.22; "K", 11, 38, 41–42,

49–56, 237n.2, 5, 238n.6–8; *LI*,
    242n.15; *LLF*, 3, 4–5, 6, 8, 16–17, 33,
    73–74, 197–98, 207, 235n.1–2,
    236n.9–10, 255n.21; "M", 66, 68,
    239n.8, 242n.22, 244n.42, 45,
    248n.20; *MAR*, 224, 242n.18,
    244n.36; *MB*, 243n.28; "MC",
    256n.10; *MJ*, 250n.17; *MO*, 3, 29,
    189–91, 193, 198, 208, 235n.3; *MP*, 4,
    105, 244n.37, 252n.2; *MPD*,
    107–108, 242n.14–15, 245n.49; *MS*,
    78–79; *N*, 103, 144, 198, 200,
    242n.14, 23, 244n.45–46, 247n.11,
    248n.15, 253n.13; "NW", 210–11,
    236n.11, 254n.18; "O", 249n.12; *OH*,
    12, 81–82, 103, 110, 240n.1, 242n.25,
    244n.42, 245n.52, 246n.2; *OS*, 77;
    "P", 194; *P*, 5, 103–4, 215–16,
    218–19, 222, 242n.16–17, 19, 26,
    243n.28, 245n.51, 248n.16, 256n.7;
    PC, 218, 222, 225, 243n.28, 256n.8;
    PF, 65, 82, 114, 128, 152, 243n.28,
    246n.2, 247n.10; *PG*, 240n.1, 257n.2;
    PM, 23–24, 66, 68, 74–75, 101, 194,
    195–96, 223, 239n.7–8, 240n.12,
    241n.5, 242n.21, 243n.33, 244n.42,
    45, 245n.54, 252n.2, 253n.5, 9, 13;
    "PMS", 66–67, 144, 239n.9; *POS*,
    240n.4; "PP", 11, 38, 40–56, 58, 60,
    209, 237n.2–4, 238n.10, 251n.4; *PSY
    II*, 16, 50, 56–60, 64, 220, 225,
    238n.8, 240n.10, 242n.21–22; *R*, 11,
    12, 32, 38–42, 47–50, 56, 60, 66,
    68–69, 81–82, 94, 106, 112–13,
    115–16, 118, 121, 123, 125–30,
    132–46, 164, 243n.32, 246n.3–5,
    247n.6, 12–13, 248n.14, 18, 257n.15;
    RES, 243n.28; "SA", 140, 242n.20;
    SM, 70, 82, 84, 88–89, 100, 103, 106,
    128–29, 132, 171, 244n.36, 246n.2;
    "SN", 217; *SP*, 16, 98, 165, 189,
    191–192, 202, 207, 208, 210,
    243n.28, 253n.7; *SQ*, 4, 6–8, 16, 63,
    189, 213, 216–17, 221, 226, 232–33,
    235n.4–6, 253n.14, 256n.9, 11,
    257n.17, 3; "SST", 101, 248n.17;
    SUR, 242n.19, 244n.39, 44; *TM*,
    241n.3, 242n.22; *TS*, 243n.28; "UG",

Hussein, Saddam, 93
Husserl, Edmund, 28, 98, 104, 120, 169, 170, 191–92, 228, 230–31, 240n.1, 257n.2
Hyppolite, Jean, 98

IMEC (Institut Mémoires de l'édition contemporaine), 94
Iraq, 12, 82, 89, 91, 123, 136, 137, 168
Irvine (University of California), 28, 99, 103, 107, 242n.22
Islam (Muslims), 13, 70, 71, 72–73, 77, 84–85, 90, 93, 106, 136, 206
Israel, 91–93
Ithaca, 103

Jabès, Edmond, 169
James, Henry, 243n.28
Jamieson, Kathleen Hall, 251n.7
Janicaud, Dominique, 239n.4
Jankélévitch, Vladimir, 94
Jennings, Theodore, 239n.5
Jenson, Wilhelm, 206
Jerusalem, 56, 220
Joan of Arc, 67
Johns Hopkins University, 98, 99
Johnson, Barbara, 237n.3
Joyce, James, 28, 46, 98, 104, 120, 210–11, 228, 243n.29, 255n.23
Judaism, 71, 73, 77, 78, 84, 93, 111, 198, 239n.5, 253n.10, 254n.17; and Derrida, 27–28, 69–70

Kafka, Franz, 104, 243n.28–29
Kamuf, Peggy, 109, 236–37n.11, 241n.2
Kant, Immanuel, 20, 24, 28, 40, 58, 67, 70, 79, 86, 104, 162, 228, 237n.5
Kearney, Richard, 242n.14
Keats, John, 119–120
Khōra, 11, 15, 38, 40–42, 48–61, 70, 118, 123, 132, 145, 146, 202, 207, 237n.2, 238n.6–9, 239n.5, 248n.21
Kierkegaard, Søren, 28, 79, 228
King, Jr., Martin Luther, 105
King, Rodney, 106
Knights of Columbus, 145
Kofman, Amy, 211, 241n.10
Kofman, Sarah, 169

Krell, David Farrell, 228
Kristeva, Julia, 98

Labyrinth Books, 167
Lacan, Jacques, 98, 104, 243n.28
La Fontaine, Jean de, 253n.14
Laguna Beach, 100, 103, 242n.22
Lang, Jack, 83
Lawlor, Leonard, 199, 253n.11
Lazarus, 120, 246n.18
Leavey, Jr., John P., 252n.15
Le Front National, 198
Leibniz, Gottfried Wilhelm, 104
Le Monde, 3, 21, 26, 33, 73
Le Monde diplomatique, 12, 83, 86–93, 240n.2, 245n.56
Le Pen, Jean-Marie, 198
Levinas, Emmanuel, 28, 34, 48, 64, 74, 98–99, 104, 169, 170, 228, 231, 257n.13
Lewinski, Monica, 106
Libeskind, Daniel, 34
Life, 4–5, 7, 11, 14, 16, 28, 30–31, 33, 35, 56, 68, 72, 114–18, 120, 155, 182, 183–85, 213–226, 253n.11, 256n.8, 257n.13; affirmation of, 7, 11, 28, 31, 60, 225 236n.10–11; and autoimmunity, 124–25, 129–31, 133, 135, 141–42; and living on, 3, 7, 14, 16, 30, 33, 60, 69, 78, 189, 201, 204, 225, 232; and phantasm, 199–208, 211, in Plato, 174–76; and sacrifice, 56, 60, 67, 131, 211; and sovereignty, 39, 56, 59–60, 248n.18
Loreau, Max, 169
Los Angeles, 28
Loyola University, Chicago, 34
Lyotard, Jean-François, 15, 94, 98–99, 169, 171–73, 179, 251n.2

Malabou, Catherine, 243n.35
Mallarmé, Stéphane, 104, 243n.28–29
Malle, Justine, 240n.2
Mallet, Marie-Louise, 255n.1
Marcel, Gabriel, 94
Marin, Louis, 169
Marriage, civil union, 73–74, 240n.13
Martin, Bill, 228–29

Perspectives in
Continental Philosophy Series
John D. Caputo, series editor

Henry, Jean-Luc Marion, and Paul Ricœur, *Phenomenology and the "Theological Turn": The French Debate.*

Karl Jaspers, *The Question of German Guilt.* Introduction by Joseph W. Koterski, S.J.

Jean-Luc Marion, *The Idol and Distance: Five Studies.* Translated with an introduction by Thomas A. Carlson.

Jeffrey Dudiak, *The Intrigue of Ethics: A Reading of the Idea of Discourse in the Thought of Emmanuel Levinas.*

Robyn Horner, *Rethinking God as Gift: Marion, Derrida, and the Limits of Phenomenology.*

Mark Dooley, *The Politics of Exodus: Søren Keirkegaard's Ethics of Responsibility.*

Merold Westphal, *Overcoming Onto-Theology: Toward a Postmodern Christian Faith.*

Edith Wyschogrod, Jean-Joseph Goux and Eric Boynton, eds., *The Enigma of Gift and Sacrifice.*

Stanislas Breton, *The Word and the Cross.* Translated with an introduction by Jacquelyn Porter.

Jean-Luc Marion, *Prolegomena to Charity.* Translated by Stephen E. Lewis.

Peter H. Spader, *Scheler's Ethical Personalism: Its Logic, Development, and Promise.*

Jean-Louis Chrétien, *The Unforgettable and the Unhoped For.* Translated by Jeffrey Bloechl.

Don Cupitt, *Is Nothing Sacred? The Non-Realist Philosophy of Religion: Selected Essays.*

Jean-Luc Marion, *In Excess: Studies of Saturated Phenomena.* Translated by Robyn Horner and Vincent Berraud.

Phillip Goodchild, *Rethinking Philosophy of Religion: Approaches from Continental Philosophy.*

William J. Richardson, S.J., *Heidegger: Through Phenomenology to Thought.*

Jeffrey Andrew Barash, *Martin Heidegger and the Problem of Historical Meaning.*

Jean-Louis Chrétien, *Hand to Hand: Listening to the Work of Art.* Translated by Stephen E. Lewis.

Jean-Louis Chrétien, *The Call and the Response.* Translated with an introduction by Anne Davenport.

D. C. Schindler, *Han Urs von Balthasar and the Dramatic Structure of Truth: A Philosophical Investigation.*

Julian Wolfreys, ed., *Thinking Difference: Critics in Conversation.*

Allen Scult, *Being Jewish/Reading Heidegger: An Ontological Encounter.*

Richard Kearney, *Debates in Continental Philosophy: Conversations with Contemporary Thinkers.*

Jennifer Anna Gosetti-Ferencei, *Heidegger, Hölderlin, and the Subject of Poetic Language: Towards a New Poetics of Dasein.*

Jolita Pons, *Stealing a Gift: Kirkegaard's Pseudonyms and the Bible*.

Jean-Yves Lacoste, *Experience and the Absolute: Disputed Questions on the Humanity of Man*. Translated by Mark Raftery-Skehan.

Charles P. Bigger, *Between* Chora *and the Good: Metaphor's Metaphysical Neighborhood*.

Dominique Janicaud, *Phenomenology "Wide Open": After the French Debate*. Translated by Charles N. Cabral.

Ian Leask and Eoin Cassidy, eds., *Givenness and God: Questions of Jean-Luc Marion*.

Jacques Derrida, *Sovereignties in Question: The Poetics of Paul Celan*. Edited by Thomas Dutoit and Outi Pasanen.

William Desmond, *Is There a Sabbath for Thought? Between Religion and Philosophy*.

Bruce Ellis Benson and Norman Wirzba, eds. *The Phenomoenology of Prayer*.

S. Clark Buckner and Matthew Statler, eds. *Styles of Piety: Practicing Philosophy after the Death of God*.

Kevin Hart and Barbara Wall, eds. *The Experience of God: A Postmodern Response*.

John Panteleimon Manoussakis, *After God: Richard Kearney and the Religious Turn in Continental Philosophy*.

John Martis, *Philippe Lacoue-Labarthe: Representation and the Loss of the Subject*.

Jean-Luc Nancy, *The Ground of the Image*.

Edith Wyschogrod, *Crossover Queries: Dwelling with Negatives, Embodying Philosophy's Others*.

Gerald Bruns, *On the Anarchy of Poetry and Philosophy: A Guide for the Unruly*.

Brian Treanor, *Aspects of Alterity: Levinas, Marcel, and the Contemporary Debate*.

Simon Morgan Wortham, *Counter-Institutions: Jacques Derrida and the Question of the University*.

Leonard Lawlor, *The Implications of Immanence: Toward a New Concept of Life*.

Clayton Crockett, *Interstices of the Sublime: Theology and Psychoanalytic Theory*.

Bettina Bergo, Joseph Cohen, and Raphael Zagury-Orly, eds., *Judeities: Questions for Jacques Derrida*. Translated by Bettina Bergo, and Michael B. Smith.

Jean-Luc Marion, *On the Ego and on God: Further Cartesian Questions*. Translated by Christina M. Gschwandtner.

Jean-Luc Nancy, *Philosophical Chronicles*. Translated by Franson Manjali.

Jean-Luc Nancy, *Dis-Enclosure: The Deconstruction of Christianity*. Translated by Bettina Bergo, Gabriel Malenfant, and Michael B. Smith.

Andrea Hurst, *Derrida Vis-à-vis Lacan: Interweaving Deconstruction and Psychoanalysis*.

Jean-Luc Nancy, *Noli me tangere: On the Raising of the Body*. Translated by Sarah Clift, Pascale-Anne Brault, and Michael Naas.

Jacques Derrida, *The Animal That Therefore I Am*. Edited by Marie-Louise Mallet, translated by David Wills.

Jean-Luc Marion, *The Visible and the Revealed*. Translated by Christina M. Gschwandtner and others.

Michel Henry, *Material Phenomenology*. Translated by Scott Davidson.